Hispano-Arabic
Poetry

Hispano-Arabic Poetry / A Student Anthology

by *James T. Monroe*

GORGIAS PRESS
2004

First Gorgias Press Edition, 2004.

 Published in the United States of America by Gorgias Press LLC, New Jersey. This edition is a facsimile reprint of the original edition published by the University of California Press, Los Angeles, London, 1974.

ISBN 1-59333-115-0

GORGIAS PRESS
46 Orris Ave., Piscataway, NJ 08854 USA
www.gorgiaspress.com

Printed and bound by CPI Group (UK) Ltd, Croydon, CR0 4YY

for juliane

Preface to the Reprint

This work was originally written in La Jolla where, in the then recently constituted Department of Literature at the University of California, San Diego, I held my first teaching position. The book was submitted to the University of California Press in 1968. There, its publication was delayed for several years because of certain difficulties encountered in reproducing the Arabic texts. In 1974, after those difficulties had been overcome, the book finally appeared in print. As a result of this delay, it was not possible to include in it references to certain works that appeared after 1968, even though they would have been relevant to a better understanding of the poems contained in the anthology.

Since 1968, the study of Arabic poetry in general, and of Andalusī poetry in particular, has made tremendous strides forward. New editions of *dīwān*s have appeared and, based on these, meticulous studies of genres, individual poets, and even key poems, have been published. Most importantly, the study of Arabic literature has advanced from a preliminary stage, largely textual and philological in nature, to one in which the principles of literary criticism are finally, and effectively, being applied to Arabic texts. To provide an adequate reflection of all these developments would require an entirely revised and updated second edition of *Hispano-Arabic Poetry* rather than the present and far less ambitious reprint.

Let me offer but one example of how the state of the art has changed: not only has the narrative *urjūza* by Ibn ʻAbd Rabbihi (which constitutes the first poem in this collection) been edited and studied by several scholars, but that author's entire extant corpus of poetry, previously dispersed throughout a variety of sources, has by now been gathered together and edited, at least thrice. Of these editions, the earliest includes a detailed study, and complete translation into English, of the author's *Dīwān*.[1] Furthermore, to my own article analyzing the *urjūza*, as cited in the Bibliography attached to this work,[2] one must now add an essential, book-length study of the same poem authored by Francisco Marcos Marín.[3]

Andalusī strophic poetry has been the subject of a major debate between one group of scholars championed by Federico Corriente,[4] who argue that this corpus is derived exclusively from the Arabic tradition, and owes little, if anything, to the local, Romance-speaking environment within which it was born and flourished, and another group of scholars (among whom I include myself), who draw their inspiration from the work of the late E. García Gómez, in maintaining that the forms and meters of Andalusī strophic poetry are Hispano-Romance in origin and, therefore, syllabic in scansion.[5] In a recent book, Pierre Cachia sums up the discussion between these two rival groups, and concludes that "the debate has somctimes been skewed by national pride."[6] This seems a rather odd conclusion to reach, considering that Corriente is a Spaniard who argues for an Arabic (*i.e.*, a non-Spanish) solution to the problem, whereas I, who am a non-Spaniard, argue for a Hispano-Romance solution to it. An entirely different factor, professional in nature, and surely more relevant to the discussion than is the concept of national pride, may possibly be found in the circumstance that Corriente, although Spanish, was trained as an Arabist, whereas I, who am non-Spanish, was trained

---

[1] Dustin Cowell, *The Poetry of Ibn 'Abd Rabbihi* (unpublished University of California doctoral dissertation in Literature, San Diego, 1976); Ibn 'Abd Rabbihi, *Shi'r Ibn 'Abd Rabbihi*, ed. Muḥammad ibn Tāwīt (Casablanca: Dār al-Maghrib li-l-Ta'līf wa-l-Tarjama wa-l-Nashr, 1978); Ibn 'Abd Rabbihi, *Dīwān*, ed. Muḥammad Riḍwān al-Dāya (Beirut: Mu'assasat al-Risāla, 1979).

[2] See below, p. 397.

[3] *Poesía narrativa árabe y épica hispánica: Elementos árabes en los orígenes de la épica hispánica* (Madrid: Gredos, 1971).

[4] See F. Corriente, *El cancionero hispano-árabe de Aban Quzmán de Córdoba (m. 555/1160) "Iṣābat al-aġrāḍ fī ḏikr al-a'rāḍ"* (Cairo: al-Majlis al-A'là li-l-Ṭaqāfa: Jumhūrīyat Miṣr al-'Arabīya, 1995).

[5] See E. García Gómez, *Todo Ben Quzmān* (Madrid Gredos, 1972), 3 vols.

[6] *Arabic Literature: An Overview* (London: RoutledgeCurzon, 2002), p. 96.

as a Hispanist and, therefore, may lay some small claim to familiarity with medieval Hispano-Romance popular poetry.

The central point to be derived from the above remarks is that, when this anthology was originally compiled, I scanned its strophic poems, *i.e.* its *muwashshaḥāt* and *azjāl*, according to the Hispano-Romance system, following in this, the only convincing method of scansion then available for that corpus, namely that of García Gómez. Moreover, and as of this writing, I have yet to come across any valid and persuasive reasons why I should radically modify my views on this issue.[7] This is not to imply, of course, that recent editions and translations of Andalusī strophic poetry, many of them published by Corriente himself, have not dramatically improved our understanding of that corpus. Specifically, "Poem 26" in this anthology, which corresponds to "Zajal 90" in the *Dīwān* of Ibn Quzmān, has been studied in an article, soon to appear, in which a thoroughly revised translation and interpretation of the poem will be offered. It will supercede the version of that text included in this reprint, not to speak of all those found in such editions as appeared after the publication of *Hispano-Arabic Poetry*.[8] One possible lesson to be learned from these considerations is that there may be more to poetry than its origin and scansion.

Among the reviews of this book that appeared soon after it was first published, I would like to single out one written by Andras Hamori,[9] not only to avail myself of this opportunity to thank him publicly, if belatedly, for the extreme care with which he went over the Arabic texts and translations, as a result of which, he was able to identify a number of errors in both, but also to warn any future student who plans to use this work, that Hamori's corrections and suggestions for improvement should not be ignored.

---

[7] On this point, see James T. Monroe, "Elements of Romance Prosody in the Poetry of Ibn Quzmān," *Perspectives on Arabic Linguistics VI*, ed. Mushira Eid, Vicente Cantarino, and Keith Walters (Amsterdam: John Benjamins Publishing Company, 1994), pp. 63-87.

[8] James T. Monroe and Mark F. Pettigrew, "The Decline of Courtly Patronage and the Appearance of New Genres in Arabic Literature: The Case of the Zajal, the Maqāma, and the Shadow Play," *Journal of Arabic Literature* 34: 2 (forthcoming).

[9] *Journal of the American Oriental Society*, 99: 2 (1979), pp. 366-373.

In conclusion, it is heartwarming to consider how much has been accomplished and learned in the field of Andalusī literature over the years that have intervened since this book's first appearance, and the present moment. At the same time, an anthology that was compiled thirty-five years ago cannot but be dated in many ways. Nevertheless, I am the constant recipient of inquiries from teachers and students of Arabic literature who ask where copies of *Hispano-Arabic Poetry*, out of print since 1989, may be obtained. I would, therefore, like to thank Gorgias Press for once again making this anthology available, despite its many and obvious shortcomings and defects, and to express my hope that it will continue to be of some use until such a time as a better compilation (for which there is an urgent need) is put together.

JAMES T. MONROE

Berkeley, California
February, 2003

Preface

All too many sources containing Hispano-Arabic poetic texts are out of print or otherwise relatively unobtainable. The purpose of this anthology is to make available in English a convenient introduction to the subject, and to facilitate the handling of the material.

In making my selection, specimens of classical poems such as the monorhymed ode (*qaṣīda*), and the *rajaz* epic rhyming in couplets (*urjūza*) have been included, as well as examples of post-classical strophic forms such as the *mukhammasa* with its five-line strophe, the *muwashshaḥa* with its varied rhymes and colloquial envoi (*kharja*), and the latter's sister form, the entirely colloquial *zajal*.

While most of the poetry included is either panegyrical, erotic, floral, or bacchic, a few mystical pieces have been added in order to provide the widest possible sampling of the literary production of Islamic Spain. The poems have all been chosen according to the prestige they enjoyed among medieval Arab critics, as well as for their appeal to the modern reader. In this way it is hoped that they will offer a faithful, yet attractive picture of al-Andalus, as Spain was called by the Arabs.

The Introduction focuses on the main currents of Hispano-Arabic poetry from a historical and literary perspective, adding to this some parallel considerations on the plastic arts. Instead of approaching the subject exclusively from the traditional, line-by-line method of interpretation initiated by the medieval writers of the great commentaries, some attention has been paid to form and its relation to content. It is hoped that the suggestions found in the Introduction will illustrate the gradual development and change that Hispano-Arabic poetry underwent with the passage of time, and that this presentation will allow the poetry to be viewed from a more modern viewpoint by literary critics, so that the usual accusations about its alleged lack of originality, slavery to theme, and resistance to change will give way to a more balanced appreciation based on purely aesthetic grounds.

In the Introduction, the fifty poems included in the Anthology are referred to by means of a boldface Roman numeral enclosed in parentheses (i.e., "**(1)**" signifies "poem number one" according to the order followed in the contents).

The Arabic texts are printed on the right-hand page, with the translations facing them on the left, following the style introduced recently by A. J. Arberry (*Arabic Poetry: A Primer for Students* [Cambridge, 1965]), a format that experience has shown to be very convenient in the classroom. The poems are numbered line by line to allow for rapid reference and comparison with the translations. Whenever possible, significant variants have been indicated in the footnotes.

The translations make no pretense at providing the only possible renderings of obscure and ambiguous passages, and the results of previous scholars' research have been taken into account whenever available, although they have not always been adopted. The margin of disagreement in translating Arabic poetry can often be surprisingly wide, hence it is not necessary to explain to those familiar with the problems involved why some of the translations differ at times from earlier efforts. For some of the poems, however, these translations are the first to have been attempted in a Western language.

The bibliography has been arranged in sections corresponding to the main historical periods of Islamic Spain. It is by no means exhaustive, but it attempts to supply a necessary and useful acquaintance with basic works in the field, both in Arabic and in Western languages.

Because summaries of Arabic prosody, poetics, thematics, and rhetorical figures are readily available in several manuals, the nature of Arabic poetry per se is not discussed in the Introduction, and knowledge of it is assumed. For prosody the student should consult W. Wright (*A Grammar of the Arabic Language* [3d ed.; Cambridge, 1951], Part IV, Prosody), where the subject is treated exhaustively. The main rhetorical figures and conventional themes used by Arab poets are listed by Arberry (*op. cit.*, Introduction, pp. 18–26). A treatise on Arabic literary criticism has been translated into English by G. E. von Grunebaum (*A Tenth-Century Document of Arabic Literary Theory and Criticism: Translation and Annotation of the Sections on Poetry of al-Baqillānī's Iʿjāz al-Qurʾān* [Chicago, 1950]), while an adequate coverage of Arabic poetics is that of Amjad Trabulsī (*La critique poétique des arabes jusqu'au Vè siècle de l'hégire* (*XIè siècle de J. C.*) [Damascus, 1956]).

Apart from the usual dictionaries used in reading Arabic poetry, R. Dozy's *Supplément aux dictionnaires arabes* (Leiden, 1881;

reprint, Leiden and Paris, 1967) is absolutely necessary for any serious philological study of Spanish Arabic texts, since it records words, meanings, and usages not commonly found in dictionaries based on Eastern sources.

The biographies of most of the poets included have been gathered together by A. R. Nykl (*Hispano-Arabic Poetry and Its Relations with the Old Provençal Troubadours* [Baltimore, 1946]), and the thematics of Hispano-Arabic poetry have been studied extensively by Henri Pérès (*La poésie andalouse en arabe classique au XI*[è] *siècle* [Paris, 1937]).

JAMES T. MONROE

La Jolla, California
June 1968

Contents

Biographical Notes

IBN ᶜABD RABBIHI, Aḥmad ibn Muḥammad Abū ᶜUmar, was born in Córdoba in 268/860. A freedman and court poet of the Umayyads, he was the author of *Kitāb al-ᶜIqd al-farīd.* He died in 328/940.

Nykl, pp. 35–42; Pérès, pp. 45, 166 ff.; Vernet, p. 103.

IBN HĀNIʾ al-Andalusī, Abū l-Qāsim Muḥammad, was born at an uncertain date, either near Mahdiyya in Tunis, in Elvira, or in Córdoba, *ca.* 320–326/932–937. Having been accused of heresy and of adhering to Greek philosophical ideas, he left al-Andalus and joined the Fatimid court of al-Muᶜizz. He died mysteriously at Barqa in 362/973.

Nykl, pp. 28–30; Pérès, pp. 43, 46 ff.; Vernet, pp. 87–88, 175.

IBN DARRĀJ AL-QASṬALLĪ, Abū ᶜUmar Aḥmad ibn Muḥammad ibn ᶜAṣī ibn Aḥmad ibn Sulaimān, was a Berber born in 347/958 either in Cazalla in the Algarve, or in Cazalilla near Jaén. He panegyrized al-Manṣūr and later traveled from court to court under the Mulūk aṭ-Ṭawāʾif until he finally settled in Saragossa. He died in 421/1030.

Nykl, pp. 56–58; Pérès, pp. 177 ff.; Vernet, pp. 112–114.

ASH-SHARĪF AṬ-ṬALĪQ, Marwān ibn ᶜAbd ar-Raḥmān ibn Marwān ibn ᶜAbd ar-Raḥmān an-Nāṣir Abū ᶜAbd al-Mālik, was an Umayyad prince born *ca.* 350/961. He was imprisoned and later freed by al-Manṣūr, and excelled in love poetry. He died *ca.* 400/1009.

Nykl, pp. 61–64; Pérès, p. 57; Vernet, p. 89.

IBN SHUHAID, Abū ᶜĀmir Aḥmad ibn Abī Marwān ᶜAbd al-Malik al-Ashjaᶜī, was a poet of aristocratic origin and a close friend of Ibn Ḥazm. He was born near Córdoba in 383/992 and composed the *Risālat at-Tawābiᶜ wa z-zawābiᶜ*. He died in 426/1035.

Nykl, pp. 47–48; Pérès, pp. 34, 296 ff.; Vernet, pp. 114–115.

IBN ḤAZM al-Andalusī, Abū Muḥammad ᶜAlī, was a distinguished philosopher, Ẓāhirite jurist, poet, and author of the *Ṭauq al-ḥamāma.* He was born in Córdoba in 383/994, became unsuccessfully involved in politics, and after suffering a life of persecution because of his ideas, he died in Montijo (Huelva) in 456/1064.

Nykl, pp. 73–103; Pérès, pp. 301–302, 414–415 ff.; Vernet, pp. 112–116.

IBN ZAIDŪN, Abū l-Walīd Aḥmad ibn ᶜAbdillāh ibn Aḥmad ibn Ghālib al-Makhzūmī, was born in Córdoba in 394/1003 and died in Seville in 463/1071. He was the purest Neoclassical poet of al-Andalus and became famous for his love affair with the Umayyad princess Wallāda.

Nykl, pp. 106–121; Pérès, pp. 412 ff.; Vernet, pp. 116–117.

IBN ᶜAMMĀR, Abu Bakr, was born near Silves in 422/1031 and became an intimate companion of al-Muᶜtamid of Seville who eventually quarreled with him and killed him in 476/1083–1084.

Nykl, pp. 154–163; Pérès, pp. 189–190 ff.; Vernet, pp. 118–119.

AL-MUᶜTAMID ᶜalā l-lāh ibn ᶜAbbād, Abū l-Qāsim Muḥammad, was the most outstanding poet of the second half of the eleventh century. He was born at Beja in 432/1040, became king of Seville, was deposed by the Almoravids and died in Morocco in 488/1095.

Nykl, pp. 134–154; Pérès, pp. 11, 222 ff.; Vernet, pp. 86, 117–119.

IBN ḤAMDĪS, ᶜAbd al-Jabbār ibn Abī Bakr ibn Muḥammad al-Azdī, aṣ-Ṣiqillī, was born at Syracuse in 447/1058. After the Norman conquest of Sicily he joined al-Muᶜtamid's Sevillian court. With the coming of the Almoravids he fled to Mahdiyya and died in Bougie in 527/1132.

Nykl, pp. 168–170; Pérès, pp. 212, 289–290 ff.; Vernet, p. 120.

ABŪ ISḤĀQ al-Ilbīrī, Ibrahīm ibn Masᶜūd ibn Saᶜīd at-Tujībī, was a Granadan *faqīh* who aroused the Berbers to revolt against the Jews of Granada. He has left a *Dīwān* of ascetic poems. His death occurred in 459/1067.

Nykl, pp. 197–200; Pérès, pp. 108, 444–445 ff.; Vernet, pp. 120–121.

IBN AL-LABBĀNA, Abū Bakr Muḥammad ibn ᶜIsā ad-Dānī, was born in Denia at an unknown date. He became a court poet of al-Muᶜtamid, and died in Majorca in 507/1113.

Nykl, pp. 163–165; Pérès, pp. 187 ff.; Vernet, p. 120.

IBN ᶜUBĀDA AL-QAZZĀZ, Abū ᶜAbdillāh Muḥammad, was a distinguished *muwashshaḥa* poet at the court of al-Muᶜtaṣim of Almería.

Nykl, p. 194; Pérès, p. 47.

IBN ARFAᶜ RAʾSUH, Abū Bakr Muḥammad, was a *muwashshaḥa* poet at the court of Maʾmūn of Toledo. His life is not well known.

Nykl, pp. 201–202.

IBN ᶜABDŪN, Abū Muḥammad ᶜAbd al-Majīd, was born at Evora, and served as a secretary under al-Mutawakkil of Badajoz. After the latter's fall he died in his hometown in 529/1134.

Nykl, pp. 175–179; Pérès, pp. 226–227 ff.; Vernet, p. 120.

IBN KHAFĀJA, Abū Isḥāq Ibrāhīm ibn Abī l-Fatḥ ibn ᶜAbdillāh, was born at Alcira, near Valencia in 450/1058. He remained in his hometown all his life and became famous for his outstanding nature poetry. He died in 533/1139.

Nykl, pp. 227–231; Pérès, pp. 159–160 ff.; Vernet, p. 121.

IBN AZ-ZAQQĀQ, ᶜAlī ibn ᶜAṭiyya Abū l-Ḥasan al-Bulughghīnī al-Mursī, was a nephew of Ibn Khafāja who, like his uncle, cultivated nature poetry. He was born *ca.* 489/1096 and died in 528/1134.

Nykl, pp. 231–233; Pérès, pp. 154 ff.; Vernet, p. 121.

AL-AᶜMĀ AT-TUṬĪLĪ, Abū l-ᶜAbbās (or Abū Jaᶜfar) Aḥmad ibn ᶜAbdillāh ibn Huraira al-ᶜAbsī, "the blind poet of Tudela," was born in that city, near Saragossa, and lived in Murcia and Seville. He died in 519/1126.

Nykl, pp. 254–256; Pérès, pp. 56, 334 ff.; Vernet, p. 122.

IBN BAQĪ, Abū Bakr Yaḥya ibn Muḥammad ibn ᶜAbd ar-Raḥmān al-Qaisī al-Qurṭubī, was a famous *muwashshaḥa* poet either from Córdoba or from Toledo, although descended from a family that came from Guadix, where he died in 540/1145 or 545/1150.

Nykl, pp. 241–244; Pérès, pp. 202, 328 ff.

IBN QUZMĀN, Abū Bakr ibn ᶜAbd al-Malik, was from Córdoba, and the greatest of the Andalusian *zajal* poets. He was born *ca.* 470–472/1078–1080, and died in his native city in 555/1160.

Nykl, pp. 266–301; Pérès, pp. 296, 397; Vernet, pp. 122–123.

AL-ABYAḌ, Abū Bakr ibn Muḥammad ibn Aḥmad al-Anṣārī al-Ishbīlī. A famous *muwashshaḥa* poet, he was born in Alhendín near Granada, and studied in Seville and Córdoba. He became famous for his satirical poetry and satirized the Almoravid governor of Córdoba az-Zubair, who had him crucified after 525/1130.

Nykl, pp. 245–247; Pérès, p. 32.

IBN BĀJJA, Abū Bakr Muḥammad ibn Yaḥya as-Saraqusṭī, Ibn aṣ-Ṣāʾigh, was born in Saragossa toward the end of the eleventh century and became vizier to the Almoravid governor Ibn Tīfalwīt. After the fall of Saragossa to the Christians he fled to Seville, Játiva, and finally to Fez where he died poisoned in 533/1138.

Nykl, pp. 251–254; Pérès, pp. 61, 379.

IBN ZUHR, Abū Bakr Muḥammad ibn Abī Marwān ᶜAbd al-Malik ibn Abī ᶜAlāʾ, called *al-ḥafīd*, "the grandson," was born near Seville in 507/1113 and became a distinguished physician, serving at the Almohad court of Yaᶜqūb ibn Yūsuf al-Manṣūr in Marrakesh. He was one of the last representatives of *muwashshaḥa* poetry in its pure form, before it was reabsorbed into the classical tradition. He died poisoned in 595/1198.

Nykl, pp. 248–251; Pérès, p. 29.

AR-RUṢĀFĪ, Abū ᶜAbdillāh Muḥammad ibn Ghālib ar-Raffā al-Andalusī, was a distinguished nature poet from La Ruzafa de Valencia who died in Málaga in 572/1177.

Nykl, pp. 326–377; Pérès, pp. 291–292; Vernet, p. 122.

ḤĀTIM IBN SAᶜĪD. Classified by Ibn Khaldūn in the *Muqaddimah* as an Almohad *muwashshaḥa* poet, his biographical data have not been compiled.

IBN SAHL, Abū Isḥāq Ibrāhīm al-Isrāʾīlī al-Ishbīlī, was a converted Jew who achieved fame in Seville for his outstanding love lyrics. He drowned in the Guadalquivir in 648/1251.

Nykl, pp. 344–345; Pérès, p. 141; Vernet, p. 122.

SHUSHTARĪ, Abū l-Ḥasan ᶜAlī ibn ᶜAbdillāh an-Numairī al-Fāsī, was born at Shushtar near Guadix *ca.* 608/1212 and became a mystic, who traveled to Morocco and then to the East, where he became friendly with Suhrawardī. He was buried in Damietta in 668/1269.

Nykl, pp. 352–353; Vernet, p. 141.

IBN AL-ᶜARABĪ, Muḥyī d-Dīn, Abū Bakr Muḥammad ibn ᶜAlī ibn Muḥammad al-Ḥātimī, was born in Murcia in 560/1165. He studied at Córdoba and Seville, went to Mecca, and settled in Damascus where he died in 630/1240, having earned his reputation as one of the greatest mystics in Islam.

Nykl, pp. 351–352; Pérès, p. 127; Vernet, pp. 140–141.

Ḥāzim al-Qarṭājannī, Abū l-Ḥasan Ḥāzim ibn Muḥammad ibn Ḥasan al-Anṣārī, was born in Cartagena in 608/1211. After the conquest of that city by the Christians he fled to Tunis where he served at the Ḥafṣid court and died in 684/1285.

Nykl, pp. 334–335; Vernet, p. 122.

ar-Rundī, Ṣāliḥ Abū l-Baqā' ash-Sharīf, was a poet from Ronda whose life is not well known, but who died in 683/1285.

Nykl, pp. 337–339; Vernet, pp. 143–144.

Ibn al-Khaṭīb, Lisān ad-Dīn Abū ᶜAbdillāh Muḥammad ibn ᶜAbdillāh ibn Saᶜīd ibn ᶜAbdillāh ibn Saᶜīd ibn ᶜAlī ibn Aḥmad as-Salmānī, was born in Loja in 713/1313 and became a vizier under Yūsuf I of Granada. He continued in this post under Muḥammad V. He was a distinguished historian, was accused of heresy by his enemies, and fled to Tlemcen and Fez where he was assassinated in 776/1374.

Nykl, pp. 363–366; Pérès, pp. 11, 74 ff.; Vernet, pp. 133–135, 145–149.

Ibn Zamrak, Muḥammad ibn Yūsuf ibn Muḥammad ibn Aḥmad ibn Muḥammad ibn Yūsuf aṣ-Ṣuraihī, Abū ᶜAbdillāh, was born in the Albaicín of Granada in 539/1333 and became a pupil of Ibn al-Khaṭīb as well as official court panegyrist whose poems are engraved on the walls of the Alhambra. After arranging his mentor's murder, he was himself assassinated by Muḥammad V's hired men in 795/1393.

Nykl, pp. 366–369; Pérès, p. 238; Vernet, pp. 144, 148.

Yūsuf III, Abū ᶜAbdillāh ibn al-Aḥmar, reigned over Granada from 810/1408 to 819/1417 when he died. He lost Antequera to the Christians but otherwise enjoyed a peaceful reign.

Vernet, p. 145.

Abbreviations

Dozy = R. Dozy, *Supplément aux dictionnaires arabes*. Leiden, 1881. Reprinted Leiden and Paris, 1967.

EI[1] = *Encyclopaedia of Islam*.

EI[2] = *Encyclopaedia of Islam*. New edition. (In progress.)

Nykl = A. R. Nykl, *Hispano-Arabic Poetry*. Baltimore, 1946.

Pérès = H. Pérès, *La poésie andalouse en arabe classique au XI*[è] *siècle*. Paris, 1937.

Vernet = J. Vernet, *Literatura árabe*. Barcelona, 1968.

Introduction

Introduction

History of Hispano-Arabic Poetry from the Islamic Conquest of Hispania to the Caliphate (A.D. 711–1009)

A crucial factor in the social and economic life of the late Roman Empire was the overtaxation of cities. As a result of it the wealthy fled to their villas and estates in the country and entrenched themselves to withstand the ever-increasing demands of the tax collector. Soon the preponderance of a local, agrarian economy over the old imperial and urban economy began to develop. Commerce was paralyzed with the decay of urban life and the symptoms of a quasi-tribal society began to perturb the smooth functioning of the centralized administrative machine. The inherent weakness of the Visigothic monarchy in the former Roman province of Hispania derived from its failure to accept the change and to adapt the older institutions to the new conditions that had been created.

By the time of the Islamic invasion (A.D. 711) Visigothic rule in Hispania had reached a stage of total exhaustion. It was neither strong enough to uphold the centralized monarchic institutions, nor could it offer a new spiritual ideal around which to rally public sentiment. This internal tension which was sapping the vigor of Hispania by the early eighth century was in turn to determine key aspects of Islamic rule.

The Arab-led invasion of Hispania was the result not of a planned effort, but of a spiritual thrust that had begun as a military adventure with no long-range goal in sight. As if by chance it succeeded, while its very lack of planning made it all the more adaptable to local conditions. After the sudden conquest was over, little had really changed. The monarchy was gone, and since the new seat of authority was in faraway Damascus the tribal society had in a sense won a battle against centralism. The conquering Arabs stayed on and married into the native nobility which had called upon them for help in the first place. These lucrative marriages plus the division of lands by right of conquest transformed the Arabs into an agrarian-based tribal aristocracy, so that the early years of peninsular Islam were filled with new anarchy until the independent Emirate founded by ᶜAbd ar-Raḥmān I (756–788) reintroduced the principle of centralism. Parallel to this there was the slow yet steady upsurge of urban life under the new regime, for medieval Islam, contrary to contemporary Western Europe, evolved into an urban civilization in which international trade revived. Merchants with their caravans, not feudal barons, were destined to become the men of action of a new order.

Hence the early history of Islam in Hispania, now called al-Andalus, was that of the gradual and repeated attempts to assert the authority of the centralizing principle, represented by the Islamized cities, over the unruly Arabized country. The cities became Islamized because of the many benefits that accrued from conversion and also because intermarriages between conquerors and conquered were performed under laws favorable to Islam, so that inevitably the Christians tended to become absorbed. The Arabs remained in the countryside, but the new converts entered the administration in the cities and fought in the army. They learned Arabic to read their new scriptures and became devout Muslims. The rapid Islamization of the converts produced the despairing reaction of those Mozarabs Eulogius and Alvarus in ninth-century Córdoba,[1] but by the tenth century not only had the Christian minority become insignificant, but also Arabism had itself been superseded by Islamism within the cities, and with it the power of the converts increased and even surpassed that of the landed Arab nobility. The new Islamic universalism found political expression in the founding of the Caliphate of Córdoba in 929. Artistically, it was expressed by a new, monumental style in architecture which was no longer intended to satisfy the needs of the agrarian world, but which by reason of its luxury and ostentation

---

[1] In A.D. 854 Alvarus described the situation predominant among Mozarabs as follows: "Our Christian young men, with their elegant airs and fluent speech, are showy in their dress and carriage, and are famed for the learning of the gentiles; intoxicated with Arab eloquence they greedily handle, eagerly devour and zealously discuss the books of the Chaldeans [i.e., Muhammadans], and make them known by praising them with every flourish of rhetoric, knowing nothing of the beauty of the Church's literature, and looking down with contempt on the streams of the Church that flow forth from Paradise; alas! the Christians are so ignorant of their own law, the Latins pay so little attention to their own language, that in the whole Christian flock there is hardly one man in a thousand who can write a letter to inquire after a friend's health intelligibly, while you may find a countless rabble of all kinds of them who can learnedly roll out the grandiloquent periods of the Chaldean tongue. They can even make poems, every line ending with the same letter, which display high flights of beauty and more skill in handling meter than the gentiles themselves possess" (Alvarus, *Indiculus Luminosus*, ¶ 35; quoted from W. Montgomery Watt, *A History of Islamic Spain* [Edinburgh, 1965], p. 56).

presented the external symbols of greatness to the new urban society.

The Great Mosque of Córdoba, the chief monument of that society, was begun by ᶜAbd ar-Raḥmān I in the eighth century, then expanded in the ninth by ᶜAbd ar-Raḥmān II (822–852). During the Caliphate al-Ḥakam II once again enlarged it between the years 961 and 968. His additions and improvements, as befitted the mature splendor of the Caliphal age, brought greater richness of decoration to the older structure. In the central nave he opened a large lighted dome to illuminate the interior, and replaced the earlier horseshoe arches with lobed ones, as well as adding the splendid mihrab made with mosaics presented to him by the Byzantine emperor. The new additions to the Mosque were carefully calculated to stir the emotion of the faithful as they entered it, for walking along the central nave in semidarkness toward the mysteriously illuminated and richly decorated chapel the faithful could catch a glimpse of the magnificent mihrab beyond and be moved to transports of religious feeling.

The last enlargement of the Mosque was made under the dictatorship of al-Manṣūr (976–1009) who merely copied the style introduced by al-Ḥakam II. Here size and mass replaced originality or quality; no longer was there a true creative force at work, and artistically as also politically the dictatorship was living off the ideals of the past.[2]

Hispano-Arabic poetry closely follows the social, political, and artistic development of al-Andalus. Its very name, *Hispano-Arabic* poetry is, however, deserving of a moment's attention. Was it Hispanic primarily, that is, native, or was it Arabic? To what extent is it either or both of these?

The thesis of Henri Pérès, to some extent deriving from and also espoused by some modern Spanish scholars, is that the poetry of al-Andalus was the native production of the Iberian race that had once expressed itself in Latin, was now doing so in Arabic, and would later write in Spanish. Furthermore, according to this thesis, a strong native tradition with its own peculiar features is traceable through the many cultural phases of the poetry of the Iberian Peninsula no matter what language it happens to be written in.[3]

This thesis contradicts the one generally in vogue among Arab

---

[2] M. Gómez Moreno, *El arte español hasta los almohades: Arte mozárabe*, Ars Hispaniae, III (Madrid, 1951), 1–171.

[3] E. García Gómez, *Poesía arábigoandaluza: breve síntesis histórica* (Madrid, 1952), pp. 17–53; H. Pérès, *La poésie andalouse en arabe classique au XI*ᵉ *siècle* (Paris, 1937).

critics who claim that Hispano-Arabic poetry is a mere transplanted version of Eastern Arabic poetry, sharing a common language and literary heritage with Arabic poetry, from which it originated. Jaudat ar-Rikābī has summed up the nature of the Andalusian poet thus: "Indeed, he is certainly an Andalusian, and yet upon reading his works and especially his poetry, we cannot deny his Arabic roots and Eastern qualities, for this Andalusian had remained Eastern in his thought, Eastern in his manner of expression . . . we cannot affirm with Henri Pérès that the Muslim Andalusian represented a racial prolongation of the original peoples who inhabited the peninsula of al-Andalus. We cannot truly agree with the Orientalist in the likes of such a peremptory judgment, nor do the facts themselves agree with what he claims."[4]

As a variation to these two antagonistic theories there is that of E. Lévi-Provençal who, basing his arguments on the bilingualism common among medieval Andalusians, suggests that the latter, who often spoke Romance at home and Arabic in public, composed poetry in a language essentially foreign to them which as a result remained awkward and artificial like the learned imitations of Latin verse written by Renaissance scholars.[5]

No doubt each of these three theories has a grain of truth in it, yet they are all inadequate if applied exclusively of one another. It cannot be questioned that Hispano-Arabic poetry, being in Arabic, is essentially Arab and Eastern in its origin and literary tradition. It is an important branch of Arabic, not Spanish literature. There is certainly much artificiality in it, particularly in the early poetry of the Caliphal period, precisely the age best known to its finest historian, Lévi-Provençal, but the artificiality is no more than that encountered in other countries where bilingualism existed after the Arab conquest, so that this trait is not peculiar to al-Andalus. It is therefore questionable whether artificiality was the result of bilingualism or of the fact that Eastern poetic styles were not at first entirely mastered, during an age when poetry was still in an experimental, imitative stage that would not reach maturity until the eleventh century. Last of all, there is no doubt that native, Romance elements have appeared in the strophic forms of Andalusian poetry, namely the *muwashshaḥa* and the *zajal*, although perhaps it could be suggested that there is some danger in explaining the organic unit that is a poem through

---

[4] Jaudat ar-Rikābī, *Fī l-adab al-andalusī* (Cairo, 1960), p. 46.

[5] E. Lévi-Provençal, *La civilisation arabe en Espagne, vue générale* (Cairo, 1938).

its sources. The way in which these elements of native origin were integrated into compositions that in essence were Arabic is aesthetically as important as the elements themselves, if not more so. Thus the true nature of Hispano-Arabic poetry is a complex matter; it depends upon the form, the period, and the aesthetic use made of its constituent elements.

According to the thirteenth-century scholar Tīfāshī, "in ancient times the songs of the people of al-Andalus were either in the style of the Christians or in the style of the Arab camel drivers."[6] Since none of the earliest and only fragments of the earlier poetry have survived, this is a broad yet vague attestation to the separate but equal coexistence of two different poetic traditions. By the ninth century the Modernist and Neoclassical schools were fiercely competing in Baghdad which had reached a stage of intense cultural activity in its development, unequaled anywhere else in the Islamic world. In al-Andalus there were no first-rate poets at the time, for poetry was in a slow process of formation as a new social order arose out of the tribal jungle. Ancient poetry, used to express warlike sentiments, was adopted to defend each local faction. ᶜAbd ar-Raḥmān II surrounded himself in Córdoba with a group of poets who sought to imitate the East. Modernism had been brought from the court of Hārūn ar-Rashīd by Ziryāb, the Persian singer who became an *arbiter elegantiarum* in the provincial capital of al-Andalus. He introduced innovations in music, poetry, fashions, manners, and even in the culinary art (several of his recipes are extant).[7] ᶜAbbās ibn Nāṣiḥ (d. 844) imitated the Modernist style of Abū Nuwās, while Muʾmin ibn Saᶜīd (d. 880) or ᶜUthmān ibn al-Muthannā adopted the Neoclassicism of Abū Tammām. Yet none of this poetry was exceptional to judge from what little has survived. Saᶜīd ibn Jūdī (d. 897) wrote love lyrics, while al-Ghazzāl ibn Yaḥya (d. 864) was more famous for his handsome features and adventures with a Byzantine princess than for his poetry. He and Tammām ibn ᶜAlqama (d. 896) introduced the historical *urjūza*, while Muqaddam ibn Muᶜāfā al-Qabrī adapted the *musammaṭ* of Abū Nuwās to native strophic forms and invented the *muwashshaḥa*. Ibn Firnās (d. 887) constructed a flying machine and was hurt while jumping off a mountain near Córdoba with it. His poetic flights were no more successful than his aerial one. In this way Córdoba was

[6] E. García Gómez, "La lyrique hispano-arabe et l'apparition de la lyrique romane," *Arabica*, V (1958), 113.

[7] A. Huici Miranda, *Traducción española de un manuscrito anónimo del siglo XIII sobre la cocina hispano-magribī* (Madrid, 1966).

introduced to the polite arts and the Muslims of the metropolis began to elaborate a cultural ideal to oppose to the vague but disruptive aspirations of tribalism. This led to the revolt of the landed aristocracy. The battle was lost by the latter and won for the principle of Cordovan centralism, while the equilibrium of forces that restored order under ᶜAbd ar-Raḥmān III (912–961) was opposed to the old Arab nobility as much as it was to the non-Arab nobility, and secured the triumph of Islamism within the community of the faithful.[8]

From the tenth century on, poetry in the East was reduced to a few brilliant but isolated names as political decline set in. In the West, however, the prosperous Caliphate was now minting gold coins for the first time since immediately after the conquest. In this atmosphere culture was favored and primary figures began to appear in the literary sphere.

Mutanabbī had been known since the time of ᶜAbd ar-Raḥmān III. Throughout the century cultural embassies from Baghdad continued to appear: Abū ᶜAlī al-Qālī arrived in 941, Saᶜīd al-Baghdādī in 990, and court poets such as Ibn ᶜAbd Rabbihi (d. 939), Ibn Hānīᵓ of Elvira (d. 972), Ibn Faraj of Jaén (976), Musḥafī (d. 982), ash-Sharīf aṭ-Ṭalīq (d. 1009), Yūsuf ibn Hārūn ar-Ramādī (d. 1022), Ibn Darrāj al-Qasṭallī (d. 1030) brought Andalusian poetry to a new level of sophistication. Poets were experimenting with every theme, from the *nauriyya* or floral poem to the historical *urjūza* and the Neoclassical *qaṣīda*. There is a parallelism in politics, social evolution, the plastic arts, and literature under the Caliphate. Ibn ᶜAbd Rabbihi was the turning point from the earlier provincialism to the new sophistication. Surviving from an earlier age his poetry is still plainer and less adorned. He embodies the aesthetics of the cultured yet provincial Emirate that is beginning to experiment with Neoclassical verse. He toys with *badīᶜ*, the rhetorical ornamentation of the new style, yet he uses it sparingly. In his poetry there is an Andalusian nationalism of sentiment yet at the same time a servile imitation of the East: his *urjūza* (**1**)[9] is an emulation of the earlier one by the Abbasid Caliph Ibn al-Muᶜtazz, yet it is about a local subject. Like the two earlier *urjūzas* written by al-Ghazzāl and Ibn ᶜAlqama the poem is a novelty in Andalusian literature; it is clearly

---

[8] Vernet, pp. 88–89; E. García Gómez, *Poemas arábigoandaluces* (Madrid, 1940), pp. 25–27.

[9] For the sake of convenience, the poems included in the anthology are designated by means of boldface numerals within parentheses according to the order followed in the anthology.

epic in nature, not panegyrical, since the poet does not merely praise his patron directly, but rather he narrates the latter's exploits in such a way that the admiration for the hero is elicited indirectly, from the listener's interpretation of the action.

In 1915 Julián Ribera claimed that Andalusian *urjūza* poetry derived from a hypothetical Mozarabic epic, now lost, and that in turn it exerted an influence on Spanish and French epic which it precedes in time.[10] It is doubtful whether a Mozarabic epic tradition ever existed, given the nonmilitary role imposed upon these people by their new Arab masters. Furthermore Ribera did not know this particular poem. Had he done so he would have recognized its Eastern derivation. It is true, however, that several of its themes, its treatment, general historicity, and even literary techniques are often remarkably similar to those found in Romance epic, and it is to be hoped that further studies will clarify the problem more fully.[11]

Ibn Hānīʾ was brought up in al-Andalus yet banished from Seville for his scandalous behavior which made him suspect of heretical views. He escaped to the Fatimid court in Tunisia and when the latter moved to Egypt he returned to the Maghreb for his family and was killed mysteriously, some claim by Umayyad agents, in 973 at Barqa. Most of his poems are panegyrics to al-Muʿizz (935–975) the fourth Fatimid Caliph. Ibn Hānīʾ imitated the Neoclassical style of Abū Tammām and in his panegyrics he fully adopts *badīʿ*, going in it one step farther than Ibn ʿAbd Rabbihi. Some Arab critics considered him to be the Mutanabbī of the West, and indeed, al-Muʿizz had hoped that his poems would outdo Mutanabbī and give lasting glory to his own Shiʿite cause. Although remarkable, the Neoclassical technique has still not been fully mastered in the poetry of Ibn Hānīʾ for his word choice is at times harsh and he sometimes lapses from true poetic height. Hence al-Maʿarrī said of him that he was "like a mill grinding corn, so little sense is there in his verse."[12]

At this time in al-Andalus the best poetry that has survived was official. The poets declaimed *qaṣīdas* in which the party line dictated to them by the state chancery was put to verse. Thus the

---

[10] J. Ribera y Tarragó, *Huellas, que aparecen en los primitivos historiadores musulmanes de la península, de una poesía épica romanceada que debió florecer en Andalucía en los siglos IX y X: Discurso leído ante la Real Academia de la Historia* (Madrid, 1915).

[11] See James T. Monroe, "The Historical Urjūza of Ibn ʿAbd Rabbihi, A Tenth-Century Hispano-Arabic Epic Poem," *Journal of the American Oriental Society*, XCI (1971), pp. 67–95.

[12] *E.I.*[1], *s.v.* "Ibn Hānīʾ."

court poets were in a sense state functionaries whose duty it was to issue bulletins of foreign policy and their art, limited as it was by these restrictions, although it handles language with superior skill, remains somewhat uninspiring. The Caliphal dignity had brought great pomp to state ceremonies, and to maintain this pomp the Caliph kept aloof from mingling with poets on too free a level. But toward the end of the century, under the dictatorship of al-Manṣūr, who was not of royal blood and could therefore mingle more intimately with his courtiers, economic prosperity favored the emergence of a new, urban poetry which was not quite so rigidly bound to expressing the official point of view. Of these new poets Ibn Darrāj al-Qasṭallī and ash-Sharīf aṭ-Ṭalīq were among the most outstanding.

Ibn Darrāj (d. 1030) also followed the Neoclassical school. He was possibly from the town of Cazalla either in Jaén or in the Algarve, of Berber ancestry, and a newcomer to Córdoba who became a pensioned court poet in 992. He stayed on in his position under al-Muẓaffar but his life and fortunes were affected by the civil disturbances after 1009 so that he fled first to Valencia and then to Saragossa.[13] In his poetry the *badīᶜ* style has finally reached maturity, but the official tone of his panegyrical poetry makes the result seem cold and artificial to the modern taste. Thus his technical skill is not matched by the content. There are in his poetry, however, faint glimmerings of a more sincere emotion to be cultivated by later poets, as when in several of his poems he substitutes the conventionalized *nasīb* with an unusual personal touch: his sorrow at parting from his wife and child. Ibn Ḥazm considered him to be the equal of the best Eastern poets, and in fact he is comparable in some ways with Mutanabbī, since he wrote several war poems narrating the campaigns of Clunia, San Esteban de Gormaz, León, Santiago de Compostela, and Cervera. Furthermore he cultivated floral poetry, the *nauriyyāt*, which had become increasingly popular in al-Manṣūr's court.[14]

The reasons for the development of floral poetry at this time must be sought in the rise of urban civilization. As the agrarian life of the countryside was superseded by Cordovan hegemony it was not surprising that the city dwellers should have rediscovered nature in much the same way that modern man goes to the countryside on weekends to avoid the maddening rush of city life. Furthermore,

---

[13] Vernet, pp. 113–114.

[14] See James T. Monroe, *Risālat at-Tawābiᶜ wa z-zawābiᶜ: The Treatise of Familiar Spirits and Demons by Abū ᶜĀmir ibn Shuhaid al-Ashjaᶜī, al Andalusī*, University of California Publications, Near Eastern Studies, XV (Berkeley, Los Angeles, London, 1971), 1–14.

under al-Manṣūr's dictatorship the ruling Umayyad aristocracy of Córdoba had been removed from positions of power and political influence; therefore it was natural for them to seek relief from their frustrated political ambitions by turning to nature and converting it into a theme of poetry. In an analogous way eighteenth-century European aristocrats sported in a pastoral setting during the declining years of their political influence. Madīnat az-Zahrāʾ, the Umayyad royal residence in the country, in more ways than one became an early version of Versailles.

This is particularly relevant to the poetry of ash-Sharīf aṭ-Ṭalīq, the Umayyad prince who was imprisoned by al-Manṣūr for murdering his own father because of their rivalry over a slave girl. He is the only writer of love poetry from this period whose work has survived, if only in fragments. According to Ibn Ḥazm, "for his poetic skill and beautiful metaphors he was among the Andalusian Umayyads like Ibn al-Muʿtazz [d. 908] among the Abbasids." The same author calls him "the best Andalusian poet of his time" and adds that "the greater part of his love poems are dedicated to blond women."[15] Being a prince, he did not need to cultivate the panegyric for a living. Although his Neoclassical technique is far more advanced than that of previous poets, it is still not entirely mature. The themes taken from the ancients and the moderns are not yet properly digested, and the allusions appear somewhat bookish, while the formal perfection he achieves does not quite harmonize with the emotion expressed, as it will in the eleventh-century poet Ibn Zaidūn whom he influenced greatly. He uses *badīʿ* to embellish each line, and to create a charming series of images. His masterpiece, the *qaṣīda* rhymed in *qāf* (= q) (**4**) contains four parts: *ghazal*, *khamriyya*, *nauriyya*, and *fakhr*. The *ghazal* presents the stock themes of Modernism crowded together in exciting new relationships that are Neoclassical in treatment. The *khamriyya* has a likewise complex use of themes quoted partly from the Eastern poet Ibn ar-Rūmī. The *nauriyya* is the forerunner of all later floral poetry in al-Andalus, particularly that of Ibn Khafāja in the twelfth century. The *fakhr* continues an embroidery on the traditional themes, so that the last line could be taken as a statement of the poet's whole Neoclassical aesthetics: "It is I who clothe in splendor the worn-out portion of their illustrious lineage with the ornaments of my resplendent poetry." Thus the Umayyad dynasty, worn out politically, turned

[15] Ibn Ḥazm, *The Dove's Neck Ring*, quoted from E. García Gómez, "El Príncipe Amnistiado y su Dīwān," *Cinco poetas musulmanes* (Madrid, 1945), pp. 67–93.

at last to the creative medium of poetry. The gradual development of the *badīʿ* style from its first faltering and sparse usage in Ibn ʿAbd Rabbihi, through its still imperfect application in Ibn Hānīʾ, to its formal mastery by Ibn Darrāj and aṭ-Ṭalīq closely parallels the political rise of the Caliphate under ʿAbd ar-Raḥmān III, its splendor under al-Ḥakam II, and prolongation under the ʿĀmirid dictatorship. In art the highly ornate additions to the Mosque of Córdoba, the building of the country residences Madīnat az-Zahrāʾ and Madīnat az-Zāhira and the palace of al-ʿĀmiriyya keep apace with the refinement, sense of balance, and good taste that harmoniously absorbed the literary influences proceeding from Baghdad in this as yet formative period.

Córdoba in Transition (1009–1031)

The collapse of the Caliphate and the political fragmentation under the Mulūk aṭ-Ṭawāʾif profoundly altered the cultural spectrum of al-Andalus. The reasons for the sudden change are obscure. One of the many contributing factors was the unprecedented, macrocephalous growth of Córdoba, largely financed by an ever-increasing burden of taxation levied from the outlying provinces. By the age of al-Manṣūr the huge revenues needed to maintain a standing army of mercenaries and a vast bureaucracy had led to increasing discontent, and the provinces eagerly seized the first chance to throw off the Cordovan yoke. Empire had brought untold wealth to the metropolis as well as a renaissance of urban civilization and its amenities. The political division that followed distributed the benefits of that civilization more evenly throughout the major cities of the land. Whereas before poets had flocked to Córdoba, they would now be welcomed in almost every petty capital of the former empire. Localism had once again overcome the principle of centralism, although with a difference, for the earlier localism of the eighth and ninth centuries had been essentially agrarian and tribal in nature, whereas the present localism was basically urban. The petty kingdoms have thus aptly been characterized as "turbaned Italian republics" by a distinguished specialist.[16] The cause of Arabism as a meaningful social force had declined along with tribalism, while the Caliphate had succeeded in cementing the different ethnic groups into a new, Islamic community under the aegis of Eastern culture. At this moment Ibn Gharsīya, a Muslim of Basque ancestry,

[16] García Gómez, *Poemas*, p. 32.

was allowed to go unpunished for writing a Shuʿūbite treatise attacking the Arabs. This indicates that the cause of the latter had ceased to have political significance.[17]

The true sense of the age must be sought in the rise of an urban, commercial oligarchy that had replaced the old Arab aristocracy. Because it was largely an upstart, parvenu society it aped the manners of the older order, imitating Baghdad even more slavishly than had Caliphal Córdoba. Recent studies based on documents from the Cairo Geniza have revealed the extraordinary significance of the middle-class revolution that took place in the Islamic world of the tenth century. In al-Andalus as elsewhere, this middle class took over the reins of power and governed through its oligarchic leaders. In the long run, however, it failed to create new and lasting institutions adequated to the new conditions, and its blind reverence for past tradition led to its eventual downfall.

The collapse of central authority naturally reduced state revenues. This, plus the luxury of the multiple royal courts and the rising offensive of the Cid Campeador's Spain brought about an economic crisis. Gold coinage virtually disappeared, adversely affecting international trade, and the silver dirham became almost pure copper. Esoteric doctrines of a communistic nature became popular among the lower classes and riots and pogroms spread. Soon a strong popular sentiment, in the name of Islam and led by the conservative Mālikite *fuqahāʾ* or jurists, resulted in the invasion of the Almoravids and the deposition of the petty kings.

The factors outlined above meant that in architecture the luxury materials used by the Caliphal builders, such as stone, alabaster, and marble, were replaced with cheaper materials such as brick, mortar, and stucco. The Toledan mosque today called El Cristo de la Luz was built in the sober Caliphal style, but with modest materials according to techniques newly imported from Iraq where stone was difficult to obtain. This new type of construction was inexpensive and efficient. It inaugurated a new departure in Hispano-Arabic building styles, for El Cristo de la Luz is the direct ancestor of Mudéjar architecture.[18]

While mosques were sober and restrained, the residences of kings were luxurious. The Aljafería of Saragossa, built by Abū Jaʿfar Aḥmad al-Muqtadir bi-llāh (1047–1081), shows a remarkable

---

[17] J. T. Monroe, *The Shuʿūbiyya in al-Andalus: The Risāla of Ibn García and Five Refutations*, *University of California Publications*, Near Eastern Studies, XIII (Berkeley and Los Angeles, 1969).

[18] Gómez Moreno, *op. cit.*, p. 201.

evolution whereby those elements that in Caliphal architecture had been functional have now been reduced to purely decorative themes. Intersecting and lobed arches like those added to the Mosque of Córdoba by al-Ḥakam II are to be found in the Aljafería, but reduced to a mere wall decoration made of stucco. Architecture has moved away from the functional toward the purely decorative. It has become "art for art's sake." Perhaps the most significant feature of this period is that elements that before had been used to embellish the public buildings of Córdoba are now adapted to serve as a luxurious setting for the private life of kings. The beauties of a building are privately located; they are to be found within doors. Palace art has been developed at the expense of the Mosque.[19]

The new desire for refinement was also to have a beneficial effect on the development of culture, for each king cultivated a special field of his own. Mutawakkil of Badajoz was a learned scholar reputed to have written hundreds of books, Ibn Razīn cultivated music, Muqtadir of Saragossa surrounded himself with scientists and philosophers, Ibn Ṭāhir of Murcia specialized in rhymed prose, ᶜAbdullāh of Granada in autobiography, Mujāhid of Denia favored the study of the Koran. Poetry, however, became everybody's patrimony and was appreciated everywhere, particularly in Seville under the Banū ᶜAbbād. Verse is composed all over al-Andalus. Not only does Neoclassical poetry flourish, but the formerly subliterary *muwashshaḥa* becomes fashionable. We are told that any peasant in Silves could improvise on any given theme at a moment's notice. Hence the collapse of the Caliphate, rather than signaling the decline of poetry, meant the beginning of a golden age.[20]

At first, most poets tried to remain in the old metropolis, and of these the two most brilliant members of the new literary group that had developed were Ibn Shuhaid (d. 1035) and Ibn Ḥazm (d. 1063). They were closely followed by the somewhat younger Ibn Zaidūn (d. 1070), and they brought an entirely fresh spirit to the bookish poetry of al-Andalus.

Like architecture, poetry was liberated from its social and political servitude and became largely personal in its choice of theme. Both Ibn Shuhaid and Ibn Ḥazm were close friends. The former was a young aristocrat of Arab extraction while the latter descended from a distinguished native family of converts. Their friendship symbolizes the triumph of Islamism within the metropolitan melting

---

[19] *Ibid.*, pp. 225–226.
[20] García Gómez, *op. cit.*, pp. 31–32.

pot. The literary school chiefly represented by these two aesthetes was revolutionary. It consciously reacted against the pedantry of earlier generations and against indiscriminate imitation of Eastern fashions. Ibn Shuhaid propounded the refreshing doctrine that poets are born, not made; that the ability to write good poetry was a gift from God and could not be acquired from one's teachers. According to him, the nature of poetry was determined by the physical and spiritual qualities of the poet. If the body of the latter was controlled by the soul, then his resulting poetry would be beautiful, he claimed. In this doctrine there is a striking departure from the attitude that prevailed among Arab critics. The novelty lies in the application of Neoplatonic doctrines positing the preeminence of spirit over matter to the creative art of poetry. As a result, Ibn Shuhaid concluded that it was the soul of the poet that determined the beauty of his poetry, not his technical mastery of language and rhetoric. This implied that meaning was more highly regarded than form.[21]

These late Caliphal poets were both aristocratically minded and traditionalists. Their ultimate objective was to raise Andalusian letters to a higher level than that of the East, and therefore they were also nationalistic. But as classicists they scorned the semipopular form of the *muwashshaḥa* and wrote in pure literary Arabic. Each of the two wrote a masterpiece of Arabic prose: Ibn Shuhaid composed the treatise entitled *Risālat at-Tawābiᶜ wa z-zawābiᶜ*, and Ibn Ḥazm the *Ṭauq al-ḥamāma*. The former is a combined voyage to Parnassus and *Divine Comedy* in which the author visits the hereafter like Dante and interviews several of the great Arab poets of antiquity. The work offers a valuable insight into his critical theories. The latter is the *Vita Nova* of al-Andalus, a delicate analysis of the psychology of love in which the major part of Ibn Ḥazm's extant poetry is contained. It too is strongly influenced by Neoplatonic doctrines.

Ibn Shuhaid's poems are stylistically superior to those of Ibn Ḥazm. They are full of passion, tinged with a philosophical pessimism derived from the life of hardship he underwent: he witnessed the civil strife that ruined his native city and suffered from a protracted disease from which he died an invalid. He was thus made painfully aware of the enormous contrast between this world and the next, between reality and the ideal.

Ibn Ḥazm's poetry was superior to Ibn Shuhaid's in content,

---

[21] J. Dickie, "Ibn Shuhaid: A Biographical and Critical Study," *Andalus*, XXIX (1964), 303–304; Monroe, *Risālat at-Tawābiᶜ wa z-zawābiᶜ*.

though inferior in style. More a philosopher in verse than a poet, he sometimes pushes his literary experiments to the extreme, as when in the *Ṭauq* he boasts of having compressed five comparisons into one line of poetry.[22] Yet he has an extraordinary intuition for love and gets at its very essence. His life was typical of the troubled times. A wealthy young aesthete, he moved in aristocratic circles and became a politician under the last Umayyads. Banished later, he was persecuted for his loyalty to the now lost Umayyad cause which he manifested by adopting the ultraconservative Ẓāhirite rite in predominantly Mālikite al-Andalus. For this he was persecuted, his books were burned, and he became an embittered polemicist fleeing from court to court until he died in Montijo (Huelva) in 1063.

A recent study of Provençal courtly love poetry written by Peter Dronke offers a new perspective from which to analyze Ibn Ḥazm's poetry.[23] Dronke has shown that "courtly love" exists universally both in popular and in courtly poetry. He further shows that the popular love songs studied by Theodor Frings and characterized by the active role of the woman who laments over her love-longing—such as occurs in the German Frauenlieder, the Galaico-Portuguese Cantigas de Amigo, and in the Arabic Ḥaufī of Tlemcen—are, properly speaking, a feminine poetry that is not courtly. Courtly poetry for Dronke is essentially masculine, and therefore there are two basic archetypes in universal love poetry: the masculine and the feminine.

Courtly love poetry, that is, the masculine archetype, has existed in classical Arabic from the earliest times. It is present in Jamīl al-ᶜUdhrī (d. 701), ᶜUmar ibn Abī Rabīᶜa (d. 719), and Ibn al-Aḥnaf (d. 813) in the East. It was this tradition that under the general name of ᶜUdhrite love made its way to Córdoba. It proclaimed the excellence of a sublimated sexuality produced by a morbid prolongation of desire, best exemplified by the following lines by Ibn Faraj of Jaén (d. 976):

> I spent the night with her like a small camel, thirsty, yet whose muzzle keeps him from drinking,
> Thus for one such as I, there can be nothing in a garden beyond looking and smelling the perfume;

---

[22] Ibn Ḥazm, *El collar de la paloma*, trans. E. García Gómez (2d ed.; Madrid, 1967), p. 110.

[23] Peter Dronke, *Medieval Latin and the Rise of European Love-Lyric* (Oxford, 1965).

> For I am not like grazing animals who use gardens as mere pasture grounds.[24]

This poetry portrays the charms of feminine beauty in order to negate sexual love. It is therefore deeply rooted in a negative and physical approach to love, which makes an ennobling virtue out of continence. In contrast, when Ibn Ḥazm says:

> Are you from the world of the angels, or are you mortal? Explain this to me, for inability [to reach the truth] has made a mockery of my understanding.
> I have no doubt but that you are that spirit which a resemblance joining one soul to another in close relationship, has directed to us.
> Were it not that our eye contemplates [your] essence we could only declare that you are the Sublime, True Reason. **(8, C)**

we are immediately aware that a philosophical superstructure has been added to the conventions of ᶜUdhrite poetry, for both language and ideology are entirely novel in Arabic poetry. The arguments of Dronke, also valid for Islam, claim that there are three types of technical vocabulary present in courtly poetry: the mystical, the noetic, and the sapiential.

In mystical language divine and human love are reconciled, although figuratively, for the two are not identical in orthodox theology since one is absolute and the other relative. In courtly poetry, however, what occurs is exactly the reverse of what takes place in mystical poetry. In the latter, the language of human love is given a divine meaning, while here the language of divine love is applied to a human subject.

The technical terminology of the noetic goes back to Aristotle's passage on the active intellect in *De Anima* (iii.5) which underwent a long process of elaboration in Islamic philosophy. It spells out the relationship between the active intellect of God and the passive intellect of man.

Finally sapiential language uses the symbolic figure of Sapientia; in the Greek tradition Hagia Sophia. This was a Christianized version of the Neoplatonic doctrine of union between the Intellect and the Anima Mundi; of the Sublime Reason and the human soul "at its divinest" (Plotinus, *Enneads* iii.5–2). The concept of a divine love union was transferred to the level of human love; the

---

[24] García Gómez, *Poemas*, p. 95. Trans. J. T. Monroe.

beloved came to be identified with the active intellect and also with Sapientia, and in this way she was related to the divine world as well as to the human. The relation, however, is not one of mere intellection, but also of love. By it the lover could aspire to reach the divine. The beloved, furthermore, received from God the power to ennoble the lover, and it became her duty to guide him along the right path. Henry Corbin sums up the Islamic manifestation of this belief as follows: "This figure [the active intellect] appears in the dominant form of a central symbol, which reveals itself to the mental vision of man under the complementary feminine form which makes a total entity of his being. . . . The union which joins the possible intellect of the human soul with the active intellect as a *Dator formarum*, Angel of Knowledge, or Sapientia-Sophia is visualized and experienced as a love union."[25]

It was the application of this philosophical superstructure to traditional Arabic love poetry that permitted Ibn Ḥazm to create a true doctrine of courtly love in al-Andalus two centuries before the poets of Provence. His system stresses the ennobling power of love, and in it the spiritual takes precedence over the material, this being one reason why his poetry is so devoid of the rhetorical ornamentation found in earlier poets. Not only does his style correspond closely to the ethics of Neoplatonism, but in contrast with the essentially negative, materially based, and morbid attitude of ʿUdhrite love he postulates a positive, spiritualized doctrine. This is the very basis of the *Ṭauq*, in which he quotes Neoplatonic traditions and expresses the belief that love is the attraction of souls now divided, yet which were once united in another world, and adds that love has no other aim than love itself. What counts for Ibn Ḥazm is not the physical beauty of bodily form so much as the spiritual harmony of character traits uniting lovers.

The main features of his system are: (1) True love is rooted in the soul. (2) It is eternal. (3) There is a desire for harmony in love. The lover agrees with the beloved in everything, delights in talking with her, is tormented by her absence. He fears avoidance and communicates with the eye, "the soul's well-polished mirrror," if all else fails. (4) Love desires secrecy. (5) Union is the ultimate bliss. He does not deny sexuality as do the ʿUdhrite poets; instead he enhances the spiritual. (6) Separation is the worst evil and can lead to death. (7) True love is ever faithful, despite infidelity on the part of the beloved. (8) The lover must submit to every whim of the

---

[25] *Avicenne et le récit visionnaire* (Tehran, 1952), II, 309.

beloved. (9) Continence is praised, but not enjoined as a virtue in itself:

> Furthermore, is one between whom and me there lies only the distance of a day's journey really far away,
>
> When the wisdom [Sapientia] of God the Creator joined us together? This mutual proximity is enough [for me]; I want nothing further. **(8, H)**

The union of souls is more important than that of bodies, although the former does not necessarily exclude the latter. In this way ᶜUdhrite love was transformed into a positive spiritual doctrine, and love poetry in al-Andalus became more humane and refined.

The most outstanding love poet of the period was Ibn Zaidūn who flourished during the last days of the Caliphate and then under the oligarchic republic of Córdoba proclaimed after the former was abolished in 1031. His stormy love for the bluestocking Umayyad princess Wallāda inspired the better part of his literary production. When Ibn Zaidūn speaks of love, he is entirely personal. His beloved is a real woman and not the conventionalized figure portrayed in the traditional erotic prelude to the Arabic ode, or *nasīb*. After a few brief months of requited love he was replaced in his lady's affections by the less literary Ibn ᶜAbdūs. Ibn Zaidūn wrote the latter a scathing satire to which he signed Wallāda's name. The epistle was divulged in Córdoba and his influential rival had the poet cast in prison. He managed to escape to Seville which had become a haven for poets as well as the new cultural capital of al-Andalus. The various episodes of Ibn Zaidūn's love for Wallāda are immortalized in poetry that fuses the consummate mastery and technical perfection attained by Caliphal poets, with the depth of meaning and tenderness of sentiment contained in Ibn Ḥazm's courtly love doctrine; a happy marriage of form and content.[26]

His poetry, linguistically perfect, is at the same time restrained. It has attained full maturity and independence from Eastern tutelage. The brilliant colors and glittering decoration of aṭ-Ṭalīq are toned down and reduced to sober and masterly contrasts between black and white which distract less from the depth and sincerity of meaning. Likewise, his language which is simple and natural like Ibn Ḥazm's, is yet embellished enough to reach an elevated poetic tone that is sometimes lacking in his philosophical contemporary.

Ibn Zaidūn's Nūniyya **(9)**, or ode rhymed in Nūn, is a master-

---

[26] Ibn Zaidūn has been studied and partially translated by A. Cour, *Un poète arabe d'Andalousie, Ibn Zaïdoûn* (Constantine, 1920).

piece of the art of persuasion and contains not only the description of his beloved's physical beauty, but also the expression of his own innermost conflicts and personal feelings. In it he uses the clever repetition of the rhyme word *nā*, "our," to suggest to his beloved that his feeling for her is mutual, and gives added stress to this impression by the abundant use of reciprocal verb forms. The pronoun *nā* which in conventional love poetry is merely a *pluralis majestatis* here acquires a subjective function difficult to explain logically for the grammatical distinction between *nā*, "our," and *kum* "your," is erased in the Nūniyya by an all-encompassing "our" that includes the "your." Its synthetic rather than antithetic value suggests the unity in diversity which was the basic idea underlying Ibn Ḥazm's courtly love poetry. The fusion and confusion of *nā* with *kum* is therefore a linguistic expression of the Neoplatonic fusion of souls. The poet's rare quality of using even the sound of the rhyme syllable to evoke the main theme of his poem is proof of his skill.

In Ibn Zaidūn's poetry nature, which in the presence of Wallāda is cheerful, grows sad in her absence. In this too, form and decor are functional and are subservient to content:

> Indeed I remembered you yearningly as you were in az-Zahrāʾ, when the horizon was clear and the face of the earth was shining,
> And the breeze had a languor in its evening hours as if it had pity for me, and so languished out of compassion.[27]

Nature is thus made to reflect the lover's inner emotional state in a way reminiscent of Renaissance poetry. All the conventions of courtly love outlined by Ibn Ḥazm appear in Ibn Zaidūn, although not as philosophical abstractions, but rather personalized by his own very real sorrow. Under the hardship of separation the Nūniyya expresses a noble attitude on behalf of the poet, for he never blames Wallāda, but merely hints delicately and indirectly at his own sorrow and her betrayal. Similarly, although he desires union with her, he sets spiritual love above the physical:

> Make open display of loyalty even if you do not generously accord me a love union; yet a dream image will satisfy us and a remembrance will suffice us. (**9**, l. 48)

The idea of love being a union of souls is expressed in line 6; as a religion it appears in line 9, while fidelity is the main theme of the poem, for neither distance (l. 11), nor another woman (l. 19), nor

[27] Arabic text and English translation in A. J. Arberry, *Arabic Poetry: A Primer for Students* (Cambridge, 1965), pp. 114–115.

impatience (ll. 38–39) can alter the poet's affection. The few reproaches are so delicately phrased that they sound more like compliments, and in this way Ibn Zaidūn lives up to the recommendations made by Ibn Ḥazm on the subject of betrayal.

Now that there was no longer a political structure to serve, poetry, like architecture, was transferred to the personal sphere. Through the union of Neoplatonic doctrines with the tradition of Arabic verse a more humane Neoclassical verse was born. In the hands of true poets the latter reached impressive heights of perfection. In a brief span of time Ibn Shuhaid had mourned the death of the old order, while Ibn Ḥazm, as a philosopher, had sought refuge in thought against the turmoil of civil war. Ibn Zaidūn, as a poet, adapted this thought to Arabic poetry. Now poets could produce a creative lyrical outburst through the cultivation of true human emotion.

The Mulūk aṭ-Ṭawāʾif (1031–1091)

Under the enlightened protection of the Banū ʿAbbād, Seville had become a paradise for poets. One of the earliest extant anthologies of Andalusian poetry, entitled *Kitāb al-Badīʿ fī waṣf ar-rabīʿ* was compiled in Seville under the Mulūk aṭ-Ṭawāʾif by Abū l-Walīd al-Ḥimyarī. A poet's residence, a sort of literary academy, was established in that city, and poets enjoyed the privilege of weekly audiences with the king during which they vied with one another in reciting their odes, and were promoted or demoted according to their success. A register of pensioned poets also existed.[28]

The eleventh-century political scene had favored the rise of religious indifference at court, which contrasted with the past. Under al-Manṣūr the orthodox Mālikite jurists had been allowed to expurgate the library of al-Ḥakam II. Their influence had repressed poetic genius. Now the latter became uninhibited. At the same time the better poets of al-Andalus had mastered the complex techniques of Arabic versification. A tradition had been established and it was in the hands of a new generation of masters. The fall of the Caliphate, resulting as it did in the crumbling of the political world left the individual alone. His personal emotion now became a subject worthy of poetic treatment.

Of the new generation one of the most skillful poets was Ibn ʿAmmār of Silves (d. 1086). He was a close friend of al-Muʿtamid

---

[28] E. García Gómez, *Un eclipse de la poesía en Sevilla: La época almorávide* (Madrid, 1945), p. 13.

and led an adventurous life, dying tragically at the hands of his own sovereign and former boon companion. Ibn ᶜAmmār came to Seville during the reign of al-Muᶜtaḍid (1042–1069) whom he praised in a panegyric that won him lasting fame among Arab critics and came to be considered his masterpiece (**10**). It shows his ability to combine themes taken from different types of poetry, in this case the *nauriyya* and the *khamriyya*, into a new unity. This he does in a way that appears natural despite its contrived artifice.

He begins his poem with a bacchic scene (l. 1) which by borrowing elements from floral poetry creates an illusion of doubly heightened sensuality and permits a more complex interplay of metaphor. The latter reaches a stage where it ceases to be merely metaphoric and becomes truly symbolic. Compared with the poetry of aṭ-Ṭalīq, Ibn ᶜAmmār has gone a step further in complicating his imagery for whereas the one merely juxtaposes the floral and bacchic passages, the other fuses them together and thereby creates exciting new relationships between old clichés.

The opening words: "Pass round the glass for the breeze has arisen" derive from bacchic poetry. But they also evoke the joyous carousing that meets the king's victory and generosity. The word *inbarā*, "has arisen," is placed in a rhymed, and therefore stressed position. In this way the idea that the poem's main theme is somehow related to the breeze and its rising is introduced. At the very end of the poem the poet will conclude: "Hence, if you find the breeze of my praise to be fragrant, I have found the breeze of your favor to be even more fragrant!" (l. 37). From this it becomes clear that the breeze which at first appears as a bacchic element possesses a dual symbolic value denoting praise and generosity, and this breeze that connects praiser and praised is the central symbol of the poem.

The words "and the stars have slackened the reins of night travel" (l. 1) are an example of the rhetorical device known as *ḥusn at-taᶜlīl* (ingenious assignment of cause).[29] They imply that the stars are like camels who are resting after a long night journey. This metaphor allows the poet to allude to the *raḥīl* or journey theme of the traditional Arabic *qaṣīda*, but the way in which this is done is typical of the *badīᶜ* style. The stage is thus set for dawn's appearance which occurs immediately following: "The dawn has

---

[29] A convenient list of the rhetorical figures common to Arabic poetry may be found in Arberry, *op. cit.*, pp. 21–26, and also in G. E. von Grunebaum, *A Tenth-Century Document of Arabic Literary Theory and Criticism: Translation and Annotation of the Sections on Poetry of al-Baqillānī's Iᶜjāz al-Qurʾān* (Chicago, 1950).

bestowed on us its camphor, after the night has claimed back [its] ambergris;" (l. 2). The *muqābala* (pair of contrasting ideas elaborated in a balanced compound) is heightened by a *ṭibāq* (two words of opposite meaning in a line, here "dawn" and "night") as well as a *takāfuʾ* (two words of opposite meaning used in a metaphorical sense in the same line, here "camphor = whiteness" and "ambergris = blackness"). The basic *muqābala* is therefore a complex one containing two other rhetorical devices used to elaborate the central antithesis. Furthermore the poet has succeeded in awakening four senses in the compact space of two lines: taste (glass), feeling (breeze), sight (stars), and smell (camphor, ambergris).

If the first two lines are bacchic in content, the following two are floral. The garden is compared with a woman and a boy, this being an inversion of the usual theme found among previous poets who compare a woman to a garden (cf. Ibn Zaidūn). By inverting the commonplace the poet succeeds in giving freshness to a banal theme. The comparisons in lines 3 and 4 are both triple ones (garden = woman; flowers = embroidered robe; dew = pearls, and likewise garden = boy; roses = cheeks; myrtle = cheek down), while the piling together of metaphor serves to capture the garden's essential beauty in a few stylized and brilliant strokes. The technique of compressing several metaphors into a single line had a long tradition in previous Arabic poetry that goes as far back as Imruʾ al-Qais,[30] but its use here serves to reduce the garden to its essential qualities. In this way the poet is enabled to capture the feeling of floral poetry succinctly, to condense a whole theme into two lines with a technique that could well be called *pointilliste*, which would be used very much in *muwashshaḥa* poetry of this period. In line 5 the garden is compared with a green robe and the river in it with a limpid wrist. This allows the poet to make another association deriving naturally from what came before, for he picks up the image of the wrist and shows in lines 6 and 7 that its function is to brandish a sword and to give generous gifts. Furthermore the idea of water immediately suggests two functions; the ripple on its surface conjures up the wavy marks on a steel blade while its flowing abundance evokes the notion of generosity to the Arab mind. Then the wind is once again introduced (l. 6), and by blowing on the water as it will later blow the fragrance of the poet's praise and of the king's favor, is here preparing the listener's mind for the plea for generosity with which the poem culminates. The wind appears again in line 16; in line 34 it is plainly a

---

[30] *Muʿallaqa*, l. 54.

symbol of generosity as also in line 37. In this way it is a leitmotiv reappearing in key passages of the poem.

Up to line 6 all is a preparation to introduce the figure of al-Muʿtaḍid. Finally his name is mentioned in an alliterative phrase (*Ibnu ʿAbbādin yubaddidu ʿaskarā*) followed by an emphatic reiteration in the enjambment with line 7 (*ʿAbbādun*). The combined effect of the enjambment, alliteration, and repetition of the name is to heighten the impression caused by the words; they produce the effect of an incantation and elevate the poetic tone of the passage to a level in which the laws of everyday reality seem to be suspended so that the extravagant metaphor and unusual relationships appear almost natural to the listener now that they are connected with the awesome presence of the monarch. In Ibn ʿAmmār's poetry, the objects of nature are therefore interwoven into complex signs of reality. They are no longer mere comparisons but go deeper until they reach the symbolic level. What is gained by the new style is that it permits the creation of startling new relationships between the objects of reality. The effect was to shock the listener into a new awareness of everyday acts. The poet wishes to draw attention to old themes for the first time and in a new light. By creating these startling relationships, he gives a freshness to reality, and is able to do so fully within the conservatism of the old tradition, without searching for new metaphors, but simply by rearranging the old ones into new patterns.

By now al-Andalus was receiving fewer significant literary influences from the East, while its poetry had reached a level of dignity and originality in the treatment of themes. Ibn ʿAmmār was more skillful in the handling of decoration, while al-Muʿtamid of Seville (r. 1068–1091) was a more accomplished poet. The latter led a life entirely devoted to poetry: he was himself a poet, he became the Western protector of poets par excellence after the Normans invaded Sicily and Kairouan was overrun by Bedouin tribes, and himself led a life full of poetry and romance. As a young man he governed Silves in the Algarve for his father. Upon becoming king, his court became like the one held by Saif ad-Daula a century earlier in Aleppo, and to it the best Western poets flocked. He married the slave girl Rumaikiyya because she was able to complete the second hemistich of a line of poetry he had composed while walking along the Guadalquivir, so the story goes. Gradually he expanded his kingdom at his neighbors' expense, conquering Córdoba and other cities. After a quarrel with his boon companion Ibn ʿAmmār he had the latter turned over to him, imprisoned, and finally he executed him in a fit of rage. Realizing that the Castilian offensive led by Alfonso VI meant a serious threat to al-Andalus' survival, he chose to be "a camel-driver in Africa rather than a swineherd in Castile"[31] and requested the aid of the Almoravid chief Yūsuf ibn Tāshufīn. The latter entered al-Andalus, defeated the Christians at al-Zallāqah in 1086, and later deposed all the petty kings. Al-Muᶜtamid was banished to Aghmāt in Morocco, where he spent his final years in poverty, writing poems filled with deep emotion in which he mourned his fall from power. His production from this period is in some ways comparable with that of the Ḥamdānid Abū Firās which the latter wrote during his captivity in Constantinople. Both poets make of their personal sorrow the main subject of their poetry, and by this means they rise above the commonplaces found in occasional verse. Every aspect of al-Muᶜtamid's life was reflected in his poetry, from the escapades of his early youth to the captivity of his later years. He died in exile in 1095.

In an early *qaṣīda* written to his father to request his forgiveness for having allowed himself to fall into a trap set for him by the Berbers of Granada (**11**), the personal tone he was to adopt in his later poetry is already present. The poem is composed in a simple, natural language containing relatively few rhetorical devices. This allows him to speak straight from the heart. When aroused, his father al-Muᶜtaḍid was known for the violence of his temper. He had executed another of his sons for betraying him, and so al-Muᶜtamid had grounds to fear the outcome of his father's displeasure at his military fiasco. For this reason he casts aside all excessive rhetoric and in the initial soliloquy, he tries to calm his own fears. In this soliloquy he employs the poetic convention of addressing himself in the second person singular *ka*, "your." But expressively the use of the pronoun *ka* suggests that the soliloquy is in reality a dialogue for it has the effect of including the father into the poet's musings. By saying (l. 1) "Rest your heart; let your cares not overcome you. What good will grief and apprehension do you?" the poet is on one level calming his own fears, as though his reason were speaking to his emotion. The device thus makes possible a lyrical dimension whereby the poet's psychology may be revealed. On another level, however, it seems to suggest that it is the father speaking to the son. It assumes sadness rather than anger on the father's part; a disposition in favor of clemency rather than punishment. By attempting to arouse the father's compassion and his nobler instincts the poet

[31] García Gómez, *Poemas*, pp. 34–35.

hopes to mitigate his wrath. On a third level, the use of *ka* might even be taken to suggest that it is the father who is sad (and therefore inclined to forgive) and that it is his son who is attempting to console him. Thus the *ka* has an expressive function that goes far beyond its mere grammatical and logical function. It serves to introduce the main theme of the poem, that is, a request for forgiveness.

Among the poets who attended the court of al-Muᶜtamid was the Sicilian Ibn Ḥamdīs (d. 1132) who had escaped to Seville after the Normans invaded his homeland. He adopted the Andalusian fashions in poetry and after the Almoravid invasion he divulged them in North Africa where he emigrated. He has left many poems in which he mourns the loss of his native Sicily. He also achieved distinction in poems which described the glories of architectural monuments in al-Andalus. The architectural theme had been cultivated in the East by al-Buḥturī, but Ibn Hamdīs seems to have popularized it in al-Andalus.[32] He remained faithful to al-Muᶜtamid during the latter's imprisonment, and refused to accept small gifts of money from his formerly munificent sovereign at a time when other, more shameless poets were importuning him for gifts he could no longer afford to make. In one such poem of refusal (**13**) he sets up an antithetically parallelistic structure (l. 1, "brought you honor—done you wrong"; l. 2, "women—masculine"; l. 4, "day—eve") to console the grieving king by showing him that the reversals of fortune can sometimes be for the better. In another poem (**14**) packed with complicated imagery based on the architectural configuration of a garden he describes a drinking scene. His last line: "For life is excusable only when we walk along the shores of pleasure and abandon all restraint!" sums up much of the bacchic poetry of the period and represents an attempt to escape by means of "art for art's sake" from the everyday threats of a politically unstable society, yet a society which eagerly pursued the pleasures of life before the coming of the Almoravid deluge.

Another of the poets faithful to al-Muᶜtamid after his fall from power was Ibn al-Labbāna of Denia (d. 1113), famous for his *qaṣīda* in which he mourns his former protector's departure into exile (**16**). The poem has not survived in its entirety, yet its fragmentary remains give evidence of a deep and sincere devotion to al-Muᶜtamid expressed with a gentle resignation to the blows of fate. Its sincere tone is typical of the personal note struck in the period by many poets.

---

[32] Vernet, p. 120.

The poetry of Abū Isḥāq of Elvira (d. 1066) is very different. Abū Isḥāq was a *faqīh* or jurist (pl. *fuqahā*ʾ) of Arab descent who had the misfortune for an Arab of living under the Zīrid dynasty of Granada who were Berbers. The latter had found it impossible to rule the Arabs without the support of a neutral element of society, and so they had raised the Jewish Banū Naghrīla family to a position of power over the hostile Arab population. The king, Bādīs ibn Ḥābbūs, was ignorant, old, and an alcoholic to boot. Insensitive to the feelings of his Muslim subjects he allowed matters to get out of control. The *fuqahā*ʾ who were orthodox and narrow-minded were forced to lead a marginal life in a kingdom ruled by a religiously indifferent dynasty. They had formerly enjoyed influence and prestige under al-Manṣūr but at present they were relegated to obscurity, and so they expressed dissatisfaction and discontent. It was natural that Abū Isḥāq, like his colleague and contemporary Ibn Ḥazm, should become embittered and write ascetic poetry renouncing the pleasures of the world that he was not allowed to enjoy. Putting his pen at the service of the prevailing anti-Jewish sentiment, he wrote a famous *qaṣīda* (**15**) in which he incited the Muslim population to rise up against the Jewish vizier Yūsuf ibn Naghrīla. The poem resulted in the pogrom of December 30, 1066, in which Yūsuf along with three thousand Jews, was massacred. It illustrates the dissatisfaction of the lower classes with Zīrid rule and explains the violent popular reaction that did away with the Mulūk aṭ-Ṭawāʾif.

García Gómez in his analysis of this poem says:

> He takes the strongest and most solid Arabic words; the words every Muslim capable of reading the Koran could understand, and arranging them in groups with a streamlined and straightforward syntax, he shoots them out in the energetic and regular syllables, like a military march, of the *mutaqārib* meter. . . . There are many concrete images: "Those Jews who once searched the dung heaps for a colored rag to shroud the dead . . . have now divided up Granada among themselves . . . they collect tributes . . . dress with elegance . . . they slaughter animals in the market places . . . that monkey, Joseph has paved his house with marble." Each of these statements is followed by its corresponding counterstatement: "You, the masters, the believers, the pure, dress in rags, you live in misery, you go hungry, they rob you, you have to beg at their door. . . ."[33]

---

[33] E. García Gómez, *Un alfaquí español: Abū Isḥāq de Elvira* (Madrid and Granada, 1944), p. 39.

As an ascetic poet Abū Isḥāq is rare in al-Andalus at this time. Living in Zīrid Granada where culture was at a low ebb, being an Arab and at the margin of society, he was a poet gone sour, and became a mouthpiece for the opposition. His poem is direct and to the point. It avoids obscure literary conceits which the Berbers would not have understood. His appeal to Islam, not Arabism, coming as it does from an Arab indicates that the cause of the latter was dead.

Along with the classical *qaṣīda* and occasional pieces, the earliest extant *muwashshaḥāt* (see Glossary for definition) composed in al-Andalus date from this period. These strophic poems had been invented much earlier, possibly by the blind poet Muqaddam ibn Muᶜāfā al-Qabrī, at the court of the Emir ᶜAbdullāh (r. 888–912). The origin and significance of Andalusian strophic poetry is not yet clear. Ibn Bassām (d. 1147) explains it as follows:

> The *muwashshaḥāt* are meters which the people of al-Andalus use abundantly in the composition of *ghazal* and *nasīb* poems, such that on hearing them there are torn open the collars—nay even the hearts—of gently nurtured ladies. The first to fashion these meters of the *muwashshaḥāt* in our country and to invent their method of composition was—according to what has reached me—Muqaddam ibn Muᶜāfā al-Qabrī, the blind, who used to fashion them out of hemistichs of poetry, except that the majority of them were based on unusual meters rarely used, taking the vernacular and *ᶜajamī* speech and calling it *markaz*, and basing on it the *muwashshaḥa*, without any internal rhyming in the *markaz* or in the *aghṣān*. It is said that Ibn ᶜAbd Rabbihi, the author of the *Kitāb al-ᶜIqd* was the first to initiate this variety of *muwashshaḥa*, after which appeared Yūsuf ibn Hārūn ar-Ramādī who was the first to make copious use of internal rhyme, by using internal rhyme at every pause [i.e., rhyming each segment together], but in the *markaz* exclusively. The poets of his age maintained this, such as Mukarram ibn Saᶜīd and the two sons of Abū l-Ḥasan. Then came our ᶜUbāda [ibn Māʾ as-Samāʾ], who introduced the innovation of *taḍfīr* [lit. "plaiting, interweaving"] for he reinforced the places of pause in the *aghṣān* by using internal rhyme just as ar-Ramādī had reinforced the pauses in the *markaz*. The meters of these *muwashshaḥāt* go beyond the scope of our book, for most of them do not follow the rules of Arabic metrics.[34]

---

[34] *Dhakhīra* (Cairo, 1942), II, 1–2.

We are fortunate in preserving a poetics of the *muwashshaḥāt* written by the Egyptian poet and critic Ibn Sanāʾ al-Mulk (d. 1211).[35] In it the author explains that the most important part of the poem was the *kharja* or "exit" which was frequently in Romance or in vernacular Arabic. The main part of the *muwashshaḥa*, which was written in classical Arabic, was adapted so that its meter and rhymes corresponded to the preexistent *kharja* in the vernacular. From this it follows that the meters in use were often syllabic as in Romance poetry and not quantitative as in classical Arabic. At other times the rarer Arabic meters mentioned by Ibn Bassām could be made to coincide with those of the vernacular *kharjāt*. Sometimes the poet composed the *kharja* himself and built his *muwashshaḥa* on it, but at times he borrowed a previously existing one. The *kharjāt* that have survived are short poems in which a woman laments her lovelornness, declares her refusal to grant her lover's desires, or seeks love in a way bordering on the obscene. The ones in Romance are sometimes rhymed like popular Spanish poetry, that is by assonance, and at others they rhyme *ū* and *ī* in the Arabic style. They are thus hybrid, popular poetry of traditional cast which on the one hand constitutes the earliest textual evidence for Romance lyrical poetry, and on the other, is an example of the feminine archetype of universal love poetry, expressed from the woman's point of view, and belongs to the kind of poetry studied by Theodor Frings.[36]

Ibn Khaldūn (d. 1406) further illuminates the problem of the origin and development of the *muwashshaḥa* as follows:

> The *muwashshaḥāt* consist of "branches" [*ghuṣn*] and "strings" [*simṭ*] in great number and different meters. A certain number [of "branches" and "strings"] is called a single verse [stanza]. There must be the same number of rhymes in the "branches" [of each stanza] and the same meter [for the "branches" of the whole poem] throughout the whole poem. The largest number of stanzas employed is seven. Each stanza contains as many "branches" as is consistent with purpose and method. Like the *qaṣīda*, the *muwashshaḥa* is used for erotic and laudatory poetry. [The authors of *muwashshaḥāt*] vied to the utmost with each other in this [kind of poetry]. Everybody, the elite

---

[35] *Dār aṭ-ṭirāz fī ʿamal al-muwashshaḥāt*, ed. by Jaudat ar-Rikābī (Damascus, 1949).

[36] See Leo Spitzer, "The Mozarabic Lyrics and Theodor Frings' Theories," *Comparative Literature, IV* (1952), 1–22.

> and the common people, liked and knew these poems because they were easy to grasp and understand. They were invented in al-Andalus by Muqaddam ibn Muʿāfā al-Qabrī, a poet under the Emir ʿAbdullāh ibn Muḥammad al-Marwānī. Aḥmad ibn ʿAbd Rabbihi, the author of the ʿIqd, learned this [type of poetry] from him. [Muqaddam and Ibn ʿAbd Rabbihi] were not mentioned together with the recent (authors of *muwashshaḥāt*), and thus their *muwashshaḥāt* fell into desuetude. The first poet after them who excelled in this subject was ʿUbāda al-Qazzāz, the poet of al-Muʿtaṣim ibn Ṣumādiḥ, the lord of Almería.[37]

Ibn Bassām, Ibn Sanāʾ al-Mulk, and Ibn Khaldūn sum up all that is known and much that has been surmised about the origin and development of the *muwashshaḥa*. Two main theories of origin have been proposed by Western critics. M. Hartmann claimed that the *muwashshaḥāt* were a local development based on Eastern strophic forms such as the *qaṣīda simṭiyya*.[38] García Gómez has shown more recently that (*a*) the strophic structure and rhyme schemes of the *muwashshaḥa* are the same as those of popular Spanish poems such as the *villancico;* (*b*) that the prosodic system used is syllabic, not quantitative, and that it follows the law of Mussafia for Romance poetry (according to whom Portuguese lyrical poetry is based on [1] syllable count, [2] contrary to modern Spanish practice a final, stressed syllable is not the equivalent of two syllables, [3] lines with an equal number of syllables may end indistinctly in words with final or penultimate stress);[39] (*c*) that the *kharjāt* in Romance, although highly Arabized, are the earliest extant examples of a popular, traditional Romance lyrical poetry betraying a common source of origin with later Galician and Castilian lyrics.

The integration of these two opposing hypotheses, the Arabic and the Romance, suggests that the eastern *qaṣīda simṭiyya* with its multiple rhymes probably made it easier to adapt native, Romance elements into the creation of a new, hybrid form.[40] Musical influences probably lie behind the origin of the new form, for the structure of the Romance *rondeau*, with a basic rhyme scheme similar to that of

---

[37] *The Muqaddimah*, trans. Franz Rosenthal (New York, 1958), III, 440–441.

[38] *Das arabische Strophengedichte. I. Das Muwashshaḥ* (Weimar, 1897).

[39] E. García Gómez, "La ley de Mussafia se aplica a la poesía estrófica arábigoandaluza," *Andalus*, XXVII (1962), 1–20.

[40] E. García Gómez, "Una pre-muwashshaḥa atribuída a Abū Nuwās," *Andalus*, XXI (1956), 406–414.

the *muwashshaḥa*, has a parallel melodic structure:

	Rhyme		Melody
simṭ	*a* *b*	*estribillo*	*a* *b*
ghuṣn	*a* *a*	*copla*	*a* *a*
simṭ	*a* *b*		*a* *b*
simṭ	*a* *b*	*estribillo*	*a* *b*

The second line of the Spanish *copla* (*ab*), corresponding to the Arabic *simṭ* is a repetition of the *estribillo*, both in the text and in the music.[41] This very elementary form, easily derived from the *qaṣīda simṭiyya* and possibly the one described by Ibn Bassām as having been invented by Muqaddam al-Qabrī, could have been later developed by the addition of further internal rhyme into the complex *muwashshaḥa* of the eleventh century. The evolution toward increased complexity of rhyme seems also to coincide with an as yet little understood but parallel evolution and complication of Hispano-Arabic music. The first extant *muwashshaḥāt* are highly decorative, structurally complex poems. Yet if the exact origin of their structure is shrouded in mystery, their themes and literary technique are not. They are basically love poems, and the type of love they describe is a curious juxtaposition of the masculine, courtly love, which is contained in the classical Arabic part of the poem, and its feminine counterpart which is uncourtly, contained in the vernacular and therefore subliterary *kharja*. The woman presented in the *kharja* is from the lower class. She is a slave girl, a Christian, and the sentiments she expresses range from ironic refusal to crude obscenity, all in an outlandish and deliberately unsophisticated patois.

The classical part of the *muwashshaḥa* furthermore is Arabic in its themes, all of which derive from the tradition of Arabic love poetry. The explanation for this curious juxtaposition of the prestigious with the uncouth lies in the fact that these poems were aristocratic. They were developed at court by cultivated Arab poets, and their view of the lower classes is essentially upper class. For them

---

[41] Adolfo Salazar, "Poesía y música en las primeras formas de versificación rimada en lengua vulgar y sus antecedentes en lengua latina en la Edad Media," *Filosofía y Letras*, VIII (1942), 287–349.

the Christians were an object of tolerant but amused ridicule. Furthermore, the juxtaposition of the high, courtly style in classical Arabic with the low style in the vernacular ironizes the former. From this point of view it could be argued that the *muwashshaḥāt* were an Andalusian version of the Modernist movement which in the East had also led to experimentation with new forms.[42] Abū Nuwās had not only poked fun at the sacrosanct themes of pre-Islamic poetry, but had written a poem in *tasmīṭ* remarkably similar in many ways to a *muwashshaḥa*.[43] By experimenting with new forms, Western poets broke up the structure of the traditional *qaṣīda* not only in content, but also in form. By ironizing the outmoded love tradition developed by ᶜUmar ibn Abī Rabīᶜa and Ibn al-Aḥnaf they were exercising a Modernist prerogative to attack the past. It even became necessary for Ibn Ḥazm, the ultraconservative loyalist, to revive and ennoble this outworn tradition by applying Neoplatonic ideas to it. Thus the *muwashshaḥāt* were another general manifestation of "art for art's sake." From their beginnings in the Modernist movement they evolved toward sheer decorativeness. They were, however, too brief in form and too ironical in theme to fit the need for the essentially dignified and social art of the Caliphate. For this reason, as Ibn Khaldūn informs us, they fell into desuetude and did not enjoy literary prestige until the Mulūk aṭ-Ṭawāᵓif whose unconcern for politics was paralleled by their fascination with "art for art's sake."

Despite the Romance elements that were present in their origin, they were absorbed so completely into the Arabic poetic tradition, that they became essentially Arabic compositions. Gradually the vernacular *kharjāt* were replaced by classical Arabic ones, while classical meters replaced the syllabic system, and in the course of time the daughter of mixed ancestry was completely absorbed, for Islamic civilization in the words of G. E. von Grunebaum, "is thoroughly syncretistic, and it proves its vitality by coating each and every borrowing with its own inimitable patina."[44]

The extremely short verses of the new poetic form made metaphoric development difficult in the traditional way. On the other hand the *muwashshaḥa* was structurally suited to develop the *pointilliste* technique found in Ibn ᶜAmmār's *qaṣīda*, a technique that leads to pure symbolism.

In this respect ᶜUbāda al-Qazzāz describes his beloved in a few

---

[42] J. T. Monroe, "The Muwashshaḥāt," in *Collected Studies in Honor of Américo Castro's Eightieth Year* (Oxford, 1965), pp. 335–371.

[43] García Gómez, *op. cit.*

[44] *Medieval Islam* (Chicago, 1961), p. 319.

brief but masterly strokes in which each image is heightened by the rhyme, and coincides with a segment of the line (**18**, ll. 13–14):

> A full moon, a midday sun, a stem on a sand dune, fragrant musk;
> None more full, none brighter, none more leafy, none more fragrant.

Decorative and apparential, the *muwashshaḥāt* carry the poetic tendencies of the eleventh century to a fragile, delicate extreme, where a fragmentary form harmonizes perfectly with a fragmentary content. The new form, moreover, with its light and musical meters, made it possible to dress the old, timeworn themes of Arabic poetry in a new garb. The result was an impressionistic, fleeting poetry of the moment, incredibly beautiful, excelling in the creation of enchanting scenery. By its very fragility and metrical brevity, however, it was prevented from compressing into its verses the meditation and psychological depth that could only be expressed in longer meters. It is sheer decorative, detailed beauty, like the stuccoes of the Aljafería.

The Almoravids (1091–1145)

The political failure of the refined Mulūk aṭ-Ṭawāʾif produced a violent reaction by the urban middle and lower classes. The religious ideals of Islamic universalism were by now strongly opposed to those of secular Arab culture, and with the aid of the Almoravids unity and commercial prosperity for a time replaced the earlier fragmentation and extravagance. The Almoravids were a fundamentalist Islamic brotherhood founded in the upper Senegal in the middle of the eleventh century which soon spread from the western Sudan to the North African coast, from the Atlantic to Algiers. They were Ṣinhajī Berbers, and wore the veil like their modern descendants the Tuaregs. When al-Muʿtamid requested the aid of their leader Yūsuf ibn Tāshufīn to repel the Christian advance, he unleashed forces that were to reduce the native Andalusian civilization to a provincial status within an African empire. Yūsuf led his veiled warriors into al-Andalus in 1086 and defeated Alfonso VI at al-Zallāqah near Badajoz. He returned twice to the peninsula, and seeing that the quarrelsome petty kings could not defend their territories from the enemy and were disliked by their subjects, he deposed all of them save for the Banū Hūd of Saragossa in 1090. His son ʿAlī later transferred the imperial capital from Marrakesh to Seville. ʿAlī

(r. 1106–1142) saw the short-lived empire at its highest peak and witnessed the beginning of its downfall. He died in 1142 and by 1147 the last Almoravid ruler Isḥāq was killed and the Almohads were crossing the straits of Gibraltar.

The irruption of the Almoravids had profound and even dislocating effects on Andalusian culture. The former were strictly orthodox and they recognized the Abbasid Caliphate of Baghdad. Their government was conducted through the support of the Mālikite *fuqahā*ʾ who constituted an intolerant, narrowly legalistic theocracy and imposed a tight control on the free expression of ideas. Scholastic theology was discouraged, the study of Koran and *ḥadīth* considered sinful, and philosophers became suspect and were forced to hide their true beliefs from the mob for fear of denunciation and persecution by a tribunal of inquisitors.[45] In this respect it is significant that Ibn Bājja "censured the fact that [the study of metaphysics] should have been mentioned . . . to the lower classes."[46] Ghazālī's books were publicly burned at the gates of the Mosque of Córdoba because of their attempt to infuse a new and more liberal Sufi spirit into orthodox theology. But it is easy to carry the condemnation of the Almoravids too far. On the other side of the balance, education in al-Andalus remained free from state intervention so that scholars could study what they wished, as before. Yūsuf who was a Berber, was not therefore a barbarian. If he did not understand the subtleties of classical Arabic poetry, his successors at least made a sincere effort to learn from the conquered Andalusians. The biographical dictionaries and bibliographical information from this period indicate that culture did not come to a halt under the Almoravids but that, quite the contrary, it continued to be productive despite a hostile atmosphere. The Almoravid government introduced a superior system of coinage which reflected the increased prosperity and put al-Andalus in a favorable position with regard to international trade. Whereas before the common people had been greatly overtaxed to pay for royal extravagance and a serious gold shortage had prevailed, under the Almoravids gold and silver became abundant.[47]

Furthermore Mālikite intolerance coincided with an astonishing outburst of poetic creativity represented by men of true genius. Although poets suffered a somewhat precarious existence after the

---

[45] García Gómez, *Un eclipse de la poesía en Sevilla.*

[46] Ibn Ṭufail, *El filósofo autodidacto,* trans. F. Pons Boïgues (2d ed.; Madrid, 1954), p. 40.

[47] García Gómez, *op. cit.*, pp. 21–26.

loss of the royal patronage they had previously enjoyed, they continued to write. Thanks also to the recent union between al-Andalus and North Africa, the former became the teacher of the latter and from this time forward Hispano-Arabic styles in art, literature, and music would reign supreme in Moroccan cities. At the same time the Almoravids' adoption of the lax morality of Andalusian society on the one hand, and their lip service to an ultraconservative puritanism on the other gave birth to an inner tension between theory and practice. From this contradiction the Almoravids never succeeded in disentangling themselves, but became prisoners of their own rigid doctrines and proved unable to adapt to changing circumstances. This condition contributed to the undermining of their moral authority. The subsequent repressions of intellectual freedom justified in the name of political expediency likewise undermined intellectual creativity and helped only to rigidify their narrow and intolerant stance. As a result moral and intellectual standards were debased and the reform movement they initiated came spiritually to a standstill. It was left to their successors the Almohads to supply a more flexible and humane ideology.

As the preceding aristocratic society was removed from power, new developments closely reflecting this social change occurred in the field of art. A new type of palatial residence was developed. It was located in the country, and its main feature was a close integration of architecture with nature. The ruined palace of El Castillejo in Monteagudo overlooking the plain of Murcia is from this period and is arranged around a central garden surrounded by private apartments. The garden is a space divided into flower beds crossed by raised walks designed so that the view of the flowers could be more readily enjoyed from above. It integrates reflection pools, running water, fountains, and flower beds into a unit central to the whole structure, and is symbolic of the current aristocratic escape to the country. In the city, large new mosques are built. A lack of marble and the magnitude of the new buildings led to the disappearance of the column and its replacement with robust, rectangular pillars that give an air of massive strength to the structure. The Mosques of Qarawiyyīn (in Fez), Tlemcen, and Algiers are masterpieces of this period. In particular the mihrab of the Tlemcen Mosque is exquisitely decorated and demonstrates the extent to which the artistic refinements developed during the eleventh century were now being adapted to public buildings as art once more regained its social function and private palaces were relegated to the countryside by the ascetic ideal of the Almoravids.

The eleventh-century tendency to overdecorate was carried to even further extremes with the invention of the *muqarnas* or "squinch"; the plain, intersecting ribs that supported the domes of Caliphal buildings are now heavily decorated and remolded into complex, three-dimensional geometric patterns suspended from the ceiling. In the cupula of the latrines of the Abū Yūsuf Mosque in Marrakesh these ribs have evolved into exuberant decorative motifs.

The tower of the Kutubiyya Mosque in Marrakesh is also Almoravid. Its elaborate external window ornamentation and rich style indicate the extent to which art had recuperated its social functions. These buildings also bear witness to the taste of the unsophisticated Berbers in adopting the exquisite Andalusian art and spreading it throughout their empire.[48]

Whereas poets had enjoyed a golden age of royal patronage under the Mulūk aṭ-Ṭawā᾿if, suddenly all had changed. The previous religious indifference was followed by an orthodox crackdown on the free expression of ideas. Seville, now ruled by Berbers who did not understand the subtleties of classical Arabic became indifferent to poets, and as a result hatred for Seville became a commonplace expressed by most major poets. It was not that Seville had become impoverished—on the contrary, it enjoyed increased prosperity—but its wealthy citizens were parsimonious with their money when it came to poets, and now that the court no longer supported them, they were suddenly left to their own devices.

Rather than signaling a decline of poetry, the new conditions gave birth to a literary renaissance. The pampered court poets of the old school, who had received their training under the Mulūk aṭ-Ṭawā᾿if all felt that they were living in a hostile milieu. Some of them, in the quiet seclusion of provincial life, seek escape through the cultivation of nature poetry at the same time when new country residences were also springing up everywhere. Such was the case of Ibn Khafāja. Some poets' escapism is expressed through a proud disdain for the present coupled with an undue reverence for the past which acquires vast proportions at this time, and is looked back upon with deep nostalgia. This is the moment when the great anthologists are busy collecting the poetry of the earlier age: Ibn Bassām (d. 1147) composes the *Dhakhīra* and Ibn Khaqān (d. 1134 or 1140) the *Qalā᾿id.* Still others modify their technique and adapt their muse to a new kind of audience, less select than formerly. A new

---

[48] Gómez Moreno, *op. cit.*, pp. 279–296.

form, the *zajal*, is invented, and Ibn Quzmān becomes its greatest exponent.[49]

One of the most serious consequences of the reverence for the past that developed out of the new situation in al-Andalus, was that it restricted the freedom of artistic expression which had existed earlier, as the *fuqahā*ʾ gained control of the country and opposed independent thinking. Later, the Almohads would reintroduce the works of Ghazālī, and a healthy intellectual renaissance would bring new life to the world of ideas, but at present the *fuqahā*ʾ, who were enjoying their period of greatest influence in Andalusian history, were narrowly legalistic; they devoted all their attention to a literalist study of the *furū*ᶜ or "ramifications" as opposed to the *uṣūl* or "sources" of jurisprudence. Hence it was natural that everywhere poets and *fuqahā*ʾ should clash head on. The former were permitted to be as scandalous and licentious as they wished in their verses, in exchange for renouncing all pretense at expressing independence of thought, or attempting to influence political events. Ibn Quzmān, who in one of his poems boasts of living in a quiet street, free from the *fuqahā*ʾ where he could conduct his immoral pursuits, was permitted to compose his indecent poems in the same city where Ghazālī's books had been burned.

Aristocratic poetry fell out of favor with the loss of royal patronage. For this reason a general feeling of bitterness, melancholy, and alienation is found in *qāṣid* poets. Ibn ᶜAbdūn, a secretary under the Afṭasid dynasty of Badajoz, wrote a long elegy (**20**) to mourn the fall of his sovereigns who were murdered by the Almoravids. The poem is traditional in style and structure, and is greatly admired by Arab critics for the complex, learned historical references it contains.[50]

The poem creates a general feeling of historical decline, for it shows that down through the ages, everything has tended to perish. There is in it a strong sense of abandonment and of powerlessness before destiny. Its handling of themes to depict the past is almost archaeological in its erudition. The poet argues that the pagan emperors, the great caliphs of the east, and the kings of al-Andalus have all come to a violent end. The poem is divided into three logical units: (1) a lament over the treachery of fate (ll. 1–9); (2) examples of this principle taken from (*a*) eastern history (ll. 10–44), (*b*) Andalusian history (ll. 45–47); (3) lament over the Afṭasids of

---

[49] García Gómez, *Poemas*, pp. 36–40.
[50] Vernet, p. 120.

Badajoz (ll. 48–75), the climax and most sincere part of the elegy. In it the expression of the poet's bitterness and despair reach a high point. The impression is given that with the death of the Afṭasids, the meaning of history has been lost: "since they have departed, [the earth], along with its inhabitants, is sundered and unsteady" (l. 64). The present is experienced as hostile to the poet whose poetry is no longer appreciated in his homeland. As the present dwindled, the immediate past loomed large in the eyes of the poet, who sought refuge in the excellence of his art and erudition.

Nature once more had become a poetic theme of significance. But unlike the Caliphal *nauriyya* in which nature was the joyous background for revelry (aṭ-Ṭalīq), or eleventh-century poetry where nature's varying moods reflect varying states of the poet's feeling (Ibn Zaidūn), nature in the twelfth century reflects a universal sadness. This is perfectly exemplified by the art of Ibn Khafāja of Alcira (d. 1138). He was born near Valencia and formed part of a group of Levantine poets who had personally known the Mulūk aṭ-Ṭawā'if generation in their youth. Ibn Khafāja is one of the very greatest of Hispano-Arabic poets. He was left to his own resources under the Almoravids and so withdrew from political activities to cultivate his farmlands and his muse. His poetry is full of charming vignettes of idyllic country life. He became known as al-Jannān, "the gardener," and also as the Ṣanawbarī of al-Andalus because in his poetry the beauty of nature is extolled to the exclusion of all else. He left a deep influence on later poetry, and his style, known as Khafājī after him, continued to be imitated until the very last days of peninsular Islam, and was then kept alive in North Africa.[51]

His masterpiece (**21**) sings the lonely grandeur of nature in hauntingly beautiful language, and expresses a feeling of universal alienation. The poem begins in the conventional way of the old Arabian *qaṣīda*, with a desert journey completely foreign to Andalusian life. The very revival of this archaic theme that had almost disappeared in the preceding century indicates the extent to which reverence for the past had developed under the Almoravids. The desert journey leads the poet to a group of stylized beloveds (l. 5) reduced to mere mouths and faces. The function of this mannerism is to exemplify the mutability of time and the instability of all human relations (l. 6). This prelude introduces the main subject of the poem: a mountain endowed with human attributes is mourning over its unrequited love and complaining that its lovers, the travelers who

---

[51] *Ibid.* p. 121; García Gómez, *op. cit.*, p. 38.

pass by it, always depart from it never to return. The mountain, a proverbial symbol of stability in Arabic poetry, here becomes a symbol of the instability of love and of universal loneliness. It is a projection of the poet's self into nature, for the broken love affairs in the prelude are now shown to be mere incidents in a vaster solitude embodied by nature itself. Nature mourns, and the whole universe is hostile to man; mountains are the mere playthings of chance. In Ibn Zaidūn's verses nature had a double attribute: it was either happy or sad depending upon his proximity to, or distance from, the beloved, but in Ibn Khafāja nature is uniformly and consistently sad. The almost Greek sense of harmony between man and nature is therefore a harmony in melancholy according to the poetry of Ibn Khafāja.

Ibn az-Zaqqāq (d. 1133) was the nephew of Ibn Khafāja. He was probably born in Valencia during the period when that city was ruled by the Cid. His main contribution to the development of Andalusian poetry was his renovation and enrichment of its metaphoric system and imagery. García Gómez writes the following on the subject: "In a moment of exhaustion of a metaphoric system that is still in use, it often happens in fact, that the worn-out images become lexicalized, and based on these once they have become lexicalized, poets build new metaphors which we could well call 'second degree' ones. This procedure which at the end of our Renaissance lyrical poetry was adopted by Góngora . . . was likewise that of Ibn az-Zaqqāq."[52]

In this way, he reworked metaphors so that, in ash-Shaqundī's words, "he renewed their form to the ear and made their rusty edge penetrate men's minds."[53]

Poets were often forced to entertain less-refined audiences than formerly and so they naturally tended to cultivate the lighter forms. For this reason the *muwashshaḥāt* enjoyed a great vogue at this time. Whereas in the eleventh century the *kharja* had been conceived as a picaresque and discordant note the function of which was to cause amusement by ironizing the courtly love substance of the poem, it now evolves in two directions: either it expresses a melancholy acceptance of love's trials (**24**) or it becomes more openly obscene (**28**).

---

[52] Ibn az-Zaqqāq, *Poesías*, ed. and trans. E. García Gómez (Madrid, 1956), p. 18. The prologue to this monograph contains a valuable study of Ibn az-Zaqqāq's use of metaphor.

[53] ash-Shaqundī, *Elogio del islam español*, trans. E. García Gómez (Madrid, 1954), p. 70.

The *muwashshaḥāt* of al-Aᶜmā at-Tuṭīlī, "the blind poet of Tudela" (d. 1126), became popular all over the Islamic world for their strain of gentle and resigned melancholy. Along with many of his colleagues, he was forced to wander from place to place looking in vain for the munificence of past royalty. His poems express an embittered disillusionment and a sense of being trapped in adverse circumstances from which there was no escape: "I would fly, yet I find no place to take flight" (**23**, l. 4).

His contemporary Ibn Baqī (d. 1145) has left a number of love poems as well as panegyrics, occasional pieces, and *muwashshaḥāt*. He also aspired to achieve fame, but was forced to conclude that his age saw "the rhymes of poetry weep intensely for an Arab lost among barbarians."[54]

Al-Abyaḍ on the other hand is a poet whose tendency to write obscene verse, much appreciated during this period, goes back to the style of the Baghdadi poet Ibn Hajjāj. This development leads to the greatest invention of the age: the *zajal* form. The *zajal* is in appearance more popular than the *muwashshaḥa*. Its origin is obscure too. Possibly it was invented by Ibn Bājja at the beginning of the twelfth century.[55] Before this time there is no record of its existence.[56] Afterward one of its earliest cultivators was a little-known poet called Yakhlaf ibn Rāshid. The recent discovery of a few of the latter's *azjāl* shows that in style they were similar to those of his illustrious successor Ibn Quzmān, and therefore it may be assumed that the peculiarities of the *zajal* were a matter of style and not the result of any particular writer's individual quirks.[57]

Generally speaking the *zajal* follows the strophic structure of the *muwashshaḥa*, but it is written entirely in the colloquial Arabic of Córdoba. There are two main types: (1) identical in everything with the *muwashshaḥa*, except for the use of the colloquial language throughout, and (2) the *zajal* proper in which the *kharja* disappears or loses its importance, while the *asmāṭ* only repeat half the rhymes of the prelude. The Romance vocabulary is no longer concentrated in the *kharja*, given the latter's disappearance, but is scattered in the form of loose words and expressions throughout the poem.

---

[54] García Gómez, *op. cit.*, p. 39.

[55] Vernet, p. 21.

[56] It is too tempting not to note in passing, however, that as early as A.D. 854 Alvarus of Córdoba was complaining that the Muslims "defile the priests of God with colloquial expressions and obscene songs" (*sacerdotes Dei . . . vulgali* [*sic*] *proverbio et cantico inhonesto sugillant*) (*Indiculus Luminosus*, ¶ 6). This passage was pointed out by Dr. Juan Gil (private communication).

[57] S. M. Stern, "Studies on Ibn Quzmān," *Andalus* XVI (1951), 379–425.

Furthermore in contrast with the *muwashshaḥa* which may have no more than seven strophes, the *zajal* is generally much longer and may have any number of strophes depending upon its purpose.[58]

The Eastern critic Ḥillī (d. 1349), in his treatise on colloquial Arabic poetry which has recently been edited and studied, devoted an extensive chapter to *zajal* poetics.[59] It contains some interesting though obscure references to music which seem to indicate that the modifications introduced into the *zajal* were related to parallel developments in music. Ḥillī was a latecomer, and he complained of the excessive simplicity and lack of rhetorical ornamentation in the early *zajal* poetry of Ibn Quzmān, claiming that it was hard to understand why the Andalusian masters should have wanted to describe a pretty girl's face as being "white as milk" instead of likening her to the full moon, or describing her hair as "black as a pot" instead of black as the night. He ends his argument by stating his preference for the copious use of *badīᶜ*. This shows that the later poets, especially in the East, missed the whole point of the *zajal* and succeeded in reabsorbing it into the classical tradition like its elder sister the *muwashshaḥa*.

This raises the question of how, by whom, and with what artistic purpose the early *azjāl* were composed. Were they street songs meant to be sung in the market places? Ribera was inclined toward this view, and even made an attempt to orchestrate a *zajal*.[60] Nykl on the other hand maintained that these songs were delivered at literary gatherings of an elitist nature by decadent and ephete young dandies.[61] A closer examination of the poetry of Ibn Quzmān will help to clarify the matter.

Ibn Quzmān (d. 1160) is without a doubt the greatest exponent of the *zajal* form and one of the very greatest poets, not only of medieval Islam, but of all medieval literature. His irony, spontaneous freshness, and rejection of the whole classical tradition are indeed a surprise in an age and a culture not known for its tendency to break with tradition. He was a noble Cordovan as well as a vizier at a time when little prestige was still attached to that title. He was a cultured person and familiar with the Eastern classical poets—

---

[58] Vernet, pp. 21–23.

[59] W. Hoenerbach, *Die vulgärabische Poetik al-Kitāb al-ᶜĀṭil al-ḥalī wa l-muraḫḫas al-ghalī des Ṣafīyaddīn Ḥillī* (Wiesbaden, 1956); "La teoría del zéjel según Ṣafī al-Dīn Ḥillī," *Andalus*, XV (1950), 297–334.

[60] J. Ribera, *El cancionero de Abén Guzmán: Discurso leído ante la Real Academia Española* (Madrid, 1912).

[61] A. R. Nykl, ed. and trans., *El cancionero de Abén Guzmán* (Madrid and Granada, 1933).

Jamīl, ʿUrwa ibn Ḥizām, Dhū r-Rumma, Abū Nuwās, Abū Tammām Mutanabbī—whom he mentions in his poems. He succeeded in making the *zajal* fashionable among his contemporaries all over the Muslim world, and says, "I cleaned it of the knots that made it ugly . . . I made it easy, but difficultly easy; common and rare at the same time, arduous to achieve and obvious. . . ."[62]

The sentiments expressed in his poem are a reaction against the rigid but external regulations of the *fuqahāʾ*. In them scenes from lower-class life, the life of taverns and market places, appear in a bawdy and ironic style. Even the use of colloquial Arabic is ironical, since it reinforces the mockery of aristocratic literary themes. The *azjāl* paint a portrait of the picaresque underworld of twelfth-century al-Andalus. Since they deal with popular life as a literary theme, and furthermore they do so in a contrivedly low style, it is clear that they are not true popular songs (although they may be based on these), but an aristocratic view of the popular life of the underworld, artificially cultivated by learned poets. The fact that aristocrats at this time indulged in all kinds of excess is attested to by Ibn Bājja in his treatise *Tadbīr al-Mutawaḥḥid*, who in speaking of those who devote their lives to the pursuit of vices says: "In most cases this class of men is found only among the offspring of aristocrats; in the hands of these the stability of human aristocracy is interrupted, and for this reason political empires have declined in different nations because of such men."[63]

The ironic elements that in the eleventh-century *muwashshaḥāt* were contained in the *kharja* have in the *zajal* become the main subject of the poem. The *kharja* has disappeared because it has invaded and taken over the whole poem. Ibn Quzmān is a city poet of some sophistication, not a popular minstrel, and he has suddenly become aware of the literary possibilities implicit in the teeming urban life that had hardly ever been reflected in poetry before. His discovery emerged from his generation's clash with the puritanical hypocrisy of the *fuqahāʾ* whose venality became the more manifest the more they mouthed their debased code of ethics. Many of his ironies were in sharp contradiction to the laws of the time, and in this he was motivated by a desire to present to society the mirror of its true and unflattering self. For this purpose he chose shock tactics and made public ostentation of his own immorality, for by implication he was the product of the corrupt society he was attempting to

[62] Quoted from Vernet, *op. cit.*, p. 123.

[63] *Tadbir al-mutawaḥḥid, El régimen del solitario*, ed. and trans. M. Asín Palacios (Madrid and Granada, 1946), pp. 71–72.

unmask. He systematically espoused the opposite of noble sentiments, noble rhetoric, noble metaphors and noble language in a way that Ḥillī, in Baghdad and two centuries later, was no longer able to understand or appreciate.

In one of his most famous *azjāl* (**26**) these tactics may be clearly discerned. He introduces his subject with the familiar bacchic theme (ll. 1–30) which in this case reflects the treatment of the latter by the Eastern poet Abū Miḥjān (d. *ca.* 637), and also possibly that of the poet's own countryman Ibn Shuhaid (cf. **7**). But here everything is distorted ironically and transformed into a low, tavern scene that contrasts sharply with the delicate and aristocratic *khamriyyāt* of aṭ-Ṭalīq or of Ibn ᶜAmmār. The effect is bawdy and humorous for the poet coarsely flaunts his own immorality (l. 12) and makes it clear that his companions in debauchery are not the noble warriors and ladies of courtly love, but drunkards (l. 9) and tavern prostitutes (l. 16). The use of the Romance words *vino, vino* (l. 5) produces a comic effect on the one hand, but it should also be remembered that the twelfth century witnessed the birth of increased intolerance and persecution of the Mozarabs. In associating himself with the traditionally Christian theme of wine-drinking like Abū Nuwās before him, Ibn Quzmān is flaunting the vices of society's most despised outcasts in the face of false piety. Since the Romance words in this poem furthermore appear in the rhyme, their comic effect and foulmouthed realism, or better, negative idealism, receives even stronger emphasis.

Next comes the traditional love theme (ll. 31–70) which was de rigueur in Arabic poetry. But it too is deformed, for the affair is not with a noble lady, nor is it even courtly, but rather it is a crude adventure with a Berber girl "with a garland [*tāj*] on her head" (l, 35). Critics have overlooked the ironic significance of the garland. but Ibn ᶜAbdūn, a twelfth-century Sevillian inspector (*muḥtasib*) in his treatise on the regulation of markets clarifies its meaning when he rules that women were to appear in public only with their heads completely and decently covered. He justifies his regulation by explaining that too many prostitutes were going about in public wearing their hair loose in order to attract their admirers.[64] Ibn Quzmān is therefore indicating that his beloved, who by the way is significantly a Berber, is also a prostitute. By wearing a garland she obeyed the the law to the letter, but not to the spirit. The discrepancies between

---

[64] Ibn ᶜAbdūn, *Sevilla a comienzos del siglo XII: El tratado de Ibn ᶜAbdūn*, trans. E. Lévi-Provençal and E. García Gómez (Madrid, 1947), pp. 156–157.

legal theory and practice were perhaps neither greater nor lesser than at other periods in Islamic history, but it is significant that Ibn Quzmān should voice his disapproval because this betrays his radical opposition to the state of the society he lived in. The supreme irony is that it is he who must escape from Córdoba whereas the Berber girl can safely stay on to practice her trade. The poet does not complain, or attempt to whitewash his own virtue. He merely makes the listener aware of the contradiction between the ideal and reality. There is in this episode even an expression of the anti-Berber feelings that were latent in al-Andalus, but it is subdued, and the poet goes beyond the merely propagandistic to touch upon the basic problems of life itself.

Courtly love according to Ibn Ḥazm and all the aristocratic poets, could not exist without secrecy on the part of the lovers, and submission of the lover to the beloved. In his poem, love—which is purely sexual—degenerates into a public brawl in which the whole neighborhood participates. In this way a picaresque tale has been substituted for the usual classical *nasīb* and it is developed in a deliberately anticourtly way.

Finally the *madīḥ* or panegyric (ll. 71–90) is itself ironized by the low language used to express solemn sentiments, as well as by the previous shamelessness that contrasts sharply with the final part of the poem. The latter comes almost as an afterthought (twenty lines) when thirty lines have been devoted to the bacchic and forty to the erotic theme, a disproportion condemned in classical poetry by critics such as Ibn Qutaiba.[65]

In his *ars poetica* (**27**) Ibn Quzmān outlines his whole anticourtly aesthetics. His beloved is from the lower class, a "dark-skinned one" (l. 6) in contrast with the earlier taste for blond princesses (cf. aṭ-Ṭalīq, Ibn Ḥazm, Ibn Zaidūn). Furthermore his love is based entirely on the physical, not the spiritual. To attain his ends he rejects ᶜUdhrite chastity: "spare me the method of Jamīl and ᶜUrwa," and adopts the more direct approach of plying his beloved with alcohol.

Ibn az-Zaqqāq had renewed the outworn themes which by now had become symbols, by rearranging them into new, algebraic patterns. Ibn Quzmān chose the path of ironizing them and produced a poetry of antithesis. In doing this both poets were able to give a new lease on life to an old tradition. They and others of their

---

[65] *Introduction au livre de la poésie et des poètes*, ed and trans. M. Gaudefroy-Demombynes (Paris, 1947).

generation are a living example of the fact that the most brilliant cultural renaissance sometimes coincides with a period of extreme political and moral decline.

The Almohads (1145–1230)

The Almohad movement was a protest against the narrow legalism and rigid conservatism of Western Mālikism as well as against the prevailing atmosphere of moral laxity. It was initiated by the Berber Ibn Tūmart who had traveled to the East and had come in contact with the ideas of Ghazālī. He adopted ascetic and reformist views which he brought back to the Maghreb with him. Meanwhile, in al-Andalus a system of local governments, a second Mulūk aṭ-Ṭawāʾif had sprung up in Valencia, Murcia, and Córdoba as a consequence of Almoravid decline. In 1145 Ibn Tūmart's successor ʿAbd al-Muʾmin (1130–1163) sent his army to the peninsula and annexed its Muslim territory. Soon an Almohad empire with its capital in Seville brought new peace and prosperity to the Muslims of al-Andalus, while order and good government were restored to provincial administration. The new dynasty ruled with efficiency and enlightenment. Its court once more became a center of art and culture, and the last flowering of medieval Islamic philosophy, represented by Ibn Ṭufail, Ibn Zuhr, and Ibn Rushd sprang up under its protection.[66]

In contrast with the Almoravids who had been fundamentalist restorers of tradition, the Almohads were true reformers and the founders of a new sect which broke with the immediate past. Ibn Tūmart (d. 1130) had witnessed the crisis undergone by Western Islam during the twelfth century, and he came to the conclusion that the Mālikite jurists were the direct source of all the West's major ills; that their blind concern with the application of the law to the exclusion of all spiritual values had corrupted the very essence of Islam. As a result he elaborated a new doctrine which may be summed up under three major headings: (1) Denial of all anthropomorphic ideas and formulation of a totally spiritual conception of God which excluded all personal or conjectural interpretation. Ibn Tūmart adopted the Muʿtazilite belief that denied the existence of divine attributes, and this gave the name of al-Muwaḥḥidūn, "the Unitarians," to the sect. (2) Suppression of the tangled legalistic

---

[66] C. E. Bosworth, *The Islamic Dynasties* (Edinburgh, 1967), pp. 30–31.

confusion created by the Mālikite jurists. The resulting simplification of the law was designed to make it easier to grasp the true essence of religion; it emphasized the spirit over the letter, and adopted the Ashᶜarite belief according to which the Koran and *ḥadīth* alone possessed legal authority to the exclusion of all later accretions. (3) Censorship of moral laxity. Ibn Tūmart preached against wine-drinking, the unveiling of women in public, and against the general corruption prevailing under Almoravid rule.[67]

If Ibn Quzmān had been a symptom of what was wrong with society, Ibn Tūmart provided the cure. Consequently his teachings were rejected by the jurists in power, since the latter were concerned only with enforcing external observance of the law in order to profit from corruption. For this reason he took his cause to the Berber tribe of the Maṣmūda by whom it was received favorably. His success was such that soon his religious reform had acquired the proportions of a popular revolt against established authority.

Among the common people there existed a belief that during the last days a Mahdi or "Messiah" would appear in the Maghreb. With profound political insight Ibn Tūmart incorporated this fourth idea into his teachings, and in 1121 he claimed to be that Mahdi. In this way his demand for a religious reform was harmonized with the social aspirations of the common people. The result was a movement dedicated both to political as well as to religious reform.

Unlike the Almoravids, Ibn Tūmart therefore founded a new sect and proclaimed himself its Imam. What had happened was not merely a political change of dynasty as before, but the launching of an authentic reform movement; the application to Western conditions of Eastern theological developments. A new spiritual force that affected the very essence of religion was introduced. Ibn Tūmart composed a sacred book; a second Koran, and those Muslims who rejected his teachings were branded unbelievers (*kuffār*) and treated accordingly.[68] In 1130 he died, and it was left to his successor ᶜAbd al-Muʾmin to translate the sect's ideals into political terms. He assumed the titles of Caliph and Commander of the Faithful, which the Almoravids had never done, and adopted as his motto the phrase "the Koran and the Prophet's Traditions, or else the sword." In 1145 his army invaded al-Andalus which was reduced to submission in five years. In 1170 Yūsuf I transferred the imperial capital from

---

[67] A. Prieto y Vives, "La reforma numismática de los almohades," in *Miscelánea de estudios y textos árabes* (Madrid, 1915), pp. 13–114.

[68] Ibn Tūmart, *Le livre de Mohammed Ibn Toumert: Mahdi des Almohades*, ed. and intro. I. Goldziher (Algiers, 1903).

Marrakesh to Seville. In 1195 Yaᶜqūb al-Manṣūr defeated the Christians at Alarcos. By 1212 the breaking point was reached with the disastrous Muslim defeat by a Christian coalition at Las Navas de Tolosa. In 1223 the death of Yūsuf al-Mustanṣir began a fierce rivalry for power that divided the empire. Decadence set in, but the dynasty's fortunes were restored by Idrīs II (1229–1232) who proclaimed himself Caliph in Seville and reconquered Morocco with the help of Fernando III of Castile in 1230. He publicly retracted the official Almohad doctrine, but the latter was restored by his son ᶜAbd al-Wāḥid II (1232–1242). A long civil war began, during which al-Andalus revolted and began a third period of local rule under the leadership of the old Andalusian families who had twice before formed separatist governments. The problem of separatism versus centralism was therefore endemic to Andalusian society. Muḥammad ibn Hūd established his authority over most of al-Andalus but was assasinated in 1237. The Almohad civil strife and the power gap left by the death of Ibn Hūd facilitated the advance of the Spanish Reconquista. Badajoz fell to the Castilians in 1230 and Córdoba in 1236. Valencia fell to the Aragonese in 1238. Then Jaén was conquered in 1246, and Seville in 1248. Ibn Hūd's descendants held out in Murcia until 1269, after which peninsular Islam was reduced to the tiny kingdom of Granada founded by Muḥammad ibn Ghālib ibn al-Aḥmar the Naṣrid (1230–1272). Meanwhile the Almohads in Africa were overwhelmed by the rising power of the Ḥafṣids in Tunisia, and that of the Marīnids in Morocco, and were extinguished by the latter in 1269.

One aspect of Almohad reform was the monetary. The new dynasty changed the shape and inscriptions of its coins as if to break with the past, and erased from them all that was irrelevant to the furtherance of its own prestige. Whereas the Almoravid dinars had weighed approximately 4.2 grams, those of the Almohads now weighed 2.3 grams, but beginning with the reign of Yaᶜqūb al-Manṣūr (1184) a new type of doubloon weighing 4.6 grams was introduced.[69]

The impact of the Almohad reform on art is clearly evident. The founder of the sect had been sober and ascetic in his personal life, while his learning was mainly theological. Therefore he condemned ostentation in art as the Protestant reformers were to do much later in Europe. When ᶜAbd al-Muʾmin conquered Fez in 1145, its inhabitants plastered over the rich decorations in the mihrab of the

---

[69] Prieto y Vives, *op. cit.*, p. 15.

Qarawiyyīn Mosque for fear they might be destroyed by the iconoclast furor of the new ruler, for it had been claimed that the mihrab was so beautiful that it distracted the faithful from their prayers.

The Almohads divested Hispano-Arabic art of its superfluous elements; they fostered a new, austere simplicity in the Mosque which harmonized well with their religious teachings. Official Almohad art is endowed with a sense of proportion, grandeur, and harmonious simplicity absent before. The universalist ideal of the Messianic and authoritarian state was translated into a monumental architecture that sought to rival that of the Cordovan Caliphate. The enormous and unfinished stone Mosque of Rabat was the ultimate exaggeration of this monumental tendency; in it size and mass have become of primary importance.

The arches of Almohad mosques are generally of the pointed horseshoe type. Their pillars are thick and the buildings are low so that the impression given is one of stark and ponderous simplicity. The sparseness of decoration is relieved by bold lines drawn on the broad, bare surfaces in large patterns that are easily grasped by the eye. By eliminating all excess detail they concentrate the attention of the beholder on the essential features of the design. The result is a sober, essential art, grandiose and dignified.

Although this official style was promoted by the government, the elaborate, native art did not entirely die out. Richly decorated stuccos proceeding from a thirteenth-century palace in Játiva have survived. The delicately carved *minbar* of the Kutubiyya was built in Córdoba between the years 1150 and 1160 and represents the exuberant Andalusian style at its best. Its exquisite geometric, epigraphic, and floral elements are a direct link between the art that flourished under the Almoravids and that of the Naṣrids of Granada, who tended to further complicate and miniaturize the already rich decorative style of the peninsula.[70]

One of the symptoms betraying the exhaustion of Andalusian culture despite the Almohad reform was its tendency to rely on its own past, and its inability to create new cultural forms. Eastern influences that had once been so fertile were now almost nonexistent. The *fuqahā*ʾ, although no longer in power, exerted a strong influence over the common people and therefore had to be reckoned with by the reigning sovereigns. The latter were often forced for reasons of political expediency to make concessions to the fanaticism of these

---

[70] L. Torres Balbás, *Arte almohade, arte nazarí, arte mudéjar*, Ars Hispaniae, IV (Madrid, 1949), pp. 9–14.

jurists. It was the jurists who caused Ibn Rushd to fall into disgrace and his books to be burned at a critical moment when the government needed the common people's support to wage war against the Christians. After the crisis was over the philosopher was restored to favor, but the incident reveals the influence still exercised by the *fuqahā*ʾ.[71] This inability of the state to provide an ideal which could be followed by all classes of society led to a compartmentalization of the latter. At this time there was a predominance of the Platonic philosophical doctrine that one level of truth was to be taught to the ignorant masses, another to the *fuqahā*ʾ, and a third to the elite, namely the philosophers. This doctrine became immensely popular among philosophical circles and is encountered repeatedly in the works of Ibn Ṭufail and Ibn Rushd.[72]

The Islamic doctrine of tolerance which had been observed in the past was rejected by the Almohads, and as a result the Mozarabs and Jews were persecuted and expelled from al-Andalus. In retaliation the Christians began to force the Muslims out of those cities they had recently captured. Whereas after the conquest of Toledo in 1085, Alfonso VI had declared himself "Emir of the two religions" and Muslims had been allowed to live in peace under Christian rule, Córdoba and Seville were now completely emptied of their inhabitants and repopulated with Christians. After Fernando III conquered Seville, he surveyed the vast and now desolate city from the top of a tower and wondered at its deathly silence.[73]

Yet the Almohad period provided the last outstanding creative movement of Islam in al-Andalus, and its scientific and philosophical productions constitute medieval Islam's last significant legacy to Europe. Poetry too reflects this productivity. The old rhetorical tradition, now complicated by the metaphorical experimentation of the twelfth century, survives and is reworked by a vast array of poets. No new forms are created, but a new spirit is introduced into the old ones that reflects the renovating spirit of the new state. Poetry found protection at the cultured court of the Almohads and as a consequence it once again became political and social. Love poetry of the dignified, courtly type was revived as the restricting influence of the jurists was relaxed. One step removed from human love, a breath of divine love enters al-Andalus with the works of

---

[71] Watt, *op. cit.*, pp. 139–140.

[72] See especially *Averroes: on the Harmony of Religion and Philosophy*, ed. and trans. George F. Hourani (London, 1962).

[73] Isidro de las Cagigas, *Sevilla almohade y últimos años de su vida musulmana* (Madrid, 1951).

Ghazālī, and mystical poetry comes to the surface and finds favor among different levels of society.

ᶜAbd al-Muʾmin had revived poetry in 1161 by presiding over a poetic contest held in Gibraltar to celebrate his conquest of al-Andalus. All the poets of the peninsula flocked there, for in every province there were skilled poets. The nature poetry of the Levantine region was now represented by ar-Ruṣāfī of Valencia (d. 1177) and Ṣafwān ibn Idrīs of Murcia (d. 1201), the latter of whom composed the anthology entitled *Zād al-Musāfir*.[74] A group of poetesses of distinction flourished in Granada, and under the new regime the capital of Seville would soon become favorable to poets once again. There the converted Jew Ibn Sahl who "joined together the two humiliations of being a lover and a Jew" composed an exquisite collection of love poems and was finally drowned in the Guadalquivir "so that the pearl might return to its home."[75]

When political decay set in, prominent Andalusian figures began to emigrate to Africa and the East; not to learn, as in former times, but to teach and to spread their own Andalusian culture. Many intellectuals displaced by the advance of the Reconquista fled to the rising Ḥafṣid court in Tunisia, such as the poet Ḥāzim al-Qarṭājannī (d. 1285), and the scholar Ibn al-Abbār (d. 1260). The anthologist Ibn Saᶜīd al-Maghribī (d. 1274 or 1281), author of the *Mughrib*, fled first to Tunisia and from there to Egypt and Syria. Ibn al-ᶜArabī (d. 1240) took his recondite mystical doctrines with him to Mecca, and Shushtarī (d. 1269) who profoundly influenced Sufism, was buried in Damietta.

Ar-Ruṣāfī of Valencia was the most prominent poet of the earlier period. He was a mere youth when ᶜAbd al-Muʾmin held his literary audience in Gibraltar, and in it he won his laurels by reciting a famous panegyric to the new ruler (**31**). Ar-Ruṣāfī of Valencia was a nature poet of the Khafājī school, yet it is significant that almost from the very outset of his career, his skill in the handling of themes is placed at the service of a political poetry that expresses a sense of optimism and elation over contemporary events, which was lacking in Almoravid poetry. In this way poets were once more reconciled with politics.

His panegyric attempts to justify the cause of the Almohads from the religious viewpoint and therefore alludes directly to the Koran as well as to the belief in the Mahdi. From lines 1 to 7 the

---

[74] Vernet, p. 122; García Gómez, *Poemas*, pp. 40–43.
[75] *Ibid.*, p. 42.

poem relates the message contained in the Koran to the Mahdi and his successor. Then, from lines 8 to 15, it identifies Gibraltar "the lofty peak" with "the peak of the Guidance" (l. 8) and the poet's elaboration of this idea transports abstract doctrine to the sphere of contemporary events. What was on the one hand a military conquest is infused with the religious significance provided by the Almohad ideology. From lines 16 to 29 ar-Ruṣāfī focuses on ᶜAbd al-Muʾmin's crossing of the Straits of Gibraltar in such a way as to imply that the conqueror was endowed with charismatic powers absent in ordinary men, for the tops of the ships bow down before him and the ropes sing out their praise of him, while the sea trembles with joy and fear over his presence (ll. 18, 20). This description of the Almohad fleet is derived partly from a *qaṣīda* in which Ibn Hānīʾ described the Fatimid fleet in Alexandria during the tenth century.[76] In its emphasis on the supernatural influence of the Caliph, there are traces of the Sufi doctrine of the *insān al-kāmil,* "the perfect man," which appear in the poetry of Mutanabbī and Ibn Hānīʾ.

After the arrival at Gibraltar a poetic description of the mountain (ll. 30–45) follows. The passage is borrowed directly from the similar theme found in Ibn Khafāja. Whereas the mountain in Ibn Khafāja's poem is a symbol of cosmic loneliness, however, here a concrete mountain is alluded to, and it becomes a symbol of fulfilled expectations. Not only is there description, but the mountain's presence is given a religious and political significance by the use of Koranic quotations (l. 39) and by introducing the idea that its function is to protect Islam in the peninsula (l. 32). Yet the description is far more elaborate than the one found in Ibn Khafāja's poem, and it shows how poetry had developed toward increased complication.

In lines 46–58, the now personified mountain is shown watching out "for the flasher of a sword" (l. 46). This transition introduces the theme of military conquest, whereby ᶜAbd al-Muʾmin is depicted as the executor of the Mahdi's goals through his own prowess in battle. He is represented as a true king, whereas his predecessors the Almoravids were considered "worthy of scorn." In this way the Caliph is raised far above the level of his followers, and it is explained that the justice of his cause was not based on the mere number of his followers, but rather on his religious authority (ll. 57–58). The final section (ll. 59–62) contains the climax of the poem, for in it ᶜAbd al-Muʾmin is once again made to approach the supernatural when he is compared with Joshua who made the sun stand still. The Almohad

[76] Partially translated in Watt, *op. cit.*, p. 74.

doctrine is likewise connected to the prophetic teachings of the Koran by the parallel drawn between the Mahdi and Moses. The whole poem furthermore expresses an optimistic attitude: a hope for the improvement of Andalusian conditions under the new state.

Ḥāzim al-Qarṭājannī (d. 1285) wrote about eighty years after ar-Ruṣāfī. A native of Cartagena, he fled after its conquest in 1241 to the Ḥafṣid court of Tunisia where he became famous for his Qaṣīda Maqṣūra, several thousand lines long, in which he eulogized Abū Zakariyāʾ Yaḥya and mourned the fall of the Levantine region of al-Andalus into Christian hands.[77] In another, shorter panegyric (**37**) addressed to the same ruler the poet appeals to him to come to the aid of the Andalusians in place of the declining Almohad dynasty (ll. 48–49). In contrast with ar-Ruṣāfī, this poem expresses a feeling of discouragement over the Andalusian situation. Thus fittingly enough, it begins with an allusion to exhaustion and old age: "Dawn for you is night and darkness is light." Here the black-white color contrast, used earlier by Ibn Zaidūn has the following meaning: "[The whiteness of your hair, like] dawn for you is night [in the despair it causes you in your old age], whereas the darkness [of your hair in youth] was like a light [in the hope of love affairs it brought you]." By this time the lexicalization of metaphor had reached such an extreme degree that it was no longer necessary to explain the allusions, while the puzzling juxtapositions that resulted allowed for new possibilities in poetic expression. Metaphors were used almost as in an algebraic equation.

All the most intense images in this poem are related to the color contrast between black and white which is woven into the poem throughout. The initial mood of dejection is expressed in terms of dawn and darkness. Later a ray of hope begins to shine when the poet reaches the Ḥafṣid court, and this is likewise expressed chromatically (ll. 21–25). Finally the reward expected by the poet induces an outburst of enthusiasm: "Were [my poem] to be written down on paper, its blackness on the whiteness of the page would be given the blackness of [dark] eyes in dowry" (l. 55). In this way, the black-white leitmotiv underlines the contrast between initial despair over exile from al-Andalus and final hope over the munificence poetic art can procure in Tunisia.

Ḥāzim al-Qarṭājannī is of particular significance in this period

---

[77] E. García Gómez, "Observaciones sobre la Qaṣīda Maqṣūra de Ḥāzim al-Qarṭājannī," *Andalus*, I (1933), 81–103.

because in his prose work *Kitāb Sirāj al-bulaghā᾽ wa minhāj al-udabā᾽* he discussed Aristotle's opinions on poetry and rhetoric in some detail.[78] Ibn Sīna, al-Fārābī, and Ibn Rushd had studied and commented on the *Poetics* and the *Rhetoric* as philosophers, but so far no poet in the Arab world had concerned himself with the subject. Ḥāzim was therefore the first poet to do so. In discussing metaphor he asserts the superiority of the Arabs in that field, and claims that if Aristotle had known Arabic metaphor "he would have added much to the rules of poetry he formulated." He goes to the very essence of Aristotle's ideas on poetry, and explains that good poetry depends on the excellence of the *imitation* whereas bad poetry results from the badness of the imitation. By imitation he understood the embellishment of nature, not a slavish copying of the latter. Nature must be embellished with moderation, however, so that the falsehood of the embellishment should not be obvious. Furthermore, embellishment of the imitation is not really falsehood, for "the descriptions and imitations that are made with restraint and without exaggeration are really truth." Neither description nor imitation can therefore be called poetic untruth, for when one thing resembles another, Ḥāzim argues, the comparison of the two is true, for the comparer informs us of the resemblance between the two. Falsehood in imitation occurs only when excess predominates, that is, in unrestrained hyperbole "for excess occurs when the poet transgresses all bounds in his description, and by this means goes from the limits of the possible to the impossible and the absurd."

The rebirth of philosophical speculation under the Almohads lies behind Ḥāzim's ideas. Ibn Rushd in al-Andalus, whom he studiously avoids quoting, had preceded him in his analysis of Aristotle by a few years. He was, however, not only the first, but also the last medieval Arab poet to attempt to apply Aristotle's views to the theory of Arabic poetry. Not only did he have no successors, but he did not apply his theoretical speculations to his own poetry which remained entirely within the tradition of Arabic poetics.

In contrast with Ḥāzim who lived securely in Tunisia, the poem by ar-Rundī (d. 1285) expresses the more profound despair of those Andalusians who were not able to emigrate. It is today generally accepted that his famous elegy on the fall of Andalusian cities (**38**) was composed after the fall of Seville in 1248. The lament over

---

[78] The relevant passage (Third Minhāj) has been published by ᶜAbd ar-Raḥmān Badawī, *Ḥāzim al-Qarṭājannī wa naẓariyyāt Arisṭū fī l-balāgha wa sh-shiᶜr* (Cairo, 1961).

Andalusian Islam, which is the central theme of the poem, is so strongly felt that the poet wastes no energy in describing the beauty of nature or in developing complex rhetorical devices. The poem is therefore bare of decorative elements and for this very reason it conveys a sincere emotion absent in more contrived poems. The elegy is structured in a way directly opposite to that of Ḥāzim; that is, it progresses from philosophical resignation to the blows of fate at the outset, to final despair. It can be divided into two main segments: the first (ll. 1–13) begins by stating philosophically that "Everything declines after reaching perfection." This introduces the *ubi sunt* theme (ll. 6–8) which presents the collapse of past empires in rapid review. The treatment of the theme is more condensed and therefore more effective than in Ibn ᶜAbdūn's elegy. The second part of the poem begins with line 14 where the transition from the remote to the immediate past; from the faraway East to the recent collapse of al-Andalus introduces the idea that "there is no consolation for what has befallen Islam" (l. 14). Then the concrete cities are enumerated: Valencia, Murcia, Játiva, Jaén, Córdoba, and finally Seville, all have fallen into enemy hands. The poet, in moving from the remote to the immediate past, has become emotionally aroused and his initial resignation now gives way to tears and lamentation. Each city is moreover introduced and characterized by a feature for which it was well known. Those objects associated with water weep: "the tap of the white ablution fount weeps in despair"(l. 21), but not only liquids weep: "even the mihrabs weep though they are solid" (l. 24). The universal lamentation now leads up to an appeal for help from the North African leaders, and indeed, from all Muslims (ll. 25–35) and then to an enumeration of the tyrannical behavior of the conquerors against the Muslims (ll. 36–42): "The heart melts with sorrow at such [sights], if there is any Islam or belief in that heart!" (l. 42).

The three political *qaṣīda*s analyzed above reflect three different stages in the rise and fall of the Almohad empire as it was experienced by three Andalusian poets. Poetry had once more become political, but in contrast with the poetry of the Cordovan Caliphate, the religious element was now much stronger than the secular; poetry was therefore at the service of a religious doctrine. It had also absorbed the complex rhetorical devices and lexicalization of metaphor developed under the Almoravids. Although the technical skill of the poet had become all important, and although no new forms were invented, the old ones were infused with a new source of inspiration and this resulted in the creation of distinguished compositions.

The reverence for tradition revived by the Almohad reform seems, however, to have impeded a new departure in poetry. With all his intellectual curiosity over Aristotle's writings, Ḥāzim al-Qarṭājannī proved unable to translate theory into practice.

In love poetry, the revival of a dignified, courtly level may be observed. Particularly in the *muwashshaḥa* the piquant function of the *kharja* begins to disappear, so that here again, a new sense of dignity invades a preexistent form. The transition may be seen in Ibn Zuhr (d. 1200) who received his education under Almoravid rule. He was a member of a learned Sevillian family and as a physician he attended the court of the Almohad sovereign Yaᶜqūb al-Manṣūr in Marrakesh. His *muwashshaḥa* (**30**) contains all the courtly themes, yet the *kharja* is no longer colloquial, but classical; neither is it spoken by the beloved, but by the lover; nor does it express any break in tone with the rest of the poem.

Ḥātim ibn Saᶜīd represents a similar tendency. His imagery is that common to Hispano-Arabic poetry, but it is highly lexicalized. The listener is expected to know that in his *muwashshaḥa* (**32**) the "sun" represents wine while the "moon" is a beautiful face. These purely symbolic meanings make it possible for the poet to begin in a striking way: "A sun drew near to a full moon" (l. 1). In this poetry there is no desire to invent new metaphors, but merely to rearrange the old ones into new patterns and combinations. If it should be asked what is gained by the new style, it could be answered that it permits the creation of a startling, new relationship between realities and has the advantage of bringing them into sharper focus by the use of contrast. If it is stated that a girl drank a glass of wine, the effect is extremely prosaic compared with the declaration that a "sun drew near to a full moon." Such an occurrence rarely takes place in nature, so that its effect is to shock the listener into a new awareness of the act of drinking. This allows the poet to handle the old themes in a fresh way. After long centuries of experimentation the poets of al-Andalus had reached a stage where they were able to manipulate a symbolic language to produce new effects of sound, image, and color, by creating excitingly new relationships between well-known images. In this poem beauty does not therefore lie in the originality of the themes, but in their juxtaposition in contrasting phrases: "my tears are a flood in which fires burn the brighter" (l. 8). The *kharja* has likewise lost all its former significance for it shows no difference in language or tone from the rest of the poem. In fact, this particular *kharja* is entirely courtly in sentiment.

Ibn Sahl (d. 1251) is considered the most outstanding love poet of the Almohad period.[79] In his poetry the same aesthetic principles are encountered as in other contemporary poets, for the themes are traditional whereas the rhetorical devices are more complex and a greater contrast of imagery is found. All the themes of courtly love outlined by Ibn Ḥazm, and the imagery contained in the odes of aṭ-Ṭalīq recur in Ibn Sahl's poems, but they are treated in a new way. One of his most famous lyrics is a *muwashshaḥa* (**33**) in which new possibilities and a new tension are introduced by equating the imagery and language of love with that of war: "I am overcome by a conqueror who conquers through the languor of his gait" (l. 8); "his two eyes drew their warring" (l. 10); "I do not blame him for what he has destroyed" (l. 20); "he appeared wearing a mark to distinguish him in combat" (l. 26). The *kharja*, rather than ironizing the poem, fuses the two antithetical themes of battle and love: "O you who have taken my heart as booty lawfully won in battle, grant the love union in exchange for the *khums*!" (l. 27). The lack of irony shows that the older conception of *muwashshaḥa* poetry was clearly not valid any longer and that the old form was being adapted to a new purpose; courtly in its inspiration, and coinciding with the reforming ideal of the Almohads.

The Almohad reform with its rehabilitation of Ghazālī's works in al-Andalus as well as its attempt to promote a more spiritualized religion among the common people, helped to encourage the emergence of a strong mystical current in Hispano-Arabic poetry. Parallel to the learned development of theology in orthodox Islamic circles, another, more spontaneous and popular movement began and was cultivated by the Sufi mystic in the East. The origins of Sufism are obscure. It seems to have begun as an ascetic reaction to the luxury and magnificence of court life. By the ninth century, authors such as Muḥāsibī (d. 837), Dhū n-Nūn al-Miṣrī (d. 861), al-Junaid (d. 910), and particularly al-Hallāj (d. 922) were busy elaborating a mystical system that gave rise to persecutions and was not incorporated into orthodox Islam until the time of Ghazālī. From its initial, ascetic stage it progressed to one of true mysticism, and then an elaborate system of theosophy was incorporated into the Sufi tradition. By the eleventh century it had spread throughout the Islamic world.[80]

In early tenth-century al-Andalus, Ibn Masarra (d. 931) appears

---

[79] A monograph has been devoted to him: M. Soualah, *Ibrāhīm ibn Sahl, poète musulman d'Espagne* (Algiers, 1914–1918).

[80] A. J. Arberry, *Sufism: An Account of the Mystics of Islam* (London, 1956), pp. 31–74.

to have been the first scholar to introduce the teachings of Dhū n-Nūn. According to M. Asín Palacios, Ibn Masarra seems to have fused the Plotinian system of the pseudo-Empedocles with Sufi elements, and to have formulated the concept of a totally spiritual eschatology that denied physical reward and punishment in the afterlife. To this he added Sufi methods of spiritual purification.[81] Then in the eleventh century Ibn al-ᶜArīf of Almería (d. 1141) introduced al-Ḥallāj's idea that the Sufi should perform an act of total renunciation of all but God, including mystical states, favors, and charismata granted by God, as a means of spiritual purification.[82] By the twelfth and thirteenth centuries this attitude of total renunciation had become central to the mysticism of Ibn al-ᶜArabī of Murcia, and it was later adopted by the Shādhilī school of which Ibn ᶜAbbād of Ronda (d. 1394) was a member. He made this idea the very basis of Western Sufism, claiming that total renunciation encouraged and promoted pure selflessness.[83]

In Islam as in other world religions, the mystical experience is ineffable; the mystic is unable to put into words and human concepts the experience he has undergone. In relating the mystical experiences of his literary character Ḥayy ibn Yaqẓān, Ibn Ṭufail says: "Do not expect me to describe a thing which the human heart has never conceived, for if it is hard to explain many things conceived by the human heart, how much more so is this the case of a thing that the human heart cannot conceive, since it neither belongs to this world in which the heart lives nor is it found within its limits."[84]

For this reason the mystic is forced to rely on the imperfect medium of human concepts, and in poetry he often turns to concepts and images taken from human love to express his intimate experience of divine love. He therefore works with a medium of symbols, allusions, or signs: "In spite of this we will not deprive you of certain signs by means of which we will point out to you something of what [Ḥayy] saw of the wonders of the [mystic] state, but we will do so by means of parables or examples. Do not yearn for [an exact] description."[85]

---

[81] M. Asín Palacios, *Abenmasarra y su escuela, orígenes de la filosofía hispano-musulmana: Discurso leído ante la Real Academia Española.* Madrid, 1914. Palacios' views on Ibn Masarra will shortly be invalidated (private communication from Dr. Muḥsin Mahdī).

[82] Ibn al-ᶜArīf, *Maḥāsin al-majālis,* ed. and trans. M. Asín Palacios (Paris, 1933).

[83] M. Asín Palacios, "Un precursor hispanomusulmán de San Juan de la Cruz," *Andalus,* I (1933), 7–79.

[84] Ibn Ṭufail, *op. cit.,* p. 112.

[85] *Ibid.*

Since the mystical experience is of the divine, the senses and the imagination play no part in it, and in the final analysis it is the result of divine illumination rather than of human intellection: "The heavens and the earth along with everything in them, all the spiritual forms, corporeal matter, and all the nonmaterial forces [which are also essences and knowers of the Supreme Being] all disappeared from [Ḥayy's] memory and his understanding; these essences vanished with his own essence and all was reduced to nothingness and dissolved like scattered atoms; while only the One, the True, the Being whose existence is permanent remained before him."[86]

The mystical experience is also transient, and although mystics are not precise about its temporal duration, it is clearly a nonpermanent state: "At times [Ḥayy's] thought became free from all admixture and he contemplated the necessary Being, but then the organic faculties returned to his body and that state was interrupted in him, bringing him back to the lowest degree, and he would return to his previous state."[87]

Mysticism is therefore experienced in Islam as a divine-human relationship or series of relationships, suprasensory in nature, transient in duration, which cannot be expressed clearly in words.

Ibn al-ᶜArabī (d. 1240) is one of Islam's greatest mystics. He came from a wealthy Andalusian family and received an unusually careful education. Until the death of his father he devoted himself to public affairs, after which he suffered a grave crisis, gave away all his wealth, and embarked upon a journey to the East. He continued to travel until his death. His orthodoxy, like that of many mystics, was questioned by the *fuqahā*ᵓ and he was accused of pantheism. Almost of necessity the mystical notion of union with God implies the dissolution of the self and its absorption into the divine essence, and this leads to pantheism. Ibn Ṭufail explains it thus: "[Ḥayy] recovered from that state which resembles drunkenness, and it occurred to him then that he had no essence whereby to distinguish himself from the essence of the Supreme, True Being."[88] Since pantheism is at variance with the basic dualism of the Koranic teaching, many mystics were persecuted and even executed for their adoption of pantheistic ideas. Ibn al-ᶜArabī

---

[86] *Ibid.*, p. 111.
[87] *Ibid.*, p. 109.
[88] *Ibid.*, p. 113.

wrote an exquisite collection of lyrical poems entitled *Tarjumān al-ashwāq*. In it he sings in appearance, the beauty of Niẓām, the fourteen-year-old daughter of a noble Meccan at whose home he stayed, although in reality he is referring to the love of God and to the joys of the mystic union. Despite the author's protestations of sincerity and purity, however, the *fuqahā*ʾ remained suspicious of his true motives, so that he was required to write a prose commentary to the poems, entitled *Dhakhā*ʾ*ir*, to prove his orthodoxy.[89]

The suspicion with which the mystic was looked upon by the orthodox led Ibn al-ᶜArabī to write in a complicated, intentionally obscure style. Ultimately the theosophic system in Sufism made it possible for Ibn al-ᶜArabī to reconcile the Koranic teaching with contemporary circumstances. This leads him in his *Fuṣūṣ al-ḥikam* to grant the immutability of the Koranic revelation, while at the same time he claims for mystics the right to change and adapt revelation by abrogating or adding to it. By this means religion could be reformed and adapted to new circumstances not foreseen in the Koran, while the innovations could be authorized by the mystics. The *Fuṣūṣ* also give mystics the right to reject any *ḥadīth* in which their illumination perceived a flaw, and this takes religion out of the hands of the tradition-bound *fuqahā*ʾ and turns it over to the reform-minded mystics. For Ibn al-ᶜArabī eschatology is purely spiritual; in the end all souls will be saved and there will be no everlasting punishment. Likewise he pleads for religious tolerance saying that "compassion towards [God's] servants [the nonbelievers] has greater claim [than destroying them]." Love, for Ibn al-ᶜArabī is the highest form in which God can be worshiped, and he claims in the *Fuṣūṣ* that God is never seen immaterially, while the vision of Him in women is the most perfect of all. The stressing of love, of tolerance, of a spiritual eschatology; the desire to make the revelation adaptable to new circumstances unforeseen by the Prophet, all betray a liberal attitude in religious matters, and a sincere desire for reform.[90]

He was forced to obscure the meaning of his writings to avoid the charge of heresy, however, and consequently his poetry is often difficult and ambiguous. In one poem from the *Tarjumān* (**36**), his attitude toward pantheism is revealed: "My heart has adopted every shape . . ." (l. 13), while his religious tolerance makes him extol the infinite God of mysticism rather than the finite God of each religious sect.

---

[89] Vernet, pp. 140–141.

[90] R. A. Nicholson, *Studies in Islamic Mysticism* (Cambridge, 1921), pp. 149–161.

As a poet, Ibn al-ʿArabī took the highly lexicalized, metaphorical diction of the Almohad period and applied it symbolically to express an entirely different, spiritual world of experience. In this poem the language of human love poetry is used symbolically to convey the emotion of divine love. The true meaning is unintelligible without the commentary that explains that the "doves of the *arak* and the *bān* trees" (l. 1) are symbols of purity and holiness. The juxtaposition of two levels of reality, the human and the divine, gives a new dimension to poetry while it also makes it hard to understand without a commentary, for it was directed to an elite circle of philosophers.

In contrast the poetry of Shushtarī (d. 1269) is addressed to the common people. It coincides therefore with the Almohad attempt to spread a simple and essential form of spirituality among the masses. Shushtarī adopts the popular *zajal* and *muwashshaḥa* forms, and speaks in a colloquial accent directly to the heart of his fellowman.

His *zajal* (**34**) betrays the influence of Ibn Quzmān in both form and language. The meter, musicality, and colloquial language as well as the deliberately antirhetorical simplicity belong to the zajalesque style. But in contrast with the shameless and bawdy love affairs of Ibn Quzmān, the poem expresses the ascetic ideal of disdain for the things of this world which was common in Sufi circles: "What have I to do with men, and what have men to do with me?" The refrain, repeated after every strophe hammers home the point with the insistence of a Sufi chant.

His second *zajal* (**35**) even quotes phrases borrowed from Ibn Quzmān (ll. 18, 19) but in theme the poem is entirely mystical. Love union, heavenly wine, illumination, the dark night of the soul, are all present in the poem. The ineffability of the sublime experience is conveyed by the use of dramatic exclamations where the use of ordinary logic is impossible: "O for his liquor! O for his wine! O for the wine seller! O for the joy! O for the song!" (l. 8), while the apparently disordered reiteration of exclamatory phrases throughout the poem serves to underline the poet's state of feeling at the expense of strict logic. Occasional references make it clear that he is speaking not about human love, but about a suprasensory experience: "He filled my glasses and cups, but not with [the juice] of grapes or of raisins!" (l. 11); "understand well my allusions" (l. 12), while the illumination received from God is not to be reduced to rational terms: "My knowledge is about what has passed and what is to come" (l. 17).

The Naṣrids (1230–1492)

When the Almohad empire disintegrated, Muḥammad ibn Ghālib ibn al-Aḥmar, an Andalusian claiming Arab ancestry, gained control of Granada and founded the Naṣrid dynasty. At first Muḥammad paid tribute to Fernando III of Castile, and later to his successor Alfonso X. Hemmed in by Castile to the north and by the Marīnids to the south, the kingdom of Granada was forced to live precariously and to play the one off against the other in order to maintain its independence from either. The Marīnids hoped to restore Islamic rule to al-Andalus but after their leader Abū l-Ḥasan ᶜAlī was defeated in 1340 at Río Salado by Alfonso XI the hope for an Islamic restoration receded. Granada's existence was under constant threat; fortified in the rugged Sierra Nevada it lived literally with its back to the wall. But despite these adverse circumstances it survived for two and a half centuries, developed a brilliant cultural milieu to which men of learning flocked from all the Islamic West, and spread its artistic influence from Burgos in the north to the Barbary states in the south.

The rivalry between Castile and Aragon delayed the advance of the Reconquista, and Granadan diplomacy exploited this rivalry as much as possible. But the union of the two crowns under Fernando V of Aragon and Isabel of Castile in 1469 signaled the end of the breathing space granted to Granada. Weakened by internal rivalries and wars of succession it fell an easy prey to Spanish might in 1492.[91]

Life was not easy in the Granadan kingdom. The small territory suffered from a serious excess of population composed of refugees from other reconquered regions of the peninsula. In order to pay its heavy tribute to Castile it had to bear a huge burden of taxation. Since many of the new taxes were not authorized by Islamic law, the latter had to be adjusted to the new conditions. Islamic law had developed during the period of expansion of the Islamic empire when conditions had been more favorable. Now it was no longer viable and so jurists issued legal decisions that sought to reconcile theory with contemporary needs. They authorized the collecting of non-Koranic taxes by means of a subtle casuistry, and one of their number, Wansharīshī, defended the innovations as follows: "If the ancient jurists did not foresee cases like this, it is because the vicinity of the infidel in the early days of Islam was not as it is today. These neighboring Christian lands have not begun to appear until the fifth

[91] Bosworth, *op. cit.*, pp. 18–19.

century of the Hijra, when the accursed Christians—may God destroy them!—conquered Sicily and certain cities of al-Andalus."[92]

To meet these heavy expenses the Granadans developed a thriving industry and export trade in fine porcelains, silks, and arms. This brought some measure of prosperity to the kingdom, and its currency became stable. But Ibn Khaldūn noted signs of weakness in Granada: "These Arabs of al-Andalus have lost the esprit de corps (*ʿaṣabiyya*) that produces political power. They preserve only their genealogies . . . they imagine that with lineage and a government position a kingdom can be conquered and men can be governed."[93] Ibn al-Khaṭīb, their greatest historian, described them as living modestly as solid, middle-class citizens, gay and carefree, scrupulous in paying their taxes.[94]

In the course of its two and a half centuries of existence the kingdom of Granada went through three distinct phases. The first lasted from the end of the thirteenth to the beginning of the fourteenth centuries. Since the Naṣrid dynasty had begun as a feudal protectorate observing allegiance to Fernando III and its early sovereigns were lukewarm Muslims at best, they and their people freely emulated Christian fashions. They decorated their homes with images, adopted Christian styles of dress, and fought in the Christian manner with Christian arms.

The middle period was the age of greatest political and cultural activity. The servile imitation of Christian manners declines in it and a Granadan culture based on Arab and Islamic ideals slowly takes shape. This phase lasted throughout most of the fourteenth century, that is, the reigns of Yūsuf I (1333–1354) and Muḥammad V (1354–1390). The last palaces of the Alhambra were built at this time, as was the madrasa, a state educational institution appearing for the first time in al-Andalus where education had traditionally remained free from state tutelage. Soon brilliant scholars and poets were living in or visiting Granada: Ibn al-Khaṭīb, Ibn Zamrak, Ibn Khaldūn.

The third phase, the fifteenth century, is the age of final disintegration. The Arabizing reaction gains increasing momentum in it. Eastern and African institutions are favored and the court is reorganized according to Oriental precedents. Royal titles used by

---

[92] J. López Ortiz, "Fatwas granadinas de los siglos XIV y XV," *Andalus*, VI (1941), p. 90.

[93] *Muqaddimah*, quoted by E. García Gómez, "Ibn Zamrak, el poeta de la Alhambra," in *Cinco poetas musulmanes* (Madrid, 1945), p. 172.

[94] *Iḥāṭa*, quoted by García Gómez in *ibid.*

the Marīnids such as muley (*maulāya*) were adopted. Likewise Arab styles in clothing and arms were introduced and became fashionable. The turban, which had not been worn by the early Naṣrids, now became common.[95]

Naṣrid art is a conservative prolongation of the ornate Andalusian style that had flourished in the peninsula ever since the tenth century. Granada's deliberate cultivation of archaism—a defense mechanism designed to arrest the advance of Christian influences—manifests itself artistically through a revival of the traditional tendency to cover flat surfaces with minute ornamentation. Naṣrid art creates no new forms; it invents nothing, yet it has a regard for formal perfection that gives rise to the exquisite art of the Alhambra. Even in a period of political instability (one third of the Naṣrid sultans were assassinated) it is fertile and rich, capable of constructing imposing, monumental buildings (Puerta de la Justicia) or of attaining an as yet unknown perfection in decorative ceilings, stuccowork, or wood carving. Marble, which had disappeared from Andalusian architecture in the twelfth century, was reintroduced in the form of slender columns designed to support the lacelike stucco-covered walls.

Being lukewarm in religious matters, the Naṣrids neglected mosque building and concentrated their efforts on embellishing their domestic surroundings. Fairy-tale palaces with intimate patios, reflection pools, fountains, landscaped gardens, bright tile decorations, and lacelike stuccowork were their strong points. As in earlier ages little concern is shown for the exterior, for the beauties of a building are always hidden away inside. Likewise, no attempt is made to build according to a vast, symmetrical plan. The basic architectural unit is the patio, and the Alhambra is a haphazard array of intimate patios placed one next to the other with little concern for regularity. As a result each individual nook has its own peculiar charm, but emphasis is placed on the isolated unit, not on the overall structure of the building.

Possibly the greatest achievement of Naṣrid architecture was the harmony with which it succeeded in blending landscapes, flowing water, and architecture into a unity in which the abstract rigidity of art serves to frame the free flow of nature with a pleasing sense of contrast. The aesthetic principle inspiring Naṣrid decoration is similar for it consisted in dividing wall surfaces into rectangular spaces enclosed by geometric borders. The result is a subtle interplay

[95] *Ibid.*, pp. 175–184.

between rigid, rectangular lines and flowing floral decoration contained within them. Beauty of detail is thus harmoniously organized with superb formal perfection.[96]

The same features are traceable in poetry: it cultivates archaism, and achieves a new stage of complication in the use of metaphor and the formal structure of the poem. One of the important poets of the fourteenth century was Ibn al-Khaṭīb (d. 1374).[97] He was a Granadan vizier, a philosopher, historian, physician, as well as a poet, and he flourished under Muḥammad V. He was on familiar terms with the great historian Ibn Khaldūn who visited Granada. In 1370 he fell out of favor and fled to Morocco where he was assassinated. His *muwashshaḥa* (**39**), possibly written after his flight, is a direct imitation of the one by Ibn Sahl (**33**), the first two lines of which it uses as its *kharja*. Both poems are written in the *ramal* meter, yet whereas Ibn Sahl's abides by the rule that a *muwashshaḥa* may not have more than seven strophes (it has five), that of Ibn al-Khaṭīb has ten. The undue length indicates that by now the *muwashshaḥa* form had been almost completely reabsorbed into the *qaṣīda*, and that the only difference between the two forms was the variety of rhymes in the former. This evolution was the result of an attempt to dignify nonclassical forms by adapting them to the prestigious classical tradition. It is one more manifestation of the archaism deliberately sought by Granadan artists to oppose to the inexorable advance of Christendom.

Ibn Zamrak was perhaps the age's greatest poet.[98] Born in 1333, the year when Yūsuf I ascended the throne, of humble, Levantine parents who had emigrated to Granada after the Christian reconquest of that region, he studied at the newly inaugurated madrasa with a brilliant group of teachers, among them Ibn al-Khaṭīb. In 1362 he was made Muḥammad V's private secretary, and became a court poet charged with the duty of composing official *qaṣīdas* to commemorate recent events. When his protector Ibn al-Khaṭīb fell out of favor in 1371 Ibn Zamrak was promoted to the vizierate in his place. Ibn al-Khaṭīb fled to Fez and was imprisoned there. Ibn Zamrak arranged soon thereafter to have his former teacher strangled in prison by a group of hired assassins. Such were the vicissitudes of the age.

---

[96] Torres Balbás, *op. cit.*, pp. 73–81.

[97] See Vernet, pp. 148–149.

[98] He has been studied by García Gómez in *op. cit.*, as well as by R. Blachère, "Le visir-poète Ibn Zumruk et son oeuvre," *Annales de l'Institut d'Études Orientales* (Paris, 1936), II, 291–312.

Ibn Zamrak continued to hold the vizierate until the death of Muḥammad V in 1391, after which he too fell out of favor and was first imprisoned, then freed. Finally one night, as the now elderly vizier was reading the Koran in his home, a group of hired assassins broke in and murdered him along with his two sons before his family's eyes. The event occurred around 1393.

The poet wrote some sixty-six *qaṣīda*s to celebrate as many court festivals. Of these around twenty have survived, as well as sixty occasional pieces and fifteen *muwashshaḥāt*. Of the latter, one is seventy strophes long, and illustrates again how the *muwashshaḥa* was reabsorbed into the *qaṣīda*. His style is Khafājī. Using all the timeworn clichés of the Neoclassical school he is able to give a glittering effect to a highly stylized poetry. His mastery of technique is perfect, particularly in harmonizing words and meter to produce smooth lines. In this respect he represents the ultimate extreme of the tendencies initiated by Mutanabbī. Furthermore, as García Gómez has pointed out, he had the good fortune to see his works published in the most luxurious of editions, for they are engraved in complex patterns on the walls of the Alhambra.[99] One of them (**40**) is particularly famous. It is a royal panegyric which organizes the metaphors common to floral, architectural, and astronomical poetry into a complex ballet. It contains no new love concepts, themes, or metaphors. Poetry now draws its inspiration entirely from the past. ʿUdhrite love still reigned supreme in western Islam at a time when Petrarch was revolutionizing European concepts of love. But the old clichés are used in an entirely fresh and original manner.

All poetry must have some vision of reality as its point of departure. Up to now, in the poems of Ibn Khafāja, ar-Ruṣāfī, or al-Qarṭājannī the point of departure had been nature, and the poet's function had been to poetize nature. But Ibn Zamrak inverts the terms and poetizes art; art becomes a new poetic springboard which relegates nature to a secondary level. In the opening line of his *qaṣīda*: "Question the horizon adorned by the bright stars, for I have entrusted a description of my condition to it," Ibn Zamrak is implying that his artistic description of his condition conveys more information about it than the actual stars themselves can gain from watching him. Likewise, the beauty of a dome in the Alhambra is greater than that of heaven's vault so that the stars wish to lodge in it (l. 62). Art has therefore improved upon and displaced nature as a

[99] García Gómez, *Poemas*, p. 45.

literary subject, for to nature's irregularity art opposes its rigid "canons of beauty" (l. 30), while from the contrast between art and nature a new poetic tension is derived which is closely akin to the aesthetic principle inspiring Naṣrid architecture.

Since poetry is based now on art, not nature, and since in Ibn Zamrak's words it is "jewels from the sea of rhetoric" (l. 141), it is therefore natural that as the old system has been inverted, inverted images should abound. Unlike Ibn Khafāja the poet does not dwell on the loftiness of a mountain, but on that of a man-made palace. In describing its trees he will add:

> In [the garden] there are all sorts of [trees] with [branches like] plaited locks hanging down, such that the hands of the breeze cause them to sway in whirling about.
>
> And in it the slender neck of the branch rose high, being devoid of ornaments, until finally its upper portions were decked in its blossoms like a necklace. (ll. 84–85)

The tree is compared with a neck and its blossoms with a necklace, while the tangled branches are likened to plaited locks. The point is that the whole image is inverted, since branches and blossoms follow an ascending order, whereas locks, neck, and necklace follow a descending order. The tree is therefore presented as a feminine bust viewed upside down, and in this way the metaphors acquire a new flexibility and a capacity for arrangement into an infinite number of new combinations and patterns.

This may be observed in the passage included between lines 32 and 36. The poet begins in line 32 by stating that the night is illuminated by the *pearls* of poetry. This implies that *pearls* which on one level stands for *verses* also means *stars*, and that consequently his *verses* are *stars*. In line 33 *dawn* is likened to a *pillar*, but also by implication it represents the king's *lineage*. Consequently the king's *lineage* is a *pillar*. Basing himself on these two syllogisms the poet claims that on this *pillar* he erects his construction of *verses*, which means secondarily, that the *stars* rest on the *pillar*, that is, that the poet's *verses* are based on the king's *lineage*. Then he states in line 34 that the king is above the *stars* (= *verses*), that is, beyond the reach of poetic description. In ascending order, line 35 places the king above the *moon*, that is, beyond the corruptible sublunar world according to the medieval philosophical doctrines that Ibn Zamrak had studied in the Granadan madrasa. Finally, after this gradual ascent from the corruptible spheres, the poet comes right out and declares: "He is the sun" (l. 36). The following chart clarifies the complex reasoning and metaphoric play:

l. 32 pearls = verses
pearls = stars

∴ verses = stars

l. 33 dawn = pillar
dawn = lineage

∴ pillar = lineage
verses = stars are raised on pillar = lineage

l. 34 king is above stars = verses
∴ king is above pillar = lineage

l. 35 king is above moon

l. 36 king = sun

What has occurred is that lexicalization has attained a new stage of complexity where metaphors represent not one but several different realities, and are organized into strictly logical though often obscure patterns to convey different levels of meaning at the same time. The image *pearls* appears six times in the poem, but in each case it denotes a different aspect of reality: tears (l. 15), teeth (l. 19), poetry (l. 32), marble (l. 70), drops of water (l. 74), flowers (l. 86). The first impression received is one of metaphoric impoverishment until one pauses to consider that with the stylized usage of one symbol, a whole series of varied natural objects are reduced to formal unity. The preoccupation with the formal regularity of the poem can be seen in the fact that different sentiments are expressed in almost identical phrases or formulas. In line 3 the poet's initial despair and love-longing is summed up in the phrase "I lay upon them that which makes mountains to be light." At the end of the poem when royal favor has brought consolation to the poet, he expresses his renewed hope in the same words: "the inheritance of a lofty majesty finds mountains to be light!" (l. 143). In this way the variety of emotions in the poem, its progression from initial despair to final hope, is framed by the use of a formula just as the variety of nature is unified through the stylization of metaphor.

The poet king Yūsuf III (r. 1407–1417) flourished during the early fifteenth century when the tendency to formal perfection outlined above became more and more pronounced as Granada became more Orientalized. His *muwashshaḥa* (**42**) is a fine example of Naṣrid concern with formal perfection in art. Like the poets before him, Yūsuf III invents nothing, yet the subtlety of form is astonishing in this poem. Its strophes are divided into two elements: (1) a *simṭ* of two lines subdivided into three segments each (= six segments) and (2) a *ghuṣn* of three lines subdivided into two segments each (= six segments); the rhyme is *abcabc dedede*, and so on. The basic pattern of alternating twos and threes is framed within the first and last two lines which are exactly the same. Furthermore, line 14 is the exact center of the poem and divides it into two parts. As the center of a three-line *ghuṣn* it further emphasizes the division, for the preceding line (l. 13) expresses the ideals of courtly love: "He has seduced me/With the spell of his eyelids," while the following line (l. 15) brings up the idea of physical union: "I'd have won my desires/By undoing his sash." These two aspects of love, the spiritual and the physical, are organized in such a way as to coincide with the formal structure of the poem, for its first half expresses the ideals of courtly love whereas the second half stresses physical union, with line 14 being the watershed in content as well as in form.

All the old commonplaces are skillfully reworked into an exquisite filigree in which the spontaneity of human emotion contrasts strongly with the rigid symmetry of an architecturally perfect structure.

Another of Yūsuf III's poems is of historical interest (**41**) because of the circumstances in which it was written, namely the fall of Antequera into the hands of the Christians in 1410. The theme is therefore analogous to that of ar-Rundī with whom it coincides in claiming that "Islam is in the clutch of unbelief" (l. 24). Yet whereas ar-Rundī's poem is an appeal to Africa for military help, and is not concerned with the poet's own private life, Yūsuf III, who after all was responsible for the loss of Antequera before his subjects, had of necessity to combine self-justification with the elegiac theme if he was to regain the confidence of his followers. Therefore, while ar-Rundī's elegy ends with a note of despair, Yūsuf III expresses instead his optimistic faith in a fortunate outcome for Islam.

After the fall of Granada in 1492, the royal family, aristocracy, and intellectuals began to drift to Africa as Spanish Christian rule became more intolerant. Those who remained behind consequently lost their educational tradition and knowledge of classical Arabic, so that when the last Muslims were expelled from Spain in the seventeenth century they went to Africa taking with them the Spanish language, and a literature written in Spanish, although with Arabic characters (Aljamiado) in which they imitated the Renaissance poetry of Lope de Vega. They also built mosques with baroque mihrabs, such as that of Testour in Tunisia, and continued to speak Spanish well into the eighteenth century.

Before this, an anonymous poem written around the year 1501 in Arabic documents the intellectual decline of the Granadan Muslims (**43**) while it also offers an insight into the political and spiritual difficulties they encountered after the conquest.[100] The poem is a *qaṣīda* addressed to the most powerful Muslim leader of the age, the Ottoman emperor Bāyazīd II (r. 1481–1512), in an attempt to enlist his support in restoring the fortunes of peninsular Islam. The poem is almost devoid of *badīᶜ* and constitutes a striking contrast with the elaborate and flowery odes of Ibn Zamrak. It is sincere and artless, in the elegiac tradition of ar-Rundī. The fact that the educational tradition of classical Arabic had declined is visible in its defects: abuse of stock phrases, which in this case are not metaphorically employed, and repetition of the same word in the rhyme foot, a defect condemned by medieval Arab critics. Yet its natural simplicity and the sincere sorrow it evokes raise it above the generality of political odes in Arabic.

Lines 1 to 8 contain an invocation to Bāyazīd on behalf of some "slaves" in al-Andalus, whose sorry state is briefly sketched (ll. 9–18). Then the surrender of Granada is justified (ll. 19–39). The emperor is informed that the Muslim population has now been converted forcibly to Christianity (l. 20), and this immediately raises the question of apostasy which in Islamic law is punishable by death. The burden is therefore on the Granadans to explain that their conversion was involuntary if they wished to obtain Muslim support. According to the doctrine of *taqiyya* which condones religious dissembling in cases of personal danger, a forced conversion was considered invalid, and therefore not a case of apostasy. *Taqiyya* was based on *niyya* or the "intention" of the believer rather than his outward observance of the ceremonial law, and therefore the poet emphasizes the good intention of the Granadans to remain Muslims in secret despite their outward observance of Christianity.

After having proclaimed the secret Islamic affiliation of the forced converts, the poet describes the treaty of surrender (ll. 40–55). Its terms, he shows, had been violated by the Christians: they had forced conversion upon the new subjects, Cardinal Cisneros had

---

[100] James T. Monroe, "A Curious Morisco Appeal to the Ottoman Empire," *Andalus*, XXXI (1966), 281–303.

burned all their books in a public auto-da-fé, those who failed to attend Mass were punished, they were compelled to eat pork and drink wine. From lines 56 to 66 their sorry state is further elaborated upon: their children were indoctrinated by the priests, their mosques had been turned into churches, the Muslims, now nominally Christians, were despised by their African brethren and could therefore not be ransomed with Muslim funds like captives, but had fallen into a state worse than slavery, for they were rejected by their coreligionaries yet unacceptable to the old Christians.

This leads to a fresh appeal to Bāyazīd (ll. 67–81) in which the poet suggests that the emperor retaliate by avenging himself on the Christians of the Holy Land, and that he urge the Pope to intercede with the Spanish sovereigns (out of politeness he mentions only Fernando) on behalf of the wretched Moriscos of Granada. It is significant that one of the strongest arguments in favor of religious tolerance is that under Muslim rule in al-Andalus, the Mozarabs "neither were converted from their faith nor expelled from their homes" (l. 79) in contrast with the intolerant policies of the Spanish sovereigns.

From lines 82 to 95 the poet exposes the duplicity of Fernando and Isabel who had informed the Egyptian and Turkish envoys to their court that the Morisco conversion had been entirely voluntary: "Rather, it was the fear of death and of burning, that caused us to convert" (l. 88), the poet says, invoking the doctrine of *taqiyya*. Then he enumerates the towns where atrocities had been committed by the Christians in putting down the first Muslim revolt of Las Alpujarras of Granada.

Lines 96 to 105 contain a final plea for help. In them the poet implores Bāyazīd to intercede so that the Moriscos could be allowed either to practice their religion, or barring that, to leave Spain taking their property with them.

The significance of this poem is considerable. Its emphasis on intention and dissimulation shifts the seat of religion from ceremonial practice to inner observance. It therefore reveals a major religious crisis. From this time forth the persecuted Moriscos would stress universal moral values rather than the narrow, sectarian doctrines of any particular religion. This would allow them to reconcile their crypto-Islam with outward observance of Catholicism. In contrasting the tolerant attitude of Islam toward other religions in the past with contemporary Christian intolerance and persecution the poet gave expression to a theme that came to predominate in later Morisco writings, for Miguel de Luna picked up the idea in his

History of the Conquest of Spain by the Moors.[101] This book is not a true history, but a historical novel; it attempts to defend the Morisco cause by contrasting medieval Islamic tolerance in al-Andalus with the Catholic intolerance of sixteenth-century Spain. Soon the theme of the tolerant, virtuous Moor would become fashionable in Golden Age Spanish literature, in chivalric ballads, plays, and novels.[102] The significance of Cervantes' imaginary Arab historian Cide Hamete Benengeli has yet to be studied in this light.

The religious crisis of the Moriscos led to the creation of an intermediate religion designed to reconcile crypto-Islam with observance of Catholic ceremonial. Toward the second half of the sixteenth century, certain leaden tablets began to appear all over Granada. These *libros plumbeos* as they were called, bore inscriptions in Arabic outlining a new syncretic religion. Claiming to be Christian revelations, they explained away the sonhood of Jesus as a figure of speech, and claimed that the chalice used in the Mass contained water—not wine, which is forbidden in Islam—and that it was used by the priest to wash his hands, face, and mouth, that is, to perform the *ghusl* or ritual ablution of Islam.[103]

Thus, important Islamic attitudes are revealed in this last farewell of Hispano-Arabic poetry, attitudes that gave birth to new solutions to the religious crisis of the late fifteenth and early sixteenth centuries. These attitudes also affected Spanish literary works that gave to the world the image and theme of the chivalrous Moor of Granada. In this way, the last poetic production of al-Andalus was blended into Spanish Renaissance literature with no break in continuity.

---

[101] London, 1687.

[102] See María S. Carrasco Urgoiti, *El moro de Granada en la literatura (del siglo XV al XX)* (Madrid, 1956).

[103] The *libros plumbeos* have been studied recently by D. Cabanelas Rodríguez, *El morisco granadino Alonso del Castillo* (Granada, 1965).

Arabic Texts, Translations, and Notes

1 Ibn ʿAbd Rabbihi

1 Praise be to Him who is not contained in any region nor reached by any vision,

2 Before whose countenance all faces are lowered in submission, for He has no rival or equal;

3 Praise be to Him for He is a mighty Creator, well informed about His creation; farseeing.

4 [He is] a first principle having no beginning and a iast one having no end.

5 His kindness and excellence have favored us, while it would be impossible to find His like,

6 Since He is far too illustrious for eyes to perceive or imagination and conjecture to grasp,

7 Although He may be perceived by the mind, the intellect and by rational proofs,

8 Since these are the most solid means of knowing subjects that are abstruse and subtle.

9 The knowledge grasped by man's intellect is more solid than that gained from ocular evidence,

10 Therefore may God be praised most plentifully for His blessings and favors;

11 And after praising and glorifying God, and thanking the Creator and Quickener of the dead,

12 I will speak about the battle days of the best of men; one who has been adorned with generosity and courage;

13 One who has destroyed unbelief and rebellion and sundered sedition and schism.

14 For we were experiencing a moment of darkness intense as the night, as well as a civil war; being like the scum and rubbish [swept] by the torrent

---

1. SOURCE: Ibn ʿAbd Rabbihi, *al-ʿIqd al-farīd*, ed. Aḥmad Amīn (Cairo, 1962), IV, 501–527.

METER: *rajaz.*

In this poem the author praises the exploits of ʿAbd ar-Raḥmān III, first Caliph of Córdoba, whose determination and courage secured the power

١

ابن عبد ربّه

١ سُبْحَانَ مَنْ لَمْ تَحوِهِ أَقْطارُ ... ولَمْ تَكُنْ تُدْرِكُهُ الأَبصارُ

٢ و مَن عَنَتْ لِوَجْهِهِ الوُجوهُ ... فما له نِدٌّ ولا شَبيهُ

٣ سُبْحانَهُ مِن خالِقٍ قَديرِ ... وعالِمٍ بِخَلْقِهِ بَصيرِ

٤ وأَوّلٌ لَيْسَ لَهُ ابْتِداءُ ... وآخِرٌ ليس له انْتِهاءُ

٥ أَوْسَعَنا إِحْسانَهُ وفَضْلَهُ ... وعَزَّ أَنْ يكونَ شيءٌ مثلَهُ

٦ وجَلَّ أَنْ تُدْرِكَهُ العُيونُ ... أَوْ يَحْوِياهُ الوَهْمُ والظُّنونُ

٧ لِكِنَّهُ يُدْرَكُ بالقَريحَهْ ... والعَقلِ والأَبْنِيَةِ الصَّحيحَهْ

٨ وهذه مِن أَثْبت المَعارِفْ ... في الأَوْجُهِ الغامِضةِ اللَّطائفْ

٩ مَعْرِفَةُ العَقْلِ مِن الإِنسانِ ... أَثبتُ مِن مَعرفةِ العِيانِ

١٠ فالحَمْدُ لِلّهِ على نَعْمائِهِ ... حمدًا جَزيلًا وعلى آلائِهِ

١١ وبعد حَمْدِ اللّهِ والتَّمجيدِ ... وبعد شُكْرِ المُبْدِئِ المُعيدِ

١٢ أَقولُ في أَيّامِ خَيرِ النّاسِ ... ومَن تحلّى بالنَّدى والباسِ

١٣ ومَن أَبادَ الكُفْرَ والنِّفاقا ... وشَرَّدَ الفِتْنَةَ والشِّقاقا

١٤ ونَحْنُ في حَنادِسٍ كاللَّيْلِ ... وفِتْنةٍ مثلِ غُثاءِ السَّيْلِ

---

of the Umayyads in al-Andalus. For a study of this type of *urjūza*, the student may consult J. Ribera, *Disertaciones y opúsculos* (Madrid, 1928), I, 93–150, and L. Abdel Badi, *La épica árabe y su influencia en la épica castellana*, (Santiago de Chile, 1964).

15 Until that worshiper of the Clement who is the most eminent of the Banū Marwān was invested with power.

16 Being supported [by God] he appointed a sword from the edges of which death flowed, to judge over his enemies,

17 While he saluted royal power at dawn along with the new moon, so that they both arose in the morning like two rivals in beauty.

18 He bore [signs of] piety on his forehead and religious and secular authority upon his right hand.

19 The land was illuminated by his light and the stirring up of evil and mischief was interrupted,

20 During a time rife with rebellion when the breaking of alliances as well as apostasy were rampant,

21 And the earth had straitened its inhabitants while war had kindled the blaze of its fires,

22 When we were enfolded in a pitch-black night blindness and a gloom without equal,

23 Such that every day we were attacked by mourning so that no eye could enjoy sleep.

24 Thus during ᶜĪd we have even had to pray under the protection of guards out of fear for an enemy intent upon revenge,

25 Until we were given in rescue, like a light putting heaven and earth next to each other,

26 The Caliph of God, whom He elected and chose over all creation,

27 From the source of the Revelation, the abode of [divine] wisdom and the best descendants of the Imams.

28 The South winds are only remotely related to his beneficence, while the clouds are shamed by his generosity;

29 In his face there is evidence of [God's] light, whereas the kissing of his hand is a religious sacrifice to God.

30 He quickens the dead with qualities generous as those of the age of Kaᶜb and of the time of Ḥātim;

---

15. The "Banū Marwān," i.e., the Umayyads.

17. ᶜAbd ar-Raḥmān III was enthroned on the first of Rabīᶜ I, 300/Oct. 16, 912 (E. Lévi-Provençal, "España musulmana hasta la caída del califato de Córdoba (711–1031 de J.C.)," trans. E. García Gómez, *Historia de España*, directed by R. Menéndez Pidal [Madrid, 1950–1957] IV, 262).

١٥ حتّى تَوَلّى عابِدُ الرحمنِ   ذاك الأَغَرُّ مِن بَني مَرْوانِ

١٦ مُؤَيَّدٌ حَكَّمَ في عُداتِه   سَيْفاً يَسيلُ المَوْتُ مِن ظُباتِه

١٧ وَصَبَّحَ المُلْكَ مع الهِلالِ   فأَصْبَحا نِدَّيْنِ في الْجَمالِ

١٨ واحْتَمَلَ التَّقْوَى على جَبينِه   والدِّينَ والدُّنْيا على يَمينِه

١٩ قد أَشْرَقَتْ بِنُورِهِ البِلادُ   وانْقَطَعَ التَّشْغيبُ والفسادُ

٢٠ هذا على حينَ طَغَى النِّفاقُ   واسْتَفْحَلَ النُّكَّاثُ والمُرّاقُ

٢١ وضاقَتْ الأَرْضُ على سُكانِها   وأَذْكَتْ الحَرْبُ لَظَى نيرانِها

٢٢ ونَحْنُ في عَشْواءَ مُدْلَهِمَّهْ   وظُلْمَةٍ ما مِثْلُها مِن ظُلْمَهْ

٢٣ تأْخُذُنا الصَّيْحَةُ كُلَّ يَوْمِ   فما تَلَذُّ مُقْلَةٌ بِنَوْمِ

٢٤ وقد نُصَلّى العيدَ بالنَّواظِرِ   مخافَةً مِن العَدُوِّ الثائرِ

٢٥ حتى أتانا الغَوْثُ مِن ضياءِ   طَبَّقَ بين الأَرْضِ والسماءِ

٢٦ خَليفَةَ اللّهِ الذى اصْطَفاهُ   على جَميعِ الخَلْقِ واجْتَباهُ

٢٧ مِن مَعدِنِ الوَحْيِ وبَيْتِ الحِكْمَهْ   وخَيْرِ مَنسوبٍ إلى الأَئِمَّهْ

٢٨ تَكِلُّ عن مَعْروفِهِ الجَنائِبُ   وتَسْتَحي مِن وجُودِهِ السَّحائِبُ

٢٩ في وَجْهِهِ مِن نُورِهِ بُرْهانُ   وكَفُّهُ تَقْبيلُها قُرْبانُ

٣٠ أَحْيَا الذى ماتَ مِن المَكارِمِ   مِن عَهْدِ كَعْبٍ وزَمانِ حاتِمِ

---

24. ᶜĪd is a Muslim festival.

30. Kaᶜb Ibn Māma and Ḥātim of Ṭaʾī were both pre-Islamic heroes proverbial for their generosity.

31 Generous qualities such that description falls short of them, and a brightness of countenance such that the eye becomes tired of it;

32 And a natural disposition [bitter as] colocynth or [sweet as] water, and a lofty ambition aspiring to reach the sky.

33 Yet gaze upon the loftiness of his construction; it will show you one of the wonders of the eminence of his condition.

34 Were the ocean to rival the generosity of his hands when those requesting his favor repair to him for protection,

35 It would not be enough, or barely so; whereas he does not shrink after having given in abundance;

36 He who caused blessings to abound after they had been destroyed and sewed this world together after it had been slit apart.

37 It is he who has united the divided community [of the faithful] and rent the obscure coverings of darkness from it,

38 Renovating a royal power that had been worn out, until its tent pegs became firm and stable,

39 And gathering together military equipment and numerous troops, organizing both armies and companies.

The First Campaign Undertaken by the Prince of the Faithful, ᶜAbd ar-Raḥmān ibn Muḥammad

40 Then he set out for Jaén on his campaign, accompanied by an army afire with his zeal

41 And he brought the wild animals down from the peaks as though they had been made to descend from the clouds.

42 For their rebels hastily submitted while their fortresses began to crumble.

43 When he aimed at them with the swords of resolute purpose whetted on the coats of mail of prudent courage,

44 They almost offered themselves up to [those swords] and the earth was almost convulsed by them.

45 Had it not been for the [One] God it would have quaked and relieved itself of its weights out of fear.

46 So he sent [our] people down to the broad plain and cut off distance from the group,

---

36. Some sources read *wa fattaqa d-dunyā wa kānat ratqā*, although the sense requires the opposite, which is recorded in some manuscripts.

٣١ مَكارِمٌ يَقْصُرُ عنها الوَصْفُ وغُرَّةٌ يَحْسُرُ عنها الطَّرْفُ

٣٢ وشِيمَةٌ كالصَّابِ أو كالمَاءِ وَهِمَّةٌ تَرْقَى إلى السَّمَاءِ

٣٣ وَٱنْظُرْ إلى الرفيعِ مِن بُنْيانِه يُرِيكَ بِدْعًا مِن عَظيمِ شانِه

٣٤ لَوْ خَايَلَ البَحْرُ نَدَى يَدَيْهِ إِذا لَجَتْ عُفاتُه إِلَيْهِ

٣٥ لَغاضَ أَوْ لَكادَ أَنْ يَغِيضَا ولا ٱسْتَحى من بعد أَنْ يَفِيضَا

٣٦ مَن أَسبغ النُّعمى وكانَتْ مَحْقَا وَرَفَّق الدُّنْيَا وكانت فَتْقَا

٣٧ هو الذى جَمَّعَ شَمْلَ الأُمَّهْ وجابَ عنها دامِساتِ الظُّلْمَهْ

٣٨ وجَدَّدَ المُلْكَ الذى قد أَخْلَقا حتَّى رَسَتْ أَوْتَادُه وٱسْتَوْسقَا

٣٩ وجَمَّع العُدَّةَ والعَدِيدا وكَثَّفَ الأَجْنادَ والحُشودا

أَوَّل غزاة غزاها أَمير المؤمنين عبد الرحمن بن محمد

٤٠ ثُمَّ ٱنْتَحَى جَيَّانَ في غَزَاتِه بِعَسْكَرٍ يَسْعر مِن حُماتِه

٤١ فَٱسْتَنْزَلَ الوَحْشَ مِن الهِضابِ كأَنَّما حُطَّتْ مِن السَّحابِ

٤٢ فأَذْعَنَتْ مُرَّاقُها سِراعَا وأَقْبَلَتْ حُصونُها تَداعَى

٤٣ لمَّا رَمَاها بِسُيوفِ العَزْمِ مَشْحونةٍ على دُروعِ الحَزْمِ

٤٤ كادَتْ لها أَنْفُسهم تَجودُ وكادت الأَرْضُ بهم تَمِيدُ

٤٥ لولا الإِلٰه زُلْزِلَتْ زِلْزالَها وأَخرجَتْ مِن رَهْبةٍ أَثْقالَها

٤٦ فأَنْزَلَ الناسَ إلى البَسِيط وقَطَّعَ البَيْنَ مِن الخَليط

47 Conquering the fortresses one after another and granting safe-conduct to all the inhabitants.

48 He did not desist until he had reached Jaén and had left not one devil in its territory,

49 So that all the people became one community after he had contracted in their favor covenants of protection with Muslims and non-Muslims.

50 Then, in his wrath, he made for Elvira since the latter was notorious for every sort of evil,

51 And he caused his horsemen and foot soldiers to tread on it until his sandal had trampled upon its cheek,

52 Leaving not one single rebellious jinn in it, nor any one of its obstinate humans.

53 But that he clothed him in humility and abasement and turbaned him and his family in ruin.

54 For this reason I have never seen the like of that year nor the like of God's favor toward Islam.

55 Then the Emir departed from his campaign, for God had made him recover from his enemies.

56 Yet before it Écija had been humbled and had submitted, a long time having elapsed that it had [not] done so,

57 And after it the city of Seville surrendered to the gleaming, sharp sword,

58 When the commander of the Emir successfully campaigned against it under the [latter's] victorious banner,

59 So that it surrendered to Islam, not having been Islamic before then, and Aḥmad ibn Maslama withdrew from it.

60 Afterward, during the last month of that year the light of which was bright,

61 Castles and fortresses quaked as though death had rushed upon them,

62 And their masters came forth in deputations requesting signs of favor from their Imam.

63 No man possessing power and strength remained behind, but rather they all went together to Bāb as-Sudda.

---

57. The text reads *shiʾil* instead of *Ishbilya*, "Seville," but from contemporary sources it is clear that Seville is alluded to.

59. Lévi-Provençal, *op. cit.*, p. 268.

٤٧ وافتتح الحصونَ حِصْناً حِصناً   وأوْسَعَ الناسَ جميعاً أمْناً
٤٨ ولم يَزَلْ حتّى انتحى جيّانا   فلم يَدَعْ بأرْضِها شَيْطانا
٤٩ فأصْبَحَ الناسُ جميعاً أُمَّهْ   قد عَقَدَ الإلّ لهم والذِّمّه
٥٠ ثم انتحى مِن فَوْرِهِ إلْبيرَهْ   وهي بِكُلِّ آفةٍ مَشهورَهْ
٥١ فداسَها بِخَيْلِهِ ورَجْلِهِ   حتى تَوَطَّا خَدَّها بِنَعْلِهِ
٥٢ ولم يَدَعْ مِن جِنّها مَريدَا   بها ولا من إنْسِها عَنيدَا
٥٣ إلّا كَسَاهُ الذُّلَّ والصَّغارَا   وعَمَّهُ وأهْلَهُ دَمَارَا
٥٤ فما رَأيْتُ مثلَ ذاك العامِ   ومثلَ صُنْعِ اللهِ للإسلامِ
٥٥ فانْصَرَفَ الأميرُ من غَزاتِهِ   وقد شَفاهُ اللهُ من عُداتِهِ
٥٦ وقبلَها ما خَضَعَتْ وأَذْعَنَتْ   إسْتِجَة وطالما قد صَنَعَتْ
٥٧ وبعدَها مدينةُ الشَّنْتيلِ   ما أذعنت لِلصّارِمِ الصَّقيلِ
٥٨ لما غَزاها قائدُ الأميرِ   باليُمْنِ في لِوائِهِ المَنْصورِ
٥٩ فأسْلَمَتْ ولم تَكُنْ بالمُسْلِمَهْ   وزالَ عنها أحْمَدُ بنُ مَسْلَمَهْ
٦٠ وبعدَها في آخِرِ الشُّهورِ   من ذلك العامِ الزّكيّ النُّورِ
٦١ أرْجَفَتِ القِلاعُ والحُصونُ   كأنّما ساوَرَها المَنونُ
٦٢ وأقْبَلَتْ رِجالُها وُفودَا   تَبْغي لَدَى إمامِها السُّعودَا
٦٣ وليس مِن ذي عِزّةٍ وشِدّهْ   إلّا تَوافَوْا عند بابِ السُّدّهْ

63. Bāb as-Sudda was the old palace of the Umayyads at Córdoba.

64 Their hearts, publicly recognizing obedience, unanimously agreed to join the Islamic community.

The Year 301/913–914

65 Then he campaigned during the end of the following year, overrunning Sidonia and the coast,

66 Not leaving Rayya and Algeciras until he had singed its yelping dogs;

67 [He campaigned] until he halted at the plain of Carmona with an army like the millstone,

68 Against the person in it who had disobeyed the law and done mischief, whose origin may be traced back to a certain black Sawāda if he should boast of his origin.

69 The latter requested that [the Caliph] grant him a delay of a few months after which he would become a servant at his orders,

70 So the Amir complied with what he had requested, requited him favorably and departed.

The Year 302/914–915

71 In it the return on the way from the campaign of the year 301 took place;

72 Therefore no campaign was undertaken during the remainder [of that year] nor was any [army] sent forth.

The Year 303/915–916

73 Then on the third year he caused his paternal uncle to campaign after having invested him with his own resolution and steadfastness.

74 So he set forth with a strongly courageous army whose commander was Abū l-ᶜAbbās,

75 Until he climbed to the summits of Bobastro and overran its plains with the army,

---

66. Rayya was the ancient Carthaginian province of Málaga, called by the Romans "Provincia Regia."

68. Lévi-Provençal, *op. cit.*, p. 269.

٦٤ قُلُوبُهُمْ بَاخِعَةٌ بِالطَّاعَةْ   قد أَجْمَعُوا الدُّخولَ في الجَمَاعَةْ

سنة إحدى وثلثمائة

٦٥ ثُمَّ غَزَا في عُقْبِ عامٍ قابِلِ   فجالَ في شَذُونةٍ والسَّاحِلِ

٦٦ ولم يَدَعْ رَيَّةَ والجَزِيرَهْ   حتى كَوَى أَكْلُبَها الهَرِيرَهْ

٦٧ حتى أَنَاخَ في ذُرَى قَرْمُونَهْ   بِكَلْكَلٍ كَمَدْرَةِ الطَّاحُونَهْ

٦٨ على الذى خالَفَ فيها وٱنتزى   يُعْزَى إلى سَوَادَةٍ إذا ٱعْتَزَى

٦٩ فسَأَلَ أَنْ يُمْهِلَهُ شُهُورَا   ثُمَّ يكون عبدَهُ المأمُورَا

٧٠ فأَسْعَفَ الأميرُ منه ما سَأَلْ   وعاد بالفَضْلِ عليه وقَفَلْ

سنة اثنتين وثلثمائة

٧١ كان بها القُفُولُ عند الجَيَّةْ   مِن غَزْوِ إحْدَى وثَلثمايه

٧٢ فلم يَكُن يُدْرَكُ في باقيها   غَزْوٌ ولا بَعْثٌ يكون فيها

سنة ثلاث وثلثمائة

٧٣ ثُمَّتَ أَغْزَى في الثلاثِ عَمَّهْ   وقد كَسَاهُ عَزْمَهُ وحَزْمَهْ

٧٤ فسار في جَيْشٍ شديدِ البَاس   وقائدُ الجَيْشِ أَبُو العَبَّاس

٧٥ حتى تَرَقَّى بِذُرَى بُبَشْتَرْ   وجالَ في ساحاتها بالعَسْكَرْ

---

73. The Caliph's paternal uncle was Abān (*ibid.*, p. 270).
74. Abū l-ᶜAbbās, Aḥmad ibn Abī ᶜUbaida.

76 Nor did he leave behind for them any crops or fruits, or any precious object or rich furnishing,

77 Cutting down its vines and trees, yet its apostate neither acknowledged his [authority] nor did he appear.

78 After that he turned back, having destroyed the crops and food supplies

79 So that the pig then became certain that no means of livelihood were to be expected therein.

80 Therefore he wrote to the Imam in recognition of his duty, [expressing his readiness] "to hear and to obey" and his repentance.

81 In this way God allayed the blaze of civil strife and the people became united in reconciliation,

82 And the sheep and the wolf grazed together after the wars had lain down their arms.

The Year 304/916–917

83 After it came the campaign of the fourth year, and what good deed did our Lord not perform

84 During its course, by cheering up the grieving sovereign both of whose hands strove in God's path!

85 This was so because he sent out two commanders who manifested both divine victory and support;

86 The one toward the frontier and its adjacent areas, against the polytheist enemy or his supporters,

87 And the other to the fragrant gardens of Murcia, while the part that went on traveled as far as Valencia.

88 He whom he sent to the coast was the Quraishite, the commander of the cavalry,

89 While Ibn Abī ᶜAbda [was sent] toward the [land of] polytheism accompanied by the crack troops and best weapons.

90 And they approached with every kind of total victory, causing bereavement that really left the enemy bereft.

---

77. "Its apostate," i.e., Ibn Ḥafṣūn, the famous rebel against the central authority of Córdoba.

٧٦ فلم يَدَعْ زَرْعًا ولا ثِمارَا   لهم ولا عِلْقًا ولا عُقَارَا

٧٧ وقَطَّعَ الكُرومَ منها والشَّجَرْ   ولم يُبايع عِلْجُها ولا ظَهَرْ

٧٨ ثم آنْثَنَى مِن بعد ذاك قافِلَا   وقد أَبادَ الزَّرْعَ والمآكِلَا

٧٩ فأَيْقَنَ الخِنْزيرُ عند ذاكا   أَنْ لا بَقَاءَ يُرْتَجَى هُناكا

٨٠ فكاتَبَ الإمامَ بالإجابَه   والسَّمْعِ والطَّاعَةِ والإنابَه

٨١ فأَخْمَدَ اللّٰهُ شِهابَ الفِتْنَه   وأَصْبَحَ الناسُ معًا في هُدْنَه

٨٢ وآرْتَعَتْ الشاةُ معًا والذِّيبُ   إذ وَضَعَتْ أَوْزارَها الحُروبْ

سنة أربع وثلثمائة

٨٣ وبعدها كانَتْ غَزاةُ أَرْبَعِ   فأَيُّ صُنْعٍ رَبُّنا لم يَصْنَعِ

٨٤ فيها بِبَسْطِ المَلِكِ الأَوَّاهِ   كِلْتَا يَدَيْهِ في سَبيلِ اللّٰهِ

٨٥ وذاك أَنْ قَوَّدَ قائدَيْنِ   بالنَّصْرِ والتَّأْيِيدِ ظاهِرَيْنِ

٨٦ هذا إلى الثَّغْرِ وما يَلِيهِ   على عَدُوِّ الشِّرْكِ أَو ذَوِيهِ

٨٧ وذا إلى شُمِّ الرُّبَا مِن مُرْسِيَهْ   وما مَضَى جَرَى إلى بَلَنْسِيَهْ

٨٨ فكان مَن وَجَّهَهُ للسَّاحِلْ   القُرَشِيُّ القائدُ القَنابِلْ

٨٩ وابن أَبى عَبْدَةٍ نَحْوَ الشِّرْكِ   في خَيْرِ ما تَعْبيةٍ وشِكِّ

٩٠ فأَقْبَلَا بكُلِّ فَتْحٍ شامِلِ   وكُلِّ نُكْلٍ للعَدُوِّ ناكِلِ

---

84. That year the Caliph lost two sons, therefore he was "grieving" (*Bayān al-Mughrib*, trans. E. Fagnan [Algiers, 1904], II, 282).

88. He was Isḥāq ibn Muḥammad al-Qurashī (*ibid.*, p. 281).

91 After that brilliant campaign there occurred the conquest of Niebla the Red:
92 At the end of that year without equal, accompanied by troops to campaign against it, he sent his freedman
93 Badr, who encompassed its two sides and harrassed it until it responded to his command
94 And delivered up its master in subjection, so that Badr brought him in captivity.

The Year 305/917–918

95 After it came the campaign of the fifth year against the descendant of Sawāda, the ally of misfortune,
96 When he was doing mischief, breaking bounds, and violating treaties and alliances,
97 And warring against the central power out of his ill luck, his enmity, and his evil opinion.
98 [The Caliph] sent the Quraishite, the commander, against him, when in erring he had swerved from the right path.
99 Then he strengthened his force by means of Badr for the latter was like an even number to that odd one
100 Who had encompassed [Carmona] by means of horsemen and footsoldiers, tucking up his robe and exerting himself in the struggle;
101 Thus he came down upon the lofty fortress accompanied by footsoldiers, archers, and cavalry,
102 While Badr continued to invest it and, in a similar manner, applied himself earnestly to the fray.
103 Yet the dog had plunged into rashness, while his throat and breath had become contracted against him,
104 So his companions deserted his banner and opened the gates against his advice,
105 And the army rushed blindly into the city, while he in it was like the shape of the woman riding in a camel litter,

---

93. Badr ibn Aḥmad was the royal Ḥājib or "chamberlain."
95. Ḥabīb ibn Sawāda (Lévi-Provençal, *op. cit.*, p. 269).

٩١ وبعد هذى الغَـزْوَةِ الغَرّاءِ كان افتتاحُ لَبْلَةَ الحَمْراءِ

٩٢ أَغْزَى بِجُنْدٍ نحوَها مَوْلاهُ في عُقْبِ هذا العامِ لا سِواهُ

٩٣ بَدْرًا فضَمَّ جانِبَيْها ضَمَّهْ وغَمَّها حتى أجابَتْ حُكْمَهْ

٩٤ وأَسْلَمَتْ صاحِبَها مَقْهورًا حتى أَتَى بدرٌ به مَأْسُورًا

سنة خمس وثلثمائة

٩٥ وبعدها كانَتْ غَزاةُ خَمْسِ إلى السَّوادِيِّ عَقِيدِ النَّحْسِ

٩٦ لَمَّا طَغَى وجَاوَزَ الحُدودَا ونَقَضَ المِيثاقَ والعُهودَا

٩٧ ونابَذَ السُّلْطانَ مِن شَقائِهِ ومِن تَعَدِّيهِ وسُوءِ رائِهِ

٩٨ أَغزَى إليهِ القُرَشِيَّ القائدَا إذْ صارَ عن قَصْدِ السَّبيلِ حائِدَا

٩٩ ثُمَّتَ شَدَّ أَزْرَه بِبَدْرِ فكانَ كالشَّفْعِ لِهذا الوِتْرِ

١٠٠ أَحْدَقَها بالخَيْلِ والرِجالِ مُشَمِّرًا وجَدَّ في القِتالِ

١٠١ فنازَلَ الحِصْنَ العَظِيمَ الشانِ بالرَّجْلِ والرُّماةِ والفُرْسانِ

١٠٢ فلم يَزَلْ بَدْرٌ بها مُحاصِرَا كذا على قِتالِهِ مُنابِرَا

١٠٣ والكَلْبُ في تَهَوُّرٍ قَدْ ٱنْغَمَسْ وضُيِّقَ الحَلْقُ عليه والنَّفَسْ

١٠٤ فٱفْتَرَقَ الأَصْحابُ عن لِوائِهِ وفَتَحوا الأَبْوابَ دُونَ رائِهِ

١٠٥ وٱقْتَحَمَ العَسْكَرُ في المَدِينَهْ وهُوَ بها كَهَيْئَةِ الظَّعِينَهْ

99. See Koran 89:3, "By the even and the odd."

106 Submitting to humility and abasement and surrendering to captivity.

107 So the chamberlain stripped the crown off his royal authority and led him off to his death with his hands tied behind his back.

108 At the end of that year the disaster to Islam brought about by Abū l-ᶜAbbās occurred:

109 He was campaigning, being the bravest of the brave as well as one of the manliest of commanders.

110 Yet he set out without any men experienced in war who could have struck out when the time was ripe for striking,

111 Waging war in the company of men who were not true warriors while the majority of the troops remained with the chamberlain.

112 The rabble of the districts joined his [forces] whereas those endowed with knowledge and foresight were far away from him.

113 Until, when he had penetrated among the enemy in such a way that he had gone neither too far nor too near [in his incursion],

114 Some hardhearted people betrayed him to the yelping dogs.

115 Thus was the commander martyred in the company of pious men who gave their souls to the Creator

116 Neither deserting nor fleeing, but rather, striking out strongly against the infidels.

The Year 306/918–919

117 Then God retaliated against His enemies and decreed victory to His friends:

118 At the beginning of the year newly commencing, truth filled the soul of the hero,

119 For the purpose of the glorious Imam; the best of those begotten and the best begetter was

120 To take up the defense of the One, the Victorious, and to vent some of his anger upon the infidels.

121 So he mustered soldiers and troops and called together with his trumpet, both lord and vassal;

122 He enrolled [the men] of the borders and frontiers and shunned pleasures and good cheer,

١٠٦ مُسْتَسْلِمًا للذُّلِّ والصَّغارِ　　ومُلْقِيًا يَدَيْهِ للإسارِ

١٠٧ فنَزَعَ الحَاجِبُ تاجَ مُلْكِهِ　　وقادَهُ مُكَتَّفًا لِهُلْكِهِ

١٠٨ وكان في آخرِ هذا العَامِ　　نَكْبُ أَبي العَبَّاسِ بالإسْلامِ

١٠٩ غَزا وكان أَنْجَدَ الأَنْجَادِ　　وقائدًا من أفحلِ القَوّادِ

١١٠ فسارَ في غَيْرِ رِجالِ الحَرْبِ　　الضّارِبينَ عند وَقْتِ الضَّرْبِ

١١١ مُحارِبًا في غَيْرِ ما مُحارِبِ　　والحَشَمُ الجُمْهورُ عند الحاجِبِ

١١٢ واجْتَمَعَتْ إليهِ أَخْلاطُ الكُوَرْ　　وغابَ ذو التَّحْصِيلِ عنه والنَّظَرْ

١١٣ حتى إذا أَوْغَلَ في العَدُوِّ　　فكان بين البُعْدِ والدُّنُوِّ

١١٤ أَسْلَمَه أهلُ القُلوبِ القَاسِيَهْ　　وأَفْرَدوه لِلكِلابِ العَاوِيَهْ

١١٥ فاسْتُشْهِدَ القائدُ في أَبْرارِ　　قد وَهَبوا نُفوسَهم لِلْبَارِي

١١٦ في غَيْرِ تَأْخِيرِ ولا فِرارِ　　إلّا شديدَ الضَّرْبِ للكُفّارِ

سنة ست وثلثمائة

١١٧ ثُمَّ أَقادَ اللّٰهُ مِن أَعْدائِهِ　　وأَحْكَمَ النصْرَ لِأَوْلِيائِهِ

١١٨ في مَبْدَأ العامِ الذى مِن قابِلِ　　أَزْهَقَ فيه الحَقُّ نَفْسَ الباطِلِ

١١٩ فكان مِن رأيِ الإمامِ الماجِدِ　　وخَيْرِ مَوْلودٍ وخَيْرِ وَالِدِ

١٢٠ أَن احْتَمَى بالواحِدِ القَهّارِ　　وفاضَ مِن غَيْظٍ على الكُفّارِ

١٢١ فجَمَّعَ الأَجْنادَ والحُشودَا　　ونَفَّرَ السَّيِّدَ والمَسُودَا

١٢٢ وحَشَرَ الأَطْرافَ والثُّغورَا　　ورَفَضَ اللَّذاتِ والحُبورَا

123 Until, when the troops were complete and recruiters and recruits had been mustered,
124 He appointed Badr to command the group, for he was held in great awe.
125 So he set forth accompanied by troops like the torrent and an army like the blackness of night,
126 Until, when he descended upon Motunia in which the worst of creatures was [lurking],
127 He waged against them an open war that gave off sparks such that fire could be kindled from it,
128 And fighting was intense among them while the foot soldiers surrounded them on all sides.
129 So they waged war all day long, then spent the night with the archers banishing their sleep,
130 So that during the long passage of the night, they were like those fatigued whose wounds fester on their limbs.
131 Then they continued warring against them for a few days until death revealed itself to them suddenly and violently.
132 When they saw the clouds of Fate raining the thunderbolts of misfortune down upon them,
133 The non-Arabs hurriedly made a break for their foreign land and reassembled under every star;
134 So the non-Arab came to their rescue on Thursday in the greatest haste:
135 In front of him went the foot soldiers and knights, and around him the crosses and bells,
136 For he was hoping to dislodge the army from the side of the fortress that had been destroyed,
137 So Badr impeded him with his own men, observing him attentively on his march toward him.
138 Until the right wing of one army met up with the left wing of the other and breaths got stuck in the windpipe.
139 Therefore God's partisans were victorious over the two infidels and the familiars of Satan were put to flight.
140 Thus they were massacred swiftly and dispersed, while the infidel retreated with blame and disgrace,
141 Whereas [our] people set out for Alcolea and met the enemy on Friday morning.

---

126. For Motunia, cf. *Bayān*, p. 286.

١٢٣ حتى إذا ما وَفت الجُنودُ ... وٱجْتَمَعَ الحُشَّادُ والحُشُودُ

١٢٤ قَوَّدَ بَدْرًا أَمْرَ تلك الطائفَهْ ... وكانَتْ النفسُ عليه خائفَهْ

١٢٥ فسَارَ في كَتائبٍ كالسَّيْلِ ... وعَسْكَرٍ مِثْلِ سَوَادِ اللَّيْلِ

١٢٦ حتى إذا حَلَّ على مُطِنيَّهْ ... وكان فيها أَخْبَثُ البَرِيَّهْ

١٢٧ ناصَبَهم حَرْبًا لها شَرَارُ ... كأنما أُضْرِمَ فيها النارُ

١٢٨ وجَدَّ مِن بينهمْ القِتالُ ... وأَحْدقت حولَهم الرِّجالُ

١٢٩ فحاربُوا يومَهمُ وباتُوا ... وقد نَفت نومَهم الرُّماةُ

١٣٠ فهم طَوالَ اللَّيْلِ كالطلائحِ ... جِراحُهم تَنْغل في الجوارحِ

١٣١ ثم مَضَوْا في حَرْبِهم أَيَّامَا ... حتى بدا المَوْتُ لهم زُؤَامَا

١٣٢ لما رأَوْا سَحَائِبَ المَنِيَّهْ ... تُمْطِرُهم صَواعِقَ البَلِيَّهْ

١٣٣ تَغَلْغل العُجْمُ بأَرْضِ العُجْمِ ... وٱنْحَشَدوا مِن تحت كلِّ نَجْمِ

١٣٤ فأَقْبَلَ العِلْجُ لهم مُغِينَا ... يومَ الخَمِيسِ مُسْرِعًا حَنِينَا

١٣٥ بين يَدَيْهِ الرَّجْلُ والفَوارِسُ ... وحوله الصُّلْبانُ والنَّواقسُ

١٣٦ وكان يَرْجُوأنْ يُزيلَ العَسْكَرَا ... عن جانبِ الحِصْنِ الذى قد دُمِّرَا

١٣٧ فٱعتاقَه بَدْرٌ بمَن لَدَيْهِ ... مُسْتَبْصِرًا في زَحْفِهِ إليْهِ

١٣٨ حتى ٱلْتَقَتْ مَيْمَنَةٌ بِمَيْسَرَهْ ... وٱعْتَنَقَتْ الأَرْواحُ عند الحَنْجَرَهْ

١٣٩ ففازَ حِزْبُ اللّٰهِ بالعِلْجَانِ ... وٱنهزَمَتْ بِطانَةُ الشَّيْطانِ

١٤٠ فقُتِّلوا قَتْلاً ذَريعًا فاشيَا ... وأَدْبَرَ العِلْجُ ذَميمًا خازيا

١٤١ وٱنصَرَفَ الناسُ إلى القُلَيْعَهْ ... فصَبَّحُوا العَدوَّ يَوْمَ الجُمْعَهْ

142 Then the two infidels met together on the road: the Pamplonan and the Galician

143 And agreed to plunder the [Muslim] army, [or else] to die before that assembly.

144 They swore by enchantment and the devil that they would not be put to flight before death's encounter.

145 So they advanced with the greatest body of unbelievers who had covered the hills in general with horsemen,

146 Until [our] people drew near on Saturday, and O, what a moment it was!

147 For spears were aimed among them and cries of "God is very great!" and shouts rose high,

148 Swords forsook their sheaths, and deaths opened wide their mouths;

149 Foot soldiers met with foot soldiers and plunged into the thick of the fray

150 In a place such that glances swerved away from it and in its length lives became too short,

151 And those gifted with patient forbearance and farseeing prudence acted with brisk energy, for they rushed upon the non-believing enemy,

152 Until there took place the routing of the Basques as though it were a stain of *wars*,

153 For the eagles and hounds arose and they cried out, calling upon the captain of the Galicians:

154 The eagles of a death that snatches away souls and satiates swords and spears.

155 Thus was the pig put to flight at that time while his shame was revealed in that place;

156 Moreover, they were massacred in every river bottom and [their] heads were carried [aloft] on poles,

157 And the commander sent forward a thousand heads of the Galicians schooled in hardship.

158 In this way God's favor toward Islam was accomplished while the joy of that year embraced us all,

159 Although the greatest joy that occurred in its course was the death in it of Ibn Ḥafṣūn, the pig!

160 Thus one conquest was added to a second and one victory to another granted by the aid of God,

---

152. *Wars* is the *Memecylon tinctorium*, a plant of Yemen used as a reddish-yellow dye.

١٤٢ ثم ٱلْتَقَى العِلْجانِ في الطَّريقِ البَنْبَلُونيُّ مع الجِلِّيقِي

١٤٣ فأَعْقَدا على ٱنْتِهابِ العَسْكَرِ وأَنْ يَمُوتا قبل ذاك المَحْضَرِ

١٤٤ وأَقْسَما بالجِبْتِ والطّاغُوتِ لا يُهْزَما دون لِقاءِ المَوْتِ

١٤٥ فأَقْبَلوا بأَعْظَمِ الطُّغْيانِ قد جَلَّلوا الجِبالَ بالفُرْسانِ

١٤٦ حتى تَداعَى الناسُ يومَ السبتِ فكانَ وَقْتًا يالَهُ مِن وَقْتِ

١٤٧ فأُشْرِعَتْ بَينهمُ الرماحُ وقد عَلا التَّكْبِيرُ والصِّياحُ

١٤٨ وفارَقَتْ أَغْمادَها السُّيُوفُ وفَغَرَتْ أَفْواهَها الحُتوفُ

١٤٩ وٱلْتَقَتْ الرِّجالُ بالرِّجالِ وٱنْغَمَسُوا في غَمْرةِ القِتالِ

١٥٠ في مَوْقِفٍ زاغَتْ بهِ الأَبْصارُ وقَصُرَتْ في طُولِهِ الأَعْمارُ

١٥١ وهَبَّ أَهْلُ الصَّبْرِ والبَصائرِ فأَوْعَقُوا على العَدُوِّ الكافِرِ

١٥٢ حتى بَدَتْ هَزيمةُ البَشْكُنْسِ كأَنَّهُ مُخْتَضِبٌ بالوَرْسِ

١٥٣ فٱنْقَضَّتِ العِقْبانُ والسَّلالِقَهْ زَعْقًا على مُقَدَّمِ الجَلالِقَهْ

١٥٤ عِقْبانُ مَوْتٍ تَخْطِفُ الأَرْواحا وتُشْبِعُ السيوفَ والرِّماحا

١٥٥ فٱنْهزَمَ الخِنْزيرُ عند ذاكا وٱنْكَشَفَتْ عَورتُهُ هُناكَ

١٥٦ فقُتِّلوا في بَطْنِ كلِّ وادِي وجاءتْ الرُّءوسُ في الأَعْوادِ

١٥٧ وقَدَّمَ القائدُ أَلْفَ راسِ مِن الجَلالِيقَ ذَوِي العماسِ

١٥٨ فتَمَّ صُنْعُ اللّٰهِ للإسلامِ وعَمَّنا سُرورُ ذاك العامِ

١٥٩ وخَيْرُ ما فيه من السُّرورِ مَوْتُ ٱبنِ حَفْصُونٍ بهِ الخِنْزيرِ

١٦٠ فٱتَّصَلَ الفَتْحُ بفَتْحٍ ثانِي والنصرُ بالنَّصرِ مِن الرحمنِ

161 Hence this campaign is called "The Decisive" because after it a great calamity was to befall [the enemy].

The Year 307/919–920

162 For after it, the campaign against Albelda took place, carrying off the apostates [to their death].

163 Its beginning occurred when the Imam, the elect of God, the most trustworthy of earth's inhabitants in matters of justice and in keeping promises,

164 Received news of the way in which the pig had died, and that he had gone to hellfire,

165 [Ibn Ḥafṣūn's] sons wrote to [the Caliph] proffering their submission and [announcing] their entry into the [Islamic] community,

166 And [requesting] that he acknowledge their right to govern in exchange for their payment of the land tax and tribute.

167 Therefore the gracious Imam chose [to comply with] that for his thoughts were constantly occupied with the granting of favors.

168 Then Satan turned Jaᶜfar's head and because of this his nose became swollen with pride,

169 So that he broke the treaties and alliances and adopted discord and apostasy,

170 Embracing pact-breakers and lawbreakers of the sort who are neither reliable nor do they keep their word.

171 But the Caliph supported [by God] impeded him, for he is the man by whom one is reduced to destitution or rendered fortunate;

172 The man over whom there are guardians watching out for any misfortune; guardians who are the [many] eyes of God.

173 So he mustered troops and companies, appointing commanders and squadrons of cavalry,

174 After which he went into campaign with the greater part of [their] number, seeking to remain in the pale of [God's] victory and support,

175 Until, when he reached the fortress of Albelda, he left a commander behind as his representative, along with a number [of men],

176 Forbidding them from dispersing their cavalry and [ordering them] to stand guard day and night.

177 Then he went forth, seeking to descend upon the [other] fortresses, and sending out lookouts and scouts.

١٦١ وهذه الغَزاةُ تُدْعَى القاضِيَهْ   وقد أَتَتْهم بعد ذاك الدّاهِيَهْ

سنة سبع وثلثمائة

١٦٢ وبعدها كانت غزاةُ بَلْدَهْ   وهي التى أَوْدَتْ بأَهْلِ الرِّدَّهْ

١٦٣ وبَدْؤُها أنّ الإمامَ المُصْطَفَى   أَصْدَقَ أهلِ الأَرْضِ عَدْلاً ووَفَا

١٦٤ لَمَّا أَتَتْهُ مِيتَةُ الخِنْزِيرِ   وأَنَّه صار إلى السَّعيرِ

١٦٥ كاتَبَه أَوْلادُه بالطَّاعَهْ   وبالدُّخولِ مَدْخلِ الجَماعَهْ

١٦٦ وأَنْ يُقِرَّهم على الوِلايَهْ   على درورِ الخَرْجِ والجِبايَهْ

١٦٧ فاْختارَ ذلك الإمامُ المُفْضِلُ   ولم يَزَلْ مِن رأيِه التَّفَضُّلُ

١٦٨ ثم لَوى الشيطانُ رأسَ جَعْفَرِ   وصارَ منه نافِخًا في المُنْخُرِ

١٦٩ فنَقَضَ العُهودَ والمِيثاقَا   واْستَعْمَلَ التَّشْغيبَ والنِّفاقَا

١٧٠ وضَمَّ أهلَ النُّكْثِ والخِلافِ   مِن غَيْرُ ما كافٍ وغَيْرُ وافِى

١٧١ فاعتاقَه الخَليفةُ المُؤَيَّدُ   وهو الذى يُشْقَى به ويُسْعَدُ

١٧٢ مَن عليه مِن عُيونِ اللّهِ   حَوافِظٌ مِن كُلِّ أمرٍ داهِى

١٧٣ فجَنَّدَ الجُنودَ والكَتائبَا   وقَوَّدَ القُوَّادَ والمَقانِبَا

١٧٤ ثم غَزا في أكثرِ العَديدِ   مُسْتَصحَبًا بالنَّصْرِ والتَّأْييدِ

١٧٥ حتى إذا مَرَّ بحِصْنِ بَلْدَهْ   خَلَّفَ فيه قائدًا في عِدَّهْ

١٧٦ يَمنعهم مِن اْنتِشارِ خَيْلِهِمْ   وحارِسًا في يَومِهم ولَيْلِهِمْ

١٧٧ ثم مَضَى يَسْتَنْزِلُ الحُصونَا   ويَبعث الطُّلَّاعَ والعُيونَا

178 Until [a messenger] bringing good news from Albelda reached him, running with the head of its chief atop a straight lance;

179 Therefore he led the horsemen swiftly toward it, alighting in it that very day by hastening toward it.

180 Then he surrounded it with horsemen, skilled archers, and all the defenders and brave warriors,

181 While the foot soldiers rushed upon its breaches and the troops thronged blindly upon its gates.

182 Thus it surrendered, though it had never surrendered before, and so an infidel [community] was delivered up to a believing one,

183 While its infidels were led before the sword and massacred for their just deserts—not out of injustice.

184 It all came about because of the good fortune of the Imam al-Murtaḍā, "the satisfied [with God's decree]," the best of those remaining, the best of those who have passed away.

185 Then, in his wrath he made for Bobastro and left not a single green stalk in it,

186 Breaking down plants and standing corn, and tearing up crops and fields.

187 So when the dog witnessed what was clearly evident of [the Caliph's] firm resolve to countervene his intention,

188 He humbly submitted to him and requested that he might be spared, with his permission,

189 And that he might be [recognized] governor under his suzerainty, in exchange for his payment of the land tax out of the tribute [he collected].

190 Hence the Imam bound him by taking hostages, so that he would not become blind to his condition,

191 And the Imam accepted his [terms] out of his own graciousness and inclination to do good, and departed from him.

The Year 308/920–921

192 Then the Imam campaigned against the land of the infidel and what a momentous affair that was!

193 To this end the chiefs of the provinces were mustered around him as well as those who enjoyed honor and rank among men,

---

184. al-Murtaḍā was the Caliph's official seal-name (*Bayān*, p. 260).

١٧٨ حتى أتاه باشرٌ مِن بَلْدَةْ — يَغْدُو بِرَأْسِ رأسِها في صَعْدَةْ

١٧٩ فقَدَّمَ الخَيْلَ إليها مُسْرِعَا — وآحْتَلَّها مِن يومِهِ تَسَرُّعَا

١٨٠ فحَفَّها بالخَيْلِ والرُّماةِ — وجُمْلَةِ الحُماةِ والكُماةِ

١٨١ فأطَّلَعَ الرَّجْلُ على أنْقابِها — وآقْتَحَمَ الجُنْدُ على أبْوابِها

١٨٢ فأذْعَنَتْ ولم تَكُنْ بِمُذْعِنَهْ — وآسْتَسْلَمَتْ كافِرَةٌ لِمُؤْمِنَهْ

١٨٣ فقُدِّمَتْ كُفّارُها لِلسَّيْفِ — وقُتِّلوا بالحَقِّ لا بالحَيْفِ

١٨٤ وذاك مِن يُمْنِ الإمامِ المُرْتَضَى — وخَيْرِ مَن بَقِيَ وخَيرِ مَن مَضَى

١٨٥ ثم آنْتَحَى مِن فَوْرِهِ بُبَشْتَرَا — فلم يَدَعْ بها قَضيبًا أخْضَرَا

١٨٦ وحَطَّمَ النَّباتَ والزُّروعَا — وهَتَّكَ الرِّباعَ والرُّبوعَا

١٨٧ فإذْ رأى الكَلْبُ الذي رآهُ — مِن عَزْمِهِ في قَطْعِ مُنْتَواهُ

١٨٨ ألْقَى إليهِ باليَدَيْنِ ضارِعَا — وسَأَلَ أنْ يُبْقَى عليه وادِعَا

١٨٩ وأنْ يكونَ عامِلاً في طاعَتِهْ — على دُرورِ الخَرْجِ مِن جِبايَتِهْ

١٩٠ فوَثَّقَ الإمامُ مِن رِهانِهِ — كَيْلَا يكونَ في عَمًى مِن شانِهِ

١٩١ وقَبِلَ الإمامُ ذاك مِنهُ — فَضْلاً وإحْسانًا وسارَ عنهُ

سنة ثمان وثلثمائة

١٩٢ ثم غزا الإمامُ دارَ الحَرْبِ — فكان خَطْبًا يا لَهُ مِن خَطْبِ

١٩٣ فحُشِّدَتْ إليه أعْلامُ الكُوَرْ — ومَن له في النّاسِ ذِكْرٌ وخَطَرْ

---

192. Cf. *ibid*, p. 291, for this campaign.

194 Including ministers, generals, all those who were connected to marks of distinction,

195 Everyone who sincerely obeyed [the law of] the Clement both in secret and in public,

196 And everyone determined to wage a Holy War or whom a saddle could hold on a generous steed.

197 So what a troop it was!—One made up of every freeborn man among us as well as every slave.

198 Thus you would have thought that the people were "locusts scattered abroad" as our Lord says of those who will be assembled [at Doomsday].

199 Then the one rendered victorious, aided [by God], upon whose forehead lies [the imprint of] the Message and the Light, set forth,

200 While before him went troops of angels seizing or sparing for their Lord's sake,

201 Until, when he went in among the enemy, the Clement made him avoid all harm,

202 While he was able to impose the poll tax and dire misfortunes upon those who had associated partners to God.

203 Thus their feet quaked in terror and they were scared away out of fear for the blaze of war,

204 Rushing blindly through mountain passes and into places of concealment, surrendering fortresses and towns,

205 So that no church or monastery belonging to any Christian monk remained in any of the provincial districts

206 But that he made it go up in smoke like a fire that has come in contact with [dry] stubble,

207 While the cavalry of the Sultan knocked down all the buildings in them.

208 One of the first fortresses they knocked down and [one of the first] enemies within it whom they attacked, was

209 A town known as Osma which they left behind like a blackened piece of charcoal.

210 Then they ascended from there to certain towns which they left behind like a yesterday that has elapsed.

---

198. Cf. Koran 54:7, "They will come forth, their eyes humbled, from their graves, [torpid] like locusts scattered abroad."

١٩٤ إلى ذَوى الدِّيوَانِ والرَّاياتِ وكُلِّ مَنسوبٍ إلى الشَّاماتِ

١٩٥ وكُلِّ مَن أَخْلَصَ لِلرّحمن بطاعةٍ في السِّرِّ والإعْلانِ

١٩٦ وكُلِّ مَن طاوع في الجِهادِ أو ضَمَّه سَرْجٌ على الجِياد

١٩٧ فكان حَشْداً يا لَهُ من حَشْدِ من كُلِّ حُرٍّ عندنا وعَبْدِ

١٩٨ فتَحْسِبُ الناسَ جَرَاداً مُنْتَشِرْ كما يقولُ رَبُّنا فيمَنْ حُشِرْ

١٩٩ ثم مَضَى المُظَفَّرُ المَنْصورُ على جَبِينِه الهُدى والنُّورُ

٢٠٠ أمامَه جُنْدٌ مِن المَلائِكَهْ آخِذَةٌ لِربِّها وتارِكَهْ

٢٠١ حتى إذا فَوَّزَ في العَدُوِّ جَنَّبَه الرحمنُ كُلَّ سُوِّ

٢٠٢ وأَنْزَلَ الجزيةَ والدَّواهي على الذين أَشْرَكوا باللهِ

٢٠٣ فزُلْزِلَتْ أَقْدَامُهم بالرُّعْبِ واسْتُنْفِروا مِن خَوْفِ نارِ الحَرْبِ

٢٠٤ واقْتَحَمُوا الشِّعابَ والمَكامِنَا وأَسْلَمُوا الحُصونَ والمَدائنَا

٢٠٥ فما بَقِيَ مِن جَنَباتِ دُورِ مِن بِيعةٍ لِراهِبٍ أو دَيْرِ

٢٠٦ إلّا وقد صَيَّرَها هَباءَ كالنّارِ إذْ وافَقَتِ الأَباءَ

٢٠٧ وزَعزعت كَتائِبُ السلْطانِ لِكُلِّ ما فيها من البُنْيانِ

٢٠٨ فكان مِن أَوَّلِ حِصْنٍ زَعْزَعُوا ومَن به مِن العَدُوِّ أَوْقَعُوا

٢٠٩ مَدينةٌ مَعْروفةٌ بِوَخْشَمَهْ فغادَرُوها فَحْمَةً مُسَخَّمَهْ

٢١٠ ثم ارْتَقوا منها إلى حَواضِرِ فغادروها مِثْلَ أَمْسِ الدابِرِ

---

209. For Wakhshama-Osma, see *Bayān*, p. 293, v. 2; E. Lévi-Provençal and E. García Gómez, *Una crónica anónima* (Madrid, 1950), pp. 63–134 (cited as *Crónica anónima*).

211 Then they moved forward with the infidel following them with his army, fearing and imitating their [movements],
212 Until they came directly to the river Daiy where orthodoxy effaced the paths of error,
213 When they met in Majmaᶜ al-Jauzain where the squadrons of the two unbelievers had been collected
214 From the people of León and Pamplona, and those of Arnedo and Barcelona.
215 The infidels were helping one another in spite of their unbelief, having gathered together from various lands;
216 For they were milling around at the foot of a lofty mountain, forming their ranks for battle
217 So [our] vanguard, raised high on their raiding horses, ran up to them,
218 And its swell was followed by another swell stretching out like an ocean of vast expanse.
219 In this way the two infidels were put to flight in the company of [their] infidels, having donned a robe of dust.
220 Each of the two looks back at times, yet in every face he sees his death,
221 Fine white [swords] and tawny [lances] are on their track, while killing and capturing penetrate deeply into their [ranks].
222 There is no fleeing for them, and heads were carried [aloft] on spears,
223 Because the Emir gave orders for putting to rout and [our] army was swift to rush against [the enemy].
224 It came upon their multitude when they had been put to flight, and watched as their commanders were destroyed.
225 For when they wished to enter their fortress, they entered one of death's enclosures.
226 O, what an enclosure, O!—In it their souls paid up the debt to death which had fallen due.
227 When they saw the waves [of our army] before them, they entrenched themselves in a stronghold that became a tether for them;
228 A rock that became a dire misfortune for them, since they turned from it to hellfire;

---

212. The river Daiy is the Duero (*Bayān*, p. 293).

213. An unidentified location. The "two unbelievers" were Ordoño of León and Sancho of Navarre.

٢١١ ثم مَضَوْا والعِلْجُ يَحْتَذِيهِمْ   بِجَيْشِهِ يَخشى ويَقْتَفِيهِمْ
٢١٢ حتى أتوا تَوًّا لِوادِي دَىّ   ففيه عَفّى الرُّشْدُ سُبُلَ الغَىّ
٢١٣ لما ٱلْتَقَوْا بِمَجْمَعِ الجَوْزَيْنِ   وٱجْتَمَعَتْ كتائبُ العِلْجَيْنِ
٢١٤ مِن أَهْلِ أَلْيُون وبَنْبَلُونَهْ   وأَهْلِ أَرْنِيط وبَرْشِلُونَهْ
٢١٥ تضافر الكُفْرُ مع الإلحادِ   وٱجْتَمَعُوا مِن سائرِ البلادِ
٢١٦ فٱضْطَرَبُوا في سَفْحِ طَوْدٍ عالِي   وصَففوا تعبيةَ القِتالِ
٢١٧ فبادَرَتْ إليهمُ المُقَدِّمَهْ   سامِيةً في خَيلِها المُسَوَّمَهْ
٢١٨ ورِدْءُها مُتَّصِلٌ بِرِدِّ   يُمده بحرٌ عَظيمُ المَدِّ
٢١٩ فٱنْهَزَمَ العِلجانِ في عِلاجِ   ولَبسوا ثَوْبًا من العَجاجِ
٢٢٠ كِلاهما يَنْظُرُ حينًا خَلْفَهُ   فَهْوَ يَرى في كُلِّ وَجْهٍ حَتْفَهُ
٢٢١ والبِيضُ في إثْرِهِمْ والسُّمْرُ   والقَتْلُ ماضٍ فيهمُ والأَسْرُ
٢٢٢ فلم يكن للناسِ مِنْ بَراحِ   وجاءَتْ الرُّءوسُ في الرِّماحِ
٢٢٣ فأَمَرَ الأَميرُ بالتَّقْويضِ   وأَسْرَعَ العَسْكَرُ في النُّهوضِ
٢٢٤ فصادَفوا الجُمْهورَ لما هُزِمُوا   وعايَنُوا قُوّادَهم تُخُرِّمُوا
٢٢٥ فدَخَلوا حَديقَةً للمَوْتِ   إذْ طَمِعوا في حِصْنِها بالفَوْتِ
٢٢٦ فَيا لَها حديقةً وَيا لَها   وافَتْ بها نُفُوسُهم آجالَها
٢٢٧ تَحَصَّنوا إذ عاينوا الأَهْوالا   لِمَعْقِلٍ كان لَهُم عِقالا
٢٢٨ وصَخْرة كانَتْ عليهم صَيْلَمَا   وٱنقلبوا منها إلى جَهَنَّمَا

229 They fell one by one asking for water, yet their souls were taken from them while they were still athirst.

230 Therefore, how many a man was present at the feast of the crows and vultures, who had fallen prey to God's sword!

231 And how many priests who summon [their followers] to crosses and bells were killed by it!

232 Then the Emir departed, while all around him shouts of "There is no God but one God!" and "God is very great!" could be heard,

233 For he was determined to wage war on the land of the infidels, and [moved forward] preceded by squadrons of Arab cavalry.

234 Hence he trampled it underfoot as well as imposing on it ignominy, disgrace, bloodshed and a smashing destruction.

235 Moreover they burned down and destroyed fortresses, and afflicted their inhabitants,

236 So look right and left and all you will see is the fierce blaze of fire;

237 In the morning their habitations appeared devastated and all you could see was a spreading pall of smoke;

238 While in the midst of them all, the Imam, [God's] elect, was granted victory, for he had quenched [his thirst for vengeance] upon the enemy and could rejoice at the evil lot that had befallen them.

The Year 309/921–922

239 Afterward there occurred the campaign of Torrox toward which his army climbed without losing breath,

240 While the vipers and all the large black serpents were beseiged in its fortress.

241 Next he constructed fortifications rising opposite it, in which commanders took turns in steadily striving,

242 Until its demons were forcibly constrained to repent and their devils abandoned their brains,

243 For it surrendered to the lord of lords, the noblest of both the quick and the dead,

244 God's Caliph over His worshipers, the best of those ruling His land.

---

239. For the campaign of Torrox, see *ibid.*, p. 299; *Crónica anónima*, p. 136.

٢٢٩ تَساقَطوا يَسْتَطْعِمُونَ الماءَ   فأُخْرِجَتْ أَرْوَاحُهم ظِماءَ

٢٣٠ فكَمْ لِسَيفِ اللّهِ من جَزُورِ   فى مَأْدبِ الغِرْبانِ والنُسُورِ

٢٣١ وكَمْ به قَتْلَى مِن القَساوِسِ   تندب لِلصُّلْبانِ والنَّواقِسِ

٢٣٢ ثم تَنَى عِنانَه الأميرُ   وحَوْلَه التَّهْليلُ والتكْبيرُ

٢٣٣ مُصمّماً بِحَرْب دارِ الحَرْبِ   قُدّامَه كَتائبٌ مِن عُرْبِ

٢٣٤ فَداسَها وسامَها بالخَسْفِ   والهَتْكِ والسَّفْكِ لها والنَّسْفِ

٢٣٥ فحَرَّقوا ومَزَّقوا الحُصونَا   وأَثْخَنوا مِن أهلِها العُيونَا

٢٣٦ فٱنْظُر عن اليَمينِ واليَسارِ   فما تَرى إلاّ لَهيبَ النارِ

٢٣٧ وأَصبحَتْ دِيَارُهم بَلاقِعَا   فما تَرى إلاّ دُخاناً ساطِعَا

١٣٨ ونُصِرَ الإمامُ فيها المُصْطَفَى   وقد شَفَى مِن العَدُوّ وٱشْتَفَى

سنة تسع وثلثمائة

٢٣٩ وبعدها كانَتْ غَزاة طُرُّشْ   سَما إليها جَيْشُه لم يُنْهَشْ

٢٤٠ وأُحْدقَتْ بِحِصْنِها الأَفاعى   وكُلُّ صِلٍّ أَسْود شُجَاعِ

٢٤١ ثم بَنَى حِصْناً عليها راتِبَا   يَعتور القُوّادُ فيه دائبَا

٢٤٢ حتى أنابَتْ عَنْوَةً جِنانُها   وغابَ عن يافوخِها شَيْطانُها

٢٤٣ فأَذْعنَتْ لِسَيِّدِ الساداتِ   وأَكْرَمِ الأَحْياءِ والأَمْوَاتِ

٢٤٤ خَليفةِ اللّهِ على عِبادِه   وخيرِ مَنْ يَحْكم فى بِلادِه

245 The death of Badr ibn Aḥmad took place after the return of the divinely supported sovereign,

246 So the Imam appointed the best of chamberlains, the best befriended, and the best of friends:

247 Mūsā the most eminent of the Banū Judair, the true ally of all mercy and good.

The Year 310/922–923

248 Afterward came the tenth campaign during which Monteleón was captured by force.

249 The Imam campaigned in the company of powerful lords, directing his steps against pact-breakers and rebels.

250 He descended upon the fortress of Monteleón, cutting off the means of livelihood of its occupant, who had repudiated his treaty obligations.

251 He traveled toward him and built [fortifications] opposite him until he came before him in submission.

252 Then he turned away from him to Sidonia, and turned its rugged ground into a flat plain,

253 Driving its adults and children to the dome of the faith by force,

254 And leaving no [castle] hard of access or well fortified, but that he humbled them all,

255 After which he returned with the most auspicious of homecomings just as he had set out with the best of good graces.

The Year 311/923–924

256 After it came the campaign of the year eleven: How many a sleeper did it not arouse from his torpor!

257 The Imam made his way to campaign against Bobastro accompanied by an army—and what a great army!

258 He occupied the courtyard of Bobastro, overrunning Jete and other [forts] like it.

---

245. I.e., the royal chamberlain (*Bayān*, p. 301).

247. He was Mūsā ibn Aḥmad ibn Judair (*ibid.*).

248. According to other contemporary accounts it was Monterrubio that was captured in A.H. 310, not Monteleón (*Crónica anónima*, p. 139).

٢٤٥ وكانَ موتُ بَدْرٍ ابنِ أحمدِ   بعدَ قُفولِ المَلِكِ المُؤَيَّدِ

٢٤٦ وٱستحجب الإمامُ خيرَ حاجبِ   وخيرَ مَصحوبٍ وخَيرَ صاحبِ

٢٤٧ مُوسَى الأَغَرَّ مِن بَنِى جُدَيْرِ   عَقيدَ كُلِّ رَأْفَةٍ وخَيْرِ

سنة عشر وثلثمائة

٢٤٨ وبعدها غَزاةُ عَشْرِ غَزْوَهْ   بها ٱفتتاحُ مُنْتِلُون عَنْوَهْ

٢٤٩ غَزا الإمامُ فى ذَوِى السُّلطانِ   يَوْمَ أَهلَ النَّكْثِ والطُّغْيانِ

٢٥٠ فٱحْتَلَّ حِصْنَ مُنتِلُونِ قاطعًا   أَسبابَ مَن أَصبحَ فيه خالِعًا

٢٥١ سارَ إليه وبَنَى عليه   حتى أتاهُ مُلْقِيًا يَدَيْه

٢٥٢ ثم ٱنثنى عنه إلى شَذُونَهْ   فعاضَها سَهْلاً مِن الحُزونَهْ

٢٥٣ وساقَها بالأَهْلِ والوِلْدانِ   إلى لُزُومِ قُبَّةِ الإيمانِ

٢٥٤ ولم يَدَعْ صَعْبًا وَلا مَنيعًا   إلّا وقد أذلَّهم جَميعًا

٢٥٥ ثم ٱنثَنى بِأَطْيَبِ القُفولِ   كما مَضَى بِأَحْسَنِ الفُضولِ

سنة إحدى عشرة وثلثمائة

٢٥٦ وبعدها غَزاةُ إحْدَى عَشَرَهْ   كم نَبَّهَتْ مِن نائمٍ فى سَكْرَهْ

٢٥٧ غَزا الإمامُ يَنْتَحِي بُبَشْتَرا   في عَسْكرٍ أعظِمْ بذاك عَسْكَرا

٢٥٨ فٱحْتَلَّ مِن بُبَشْتَر ذَراها   وجالَ فى شاطٍ وفى سِواها

---

253. The Arabic source reads *lurūm*, perhaps identifiable as the Morón of the *Crónica anónima*, p. 142, but more probably a misprint for *luzūm*.

258. For Jete, see *Bayān*, pp. 304–305.

259 Moreover he laid waste the flourishing crops of Bobastro whereas Jete surrendered to the lord of the army,

260 So that he introduced military equipment and numerous soldiers into it, leaving not one single obstinate rebel therein.

261 Next he made his way to the fortresses of the non-Arabs which he crunched with his front teeth after having ground them with his back teeth,

262 [Fortresses] that rose on the seashore, on the lowlands and on steep, rugged terrain.

263 In this way he introduced obedience [to his rule] into an area that had never known obedience to the central power.

264 Then he attacked the [northern] frontier with the best of commanders, driving [the infidel] from it with the best of drivers.

265 By his means God subdued the polytheists and rescued the frontier from imminent destruction,

266 And he saved Tudela from the pit of perdition for its blood had been spilled like dew, going unavenged,

267 And he purified the frontier and its adjacent areas of the infidel sect and its followers,

268 After which he came back with victory and success, having turned wrongdoing into righteousness.

The Year 312/924–925

269 Afterward the campaign of the year twelve took place. How many misfortunes and warning examples occurred during its course!

270 The Imam campaigned with his squadrons around him, like the full moon surrounded by its stars;

271 He campaigned with the sword of victory in his right hand and the rising star of good fortune on his forehead,

272 While the officer in charge of the army and the government was the eminent Mūsā, the Emir's chamberlain.

273 He destroyed the fortresses of Todmir and made the wild animals descend from the rocky peaks.

274 So that the people unanimously agreed [to obey] him and the leaders of the rebellion acknowledged him as chief,

275 Until, when he had taken all their fortresses and inscribed the truth elegantly on their texts,

---

273. Todmir was a province in the east of al-Andalus corresponding to the present-day Murcia.

٢٥٩ فخَرَّبَ العُمْرانَ من بُبَشْتَرِ   وأذعنتْ شاطُ لِرَبِّ العَسْكَرِ

٢٦٠ فأدْخلَ العُدَّةَ والعَديدَا   فيها ولم يَتْرُكْ بها عَنيدَا

٢٦١ ثم آنتَحى بعدُ حُصونَ العُجْمِ   فداسَها بالقَضْمِ بعد الخَضْمِ

٢٦٢ ما كان في سَواحِلِ البُحورِ   منها وفى الغاباتِ والوُعورِ

٢٦٣ وأدخلَ الطاعةَ فى مكانِ   لم يَدْرِ قَطُّ طاعةَ السلطانِ

٢٦٤ ثم رَمَى الثَّغْرَ بِخَيْرِ قائدِ   وذادَهم عنه بِخَيْرِ ذائِدِ

٢٦٥ بهِ قَما اللّٰهُ ذَوى الإشراكِ   وأنقذ الثغرَ مِنَ الهلاكِ

٢٦٦ وآنتاشَ من مَهْواتها تُطيلَهْ   وقد جَرَتْ دِماؤُها مَطْلولَهْ

٢٦٧ وطَهَّرَ الثغرَ وما يَليهِ   مِن شِيعَةِ الكُفْرِ ومن ذَوِيهِ

٢٦٨ ثم آنثنى بالفَتحِ والنَّجاحِ   قد غَيَّرَ الفسادَ بالصلاحِ

سنة اثنتى عشرة وثلثمائة

٢٦٩ وبعدها غَزاةُ ثِنْتَى عَشَرَهْ   وكَم بها من حَسْرَةٍ وعِبْرَهْ

٢٧٠ غزا الإمامُ حَوْلَه كَتائِبُهْ   كالبَدْرِ مَحْفوفًا به كَوَاكِبُهْ

٢٧١ غَزا وسَيْفُ النَّصْرِ فى يَمينِهِ   وطالِعُ السَّعْدِ على جَبينِهِ

٢٧٢ وصاحبُ العَسْكَرِ والتَّدْبيرِ   مُوسَى الأَغَرُّ حاجِبُ الأَميرِ

٢٧٣ فدَمَّرَ الحُصونَ مِن تُدْميرِ   وآسْتَنْزَلَ الوَحْشَ مِنَ الصُّخورِ

٢٧٤ فآجْتَمَعَتْ عليه كُلُّ الأُمَّهْ   وبايَعَتْهُ أُمَراءُ الفِتْنَهْ

٢٧٥ حتى إذا أوعبَ مِن حُصونِها   وجَمَّلَ الحَقَّ على مُتونِها

276 There set forth, traveling in the shadow of the army, under the banner of the great lion,

277 The men of Todmir and their kinfolk, of every tie that could trace back its lineage to them.

278 Until, when he occupied Tudela, it was mourning over its blood that had gone unavenged,

279 Over the magnitude of what it had suffered at the hands of the enemy, and over the constant warring, evening and morning.

280 Therefore he became anxious to humiliate the land of the infidel and that supporting [troops] should occupy the mountain pass.

281 Next he consulted those of his friends and of the frontiersmen who were endowed with wisdom and intelligence,

282 But they all advised him not to invade [the enemy territory] through the mountain pass, nor to cross through the densely tangled mountain,

283 For he was accompanied by an army weakened by the loss of all the officers and [main] troops,

284 And they spread the rumor that fifty thousand of the infidel's men were stationed beyond the ravine.

285 Yet he declared: "I will most definitely enter [the pass], there being no road for me but the one leading to it,

286 And to my subduing the territory of Pamplona and the courtyard of that accursed city."

287 Yet no one but the chamberlain supported him in this decision.

288 Thus he asked God for assistance, set his troops in battle formation, and entered, following which a victory without equal ensued.

289 Once he had set out and was crossing the mountain passes, wearing the breastplate of war,

290 A certain infidel placed his squadrons of cavalry in battle formation to attack him, and they plunged over the ravines.

291 Therefore the Imam asked for the assistance of the Lord of mankind, after which he sought the help of generosity and courage.

292 Then he took refuge in both private oration and prayer, to bring victory down from heaven.

293 Next he put the commanders at the head of the [main] troops making auxiliaries follow one after another.

٢٧٦ مَضَى وسارَ في ظلالِ العَسْكرِ   تحت لِواءِ الأسدِ الغَضَنْفَرِ

٢٧٧ رِجالُ تُدْمِيرَ ومَن يَليهمُ   مِن كُلِّ صِنْفٍ يعتزى إليهمُ

٢٧٨ حتى إذا حَلَّ على تُطيلَهْ   بَكَتْ على دِمائِها المَطْلُولَهْ

٢٧٩ وعِظْمِ ما لاقتْ مِن العَدُوِّ   والحَرْبِ فى الرَّواحِ والغُدُوِّ

٢٨٠ فَهَمَّ أن يُديخَ دارَ الحَرْبِ   وأن تَكونَ رِدْأةً فى الدَّرْبِ

٢٨١ ثم آستشارَ ذا النُّهى والحِجْرِ   مِن صَحْبِه ومِن رِجالِ الثَّغْرِ

٢٨٢ فكُلُّهم أشارَ أن لا يُدْرِبَا   ولا يَجُوزَ الجَبَلَ المُوَشَّبا

٢٨٣ لأنَّه فى عسكرٍ قد آنخرمْ   بِنَدْبِ كلِّ العُرفاءِ والحَشَمْ

٢٨٤ وشَنَّعوا أنَّ وَراءَ الفَجِّ   خَمْسِينَ ألْفًا مِن رِجالِ العِلْجِ

١٨٥ فقالَ لا بُدَّ مِن الدُّخولِ   وما إلى حاشاهُ مِن سَبيلِ

٢٨٦ وأن أُديخَ أرضَ بَنْبَلُونَهْ   وساحةَ المَدينةِ المَلْعُونَهْ

٢٨٧ وكان رأيًا لم يكُن من صاحبِ   ساعَدَه عليه غيرُ الحاجِبِ

٢٨٨ فآستنصرَ اللهَ وعَبَّى ودَخَلْ   فكان فَتْحًا لم يكُن له مَثَلْ

٢٨٩ لمَّا مَضَى وجاوزَ الدُّروبَا   وآدَّرعَ الهَيْجاءَ والحُروبَا

٢٩٠ عَبَّى له عِلْجٌ مِن الأعْلاجِ   كَتائبًا غَطَّتْ على الفِجاجِ

٢٩١ فآستنصرَ الإمامُ رَبَّ الناسِ   ثم آستعانَ بالنَّدى والباسِ

٢٩٢ وعاذ بالرَّغْبةِ والدُّعاءِ   وآستنزلَ النصرَ مِن السَّماءِ

٢٩٣ فقدَّمَ القُوّادَ بالحُشودِ   وأتْبعَ المُدودَ بالمُدودِ

294 In this way the infidel was put to rout, while a slaughter took place in which the rearguard outdid the vanguard,

295 So that they were massacred in such a way as to be reduced to nought; moreover the white [swords] were abundantly watered with blood.

296 Then he turned toward Pamplona and the army rushed blindly upon the city

297 Until, when "they entered to search the very inmost parts of its homes" and ruin rushed into the flourishing state of its civilization,

298 Onlookers wept over what befell it, when hooves first began to pound on it,

299 For the loss of its men who were slaughtered and for the abasement of its children who were orphaned.

300 How many uncircumcised ones [lie dead] in and around it, over whom the eye of the bishop sheds [bitter] tears:

301 And how many churches in it have been held in contempt, while their bells have been replaced by the muezzin's call;

302 Both bell and cross weep over [Pamplona] for to each of them weeping is a [last remaining] duty!

303 Meanwhile the Imam departed with success, victory, divine support, and prosperity;

304 Then, while on his way back, he turned the banners in the direction of the Banū Dhī n-Nūn, because of his success,

305 So that after a period of prosperity, the latter entered one of hardship, while their cheeks were glued to the ground,

306 Until they appeared before him with hostages consisting of both the eldest of the parents and of the offspring.

307 Therefore let there be great praise to God for supporting him and giving him right guidance!

The Year 313/925–926

308 Then, in his good fortune, he campaigned against Osuna after having destroyed several fortresses around it,

309 Besieging it with cavalry and foot soldiers who fought against [the enemy] with the utmost tenacity,

---

297. Cf. Koran 17:5.
304. The Banū Dhī n-Nūn were lords of Toledo.

٢٩٤ فآنهزم العِلْجُ وكانت مَلْحَمَهْ   جاوزَ فيها الساقةُ المُقدِّمَهْ

٢٩٥ فقُتِّلوا مَقْتَلَةَ الفَنَاءِ   فآرْتَوَتْ البِيضُ مِن الدِّماءِ

٢٩٦ ثم أمال نحوَ بَنْبَلُونَهْ   وآقتحم العسكرُ فى المَدينَهْ

٢٩٧ حتى اذا جاسوا خلالَ دُورِها   وأسْرَعَ الخَرابُ فى مَعْمُورِها

٢٩٨ بَكَتْ على ما فاتَها النَواظِرُ   إذ جَعَلت تَدُقُّها الحَوافِرُ

٢٩٩ لِفَقْدِ مَن قُتِّلَ مِن رِجالِها   وذُلِّ مَن أيْتَمَ مِن أطْفالِها

٣٠٠ فكَم بها وحولها مِن أغْلَفِ   تَهمى عليه الدمعَ عَيْنُ الأُسْقُفِ

٣٠١ وكَم بها حُقِّرَ مِن كَنائِسِ   بَدَّلت الآذانَ بالنَّواقِسِ

٣٠٢ يَبْكِى لها الناقوسُ والصَّليبُ   كِلاهما فَرْضٌ له النَحيبُ

٣٠٣ وآنصرَفَ الإمامُ بالنَّجاحِ   والنصرِ والتأييدِ والفلاحِ

٣٠٤ ثم ثَنَى الراياتِ فى طريقِه   إلى بَنِى ذى النُونِ مِن تَوْفيقِه

٣٠٥ فأصْبَحُوا مِن بَسْطِهِم فى قَبْضِ   قد أُلْصِقَتْ خُدودُهم بالأرْضِ

٣٠٦ حتى بَدَوْا إليه بالرِّهانِ   مِن أكْبَرِ الأباءِ والوِلْدانِ

٣٠٧ فالحَمْدُ لِلّهِ على تأْييدِهِ   حَمْدًا كثيرًا وعلى تَسْديدِه

سنة ثلاث عشرة وثلثمائة

٣٠٨ ثم غَزا بيُمنِه أُشُونَا   وقد أشادُوا حولها حُصونَا

٣٠٩ وحَفَّها بآلخَيْلِ والرِجالِ   وقاتَلوهم أبْلَغَ القِتالِ

306. The Arabic sources read *bi-l-burhān* which should be corrected to *bi-r-rihān.*

310 Until, when they were faced with imminent destruction, they all finally hastened to offer their obedience,

311 Surrendering their inexpugnable fortress and humbly complying with the payment of their land tax.

312 Yet before them in that campaign rebel strongholds had already been demolished;

313 Furthermore, out of the excellence of his rule, the Imam meted out justice during his journey against the Banū Hābil,

314 And against others of their tribe as well as the leaders of the revolt that had caused discord,

315 When they were all detained and guarded carefully until they handed over all that they possessed

316 In the way of sons, families, and guards as well as all the servants lodged in their homes.

317 Thus they came down from all the districts and were lodged in the city of the Sultan.

318 Furthermore, at the end of that year, after the submission of the infidel to Islam,

319 Certain most exalted martyrdoms occurred under the leadership of the commander ᶜAbd al-Ḥamīd,

320 While he was campaigning against the Banū Dhī n-Nūn—moreover it was an unequaled victory—

321 When the latter exceeded all limits in their wickedness and injustice, by killing the Sultan's governor,

322 And once again incurred in wrongdoing until the most courageous of creatures campaigned against them.

323 Therefore he hindered them from achieving all they had hoped for, by destroying all they had built,

324 And seizing control of the great fortress of San Esteban with foot soldiers and knights.

325 Then the mighty lion set out toward them, advancing slowly with his army in order to snatch their souls violently away.

326 Thus they were routed in such a way that their flight could not be withstood, and surrendered their brother Muḥammad

---

313. For the campaign against the Banū Hābil, see *Bayān*, p. 225. They owned a castle in Jaén.

319. ᶜAbd al-Ḥamīd ibn Basīl (*ibid.*, p. 316).

٣١٠ حتى إذا ما عايَنُوا الهَلاكَا تبادروا بالطَّوْعِ حِينَئذَ اكَا

٣١١ وأَسلَمُوا حِصْنَهمُ المَنِيعَا وسَمحوا بِخَرْجِهِم خُضوعَا

٣١٢ وقَبْلَهم فى هذه الغَزاةِ قد هُدِّمت مَعاقِلُ العُصاةِ

٣١٣ وأَحكَمَ الإمامُ فى تَدبيرِهِ على بنى هابِلَ فى مَسيرِهِ

٣١٤ ومَن سِواهم من ذوى العَشيرَهْ وأُمَراءِ الفِتْنةِ المُغيرَهْ

٣١٥ إذ حُبِسوا مراقبًا عليهمُ حتى أَتوا بكُلِّ ما لديهمُ

٣١٦ من البَنِينَ والعِيالِ والحَشَمْ وكلّ مَن لاذ بهمْ مِن الخَدَمْ

٣١٧ فَهَبطُوا مِن أَجْمَع البُلْدَانِ وأُسْكِنُوا مَدينَةَ السلطانِ

٣١٨ فكانَ فى آخِرِ هذا العامِ بعد خُضوعِ الكُفْرِ للإِسْلَامِ

٣١٩ مَشاهِدٌ مِن أَعظمِ المَشاهِدِ على يَدَىْ عبدِ الحميدِ القائدِ

٣٢٠ لما غَزا إلى بنى ذى النُّونِ فكان فَتْحًا لم يَكُنْ بالدُّونِ

٣٢١ إذ جاوزوا في الظُّلْم والطُّغْيَانِ بِقَتْلِهم لِعامِلِ السُّلْطَانِ

٣٢٢ وحاوَلوا الدُّخولَ في الأَذِيَّةَ حتى غَزاهمْ أَنجدُ البَرِيَّةَ

٣٢٣ فعاقَهم عن كُلِّ ما رَجَوْهُ بِنَقْضِه كُلَّ الذى بَنَوْهُ

٣٢٤ وضَبْطِه الحِصْنَ العظيمَ الشانِ أَشْتِين بالرَّجْلِ وبالفُرْسَانِ

٣٢٥ ثم مَضَى اللَّيْثُ إليهم زَحْفًا يَخْتَطِفُ الأَرواحَ منْهم خَطْفَا

٣٢٦ فانهزموا هَزِيمةً لَنْ تُرْفَدَا وأَسْلموا صِنْوَهم مُحَمَّدَا

---

324. The original reads *shān ashtīn*, but the sense requires Shān Ashtaban (San Esteban), from *ibid.*, p. 313.

327 As well as others from among the most distinguished knights, banished to the funeral meeting of the crows;
328 His limbs were cut to pieces with swords, after he had been torn apart with short spears.
329 Only then did they become insistent upon claiming safe-conduct and being granted alliances in exchange for hostages,
330 So their hostages were taken, they were granted safe-conduct, they wagged their heads [to signify approval], and surrendered.
331 Then, enjoying support, victory, and right guidance, all granted by the Lord of the heavenly throne, the commander moved forward
332 Until he reached the fortress of the Banū ᶜImāra and war was waged with success and dispatch,
333 For he conquered the fortress, seized its lord, and granted safe-conduct to all around him.

The Year 314/926–927

334 During [the course of that year], [the Caliph] did not campaign, though his commanders did, and his troops came within reach of Bobastro.
335 Thus did they all afflict [the enemy] and give satisfaction and content, while easing their breasts and becoming contented.
336 Then the lion of the thicket, ᶜAbd al-Ḥamīd of the Banū Basīl, followed in their path.
337 It was he who stood in place of [that other] lion, bringing misfortune [upon the enemy] with his campaign;
338 [By bringing] the head of the Goliath of apostasy and envy, he in whom the qualities of the pig and the lion were conjoined.
339 For here you have him in the company of his comrades, all of whom are crucified at Bāb as-Sudda.
340 He is mounted on a certain beast which stands ever still and upright, without galloping away;
341 A beast such that if it should break down, it is the carpenter and not the farrier who will make it sound.
342 It is as though he, on top of it, were a skilled archer [riding along] with a nail driven into each of his eyes;

---

337. The "other lion" is the Caliph.
338. The poet refers to Sulaiman ibn ᶜUmar ibn Ḥafṣūn, whose head,

٣٢٧ وغيرُه مِن أَوْجُهِ الفُرسانِ   مُغَرَّبٍ في مَأْتَمِ الغِرْبانِ
٣٢٨ مُقَطَّعِ الأَوْصالِ بالسَّنابِكِ   مِن بعد ما مُزِق بالنَّيازِكِ
٣٢٩ ثم لجّوا إلى طِلابِ الأَمْنِ   وبَذْلِهم ودائعًا من رَهْنِ
٣٣٠ فقُبضت رِهانُهم وأُمِّنوا   وأَنْغَضوا رُءوسَهم وأَذْعنوا
٣٣١ ثم مَضَى القائدُ بالتأْييدِ   والنَّصْرِ مِن ذي العَرْشِ والتَّسديدِ
٣٣٢ حتى أتى حِصْنَ بَنِي عِمَارَهْ   والحَرْبُ بالتَّدْبيرِ والإدارَهْ
٣٣٣ فٱفتتح الحِصْنَ وخلّى صاحِبَهْ   وأَمَّنَ الناسَ جميعًا جانِبَهْ

سنة أربع عشرة وثلثمائة

٣٣٤ لم يَغْزُ فيها وغَزَتْ قُوّادُهُ   وٱعتورت بُبَشْتَرا أَجْنادُهُ
٣٣٥ فكُلُّهم أَبْلَى وأَغْنَى وٱكْتَفَى   وكُلُّهم شفَى الصُّدورَ وٱشْتَفَى
٣٣٦ ثم تلاهم بعدُ لَيْثُ الغِيلِ   عبدُ الحَميدِ من بني بَسيلِ
٣٣٧ هو الذي قامَ مقامَ الضَّيْغَمِ   وجاءَ في غَزاتِه بالصَّيْلَمِ
٣٣٨ برأسِ جَالُوتِ النِّفاقِ والحَسَدْ   مَن جُمِّعَ الخِنْزيرُ فيه والأَسَدْ
٣٣٩ فَهاكَهُ مع صَحْبِهِ في عِدَّةْ   مُصَلَّبِينَ عند بابِ السُّدَّةْ
٣٤٠ قد ٱمتطَى مَطِيَّةً لا تَبْرَحُ   صَائمَةً قائمَةً لا تَرْمَحُ
٣٤١ مَطيّةً إنْ يَعْرُها ٱنْكِسارُ   يُطِبُّها النَّجّارُ لا البَيْطارُ
٣٤٢ كأنَّه مِن فَوْقِها أُسْوارُ   عَيْناهُ في كِلْتَيْهِما مِسْمارُ

hands, and feet were cut off and sent to Córdoba along with his body, where they were all displayed at Bāb as-Sudda on a pole (*ibid.*, p. 317).

343 Gazing at the sun and the winds astride a swift steed which is not inclined to run away;

344 Speaking the words of a friend giving sincere advice to the passerby on the road:

345 "This is the place of the servant of Satan and of one who rebelled against the Caliph of the Compassionate";

346 For we have never beheld a preacher who does not talk, offer a truer warning by that which he does not say.

347 Therefore say to the man deceived by his evil thoughts who, when he does harm, is connected with the likes of [Sulaimān's] disease:

348 "How many apostates who have passed away, and how many religious hypocrites in the company of that wretch, who have enjoyed high rank,

349 Have then suffered a reversal of fortune, being crucified on a pole with their heads placed upon its trunk,

350 So how can the lawbreaker not take warning from the fate of one whom Caliphs have pursued?

351 Do you not see him raised up high in abjection, serving as a warning to whomsoever would see or hear?"

The Year 315/927–928

352 In it he campaigned against Bobastro, resolving to overrun and destroy its courtyard.

353 Then he built [the castle of] Taljīra on the way to it to obstruct the gullet [lying] between its two neck veins.

354 He put [Taljīra] in charge of Ibn Salīm, one fighting hard, tucking up [his garment] from his shank to wage war,

355 Until Ḥafṣ perceived the path leading to his own right guidance, after having exerted himself to the limit,

356 So that he submitted to the Imam, repairing humbly to him and obediently surrendering the fortress.

---

347. The Arabic source reads *shāʾa* rather than *sāʾa*.

351. The Arabic source reads *yartaᶜu* though the variant *yurfaᶜu* is recorded.

٣٤٣ مُبَاشِرًا للشَّمْسِ والرِيَاحِ — على جَوَادٍ غيرِ ذى جِمَاحِ

٣٤٤ يقولُ للخاطرِ بالطَّرِيقِ — قَوْلَ مُحِبٍّ ناصحٍ شَفِيقِ

٣٤٥ هذا مَقامُ خادِمِ الشَّيْطانِ — ومَن عَصَى خَليفةَ الرحمنِ

٣٤٦ فما رأينا واعظًا لا يَنْطقُ — أَصْدَقَ منه فى الذى لا يَصْدقُ

٣٤٧ فقُلْ لِمَن غُرَّ بسُوءِ رائِه — يَمُتُّ إذا ساءَ بمثل دائِه

٣٤٨ كَم مارقٍ مَضَى وكَم مُنافِقِ — قد ٱرْتَقَى فى مِثْلِ ذاك الحالِقِ

٣٤٩ وعادَ وَهْوَ فى العَصَا مُصَلَّبُ — ورأسُه فى جِذْعِه مُرَكَّبُ

٣٥٠ فكيف لا يَعْتَبِرُ المُخَالِفُ — بِحالِ مَن تَطْلُبُه الخَلَائِفُ

٣٥١ أَمَا تَرَاهُ فى هَوَانٍ يُرْفَعُ — مُعْتَبَرًا لِمَنْ يَرَى ويَسْمَعُ

سنة خمس عشرة وثلثمائة

٣٥٢ فيها غَزا معتزما بُبَشْتَرَا — فجالَ فى ساحتِها ودَمَّرَا

٣٥٣ ثم بَنَى طَلْجِيرَةً إليها — وهي الشجَى مِن بين أخدعَيْها

٣٥٤ وٱمتدَّها بابنِ السَّلِيم راتبًا — مُشَمِّرًا عن ساقِهِ مُحارِبًا

٣٥٥ حتى رأى حَفْصٌ سَبِيلَ رُشْدِه — بعد بُلوغِ غايةٍ مِن جُهْدِه

٣٥٦ فدانَ لِلإمامِ قصدًا خاضِعًا — وأسلَمَ الحِصْنَ إليه طائِعًا

---

353. For the castle of Taljīra, see *Crónica anónima*, p. 147. Some texts read *ghazā taljīratan.*

355. Ḥafṣ was the son of ᶜUmar ibn Ḥafṣūn.

The Year 316/928–929

357 [That year] he did not compaign, but he went to Bobastro to repair and manage it in accordance with his views,
358 Filling it with power and glory, while also erasing the traces of the Banū Ḥafṣūn
359 By restoring it from the corrupt [state] in which it had lain because of them, and purifying [its] tombs by [removing] their bodies,
360 Until the hollow of every grave was empty of each profoundly disbelieving apostate.
361 [They were all] a party belonging to Satan's sect, hostile to God and the Sultan,
362 Therefore their bodies were violently destroyed whereas their souls roasted in hellfire,
363 While that year the Imam sent out the lionlike ᶜAbd al-Ḥamīd
364 Against Ibn Dāwud who had inexpugnably fortified himself between the two mountains of Sidonia,
365 Yet [ᶜAbd al-Ḥamīd] made him come down from [Sidonia] to the plain like a bird falling [to the ground],
366 After which he brought him to the Imam; to the man faithful to his agreements with Muslims and non-Muslims.

The Year 317/929–930

367 Then came the seventeenth year, during which he campaigned against Badajoz and its outlying regions,
368 Never ceasing to impose ignominy upon it or to carry to it the swords of death,
369 Until, when he had encompassed its two sides while besieging it, and constructed [fortifications from which to attack it],
370 He loosed Ibn Isḥāq against it; one fighting hard, assiduously striving and persevering in battle.
371 While he went off to the furthest castles of the Algarve, afflicting them with the heavy blow of war
372 Until he had accomplished everything [he planned to do] to them, and Ocsonoba and Beja had been conquered.

---

364. For the campaign against Ibn Dāwud see *ibid.*, p. 325.

372. The mysterious town of Ocsonaba has been recently identified with Santa María de Algarve in Portugal.

سنة ست عشرة وثلثمائة

٣٥٧ لم يَغْزُ فيها وانتحَى بُبَشْتَرَا — فرمَّها بما رَأى ودَبَّرَا

٣٥٨ واحتلّها بالعزّ والتَّمكينِ — ومَحْو آثارِ بَنِي حَفْصونِ

٣٥٩ وعاضَها الإصلاحَ مِن فسادِهِمْ — وطَهَّرَ القُبورَ مِن أجْسادِهِمْ

٣٦٠ حتى خلا مَلْحودُ كل قَبْرِ — من كل مُرتدٍّ عظيمِ الكُفْرِ

٣٦١ عِصابةٌ من شِيعَةِ الشَّيْطانِ — عَدُوَّةٌ لِلّهِ والسلطانِ

٣٦٢ فخُرِّمَتْ أجْسادُها تخرّما — وأُصْلِيَتْ أرْواحُهم جَهنَّمَا

٣٦٣ ووَجَّهَ الإمامُ فى ذا العَامِ — عبدَ الحميد وهو كالضِّرْغامِ

٣٦٤ إلى آبن داودَ الذى تقلّعا — في جَبَلَىْ شَذُونَة تمنّعا

٣٦٥ فحطّه منها الى البَسيطِ — كطائر آذنَ بالسُّقوطِ

٣٦٦ ثم أتى به إلى الإمامِ — إلى وَفِيِّ العهد والذِّمامِ

سنة سبع عشرة وثلثمائة

٣٦٧ وبعد سَبعَ عَشرةَ وفيها — غَزا بَطَلْيَوْسَ وما يَلِيها

٣٦٨ فلم يَزَلْ يَسومُها بالخَسْفِ — ويَنْتحيها بسُيوفِ الحَتْفِ

٣٦٩ حتى إذا ما ضَمَّ جانِبَيْهَا — مُحاصِرًا ثم بَنَى عَلَيْهَا

٣٧٠ خلّى آبْنَ إسحاقٍ عليها راتِبًا — مُنابِرًا فى حَرْبِه مُواظِبًا

٣٧١ ومَرَّ يَسْتَقْصِى حُصونَ الغَرْبِ — ويَبْتليها بوَبيلِ الحَرْبِ

٣٧٢ حتى قَضَى مِنهنَّ كلَّ حاجَهْ — وآفْتَتِحَتْ أُكْشُونُبَة وباجَهْ

373 Yet after the conquest of, and expedition to the furthest limits of the Algarve, as well as his stopping the disease of his enemies,

374 Badajoz persisted in its rebelliousness, being deceived by the obstinacy of its apostates

375 Until, when it had tasted death and sheathed both spears and swords,

376 Ibn Marwān called upon the Sultan, coming to him in search of alliance and safe-conduct,

377 Therefore he came to enjoy the Imam's gracious generosity and to dwell in the Dome of Islam.

The Year 318/930–931

378 In it he resolutely campaigned against Toledo while [its leaders] were fortified in a castle without equal.

379 Until he fortified [Mount] Chalencas next to it, an inexpugnable fortress [intended to] bear the brunt of the attack.

380 He strengthened it by appointing Ibn Salīm to be its commander and to fight and wage holy war against the people [of Toledo].

381 Moreover, he visited it throughout the length of that year, with ignominy, destruction, and the cutting off of its heads.

The Year 319/931–932

382 Then Durrī came as his second in command with an army the decisions of which were wont to be carried out.

383 Thus they besieged it during the nineteenth year with every mighty fellow endowed with great strength.

384 Then they brought foot soldiers forward against [the enemy] and fought them in the most devastating manner.

The Year 320/932–933

385 Until, when a few destruction-filled months of the twentieth year had elapsed,

---

376. The poet refers to ᶜAbd ar-Raḥman ibn Marwān al-Jilliqī (*Crónica anónima*, p. 154).

377. The "Dome of Islam" is Córdoba.

٣٧٣ وبعد فَتْحِ الغَرْبِ وٱسْتِقْصائِه   وحَسْمِهِ الأَدْواء مِن أَعدائِه

٣٧٤ لَجَّتْ بَطَلْيَوْس على نِفاقِهَا   وغَرَّها اللَّجاجُ مِن مُرَّاقِهَا

٣٧٥ حتى إذا شافهت الحُتوفَا   وشامت الرِّماحَ والسُّيوفَا

٣٧٦ دَعا ٱبنُ مَرْوان إلى السُّلطانِ   وجاءَهُ بالعَهْدِ والأَمانِ

٣٧٧ فصارَ فى تَوْسِعَةِ الإمامِ   وساكِنًا فى قُبَّةِ الإسْلامِ

سنة ثمانى عشرة وثلثمائة

٣٧٨ فيها غَزا بعَزْمِهِ طُلَيْطُلَهْ   وٱمتنعوا بمَعْقِلٍ لا مِثْلَ لَهْ

٣٧٩ حتى بَنَى جَرَنْكَشَه بِجَنْبِها   حِصْنًا مَنيعًا كافِلاً بِحَرْبِهَا

٣٨٠ وشَدَّها بٱبنِ سَلِيم قائدًا   مُجالِدًا لأَهْلِهَا مُجاهِدًا

٣٨١ فجاسَها فى طُولِ ذاك العامِ   بالخَسْفِ والنَّسْفِ وضَرْبِ الهامِ

سنة تسع عشرة وثلثمائة

٣٨٢ ثم أَتَى رِدْفًا له دُرِّىٌّ   فى عسكرٍ قَضَاؤُهُ مَقْضِىٌّ

٣٨٣ فحاصروها عامَ تسعَ عشْرَهْ   بكلِّ مَحْبُوك القُوَى ذى مِرَّهْ

٣٨٤ ثم أتاهم بعدُ بالرِّجالِ   فقاتلوهم أَبلغَ القِتالِ

سنة عشرين وثلثمائة

٣٨٥ حتى إذا ما سَلَفت شُهورُ   مِن عامِ عِشْرين لها نُبورُ

---

379. Chalencas is an unknown site (*Bayān*, p. 336).
382. Durrī ibn ᶜAbd ar-Raḥmān aṣ-Ṣiqlabī Abū ᶜUthmān (*ibid.*, p. 344).

386 [Toledo] obediently surrendered to the Imam, submitting to him under constraint and publicly recognizing his suzerainty.

387 Thus was it humbled, never having been so [before], for it had not been governed, having been independent,

388 And not recognizing the faith pertaining to its Lord for seventy-seven years.

389 Moreover, at the beginning of the twentieth year, the chamberlain Mūsā, the piercing warrior, died.

390 But the Imam set out with divine support, accompanied by his military apparatus and numerous contingents,

391 Making his way to the accursed city—may the Clement destroy it among all cities!—

392 The city of schism and sacrilege, the shelter of lawbreakers and apostates,

393 Until, when he was before it and the midday heat was fiercely blazing,

394 Its governor and the town elders came to him, surrendering to the Imam who enjoys divine trust,

395 So they encountered generosity on the part of the Imam and were lodged in [the home of] benevolence and honor.

396 Yet at noon, the Imam sent some horsemen, so that into [Toledo,] the peninsula [of the Tajo], there might enter,

397 Commanded by Durrī, a detachment of cavalry upon whose backs light coats of mail were shining.

398 So they rushed blindly both over its rugged and its smooth areas at [a time] when its inhabitants had grown heedless;

399 Yet [these same] people were unable to ward off or protect themselves from Durrī's horsemen,

400 Whereas the Imam wrought destruction at that moment for his heart was hardened by what there was therein,

401 Until, when he reached the town, since its people were submissive and weak,

402 He took it with horsemen and foot soldiers without [even] engaging in war or in battle.

403 One of the first things he saw to, spoke of, and to which he attended, was

404 The knocking down of its gateway and walls, this being the best way to handle the [situation].

٣٨٦ أَلْقَتْ يَدَيْها لِلإمامِ طائعَهْ   وٱستسلمَتْ قَسْرًا إليه باخِعَهْ

٣٨٧ فأَذعنَتْ وقبلَها لم تُذْعِن   ولم تَقُدْ من نَفْسِها وتُمْكِنِ

٣٨٨ ولم تَدِنْ لِرَبِّها بِدِينِ   سبعًا وسَبعينَ من السِّنينِ

٣٨٩ ومُبْتَدَى عشرين ماتَ الحاجِبْ   مُوسَى الذى كانَ الشِّهابَ الناقِبْ

٣٩٠ وبَرزَ الإمامُ بالتأْيِيدِ   فى عُدَّةٍ منه وفى عَديدِ

٣٩١ صَمْدًا إلى المدينةِ اللَّعِينَهْ   أَتْعَسَها الرحمنُ مِن مَدينَهْ

٣٩٢ مدينةُ الشِّقاقِ والنفاقِ   ومَوْئلُ الفُسَّاقِ والمُرَّاقِ

٣٩٣ حتى إذا ما كانَ منها بالأَمَمْ   وقد ذَكا حَرُّ الهَجيرِ وٱحتدَمْ

٣٩٤ أَتاهُ وَالِيها وأشياخُ البَلَدْ   مُسْتَسْلِمِينَ لِلإمامِ المُعْتَمَدْ

٣٩٥ فوافَقوا الرَّحْبَ من الإمامِ   وأُنْزِلوا فى البِرِّ والإكْرامِ

٣٩٦ ووَجَّهَ الإمامُ فى الظَّهِيرَهْ   خَيْلاً لِكَىْ تدخلَ فى الجَزِيرَهْ

٣٩٧ جريدةً قائدُها دُرِّىُّ   يَلمع فى مُتونِها الماذِىُّ

٣٩٨ فٱقتحمُوا فى وَعْرِها وسَهلِهَا   وذاك حِينَ غَفْلَةٍ من أَهْلِهَا

٣٩٩ ولم يكن للقَوْمِ من دِفاعِ   بِخَيْلِ دُرِّىٍّ ولا ٱمتناعِ

٤٠٠ وقَوَّضَ الإمامُ عند ذلكا   وقَلْبُهُ صَبٌّ بما هُنالكَا

٤٠١ حتى إذا ما حَلَّ فى المَدينَهْ   وأَهْلُها ذَليلةٌ مَهينَهْ

٤٠٢ أَقْمعها بالخَيْلِ والرِّجالِ   من غيرِ ما حَرْبٍ ولا قِتالِ

٤٠٣ وكانَ مِن أَوَّلِ شىءٍ نَظَرا   فيه وما رَوى له ودَبَّرا

٤٠٤ تَهدُّمُ لِبابِها والسُّورِ   وكانَ ذاك أَحْسَنَ التدبيرِ

405 Until, after he had turned it into a flat desert and [its inhabitants] had perceived that entry into the inviolate sanctity of its women's quarters had become lawful,

406 He cheered [them] up by fortifying [the town] and laying [new] foundations on the mountain of ᶜAmrūs,

407 Until a well-constructed building was completed therein, and his governor and troops had occupied it.

408 In this way the city flowing in blood surrendered and submitted after having behaved in so haughty a manner.

The Year 321/933–934

409 During its course, ᶜAbd al-Ḥamīd set out accompanied by military apparatus and a contingent of troops,

410 Until he reached the fortress in which Yaḥya ibn Dhī n-Nūn was fortified and entrenched;

411 He made him come down from the hills of Walb without having to resort to constraint or to engage in battle,

412 But rather, by inspiring him with a desire for obedience and for entering the fold of the [Muslim] community,

413 Until he brought him to the Imam, longing for the forgiveness of his sins, in a state of repentance.

414 Therefore the Imam forgave his offense, accepting the repentance he offered,

415 And sent him back once more to [his] fortresses, confirming his governorship over them by written contract.

The Year 322/934–935

416 Then the Imam endowed with a twofold glory campaigned at the beginning of the twenty-second year,

417 Accompanied by a force of five thousand men gathered into a vast multitude, a huge army crushing heads as well as hills.

418 The hillsides muster toward his slowly advancing army just as troops muster to his sides,

---

406. The "mountain of ᶜAmrūs": ᶜAmrūs was the governer of Toledo appointed by al-Ḥakam I. He built a castle on the site of the present-day Alcazar and invited the nobility of Toledo to a feast in it, killing them all, one by one, as they entered (R. Dozy, *Spanish Islam*, trans., F. G. Stokes [New York, 1913], II, 246, 249).

٤٠٥ حتى إذا صَيَّرَها بَراحَا … وعاينوا حَريمَها مُباحَا

٤٠٦ أقرَّ بالتَّشْييدِ والتَّأْسيسِ … في الجَبَلِ النّامي إلى عَمّروسِ

٤٠٧ حتى آستوى فيها بِناءٌ مُحْكَمُ … فحَلَّهُ عامِلُهُ والحَشَمُ

٤٠٨ فعند ذاك أسلَمَتْ وآستسلَمَتْ … مدينةُ الدِّماءِ بعد ما عَتَتْ

سنة إحدى وعشرين وثلثمائة

٤٠٩ فيها مَضَى عبدُ الحميدِ مُلتئِمْ … فى أُهبةٍ وعُدّةٍ من الحَشَمْ

٤١٠ حتى أتى الحصنَ الذى تقَلّعَا … يَحْيَى بنِ ذى النُّونِ به وآمتنعَا

٤١١ فحطَّهُ من هَضَبَاتِ وَلْبِ … من غيرِ تعْنيتٍ وغيرِ حَرْبِ

٤١٢ إلّا بتَرْغيبٍ له فى الطاعَهْ … وفى الدُّخولِ مَدْخَلَ الجماعَهْ

٤١٣ حتى أتى به الإمامَ راغبًا … في الصَّفحِ عن ذُنوبِهِ وتائبًا

٤١٤ فَصفحَ الإمامُ عن جِنايتِهْ … وقَبِلَ المَبْذولَ مِن إنابتِهْ

٤١٥ ورَدَّهُ إلى الحُصونِ ثانيًا … مُسَجّلاً له عليها وَاليَا

سنة اثنتين وعشرين وثلثمائة

٤١٦ ثم غزا الإمامُ ذو المَجْدَيْنِ … فى مُبْتَدا عِشْرينَ وآثنتَيْنِ

٤١٧ فى فَيْلَقٍ مُجَمْهَرٍ لُهامِ … مُدَكْدِكِ الرُّؤوسِ والآكامِ

٤١٨ حافُ الرُّبى لِزَحْفِهِ تَجَيُّشُ … تَجَيُّشٌ فى حافاتِهِ الجُيُوشُ

---

410. Yaḥya ibn Dhī n-Nūn was the lord of Toledo.

411. Walb is the present-day Huélamo, of which Yaḥya was also governor (Lévi-Provençal, *op. cit.*, p. 278). It is unlikely that it refers to Huelva.

419 As though they were jinns astride female ghouls, all of them being more penetrating [in an attack] than lions.

420 Then they rushed upon Molonda, Rūma, and the nearby fortresses of Ḥīma,

421 Until the Tujībite apostate came to beseech his favor like a repentant man returning to God.

422 Therefore the Imam granted him an exclusive welcome as well as pardon and forgiveness of his sins,

423 After which he gave him [gifts], clothed him [in a robe of honor] and presented him with a braying [mule] and a neighing [horse] which had no equal.

424 Both were the mounts of Caliphs, decked in trappings such that they defy the description of anyone who would describe them.

425 He further said: "Be one of ours and make your home in Córdoba that we may bring you close to the highest rank in it;

426 You will be a vizier, the noblest of men in rank, as well as a commander collecting taxes from this frontier in our name."

427 So he replied: "I am recovering from my illness, for you can well observe the change in my complexion and my yellowish pallor;

428 Therefore, if you think fit, O my lord, to grant me a delay until I am restored to good health,

429 Then will I come to you in all haste with my kinsfolk, children, and immediate family."

430 And he gave assurance [of this] to the Imam by swearing oaths and calling upon God to witness them.

431 Hence the Imam accepted his oaths and sent him back to his abode with forgiveness.

432 Then the lady of the Basques came to offer him her sincere affection,

433 And [to acknowledge] that she was his vassal, for her grandfather was related to his.

---

420. Molonda was near Saragossa. Ḥīma appears to be Alhama de Aragón.

421. The Banū Tujīb were lords of Saragossa.

٤١٩ كأنّهم جِنٌّ على سَعَالِي — وكُلُّهم أمْضَى من الرِّئبالِ

٤٢٠ فاقْتَحَمُوا مُلُونْدَةَ ورُومَهْ — ومِن حَوالِيها حُصونَ جِيمَهْ

٤٢١ حتى أتاه المَارِقُ التُّجيبي — مُستجدِيًا كالتائبِ المُنيبِ

٤٢٢ فخَصَّهُ الإمامُ بالتَّرْحيبِ — والصَّفْحِ والغُفْرانِ لِلذُّنوبِ

٤٢٣ ثم حَباهُ وكَساهُ ووَصَلْ — بشاحجٍ وصاهلٍ لا يُمْتَثَلْ

٤٢٤ كِلاهُما مِن مَرْكَبِ الخَلائفِ — في حِلْيَةٍ تُعْجِزُ وَصْفَ الواصِفِ

٤٢٥ وقال كُنْ مِنّا وأَوْطِنْ قُرْطُبَهْ — تُدْنيكَ فيها مِن أجلِّ مَرْتَبَهْ

٤٢٦ تكن وَزيرًا أعْظَمَ الناسِ خَطَرْ — وقائدًا تَجْبى لنا هذا الثَّغَرْ

٤٢٧ فقال إنّي ناقِهٌ من عِلَّتِي — وقد تَرَى تَغَيُّرِي وصُفْرَتي

٤٢٨ فإنْ رأيتَ سَيِّدِي إمْهالِي — حتى أُرَمَّ مِن صَلاحِ حالي

٤٢٩ ثم أُوافيكَ على آستِعْجالِ — بالأَهْلِ والأَوْلادِ والعِيالِ

٤٣٠ وأَوثَقَ الإمامَ بالعُهودِ — وجَعَلَ اللّهَ من الشُّهودِ

٤٣١ فقَبِلَ الإمامُ من أيمانِه — ورَدَّه عَفْوًا إلى مكانِه

٤٣٢ ثم أتَتْهُ رَبَّةُ البَشاقِصِ — تُدْلِي إليه بالوِدادِ الخالِصِ

٤٣٣ وأنّها مُرْسَلَةٌ مِن عندِه — وجَدُّها مُتَّصِلٌ بِجَدِّه

---

432. The "lady of the Basques" is Queen Toda or Theuda of Navarre who visited the Caliph in Córdoba (al-Maqqarī, *History of the Mohammedan Dynasties in Spain*, trans. Pascual de Gayangos [London 1840–1843] II, 135).

434 She traveled at the head of every citizen of Pamplona, setting free the prisoners taken from the Banū Dhī n-Nūn,

435 Therefore the Imam promised her safe-conduct and removed his squadrons from the vicinity of her fortresses.

436 After that he set forth in full strength and power, giving victory to the followers of this religion,

437 Amidst banners and troops and in the company of forbearing and intelligent men,

438 Against God's enemies the Galicians; the worshipers of the creature rather than the Creator.

439 Moreover they destroyed plains and fortresses, tearing up fields and crops;

440 Laying waste castles and towns and dispersing their inhabitants,

441 So that no inhabitants were left in the towns, nor was anyone left in them to light the fire,

442 For they left their flourishing civilization in a state of ruin, turning its fields into a wasteland,

443 While along with castles they burned down forts, sorely afflicting their inhabitants.

444 Finally the Imam turned back, having eased the pain from his sorrows,

445 Having freed the wilds from their defilements, and having cleansed the towns of their impurities.

---

435. The Arabic source reads *takkaba*, a misprint for *nakkåba*.

٤٣٤ وٱكتفلتْ بكُلِّ بَنْبَلُونِى   وأَطلقتْ أَسْرَى بنى ذى النُّونِ
٤٣٥ فأَوْعَدَ الإمامُ فى تَأْمِينِهَا   ونَكَّبَ العَسْكَرَ عن حُصونِهَا
٤٣٦ ثم مَضى بالعِزِّ والتَّمْكينِ   وناصرًا لِأَهْلِ هذا الدِّينِ
٤٣٧ فى جُمْلةِ الراياتِ والعَساكِرِ   وفى رِجالِ الصَّبْرِ والبَصائِرِ
٤٣٨ إلى عِدَى اللّٰهِ مِن الجَلالِقِ   وعابِدِى المَخْلوقِ دونَ الخالِقِ
٤٣٩ فدمَّروا السُّهولَ والقِلاعَا   وهَتَّكوا الرُّبوعَ والرِّباعَا
٤٤٠ وخَرَّبوا الحُصونَ والمَدائنَا   وأَنفروا من أَهْلِها المَساكِنَا
٤٤١ فلَيْسَ فى الدِّيارِ مِن دَيَّارِ   ولا بها من نافِخٍ لِلنَّارِ
٤٤٢ فغادروا عُمْرانَها خَرابَا   وبَدَّلوا رُبوعَها يَبَابَا
٤٤٣ وبالقِلاعِ أَحْرَقوا الحُصونَا   وأَسْخَنوا من أَهْلِها العُيونَا
٤٤٤ ثم ثَنى الإمامُ مِن عِنانِهِ   وقد شَفَى الشَّجِىّ من أَشْجانِهِ
٤٤٥ وأَمَّنَ القِفارَ مِن أَنْجاسِهَا   وطَهَّرَ البِلادَ مِن أَرْجاسِهَا

436. I.e., Islam.

2 Ibn Hānī'

1 The sons of al-ʿAbbās say: "Has Egypt been conquered?" Therefore reply to the sons of al-ʿAbbās: "The matter has already been accomplished

2 For Jauhar has captured Alexandria, good tidings appear to him and victory precedes him.

3 Egypt has sent him its embassies [of peace] and another bridge has been added to its arched bridge.

4 Thus this day has not dawned but that your hands have been emptied of [Egypt] and other [countries] like it.

5 So do not prolong your remembrance of the time that has gone by, for that is an age that has come to an end whereas this is [a new] age.

6 Were you doubting the army? Go gently, for here are the the supple lance and the vast army!

7 For the horsemen of God have won glory by shining out over religion and this world as does the early dawn!

8 Here is the descendant of God's Prophet who is seeking his vengeance, for it is unfitting that any of his vengeance should remain unsought for.

9 Leave the drinking of the water of the Euphrates to his horsemen, and moreover, do not deny them either its shallows or its mainstream.

10 Regarding the sun, is there any doubt that it is the sun after it has risen and is clear to the naked eye, there being no veil before it?

11 For it is only one miraculous portent coming after another, as well as a warning to you, were warning to suffice you,

12 So either be like unto "wheat in a field mowed down," or else submit to a ruler in whose hand lies [the power to dispense] death and resurrection.

13 Obey an Imam who surpasses all other Imams in excellence just as piety surpasses works.

---

2. SOURCE: Ibn Hānī', *Dīwān*, ed. Karam al-Bustānī (Beirut, 1964), pp. 131–139. METER: *ṭawīl.*

This poem was recited before the Fatimid Caliph al-Muʿizz in the Tunisian capital of Manṣūriyya after the news arrived that Jauhar, the Fatimid general, had just conquered Egypt. The conquest occurred in A.D. 969. The poem defends the Shiʿite cause.

٢

ابن هانىء

١ تقولُ بنو العبَّاسِ هل فُتِحَتْ مِصْرُ … فقُلْ لبني العبَّاسِ قد قُضِيَ الأمْرُ!

٢ وقد جاوزَ الإسكندريَّةَ جوهرٌ … تُطالِعُهُ البُشْرى ويَقْدُمُهُ النَّصْرُ

٣ وقد أوفدَتْ مِصْرٌ إليهِ وُفودَها … وزِيدَ إلى المَعْقودِ مِن جِسْرِها جِسْرُ

٤ فما جاءَ هذا اليومُ إلّا وقد غدَتْ … وأيْديكُمُ مِنها ومِن غيرِها صِفْرُ

٥ فلا تُكْثِروا ذِكْرَ الزَّمانِ الذي خلا … فذلك عَصْرٌ قد تَقَضَّى وذا عَصْرُ

٦ أفي الجَيْشِ كنتمْ تمْترونَ، رُوَيْدكمْ! … فهذا القَنا العَرَّاصُ والجَحْفَلُ المَجْرُ

٧ وقد أشرَفَتْ خَيْلُ الإلهِ طَوالِعًا … على الدينِ والدنْيا كما طَلَعَ الفَجْرُ

٨ وذا ابنُ نبيِّ اللّهِ يَطْلُبُ وِتْرَهُ … وكانَ حَرٍ أن لا يضيعَ لهُ وِتْرُ

٩ ذَرُوا الوِرْدَ في ماءِ الفُراتِ لِخَيْلِهِ … فلا الضَّحْلُ منه تمنعون ولا الغَمْرُ

١٠ أفي الشمسِ شَكٌّ أنها الشمسُ بعدما … تَجَلَّتْ عِيانًا ليس مِن دونِها سِتْرُ

١١ وما هيَ إلّا آيةٌ بعدَ آيةٍ … ونُذْرٌ لكم إن كان يغنيكمُ النُّذْرُ

١٢ فكونوا حَصيدًا خامِدينَ أوِ ارْعَوُوا … إلى مَلِكٍ في كَفِّهِ المَوْتُ والنَّشْرُ

١٣ أطيعوا إمامًا للأئمَّةِ فاضِلًا … كما كانَتِ الأعمالُ يَفْضُلُها البِرُّ

1. The reference is to the Abbasids of Baghdad.

3. Jauhar entered Egypt with a hundred thousand men and a second bridge had to be constructed to transport his huge army across the Nile.

12. "Wheat in a field mowed down" is quoted from Koran 26:28.

14 Approach one giving to drink, whose flow is inexhaustible; one whose pouring is endless, in the same way as small ants do not exhaust the seas,

15 For if you become his followers it is [only] because he is your [rightful] lord who, through God's Prophet, enjoys priority over you in [the validity of] his claim to glory.

16 Yet if you do not [approach him], then may God alienate the estranged one from prosperity! For between him and you there will be that which not even time can reconcile.

17 Was it to the son of the father of the two grandsons or to your fellow who was brought within the pale of Islam against his will that the noble verses and chapters of the Koran were revealed?

18 Sons of Natla, God did not cause any [descendants of] Natla to inherit [authority], neither did she beget sons. Surely the slave and the freeborn are not equal?

19 For he impeded the matter, since she had caused her condition of slavery as well as a heretical claim to cleave to your father; therefore beware!

20 Leave the people [in peace]; restore them to their [rightful] ruler, for you have no recognizable claim to authority, neither any unrecognizable one.

21 You made captive mighty chieftains in Iraq, yet that bondage has now been loosened from their necks,

22 And the factions of orthodoxy, the helpers of God's religion, the white swords and tawny lances, have despoiled you of your days [of undisputed power].

23 [You have also been despoiled by] one whose days are beginning, to whom fresh youth and bright time present a smiling countenance.

24 He has governed mankind according to his will, while his ten fingers have contained the seven spheres.

25 Do you perceive who is the purest of all creatures in nobility, as well as the most excellent, were both nomads and sedentary dwellers to be included in the reckoning?

26 Come up to [the councils] of the judges of every tribe, for on earth there are bright princes and assemblies,

---

17. The "son" is Ḥusain, the "father" ʿAlī ibn Abī Ṭālib, and the "two grandsons" are al-Ḥusain and al-Ḥasan. For this meaning of *ṭalīq*, cf. E. W. Lane, *Arabic-English Lexicon* (London, 1863–1885), V, 1874. The reference is to al-ʿAbbās ibn ʿAbd al-Muṭṭalib, ancestor of the Abbasids who is compared unfavorably with the ʿAlids.

١٤ رِدُوا ساقيًا لا تَنزِفونَ حِياضَهُ … جَموماً كما لا تَنزِفُ الأَبحُرَ الذَّرُّ

١٥ فإن تتبعوهُ فهو مَولاكُمُ الذي … له بِرَسولِ اللهِ دونكُمُ الفَخْرُ

١٦ وإلّا فَبُعْداً للبعيدِ فبَيْنَهُ … وبَيْنَكُمُ ما لا يُقرِّبُهُ الدَّهرُ

١٧ أفي ابنِ أبي السِّبْطَيْنِ أم في طَليقِكم … تَنَزَّلَتِ الآياتُ والسُّوَرُ الغُرُّ؟

١٨ بَني نَتْلَةٍ ما أوْرَثَ اللهُ نَتْلَةً … وما نَسَلَتْ هل يَسْتَوي العَبْدُ والحُرُّ؟

١٩ وأنّى بهذا وهي أعْدَتْ برِقِّها … أباكم فإياكم ودعوى هي الكُفْرُ

٢٠ ذَرُوا الناسَ رُدُّوهم إلى مَن يَسوسهم … فما لكُمُ في الأمرِ عُرْفٌ ولا نُكْرُ

٢١ أَسَرْتُمْ قُروماً بالعِراقِ أعِزَّةً … فقد فُكَّ مِن أعناقِهم ذلك الأَسْرُ

٢٢ وقد بَزَّكم أيّامَكُم عُصَبُ الهُدى … وأنصارُ دينِ اللهِ والبِيضُ والسُّمْرُ

٢٣ ومُقْتَبَلٌ أيامُهُ مُتَهَلِّلٌ … إليه الشبابُ الغَضُّ والزَّمنُ النَّضْرُ

٢٤ أدارَ كما شاءَ الوَرى وتَحَيَّزَتْ … على السَّبْعةِ الأفلاكِ أَنْمُلُهُ العَشْرُ

٢٥ أتدرونَ مَن أزكى البَرِيَّةِ مَنصِباً … وأفْضَلُها إنْ عُدِّدَ البَدْوُ والحَضْرُ؟

٢٦ تَعالَوْا إلى حُكّامِ كُلِّ قَبيلةٍ … ففي الأرضِ أقيالٌ وأنديةٌ زُهْرُ

---

18. Natla (diminutive: Nutaila) was the mother of al-ʿAbbās.

23 The poet refers to the fourth Fatimid Caliph al-Muʿizz who was in the prime of youth.

27 And do not turn away from the family of Hāshim; and do not abandon Fihr, nor that which Fihr has organized.

28 Therefore come along with the one whom [the tribe of] Luʾaiy ibn Ghālib contained, and come along with the one whom Kināna and Naḍr supported.

29 And do not abandon the elevated station of Maʿdd and others, so that from you it may be known to whom right and command are due.

30 Although it was a wonder that the tongue ever uttered a word in their favor and mentioned them, in view of the fact that they had passed away and even their very memory had passed away,

31 For they perished and God erased the traces of their royal authority so that no [indirect] information or any [direct] experience of them ever reached you."

32 Lo! This broad earth has appeared in the morning, nor does there remain of its breadth even the space between the thumb and forefinger for the sons of al-ʿAbbās,

33 For the world has turned to the rule of the family of Muḥammad while the newborn government has dragged the ends of its robes [in proud pomp].

34 And he whose family's works, as well as [those] of his own personal store, have been righteous, has restored the rights due the descendants of Abū Ṭālib;

35 The strengthener of orthodoxy as well as of religion and of the blood kindred whose ties are conjoined in him and to whom gratefulness is due,

36 Is the one who rescued [those descendants] in every Eastern and Western region in such a wise that their fear and panic have been transformed into security,

37 And every Imami advances as if Sirius were opposite him and the full moon in his face.

38 And when the false state was removed from [the Imamis], blindness and ignorance, blame and treason were removed [with it].

39 Rights [that were long over-]due appeared, previous to which several ages had elapsed, for no time or age had restored [these rights] to them;

---

28. Luʾaiy ibn Ghālib was an ancestor of Quraish as was Naḍr ibn Kināna. It was the Shiʿite argument that the ʿAlids had a prior claim to rule over the Abbasids.

٢٧ ولا تعدلوا بالصيد من آل هاشم   ولا تتركوا فهرا وما جمعت فهر
٢٨ فجيئوا بمن ضمّت لؤيّ بن غالب   وجيئوا بمن أدّت كنانة والنضر
٢٩ ولا تذروا عليا معدّ وغيرها   ليعرف منكم من له الحقّ والأمر
٣٠ ومن عجب أنّ اللسان جرى لهم   بذكر على حين انقضوا وانقضى الذكر
٣١ فبادوا وعفّى الله آثار ملكهم   فلا خبر يلقاك عنهم ولا خبر
٣٢ ألا تلكم الأرض العريضة أصبحت   وما لبني العبّاس في عرضها فتر
٣٣ فقد دالت الدنيا لآل محمّد   وقد جرّرت أذيالها الدولة البكر
٣٤ وردّ حقوق الطالبيّين من زكت   صنائعه في آله وزكا الذخر
٣٥ معزّ الهدى والدين والرحم التي   به اتّصلت أسبابها وله الشكر
٣٦ من انتاشهم في كلّ شرق ومغرب   فبدّل أمنا ذلك الخوف والذعر
٣٧ فكلّ إماميّ يجيء كأنّما   على يده الشعرى وفي وجهه البدر
٣٨ ولمّا تولّت دولة النصب عنهم   تولّى العمى والجهل واللؤم والغدر
٣٩ حقوق أتت من دونها أعصر خلت   فما ردّها دهر عليهم ولا عصر

34. I.e., the ʿAlids, from whom the Fatimids claimed descent.
35. Note the pun on the Caliph's title Muʿizz.
37. "Imami," i.e., Shiʿite, or follower of the ʿAlid descendants.
38. "The established state," i.e., the Abbasid regime.

40 So the wearer of the crown unsheathed appointed terms of life standing between him and his rights just as white swords whose edges are red are unsheathed.

41 In this way he rescued [his rights] from the clutches of fate after the biting gnat and the fanged lion had held them by turns.

42 Then he apportioned them out according to God's revelation in such a manner that neither little nor much of it was broken.

43 Thus, before your eyes, O people of the house of Muhammad, the muddied fountainheads [of these rights] have become pure thanks to Muʿizz ad-Dīn.

44 For the world has fallen to your share while to him there has fallen redoubled praise and thanks;

45 Because he is an Imam of such a nature that I perceive religion to be closely connected to him, for obedience to him is safety while rebellion against him is to stray.

46 I consider praising him to be like praising God; indeed, it is a form of divine obedience as well as a glorification [of God] whereby the burden of sin is lessened.

47 It is he who is heir to the earth and the one among all men for whom it was created until [the day when] the one end of the earth shall be joined to the other.

48 And al-Manṣūr was not unaware of his superiority while he was yet in the cradle, for the signs and the beauteous mark had appeared.

49 He perceived that he would most certainly be named the lord of all the earth and when he perceived him he said: "This is the one and only lord."

50 Nor was this [firmly held opinion] derived from the art of physiognomy alone; much less was he restricted [in his conclusions] to mere [doubtful] conjecture.

51 But rather it was perceived [with certainty] from the trace he came across written in priceless ink, wherein beauty lay.

52 And it was a treasure stored up from the knowledge of divine things; indeed the latter is the true knowledge, and not divining from footprints nor from observing the direction of the flight of birds.

---

46. A Shiʿite belief related to the doctrine of Caliphal infallibility.
48. al-Manṣūr was the father of al-Muʿizz.

٤٠ فجرَّدَ ذو التَّاجِ المَقاديرَ دونها   كما جُرِّدَتْ بِيضٌ مَضارِبُها حُمْرُ
٤١ فأَنقَذَها من بُرْثُنِ الدَّهْرِ بعدما   تَواكَلَها القِرْنُ المُنَيَّبُ والهِصْرُ
٤٢ فأَجْرَى على ما أنْزَلَ اللّهُ قَسْمَها   فلم يُتَخَرَّمْ منهُ قُلٌّ ولا كُثْرُ
٤٣ فَدُونَكُمُوهَا أهْلَ بَيْتِ محمّدٍ   صَفَتْ بمُعِزِّ الدينِ جمّاتُها الكُدْرُ
٤٤ فقد صارتِ الدُّنيا إليكم مصيرَها   وصار له الحَمْدُ المضاعَفُ والشُكْرُ
٤٥ إمامٌ رَأَيْتُ الدِّينَ مُرْتَبِطًا بِهِ   فطَاعَتُهُ فَوْزٌ وعِصْيانُهُ خُسْرُ
٤٦ أَرَى مَدْحَهُ كالمَدْحِ لِلّهِ إنَّهُ   قُنوتٌ وتَسْبيحٌ يُحَطُّ به الوِزْرُ
٤٧ هو الوارِثُ الدُّنْيَا ومَن خُلِقَتْ لَهُ   مِن النَّاسِ حتى يَلْتَقي القُطْرُ والقُطْرُ
٤٨ وماجَهِلَ المَنْصورُ في المَهْدِ فَضْلَهُ   وقد لاحَتِ الأَعلامُ والسِّمَةُ البَهْرُ
٤٩ رَأَى أن سَيُسْمَى مالكَ الأَرضِ كلِّها   فلَمَّا رآهُ قالَ ذا الصَّمَدُ الوَتْرُ
٥٠ وما ذاك أخذًا بالفِراسةِ وَحْدَها   ولا أنّه فيها إلى الظنِّ مضطَرٌّ
٥١ ولكنَّ مَوْجودًا مِن الأثَرِ الذى   تَلَقَّاهُ من حِبرٍ ضَنِينٍ به حِبْرُ
٥٢ وكَنْزًا من العِلْمِ الرَّبوبيِّ إنّهُ   هو العِلْمُ حَقًّا لا القِيافةُ والزَّجْرُ

---

49. I.e., "The Imam."

53 So carry good tidings about him swiftly to the Holy House when the circuit [round the Kaʿba] and the journeying [of the pilgrims from Mina to Mecca] is in progress among men.

54 And lo, it is as if he had already visited it and Ṭaiba and as-Surr had seceded from the palaces of royal power [belonging to the Abbasids], in his name.

55 Surely the House is not God's House save by reason of its being his sacred precinct, and surely to the man far from his abode there is no patience [that will restrain him from returning] home?

56 It is his own original mansions which yearn for him, for he has no shelter or palace away from them;

57 [As well as those] wherein his ancestor encountered holiness when the words of God and what was secret or public reached him.

58 So if the House has requested the favor [of his return], it is because the meeting places of the pilgrimage have become debased, yet after hardship comes ease.

59 And if it has mourned out of yearning for you, it is because the fragrance of your sweet odor is to be found in its air.

60 Are you not the descendant of its founder, so that if you were to visit it, its veils would be removed and its dust-colored places of pilgrimage would turn white?

61 Beloved one traveling on the pilgrimage to the valley of Mecca, salute a place where men are counted in which lie Mecca and the forbidden sanctuary.

62 There, the whole earth is filled with light, and [all men] meet in close proximity, nor does the traveler consider the journey to be long,

63 And [there] you will be able to distinguish the divine ordinances of the pilgrimage from its supererogatory works, while the difference between good and evil will be distinguished by the Muslim community.

64 I have witnessed the great strength you have lent to this religion; [a strength so great] that I have feared lest greatness should be entirely monopolized by it,

65 For you have promoted a matter on which your mind has been resolutely fixed so that after it [has been achieved] no man will rebel against you save for one who remains heedlessly ignorant of you; self-deceived.

---

53. The "Holy House" is the Kaʿba.

٥٣ فَبَشِّرْ بِهِ البَيْتَ المُحَرَّمَ عاجِلاً   إذا أَوْجَفَ التَّطْوافُ بالناسِ والنَّفْرُ

٥٤ وها فكأنْ قد زارَهُ وتَجانَفَتْ   به عن قُصورِ المُلْكِ طَيْبَةُ والسِّرُّ

٥٥ هل البَيْتُ بَيْتُ اللهِ إلاّ حَريمُهُ   وهل لِغَريبِ الدارِ عن دارِه صَبْرُ؟

٥٦ مَنازِلُهُ الأُولَى اللَّواتي يَشُقْنَهُ   فليس له عنهنَّ مَعْدًى ولا قَصْرُ

٥٧ وحَيْثُ تَلَقَّى جَدُّهُ القُدْسَ وانْتَحَتْ   له كَلِماتُ اللهِ والسِّرُّ والجَهْرُ

٥٨ فإن يَتَمَنَّ البَيْتُ تلك فقد دَنَتْ   مَواقيتُها والعُسْرُ من بعدِه اليُسْرُ

٥٩ وإن حَنَّ من شَوْقٍ إليكَ فإنَّهُ   لَيُوجَدُ من رَيّاكَ في جَوِّه نَشْرُ

٦٠ أَلَسْتَ ابنَ بانيهِ فلو جِئْتَهُ انْجَلَتْ   غَواشيه وابْيَضَّتْ مَناسِكُهُ الغُبْرُ

٦١ حَبيبٌ إلى بَطْحاءِ مكّةَ مَوْسِمٌ   تُحَيِّي مَعَدًّا فيه مكّةُ والحِجْرُ

٦٢ هُناكَ تُضيءُ الأرضُ نُورًا وتَلْتَقِي   دُنُوًّا فلا يَسْتَبْعِدُ السَّفَرَ السَّفْرُ

٦٣ وتَدْري فُروضَ الحَجِّ من نافِلاتِهِ   ويَمتازُ عندَ الأُمَّةِ الخَيْرُ والشَّرُّ

٦٤ شَهِدْتُ لقد أعززتَ ذا الدِّينِ عِزَّةً   خَشيتُ لها أن يَسْتَبِدَّ به الكِبْرُ

٦٥ فأَمْضَيْتَ عَزْمًا ليس يَعْصِيكَ بعدَه   مِن الناسِ إلاّ جاهِلٌ بكَ مُغْتَرُّ

54. *Ṭaiba* is an epithet applied to Medina; as-Surr is a place in Hijāz.

66 I congratulate you upon the victory which I observe with an eye which unbelief does not close,

67 For there remain only the posts stretching out at intervals one after the other, nor does a term the furthest limit of which is one month separate you [from the goal of your journey].

68 Furthermore, what harm came to Egypt when it surrendered to you? Did the Nile rise or did an ebbing tide cause it to perish?

69 In it sermons have been written in your name, the rhetorical ornaments of which are poetry though their words are in prose,

70 While in it the blood of not one single non-Muslim has been shed unlawfully nor has any crime been [falsely] imputed to a Muslim.

71 Jauhar appeared [in Egypt] in the morning, like unto the clouds of mercy, preserving its two shores from any new accident of fortune that might befall it.

72 It is as though I see him as a tale that has become current among men, a tale which Baghdad loves as much as Egypt,

73 And because of him the Eastern countries envy the latter, for he has committed an evil deed by alighting in that land and that region;

74 Yet on what basis will a government like that [of Baghdad] show him hostility, when in wartime the waist wrapper has already been tucked up from his shank,

75 And spears of Rudaina have been straightened, since there is no thoroughbred horse whom leanness will not take the fat off?

76 Nor was that which he undertook even the beginning of what would be enough, and yet royal power was strengthened and a breach in the frontier was closed up by him.

77 Thus there is no holding back in his goal [on his part] this side of glory, nor is there any breathlessness in his pace this side of an upright deed.

78 Through him you have established over the Egyptians a just religious law which is the [only] manifestly revealed miracle in the proof of which lies enchantment,

79 According to that revealed law which passed away when it did, and thus the hems of [our law] flow and are dragged over them.

---

67. For *tatrā*, 'stretching out at intervals,' cf. Biberstein Kazimirski, *Dictionnaire arabe-français* (2d ed.; Paris, 1960), II, 1481.

73. I.e., the Abbasid lands envy Egypt for having been conquered by the Fatimids.

٦٦ أُهَنِّيكَ بالفَتْحِ الذى أنا ناظِرٌ   إليه بعَينٍ ليسَ يُغمِضُها الكُفْرُ
٦٧ فلم يَبْقَ إلّا البُرْدُ تَتْرَى وما نَأَى   عليكَ مدًى أَقْصَى مَواعِيدِه شَهْرُ
٦٨ وما ضَرَّ مِصْرًا حينَ أَلقَتْ قِيادَها   إليكَ أمَدَّ النِّيلُ أم غالَهُ جَزْرُ؟
٦٩ وقد حُبِّرَتْ فيها لكَ الخُطَبُ التي   بَدائعُها نَظْمٌ وألْفاظُها نَثْرُ
٧٠ فلم يُهَرَّقْ فيها لِذي ذِمَّةٍ دَمٌ   حَرامٌ ولم يُحْمَلْ على مُسْلِمٍ إصْرُ
٧١ غَدا جَوْهَرٌ فيها غَمامةَ رَحْمَةٍ   يَقي جانبَيْها كلَّ حادِثةٍ تَعْرُو
٧٢ كأنّي بهِ قد سارَ في الناسِ سِيرةً   تَوَدُّ لها بَغْدادُ لو أنَّها مِصْرُ
٧٣ وتَحْسُدُها فيهِ المَشارِقُ أنّهُ   سَواءٌ إذا ما حلَّ في الأرضِ والقَطْرُ
٧٤ ومِن أينَ تَعْدوهُ سِياسةُ مِثْلِها   وقد قَلَّصَتْ في الحَرْبِ عن ساقِهِ الإزْرُ
٧٥ ونُقِّفَ تَثْقِيفَ الرُّدَيْنيِّ قَبْلَها   وما الطِّرْفُ إلّا أن يُهَذِّبَهُ الضُّمْرُ
٧٦ ولَيسَ الذى يأتي بأوّلِ ما كَفَى   فشُدَّ بهِ مُلْكٌ وسُدَّ بهِ ثَغْرُ
٧٧ فما بمَداهُ دونَ مَجْدٍ تَخَلُّفٌ   ولا بِخُطاهُ دونَ صالِحةٍ بُهْرُ
٧٨ سَنَنْتَ له فيهم من العَدْلِ سُنّةً   هي الآيةُ المُجْلَى بِبُرْهانِها السِّحْرُ
٧٩ على ما خَلا من سُنّةِ الوَحْيِ إذْ خَلا   فأذيالُها تضفو عليهم وتنجَرُّ

---

75. *Ṭirf* means 'a thoroughbred horse, though not of his owner's breeding, or recently acquired' according to Lane. The implication is that the nobility of the Abbasids is upstart and recent. Spears of Rudaina were famous for their excellence from pre-Islamic times.

80 And insofar as they are concerned you have enjoined upon [Jauhar], out of your mercy which follows behind your liberality to which in turn your inviolate oath is attached,

81 An order such as God enjoined upon his Prophet, nor is there any deafness in an ear you cause to listen;

82 And you folded it up in writings composed every one of them of a scroll such that all good seemed to be penned in its folds.

83 Certain men who beheld the day when he passed judgment said: "By this man would the world be made prosperous even though it were barren!

84 "By this man, rather than by those in error, would the forbidden places and plots of land of [this world] become lawful so that the best portion of the smooth and rough terrain could be chosen!"

85 Therefore, O people of Egypt, may his justice suffice you as a guide to the justice which is revealed from him [as a beautiful laugh reveals bright teeth];

86 For this is a clear explanation [on the subject of] a Caliph such that the abundance of others is a scanty thing when compared with his favor.

87 We have shown our pleasure toward you, O people of Egypt [by granting you] a government in the shadow of which safety and abundance have been at our beck and call.

88 You have an exemplary model in us of old, for there is no secrecy or veiling of our circumstances from you.

89 Yet are we other than a [small] company of those who request his favors and to whom belong the short-haired mares [having the shank of one foreleg tied up to the arm] as well as the numerous herd of camels?

90 All the more [is the wealth] of his allies who seem as though they are a sky whose rain is silver unalloyed [pouring down] upon those who request their favors!

91 We have enjoyed the days of time through him as if in them there were a deep lethargy or as if intoxication had bent them down.

92 So O Lord whose way is the way of the angels while his nobility is the nobility of the prophets!

93 And O supplier of sustenance from whose hand an abundant harvest has grown; and if not, then from [that hand's] lines does the sea issue forth!

94 Lo, the days are your days; days one half of whose blessings you enjoy while we enjoy the other half:

٨٠ وأوصيتَهُ فيهم برفقِكَ مُرْدَفًا — بجُودِكَ مَعْقودًا به عَهْدُكَ البَرُّ

٨١ وصاةً كما أَوْصَى بها اللهُ رُسْلَهُ — وليس بأُذْنٍ أَنْتَ مُسْمِعُها وَقْرُ

٨٢ ونَنَيْتَها بالكُتْبِ من كُلِّ مُدْرَجٍ — كأَنَّ جميعَ الخَيرِ في طَيِّهِ سَطْرُ

٨٣ يَقولُ رِجالٌ شاهَدوا يَوْمَ حُكْمِهِ — بِذا تُعْمَرُ الدُّنْيا ولو أنّها قَفْرُ

٨٤ بِذا لا ضِياعٍ حَلَّلوا حُرُماتِها — وأَقْطاعَها فاسْتُصْفِيَ السَّهْلُ والوَعْرُ

٨٥ فحَسْبُكُمُ يا أَهْلَ مِصْرٍ بعَدْلِهِ — دليلاً على العَدْلِ الذي عنه يَفْتَرُّ

٨٦ فذاكَ بيانٌ واضِحٌ عن خَليفةٍ — كنيرٍ سِواهُ عند مَعْروفِهِ نَزْرُ

٨٧ رَضينا لكُمْ يا أَهْلَ مِصْرٍ بدَوْلَةٍ — أطاعَ لنا في ظِلِّها الأَمْنُ والوَفْرُ

٨٨ لَكُمْ أُسْوَةٌ فينا قديمًا فلم يَكُنْ — بأَحْوالِنا عنكم خَفَاءٌ ولا سَتْرُ

٨٩ وهل نَحْنُ إلاّ مَعْشَرٌ مِن عُفاتِهِ — لنا الصافِناتُ الجُرْدُ والعَكَرُ الدَّثْرُ

٩٠ فكَيْفَ مَواليهِ الّذينَ كأنّهم — سَماءٌ على العافينَ أَمْطارُها التِّبْرُ

٩١ لَبِسْنَا به أَيّامَ دَهْرٍ كأنّما — بها وَسَنٌ أو مالَ مَيْلاً بها السُّكْرُ

٩٢ فَيا مالِكًا هَدْيُ المَلائكِ هَدْيُهُ — ولكنَّ نَجْرَ الأنْبِياءِ لهُ نَجْرُ

٩٣ ويا رازِقًا من كفِّهِ نَشَأَ الحَيا — وإلاّ فمِنْ أَسرارِها نَبَعَ البَحْرُ

٩٤ ألا إنّما الأيّامُ أيّامُكَ التي — لك الشَّطْرُ مِن نَعمائها ولنا الشَّطْرُ

95 You enjoy the glory of them; yea, you enjoy the good and the noblest rank, while there is left to us the milch camel and the milk of them.

96 You have been generous to the point that there is no one to seek wealth, and you have spent money until no vast sum has power any longer;

97 For he who does not climb to the stars entertains no lofty ambition, and he who does not accumulate wealth has no excuse.

98 I wish that a generation whose age has gone before could remain behind or return to the assembly of life,

99 And that they could witness the times, for life after them [has become like] flourishing gardens and hopes are like pleasing, bright green [pastures];

100 For were he who now consists of broken and rotten bones to hear the summons, and were he whom the grave enfolds to answer the voice,

101 I would most certainly announce to one who has died: "Long life to a government for whom the dead are raised and life is restored!"

٩٥ لكَ المَجْدُ منها يا لكَ الخَيرُ والعُلَى وتَبقى لنا منها الحَلُوبَةُ والدَّرُّ

٩٦ لقد جُدْتَ حتى ليس لِلْمَالِ طالِبٌ وأَنْفَقْتَ حتى ما لِمُنْفِسَةٍ قَدْرُ

٩٧ فليسَ لِمَن لا يَرْتَقِي النَّجْمَ هِمَّةٌ وليس لِمَن لا يَسْتَفِيدُ الغِنَى عُذْرُ

٩٨ وَدِدْتُ لِجِيلٍ قد تَقَدَّمَ عَصْرُهم لَوِ آستأخروا في حَلْبةِ العُمرِ أو كَرُّوا

٩٩ ولو شَهِدوا الأيامَ والعيشُ بعدهم حدائقُ والآمالُ مونِقَةٌ خُضْرُ

١٠٠ فلو سَمِعَ التَّنْويبَ مَن كان رِمَّةً رُفاتًا ولَبَّى الصوتَ مَن ضَمَّه قَبْرُ

١٠١ لَنادَيتُ مَن قد ماتَ: حَيَّ بدَوْلةٍ تُقامُ لها المَوْتَى ويُرْتَجَعُ العُمْرُ

3 Ibn Darrāj al-Qasṭallī

1 May [God's] mercy and power be bestowed plentifully upon this kingship, and may safety and piety be granted to both the religious and the secular [branches],

2 For the throne of the comrade of unbelief has been destroyed since the Prince of the Faithful, Sulaimān,

3 Is the namesake of him whose command was obeyed by [all] creatures, for on earth neither man nor jinn rebelled against him,

4 And he is the builder of the loftiest constructions, who rises early in the morning and retires late in the evening to give praise [to God]; who consents to uphold the covenant of piety and manifests anger in the service of God.

5 By means of [that covenant] he restored to the empty desolation of the Caliphate, the light that was peculiar to it, for both its private apartments and homelands had entered a period of darkness.

6 He rescued God's religion from the grasp of the enemy, for abjectness and submissiveness had led it into unbelief;

7 He arose, and signs arose in honor of deeds of merit, market places in honor of good, and scales in honor of justice.

8 He renovated for Islam, the robe of a Caliphate favored by a light and a proof deriving from no less than the Clement,

9 While a pact in favor of the noblest of those who keep their pacts, consolidated [the Caliphate]; one such that his pacts and oaths are sincere.

10 Thanks to him the loins of the kingdom have been girded, orthodoxy has rejoiced, and goodness and well-doing flowed out over Islam,

11 A young warrior from whom eyes turn away out of fear so that none but aspirations remain to face him.

12 On the day he waters his swords with blood it is easy in his case for darkness to come to his encounter while he is still athirst.

---

3. SOURCES: Ibn al-Khaṭīb, *Kitāb Aʿmāl al-aʿlām*, ed. E. Lévi-Provençal (Beirut, 1956), pp. 123–125; Ibn Darrāj al-Qasṭallī, *Dīwān*, ed. Maḥmūd ʿAlī Makkī (Damascus, 1961), pp. 57–59; Ibn Bassām, *Dhakhīra* (Cairo, 1942), I, 53–54.

METER: *ṭawīl*.

Sulaimān ibn al-Ḥakam ibn Sulaimān ibn an-Nāṣir was elevated to power by the Berbers in Córdoba in July, 1010. He took the title of al-Mustaʿīn bi-llāh.

٣

ابن درّاج القسطلّي

١ هَنِيئاً لِهذا المُلْكِ رَوْحٌ ورَيْحانُ ‏ ‏ ‏ ‏ ولِلدِّينِ والدُّنْيا أَمانٌ وإيمانُ
٢ فإِنَّ قَعِيدَ الشِّرْكِ قَدْ ثُلَّ عَرْشُه ‏ ‏ ‏ ‏ وإِنَّ أَميرَ المُؤْمِنينَ سُلَيْمانُ
٣ سَمِيُّ الذى آنْقادَ الأَنامُ لأَمْرِهِ ‏ ‏ ‏ ‏ فلم يَعْصِهِ في الأَرْضِ إِنْسٌ ولا جانُ
٤ وبَانِي العُلَى لِلْحَمْدِ غادٍ ورَائحٌ ‏ ‏ ‏ ‏ وحِلْفُ التُّقَى لِلّهِ راضٍ وغَضْبانُ
٥ به رَدَّ في جوِّ الخِلافةِ نُورَها ‏ ‏ ‏ ‏ وقد أَظْلَمَتْ منها قُصورٌ وأَوْطانُ
٦ وأَنْقَذَ دِينَ اللّهِ من قَبْضَةِ العِدا ‏ ‏ ‏ ‏ وقد قادَهُ لِلشِّرْكِ ذُلٌّ وإِذْعانُ
٧ وقامَ فقامَتْ للمَعالي مَعالِمٌ ‏ ‏ ‏ ‏ ولِلخَيْرِ أَسْواقٌ ولِلعَدْلِ مِيزانُ
٨ وجَدَّدَ لِلإِسْلامِ ثَوْبَ خِلافةٍ ‏ ‏ ‏ ‏ عَلَيْها من الرَّحْمنِ نُورٌ وبُرْهانُ
٩ وأَكَّدَها عَهْدٌ لأَكْرَمِ مَنْ وَفَى ‏ ‏ ‏ ‏ بِعَهْدٍ زَكَتْ منه عُهودٌ وأَيْمانُ
١٠ به شُدَّ أَزْرُ المُلْكِ وَابْتَهَجَ الهُدَى ‏ ‏ ‏ ‏ وفاضَ على الإِسْلامِ حُسْنٌ وإِحْسانُ
١١ فَتًى نَكَصَتْ عنه العُيونُ مَهابةً ‏ ‏ ‏ ‏ فَلَيْسَ له إِلاَّ الرَّغائبُ أَقْرانُ
١٢ يَهونُ عليه يَوْمَ يُرْوِي سُيوفَه ‏ ‏ ‏ ‏ دَماً أَن يُوافيهِ الدُّجَى وَهْوَ ظَمْآن

He was dethroned and then brought back to power again in 1012 at which time this congratulatory ode was composed. His second reign lasted until 1015. The poem justifies the Berber interventions in the civil wars that eventually destroyed Umayyad power in al-Andalus.

3. A reference to Sulaimān, namesake of the Biblical Solomon.

13 The relative of the Prophet, God's elect, and of his paternal cousin, as well as the heir to [the house] raised up by Quraish and ᶜAdnān,

14 And to [the affairs] conducted by the royal council, to what is required by piety, to what has been bequeathed by the possessor of the two lights, your paternal cousin ᶜUthmān,

15 To what swords have ordained for you, and to what the father of kings, your ancestor Marwān conquered for you.

16 These are the inherited possessions of kings and the confirmation of a royal investiture such that nearby victory and approval are worthy of them,

17 As well as a lofty tree of glory [rising to] the sky, as though the latter's stars were twigs and branches of the former.

18 If it is of lofty stature it is because the assistance it was given was powerful, by reason of the charges made by certain horsemen gifted with power.

19 [They are] tribes consisting of the descendants of ᶜĀd and Jurhum; they possess the choicest part of what is derived from Hūd and Qaḥṭān.

20 They are the sons of those kingdoms where royal authority has been detained; an authority such that in its [enjoyment] centuries and ages have gone by for their forefathers in them.

21 Hence it was they who acknowledged your house in the whirlwind of destruction when a stipulated pact was doubted and a benefit had been disacknowledged,

22 When in the soul of the brave there had been a foreboding of death, and in the eye of dangers fear had many hues.

23 So they granted you and asked you to grant solemn promises in the thick of battle: even if your own soul should betray you, they would never betray!

24 It is as though the sky, both its full moon and its stars, were your brave warriors when hoary-headed elders and young men surrounded you

25 And their spearheads flashed around you so that you would think that both the rugged and the even ground were on fire.

26 [They are] lions aroused to anger in battle; you will not cease to observe eagles flying off with them on the day of war.

---

13. ᶜAdnān was the group from which the northern Arabs descended; Quraish, the tribe of Muhammad.

14. ᶜUthmān was the third Caliph (r. 644–656). The "two lights" are a reference to the fact that he was married to two daughters of the Prophet who were "lights."

١٣ قَرِيبُ النَّبِيِّ المُصْطَفَى وٱبْنُ عمِّهِ ووَارِثُ ما شادَتْ قُرَيْشٌ وعَدْنَانُ
١٤ وما ساقَتْ الشُّورَى وأَوْجَبَتْ التُّقَى وأَوْرَثَ ذو النُّورَيْنِ عمُّكَ عُثْمانُ
١٥ وماحاكَمَتْ فيه السُّيوفُ وحازَهُ إليك أَبُو الأَمْلاكِ جَدُّكَ مَرْوانُ
١٦ مَوارِيثُ أَمْلاكٍ وتَوْكِيدُ بَيْعَةٍ جَدِيرٌ بها فَتْحٌ قَرِيبٌ ورِضْوانُ
١٧ ودَوْحةُ مَجْدٍ في السَّماءِ كأَنَّها كَواكِبُها مِنْها فُروعٌ وأَغْصانُ
١٨ لَئِنْ عَظُمَتْ شَأْنًا لقد عَزَّ نَصْرُها بِكَرَّاتِ فُرْسانٍ لأَقْدارِها شَانُ
١٩ قَبائلُ مِن أَبْناءِ عادٍ وَجُرْهُمٍ لهم صَفْو ما تُنْمِيه هودٌ وقَحْطانُ
٢٠ بَنُو دُوَلِ المُلْكِ الذي سَلَفَتْ به لآبائهم فيها قُرُونٌ وأَزْمانُ
٢١ فهم عَرَفُوا مَنْوَاكَ في هَبْوَةِ الرَّدَى وقد رابَ مَعْهودٌ وأُنْكِرَ عِرْفانُ
٢٢ ولِلْمَوْتِ في نَفْسِ الشُّجاعِ تَخَيُّلٌ ولِلذُّعْرِ في غَبْنِ المخاطِرِ أَلْوانُ
٢٣ فأَعْطَوْكَ وٱسْتَعْطَوْكَ في حَوْمَةِ الوَغَا مَوَاثِيقَ لو خانَتْكَ نَفْسُكَ ما خانُوا
٢٤ كأَنَّ السَّماءَ بَدْرُها ونُجومَها سُرَاكَ وقد حَفُّوكَ شِيبٌ وشُبَّانُ
٢٥ وقد لَمَعَتْ حَوْلَيْكَ مِنْهم أَسِنَّةٌ تُخَيِّلُ أَنَّ الحَزْنَ والسَّهْلَ نِيرَانُ
٢٦ أُسُودُ هَيَاجٍ ما تَزالُ تَرَاهُمُ تَطِيرُ بهم يَوْمَ الكَرِيهةِ عِقْبانُ

---

15. Marwān I (r. 684–685) was the ancestor of the Andalusian Umayyads.
19. The reference is to the Berbers, who had come to claim descent from the legendary Arabian people of ʿĀd and the Yemenite grouping of Qaḥṭān.

27 [They are] moons of war rising up as if their turbans were crowns in the place of fear.

28 And on the day of the onrush into the grave I have ascertained that they desire in it that you should be exhalted even though they become abased.

29 You advanced slowly to war with them under a dust cloud the two raisers of which seemed to be ʿAlī and Hamdān,

30 Accompanied by every Zanātī whose blade and the head of him whom it reached seemed to be a fire and an offering [to God],

31 As well as [every] white Ṣinhājī spear, the head of which seemed to be a bright meteor and a devil when it rushed upon an opponent.

32 They knew well, O Mustaʿīn, that in helping you they were helpers of God.

33 And were it not for you and the white swords with which they rushed upon [the enemy], no empire would have been established on earth for Islam,

34 And the ringing of bells in broad daylight would never have been exchanged for the minaret, while crosses would have arisen in the mihrabs.

35 It was they who heard your calling when you called them, and it was they who looked when [other] men were dumb and blind,

36 Being mere images of people looking at another image of which a fool or liar spoke to them.

37 So to God belongs a firm purpose the soul of which has returned to its rightful heritage after falsehood and calumny had defamed it!

38 I said: "Arise!" to those who had stumbled, as if to resurrect a people who had perished, namely them, since they had perished,

39 And the family representing Truth came to dwell in the abode that was rightfully theirs, while we are their family and brethren in God.

40 Praise be to Him who has redeemed souls so that they came to be like we were, having been like what they were.

---

29. ʿAlī was the fourth Caliph.

30. The Zanāta and Ṣinhāja were the two great tribal groupings of the Berbers.

٢٧ وأقمارُ حَرْبٍ طالِعاتٌ كأنَّما   عَمائمُهم في مَوْقِفِ الرَّوْعِ تيجانُ

٢٨ ويَوْمَ ٱقْتِحامِ الحَفْرِ أيقَنْتُ أنَّهم   يُريدونَ فيه أن تُعَزَّ ولَوْ هانُوا

٢٩ دلفتَ بِهِم للحَرْبِ تحت عَجاجةٍ   كأنَّ مُنيرَيْها عَلِيٌّ وهَمْدانُ

٣٠ بكُلِّ زَناتِيٍّ كأنَّ حُسامَهُ   وهامَةَ مَنْ لاقاهُ نارٌ وقُرْبانُ

٣١ وأبيضَ صِنْهاجٍ كأنَّ سِنانَه   شِهابٌ إذا أهْوَى لِقِرْنٍ وشَيْطانُ

٣٢ لقَدْ عَلِمُوا يا مُسْتَعِينُ بأنَّهم   لِرَبِّهِمُ لَمَّا أعانوكَ أعْوانُ

٣٣ ولَوْلاكَ والبِيضُ التي نَهَدُوا بها   لَمَا قامَ للإسْلامِ في الأَرضِ سُلْطانُ

٣٤ ولا ٱسْتُبْدِلَتْ قَرْعُ النَّواقيسِ بالضُّحَى   مَنارًا وقامَتْ بالمَحاريبِ صُلْبانُ

٣٥ وهم سَمِعُوا داعِيكَ لمَّا دَعَوْتَهم   وهم أبْصَرُوا والنّاسُ صُمٌّ وعُمْيانُ

٣٦ تَصاويرُ ناسٍ مُهْطِعينَ لِصُورةٍ   يكلِّمُهم منها سَفِيهٌ ومَيّانُ

٣٧ فللّهِ عَزْمٌ رُدَّ في الحَقِّ رُوحُه   ونَدَّ بهِ في الأَرضِ زُورٌ وبُهْتانُ

٣٨ وقُلْتُ لَعًا لِلْعاثِرينَ كَأنَّه   نُشُورٌ لِقَوْمٍ حانَ منهم وقَدْ حانُوا

٣٩ وأصْبَحَ أهْلُ الحَقِّ في دارِ حَقِّهم   ونَحْنُ لهم في اللّهِ أهلٌ وإخْوانُ

٤٠ فَحَمْدًا لِمَنْ رَدَّ النُّفوسَ فأصْبَحَتْ   لهم كالذى كُنّا وهُمْ كالذى كانُوا

---

32. Note the pun on Mustaᶜīn, 'asker of help [from God].'

41 A group disassociated by reason of its dispersal has become united, while an affectionate tribe now shows affection.

42 Stubbornness of error was made inoffensive, and a heart burning with zeal was cooled,

43 Since Joseph's brothers were saved from reproach while pardon and forgiveness caused them to attain to God,

44 And the sons of Qaila brought about during the war, a purity and mercy in which lies safety and belief.

45 Bakr and Taghlib yearned for the call of peace, while ʿAbs and Dhubyān joined their blood kindred to one another;

46 The divining arrows of Jupiter obtained good fortune for them since Mars gave peace and Saturn, contentment;

47 Well-doing was acknowledged and immorality was disowned, since injustice and oppression have flown off with the legendary bird of misfortune;

48 The sword of iniquity was sheathed from us since fetters and manacles, jail and jailer were forgiven;

49 Nor was the living clad by us in a garment of humility, so that he should so rise up from among those contained in a grave and in shrouds;

50 Strength was granted to those considered weak, the promises made to apportion power were fulfilled, and power gave information

51 Concerning the good fortune of the victorious, merciful Imam; whose inner and outer [natures] were sincerely favorable to Islam;

52 One unsheathing the sword of vengeance against him who revolted against his inviolate [rights], the latter being [a fellow] in whom there is religious backsliding and dissembling.

53 For him who would rather live let there be "hearing and obeying," and for him who envies the dead let there be unbelief and rebellion.

---

44. The Banū Qaila were the Arab tribes of Aus and Khazraj, so named after Qaila bint Kāhil, their common ancestress.

45. A reference to pre-Islamic tribal wars. The tribes of Bakr and Taghlib

٤١ وَأُنسَ شَمْلٌ بالتَّفَرُّقِ موحِشٌ وحَنَّ خَليطٌ بالصَّبابةِ حَنَّانُ
٤٢ ورُدَّ جماحُ الغيِّ مِن غَرْبِ شأْوِه وبُرِّدَ قَلْبٌ بالحَفيظةِ حَرَّانُ
٤٣ وقد أَمِنَ التَّثْريبَ إخْوَةُ يُوسُفٍ وأَدْرَكَهم لله عَفْوٌ وغُفْرانُ
٤٤ وأَعْقَبَ طُولَ الحَرْبِ أَبْناءُ قَيْلَةٍ زَكاةً ورحْمى فيه أَمْنٌ وإيمانُ
٤٥ وجَنَّتْ لِداعي الصُّلحِ بَكْرٌ وتَغْلِبٌ وشَفَّعَتِ الأَرْحَامَ عَبْسٌ وذُبْيانُ
٤٦ وفازَتْ قِداحُ المُشْتَرى بسُعُودِها وسَالَمَ بَهْرامٌ وأَعْتَبَ كِيوَانُ
٤٧ وعُرِّفَ مَعْروفٌ وأُنْكِرَ مُنْكَرٌ وطارَ مع العَنْقاء ظُلْمٌ وعُدْوانُ
٤٨ وأُغْمِدَ سَيْفُ البَغْي عنَّا وعُطِّلَتْ قيودٌ وأَغْلالٌ وسِجْنٌ وسُجَّانُ
٤٩ وما كان منَّا الحَيُّ في نَوْبِ ذُلَّةٍ فأَنْهَضَ مِمَّنْ ضَمَّ قَبْرٌ وأَكْفانُ
٥٠ ومَنَّ على المُسْتَضْعَفِين وأُنْجِزَتْ مَواعيدُ تَمْكينٍ وآذن إمْكانُ
٥١ بِيُمْنِ الإمامِ الظافِرِ الغافِرِ الذى صَفَا منه للإسْلامِ سِرٌّ وإعْلانُ
٥٢ مُجرِّدِ سَيْفِ الانْتقامِ لِمَنْ عَتَا حماهُ به في الدِّينِ زيغٌ وإدْهانُ
٥٣ فَمَنْ سَرَّه المَحْيا فسَمْعٌ وطاعةٌ ومَنْ يَحْسدُ المَوْتَى فكُفْرٌ وعِصْيانُ

---

fought the war of Basūs, while the ʿAbs and the Dhubyān fought the war of Dāhis and Ghabrāʾ (R. A. Nicholson, *A Literary History of the Arabs* [Cambridge, 1962] pp. 55–62).

4 ash-Sharīf aṭ-Ṭalīq

1 A branch which sways on a rounded sand dune, and from which my heart gathers [a harvest of] fire,

2 [Is such that] beauty causes a never-waning moon to arise from his face.

3 He charms [us] with the intensely white and black eyes of a white antelope whose glance is an arrow notched [to be aimed] at my heart;

4 He smiles from a necklace of pearls, so that I thought he wrested it from [our] necks [to adorn] his gums.

5 The *lām* described by the hair of his temples flowed down over his cheek as gold flows over silver plate.

6 Thus beauty reached its maximum proportions in him, [for] a branch becomes beautiful only when it has borne leaves.

7 His waist is so slender that I thought, from the degree of its thinness, that it was madly in love.

8 It is as though the hips had caught [the waist] in love's snares so that [the latter] had become troubled and anxious over [the former].

9 Being thin from emaciation it came along and attacked [the hips] which were in a state of ample luxury, like my beloved when she tarries in my embrace,

10 While it is wondrous indeed, if they both resemble us, that they have not begun to part and that they have not both been separated.

. . . .

11 Many a cup which dressed the wing of gloom with a tunic of light which shone from its flash,

---

4. Sources: Main text in Ibn al-Abbār, *apud* R. Dozy, *Notices sur quelques manuscrits arabes* (Leiden, 1847–1851) pp. 116–118; scattered lines in al-Maqqarī, *Analectes sur l'histoire et la littérature des arabes d'Espagne* ed. R. Dozy, G. Dugat, L. Krehl, W. Wright (Leiden, 1855 1861), II, 398; Ḥimyarī, *Kitāb al Badīᶜ fi waṣf ar-rabīᶜ*, ed. Henri Pérès, *Publications de l'Institut des Hautes Études Marocaines*, VIII (Rabat, 1940), 33–34; Ḍabbī, *Bughyat al-multamis*, ed. F. Codera and J. Ribera, Bibliotheca Arabico-Hispana, III (Madrid, 1885), p. 447; Ibn Saᶜīd al-Maghribī, *ᶜUnwān al-murqiṣāt*

٤

الشريف الطليق

١ غُصُنٌ يَهْتَزُّ فِي دِعْصٍ نَقَا   يَجْتَنِي مِنه فُؤَادِي حُرَقَا

٢ أَطْلَعَ الحُسْنُ لَنَا مِن وَجْهِهِ   قَمَرًا لَيْسَ يُرَى مُمَحَّقَا

٣ ورَقًا عن طَرْفِ رِيمٍ أَحْوَرَ   لَحْظُهُ سَهْمٌ لِقَلْبِي فُوِّقَا

٤ باسِمٌ عن عِقْدِ دُرٍّ خِلْتُهُ   سَلَبَتْهُ لِلِثَاهُ العُنُقَا

٥ سَالَ لامُ الصُّدْغِ فِي صَفْحَتِهِ   سَيَلَانَ التِّبْرِ وَافَى الوَرَقَا

٦ فَتَنَاهَى الحُسْنُ فِيهِ إِنَّمَا   يَحْسُنُ الغُصْنُ إِذَا مَا أَوْرَقَا

٧ رَقَّ مِنهُ الخَصْرُ حَتَّى خِلْتُهُ   مِن نُحُولِ شَفَّهِ قَد عَشِقَا

٨ وكَأَنَّ الرِّدْفَ قَد تَيَّمَهُ   فَغَدَا فِيهِ مُعَنًّى قَلِقَا

٩ نَاحِلًا جَا ورَمَتْهُ نَاعِمًا   كَحَبِيبِي ظَلَّ لِي مُعْتَنِقَا

١٠ عَجَبًا إِذْ أَشْبَهَانَا كَيْفَ لم   يُحْدِثَا هَجْرًا ولَم يُفْتَرَقَا

. . . .

١١ رُبَّ كَأْسٍ قد كَسَتْ جِنْحَ الدُّجَا   ثَوْبَ نُورٍ مِن سَنَاهَا أَشْرَقَا

---

wa l-muṭribāt, ed. ᶜAbd al-Qādir Maḥdād, Bibliothèque arabe-française, IV (Algiers, 1949), p. 16; Ibn Saᶜīd al-Maghribī, *Kitāb Raiyāt al-mubarrizīn: Libro de las banderas de los campeones*, ed. and trans. E. García Gómez (Madrid, 1942), p. 38. For a study and Spanish translation cf. E. García Gómez, *Cinco poetas musulmanes* (Madrid, 1945), pp. 53–75.

METER: *ramal.*

2. Lines 2 and 3 are missing from Ibn al-Abbār, but appear in Ḍabbī.

12 Did I spend the night offering to drink to a young gazelle in whose glance there was a sleepy languour the sight of my eye kept awake.

13 [The cup] hid itself from the eye until I thought that it feared from his glance what was feared [by us].

14 [Then] it shone in a certain pure [receptacle] consisting of the palm of his hand, like the sun's rays as they meet the dawn.

15 It is as though the cup, in his fingers, were a yellow narcissus rising from a silver [vase],

16 Which arose like a sun, his mouth being the West, and the hand of the shy cupbearer, the East,

17 So that when it set in his mouth, it left a [rosy] twilight on his cheek.

. . . .

18 And many a cloud sending forth rain is such that its showers are a drinking companion to the garden, for it sings and pours out drink.

19 Moreover, it is as though the earth were its jail and as though the plants were a criminal who has been imprisoned.

20 The lightning clothes [the cloud's] sides with its glittering brocade robe when it flashes,

21 And it is as though the dark thundercloud in it were a black [horse] on whom [the lightning] has cast a motley hue,

22 And as though the wind, when it blows along [that horse] starts a flock of magpies consisting of [its own substance] into flight.

23 On certain nights of which the planets wander astray, losing their way without being able to distinguish their orbits,

24 The lightning lights up its lantern for them so that the face of their gloom turns into a sunrise,

25 While the thunder softly mourns, so that the cups of the rain flow over [the garden] exuding moisture.

26 The sun rose, weaning [the garden] having wrapped it in a cloak which submerges it, consisting of its own light.

---

15. Ḥimyarī records *anmulihi* in place of *namlihi*. The former fits the meter and is therefore preferable. Furthermore, Ibn Saʿid records *shafaqu aṣbaḥa* in place of *ṣufratu n-narjisi*, though the sense requires the latter.

١٢ بِتُّ أَسْقِيها رَشًا في طَرْفِهِ   سِنَةٌ تُورَثُ عَيْنِي أَرَقَا

١٣ خَفِيَتْ لِلْعَيْنِ حتى خِلْتُها   تَتَّقِي مِن لَحْظِهِ ما يُتَّقَا

١٤ أَشْرَقَتْ فى نَاصِعٍ مِن كَفِّهِ   كَشُعَاعِ الشَّمْسِ لاَقَا الفَلَقَا

١٥ وكأَنَّ الكَأْسَ في أَنْمُلِهِ   صُفْرَةُ النَّرْجِسِ تَعْلُو الوَرَقَا

١٦ أَصْبَحَتْ شَمْسًا وَفُوهُ مَغْرِبًا   ويَدُ السَاقِى ٱلْمُحَيِّيٰ مَشْرِقَا

١٧ فإِذا ما غَرِبَتْ في فَمِهِ   تَرَكَتْ فى الخَدِّ مِنه شَفَقَا

. . . .

١٨ وغَمَامٍ هَطَلٍ شُؤْبُوبُهُ   نَادِمُ الرَّوْضِ فغَنَّى وسَقَا

١٩ فكأَنَّ الأَرْضَ مِنهُ مُطْبِقٌ   وكأَنَّ النَّصْبَ جانٍ أُطْبِقَا

٢٠ خَلَعَ البَرْقُ على أَرْجائِهِ   ثَوْبَ وَشْيٍ مِنه لَمَّا بَرَقَا

٢١ وكأَنَّ العَارِضَ الجَوْنَ بِهِ   أَدْهَمٌ خَلَى عليه بَلَقَا

٢٢ وكأَنَّ الريحَ إِذْ هَبَّتْ لَهُ   طَيَّرَتْ في الجَوِّ مِنه عَقْعَقَا

٢٣ في لَيَالٍ ضَلَّ سارِى نَجْمِها   حَائِرًا لا يَسْتَبِينُ الطُرُقَا

٢٤ أَوْقَدَ البَرْقُ لَها مِصْبَاحَهُ   فَٱنْثَنَى وَجْه دُجَاها مشرقَا

٢٥ وشَدَا الرَّعْدُ حَنِينًا فجَرَتْ   أَكْؤُسُ المُزْنِ عليه عَرَقَا

٢٦ وغَدَتْ تَجْذِبُهُ الشَّمْسُ وقد   أَلْحَفَتْهُ من سَنَاها غرقَا

---

17. This extraordinary delicate series of images was borrowed from Ibn ar-Rūmī (F. M. Pareja, *Islamología* [Madrid, 1952–1954], II, 988).

27 Thus it is as though the sun which revives [the garden's] breath were the brightness of the beloved reviving the lover burning with desire,

28 And as if the rose, covered with dew, were the cheek of the beloved sprinkled with drops of perspiration,

29 Which bursts open beside a pure yellow narcissus, that I thought was concealing a tender love for the rose,

30 Like two lovers intimately joined together, of whom the one appears [blushing] with shame while the other is [pale] with fear.

31 How lovely are they, namely certain stars of the garden that have risen to the horizon from their flowerbeds.

32 And gazed with delight from it at the morning sun [like] flower pupils which ensnare [our] pupils.

33 It is as though the rain, when it flowed generously upon [the starflowers], came to deposit drops of quicksilver on their petals.

. . . .

34 What noble youth is like me in courage and generosity, in word, in deed, and in piety?

35 My nobility is my own soul; my ornaments are my knowledge, and in the encounter my sword is my eloquence,

36 Because, for him who tries it, my tongue is a viper which no spells can avert.

37 My right hand is the good fortune of any destitute seeker after largesse; it joined a praise that had come to be scattered.

38 My grandfather is an-Nāṣir li-d-Dīn, he whose hands dispersed dispersal from him,

39 The noblest of the noble both in himself and in his ancestors when they rival with him in superiority, the loftiest in rank.

40 It is I who am the glory of the descendants of ᶜAbd ash-Shams, while by me the worn-out portion of their glory is renewed.

41 It is I who clothe in splendor the worn-out portion of their illustrious lineage with the ornaments of my resplendent poetry.

---

31. This line is missing in Ibn al-Abbār, but included in Ḥimyarī.

38. I.e., ᶜAbd ar-Raḥmān III, first Caliph of Córdoba.

٢٧ فكأنَّ الشَّمْسَ تُحْيِي نَفْسَه   غُرَّةُ المَعْشوقِ تُحْيِي الشَّيِّقا

٢٨ وكأنَّ الوَرْدَ يَعْلُوهُ النَّدَى   وَجْنَةُ المَحْبُوبِ تَنْدِى عَرَقَا

٢٩ يَتَفَقَّا عن بَهَارٍ فاقِعٍ   خِلْتُه بالوَرْدِ يطوي وَمَقَا

٣٠ كالمُحِبَّيْنِ الوَصِيلَيْنِ غَدَا   خَجِلًا هذا وهذا فَرِقَا

٣١ يَا لَهَا مِن أَنْجُمٍ في رَوْضَةٍ   قد تَرَقَّتْ من رُبَاها أُفُقَا

٣٢ ورَنَتْ منه إلى شَمْسِ الضُّحَى   حَدَقٌ لِلنَّوْرِ تُصْبِي الحَدَقَا

٣٣ وكأنَّ القَطْرَ لَمَّا جادَها   صارَ في الأَوْراقِ مِنها زِئْبَقَا

. . . .

٣٤ مَنْ فَتًى مِثْلِي لِبَأْسٍ ونَدَى   ومَقَالٍ وفِعَالٍ وتُقَى

٣٥ شَرَفِي نَفْسِي وحَلْيِي أَدَبِي   وحُسامِي مِقْوَلِي عند اللِّقَا

٣٦ ولِسانِي عند مَن يَخْبُرُهُ   أَفْعَوانٌ لَيْسَ يثنيه الرُّقَا

٣٧ ويَمِينِي يُمْنُ عافٍ مُعْسِرٍ   جمعَتْ حَمْدًا غَدَا مُفْتَرِقَا

٣٨ جَدِّيَ النَّاصِرُ لِلدِّينِ الذى   فَرَّقَتْ كَفَّاهُ عنه الفَرَقَا

٣٩ أَشْرَفُ الأَشْرافِ نَفْسًا وأَبًا   حِينَ يَعْلُوهُ وأَعْلَى مُرْتَقَا

٤٠ أَنَا فَخْرُ العَبْشَمِيِّينَ وَبِي   جَدَّ مِن فَخْرِهِمُ ما أَخْلَقَا

٤١ أَنَا أَكْسُو ما عَفَى مِنْ مَجْدِهِم   بِحُلَى رَوْنَقِ شِعْرِي رَوْنَقَا

---

40. Ancestor of the Umayyads (P. K. Hitti, *History of the Arabs* [7th ed.; London, 1961], p. 111).

5 Ibn Shuhaid

1 There is no one in the abandoned encampment to inform us of the beloved ones, so from whom will we seek information about their condition?

2 Ask none but separation for it is what removes you from them whether they go to the lowlands or to the highlands.

3 Time has done them injury so that they have dispersed in all directions while the majority of them have perished.

4 The vicissitudes of fortune have run over the places where their abodes were established as well as running over them, so that the two have decayed.

5 So call upon time to embellish their courtyards with blossoms so bright that hearts are almost lighted up [with joy] by them.

6 For the weeping of one who weeps with an eye the tears of which flow endlessly is not enough [to lament the loss of] such as Córdoba.

7 [It is] a city such that [we pray] that God may forgive its inhabitants' lapse, for they became Berberized, mingled with Moroccans, and adopted the creed of the Egyptians.

8 In every direction a group of them is scattered, perplexed by separation.

9 I was well acquainted with it when its state of affairs unified its people and life in it was green.

10 And the prevalence of its splendor shone over them [like the breath of a flower] [exuding] fragrance from which ambergris escapes.

11 And perfection had pitched its tent in that abode while it was beyond any decrease [in its splendor].

12 And its people were in safety from any reversal of its beauty so that they donned its beauties as a turban and as a veil.

13 O for their pleasant circumstances in its palaces and curtained apartments when its full moons were concealed in its palaces!

14 And the palace, being the palace of the sons of Umayya, abounded in all things, while the Caliphate was even more abundant!

15 And Madīnat az-Zāhira shone brightly with pleasure boats and al-^{c}Āmiriyya was rendered flourishing by the stars.

---

5. SOURCE: Ibn Shuhaid, *Dīwān*, ed. Charles Pellat (Beirut, 1963), pp. 64–67. METER: *kāmil.*

This poem was written during the civil wars that ruined Córdoba.

7. The reference is to the Ḥammūdid dynasty of Córdoba which was of Berber origin and Shi^{c}ite persuasion. Therefore the inhabitants adopted the

٥

ابن شهيد

١ ما في الطُّلولِ من الأَحِبَّةِ مُخْبِرُ   فَمَن الذى عن حالِها نَسْتَخْبِرُ ؟

٢ لا تَسْأَلَنَّ سِوَى الفِراقِ فإنَّه   يُنْبِيكَ عنهم آنْجَدوا أَم أَغْوَرُوا

٣ جَارَ الزَّمانُ عليهمُ فتَفَرَّقوا   في كُلِّ ناحِيَةٍ وبَادَ الأَكْثَرُ

٤ جَرَتِ الخُطوبُ على مَحَلِّ دِيارِهم   وعليهمِ فتَغَيَّرَتْ وتَغَيَّروا

٥ فَدَعِ الزَّمانَ يَصوغُ في عَرَصَاتِهم   نَوْرًا تكاد له القُلوبُ تَنَوَّرُ

٦ فَلِمِثْلِ قُرْطُبَةٍ يقلُّ بُكاءُ مَن   يَبْكِي بِعَيْنٍ دَمْعُها مُتَفَجِّرُ

٧ دَارٌ أَقالَ اللّٰهُ عثْرةَ أَهْلِها !   فَتَبَرْبَرُوا وتَغَرَّبُوا وتَمَصَّرُوا

٨ في كُلِّ ناحيةٍ فَريقٌ منهمُ   مُتَفَطِّرٌ لِفِراقِها مُتَحَيِّرُ

٩ عَهْدِي بها والشَّمْلُ فيها جامِعٌ   مِن أَهلِها والعَيْشُ فيها أَخْضَرُ

١٠ ورِياحُ زهْرَتِها تَلوحُ عليهمُ   بِرَوائحٍ يَفْتَرُّ مِنها العَنْبَرُ

١١ والدارُ قد ضَرَبَ الكَمالُ رِواقَهُ   فيها ، وباعُ النقْصِ فيها يَقْصُرُ

١٢ والقَوْمُ قد أَمِنُوا تَغَيُّرَ حُسْنِها   فتَعَمَّموا بِجَمالِها وتَأَزَّروا

١٣ يا طِيبَهم بقُصُورِها وخُدُورِها   وبُدُورُها بقُصُورِها تَتَخَدَّرُ

١٤ والقَصْرُ قَصْرُ بَنِي أُمَيَّةَ وافِرٌ   مِن كلِّ أَمْرٍ والخِلافةُ أَوْفَرُ

١٥ والزَّاهِرِيَّةُ بالمَراكِبِ تَزْهَرُ   والعَامِرِيَّةُ بالكَواكِبِ تُعْمَرُ

Shiʿite creed of the Fatimids of Egypt (Pérès, p. 123 n. 1; p. 97, v. 5).

15. Madīnat az-Zāhira was on the shores of the Guadalquivir (E. Lévi-Provençal, *España musulmana hasta la caída del califato de Córdoba* [*711–1031 de J.C.*], trans. E. García Gómez, *Historia de España*, directed by R. Menéndez Pidal [Madrid, 1950–1957], IV, 408). Al-ʿĀmiriyya was the palace of al-Manṣūr ibn Abī ʿĀmir.

16 And the Great Mosque was packed by all those who recited and studied whatsoever they wished [of the Koran] as well as [those who] looked on.

17 And the alleys of the markets bore witness that because of those who crossed them, doomsday's assembly would hold not a few.

18 O Paradise such that the wind of separation has blasted it and its people so that both have been destroyed,

19 I am afflicted by death over you, and it is my duty to be so afflicted, for we did not cease to boast of you during your life!

20 Your courtyard was, to the one making for it, a Mecca in which the fearful used to take shelter, and they were given help [therein].

21 O dwelling place on which and on whose inhabitants the bird of separation has alighted so that they have decayed and have become unknown,

22 The Euphrates and the Tigris; the Nile and Kauthar caused [their waters] to flow generously through your two shores!

23 While you were given to drink the water of life by a cloud such that your gardens flourished and blossomed by means of it!

24 My affliction is for an abode whose spring encampments I was well acquainted with when its young she-gazelles walked with a stately gait in its courtyard,

25 During the days when the eye of every respectful regard looked upon it from all directions;

26 During the days when command was one in it, possessed by its commander and by the commander of him who was invested with command;

27 During the days when the palm of every security was raised up to it in greeting and was hastening toward it.

28 My mourning is reiterated for its generous leaders, the narrators of its Traditions, its honest ones, its defenders;

29 My soul sighs for its graces, its happy life, its elegance, and its high rank;

30 My heart is torn apart for its wise and forbearing men, its men of letters and its men of taste.

---

22. Kauthar is a river of Paradise.

١٦ والجامِعُ الأَعلَى يَغصُّ بكلِّ مَن يَتْلُو ويَسْمَعُ ما يَشاءُ ويَنْظُرُ
١٧ ومَسالِكُ الأَسْواقِ تَشْهَدُ أَنَّها لا يَسْتَقِلُّ بسالِكِيها المَحْشَرُ
١٨ يا جَنَّةً عَصَفَتْ بها وبأَهْلِها رِيحُ النَّوَى فتَدَمَّرَتْ وتَدَمَّروا!
١٩ آسِي عليكِ مِن المَماتِ وحُقَّ لي إِنْ لم نَزَلْ بك في حَياتِكِ نَفْخَرُ
٢٠ كانَت عِراصُكِ لِلمُيَمِّمِ مَكَّةً يَأْوِي إِليها الخائفُونَ فَيُنْصَرُوا
٢١ يا مَنْزِلاً نَزَلَتْ بِهِ وبأَهْلِهِ طَيْرُ النَّوَى فتَغَيَّروا وتَنَكَّروا!
٢٢ جادَ الفُراتُ بساحَتَيْك ودِجْلَةٌ والنِّيلُ جادَ بها وجادَ الكَوْثَرُ
٢٣ وسُقِيتَ مِن مَاءِ الحَياةِ غَمامةً تَحيا بها منك الرِّياضُ وتزهَرُ
٢٤ أَسَفِي على دارٍ عهدتُ رُبوعَها وظِباؤُها بفِنائِها تَتَبَخْتَرُ
٢٥ أَيّامَ كانَتْ عينُ كُلِّ كَرامَةٍ مِن كلِّ ناحيةٍ إِليها تنظرُ
٢٦ أَيّامَ كان الأَمْرُ فيها واحِدًا لِأَميرِها وأَميرِ مَن يَتَأَمَّرُ
٢٧ أَيّامَ كانَتْ كَفُّ كُلِّ سَلامةٍ تَسْمُو إِليها بالسَّلامِ وتبدُرُ
٢٨ حُزْنِي على سَرَواتِها وَرُواتِها وَنِقاتِها وَحُماتِها يَتَكَرَّرُ
٢٩ نَفْسِي على آلائِها وصَفائِها وبَهائِها وسَنائِها تَتَحَسَّرُ
٣٠ كَبِدِي على عُلَمائِها حُلَمائِها أُدَبائِها ظُرَفائِها تَتَفَطَّرُ

6 Ibn Shuhaid

1 I observe certain eyes gazing steadily at me as if speckled snakes [issuing from them] were attacking me from both sides.

2 I turn around, yet all I encounter is [another] assailant, and I run forward, yet I meet no man who may be reconciled to me.

3 And my mind grasps different sorts of harm directed at me for the most miserable of men is the one who is learned in the province of the ignorant,

4 While the longest suffering of those endowed with intelligence, oppressed by a reversal of fortune, is a young hero of Arab descent disparaged by non-Arabs!

5 You can manage without [superior] humans, according to your claim. Well, minds making such [false] claims are indeed foolish;

6 For, can the falcon rush upon its prey in the late forenoon, if the fore feathers are missing from the feathers of its wings?

7 A farewell said to you is not the leave-taking of a grateful man, but rather it is a bone with which gullets are obstructed.

8 Nor have my teeth been gnashed in regret [at parting] from you, though a certain regretful one may well be on the eve of gnashing his teeth.

9 Keep my house and tear it down column by column, for on earth there are [other] builders and columns for me.

10 Indeed, if the worst of factions has expelled me from you, well, on earth there are brethren who will treat me generously.

11 And if the Umayyads have crushed what is my due right from them, then a Hāshimite crusher has now trodden on the surface of the main highway.

12 And it is no wonder that those peaked caps are nearby, when the turbans have recognized my due rights in this place,

13 And when the secret of our sorrow that hearts conceal was disclosed to those who nurture a secret hatred for us, by means of [our] tears.

---

6. SOURCE: Ibn Shuhaid, *Dīwān*, ed. Charles Pellat (Beirut, 1963), pp. 138–140. METER: *ṭawīl*.

This poem was written when the poet fled from Córdoba to join the party of the Ḥammūdids in Málaga.

5. The "superior humans" are the Arabs, in contrast with whom the non-Arabs are considered by the poet to be a subhuman species.

٦

ابن شهيد

١ أَرَى أَعْيُنًا تَرْنُو إِليَّ كأَنَّما   تُساوِرُ مِنهما جانِبَيَّ أَراقِمُ

٢ أَدورُ فلا أَعْتَامُ غَيْرَ مُحارِبٍ   وأَسْعَى فلا أَلقَى آمْرءًا لي يُسالِمُ

٣ ويجلبُ لي فَهْمِي ضُروبًا مِن الأَذَى   وأَشْقَى آمْرِئٍ في قَرْيةِ الجَهْلِ عالِمُ

٤ وأَوجَعُ مَظْلومٍ لقَلْبٍ وذى حِجًى   فَتًى عَرَبيٌّ تَزْدَرِيهِ أَعاجِمُ

٥ غَنِيتُمْ على ما تَزْعُمُونَ عن الوَرَى   لقد سَفِهَتْ تلك الحُلُومُ الزَّواعِمُ

٦ وهل يُقْدِمُ البَازي على الطَّيْرِ في الضُّحَى   إذا زالَ عن رِيشِ الجِناحِ القَوادِمُ ؟

٧ سَلامٌ عليكم لا تحيَّةَ شاكِرٍ   ولَكِنْ شَجًى تَنْسَدُّ مِنه الحَلاقِمُ

٨ وما قُرِعَتْ سِنِّي عليكم نَدامةً   وأَوشِكْ غدًا أَن يَقْرَعَ السِّنَّ نادِمُ

٩ عليكمْ بِدارِي فآهْدِمُوها دَعائِمًا   فَفي الأَرْضِ بَنَّاؤُونَ لي ودَعائِمُ

١٠ لَئِنْ أَخْرَجَتْنِي عنكُمُ شَرُّ عُصْبَةٍ   فَفي الأَرْضِ إِخْوانٌ عليَّ أَكارِمُ

١١ وإِن هَشَمَتْ حَقِّي أُمَيَّةُ عندها   فهاتا على ظَهْرِ المَحَجَّةِ هاشِمُ

١٢ ولا غَرْوَ مِن تلك القَلانِسِ جانِبًا   إذا عَرفَتْ حَقِّي هُناك العَمائِمُ

١٣ ولَمَّا فَشَا بالدَّمْعِ مِن سِرِّ وَجْدِنا   إلى كاشِحِينا ما القُلوبُ كَواتِمُ

---

11. The Ḥammūdids were an ᶜAlid dynasty descended from the Idrīsids of Morocco. They were therefore Hāshimites. The reference is to Yaḥya ibn ᶜAlī ibn Ḥammūd, al-Muᶜtalī of Málaga, who is called a "crusher" (*hāshim*).

12. The *qalansuwa* was a tall peaked cap worn in Abbasid times; here it denotes the *fuqahā᾽* at the service of the Ḥammūdids, whereas "turbans," the crowns of the Arabs, refer to the Umayyads of Córdoba.

14 We ordered our eyelids to hold back the tears so that the severe censor and the blamer might be choked by what was in them.
15 Thus the tears of the eye remained perplexed as if around our tear ducts they were clusters of pearls.
16 Our tears refused to flow [any longer] from fear of one who might rejoice over our evil lot, and thus a stringer strung them together like pearls between the eyelids.
17 And our noble eyes dissipated our passion, eyes that maintained a smiling air until our mouth smiled again.

١٤ أَمَرْنا بِإِمْساكِ الدُّموعِ جُفونَنا   لِيَشْجَى بما يَطوِي عَذولٌ ولائِمُ

١٥ فظَلَّتْ دُموعُ العَيْنِ حَيْرَى كَأَنَّها   خِلالَ مآقينا لآلٍ تَوائِمُ

١٦ أَبَى دَمْعُنا يَجْري مَخافَةَ شامِتٍ   فنَظَّمَه بَيْنَ المَحاجِرِ ناظِمُ

١٧ وَرَاقَ الهوَى منّا عُيونٌ كريمةٌ   تبسَّمْنَ حتّى ما تَروقُ المَباسِمُ

7 Ibn Shuhaid

1 When I observed that life had turned away its head and I became assured beyond doubt that death would seize me

2 I desired only to dwell in a cave at the summit of a windblown, lofty peak,

3 Drawing sustenance from seeds scattered on the ground for the remainder of my life—alone—and sipping the water concealed in rocky crevices.

4 My boon companion is the man who has sought death once, for I, to say the truth, have sought it fifty times.

5 Now that the hour of my departure draws near, it is as though I had gained in the past from this world only one moment brief as a flash of lightning.

6 So who will carry a message from me to Ibn Ḥazm, for he has been a mainstay in my misfortunes and during my hours of difficulty,

7 [A message saying:] "The peace of God be upon you. I am about to die, so let [the peace of God] invoked by a beloved one on the point of death suffice you as a means of sustenance.

8 Moreover, do not forget to perform my funeral oration when you shall have been deprived of me, or to speak well of the days when I was alive and of the excellence of my character.

9 And move with [your words], by God, each time you mention me, every clever and comely youth while they are burying me.

10 Perchance my corpse will hear part of it from the grave, thanks to the trilling voice of a singer or the music-making of an instrumentalist.

11 In this way I shall take joy in being remembered after my death, so do not begrudge me [joy], thinking that it is a distraction [unworthy of] the dead.

12 And I hope God will forgive [the punishment] my sins have deserved because of what he knows of my true nature."

---

7. SOURCE: Ibn Shuhaid, *Dīwān*, ed. Charles Pellat (Beirut, 1963), pp. 110–111. METER: *ṭawīl.*

Shortly before his death, the poet wrote this poem to his close friend Ibn Ḥazm.

٧

ابن شهيد

١ وَلَمَّا رَأَيْتُ العَيْشَ وَلَّى بِرَأْسِهِ   وَأَيْقَنْتُ أَنَّ المَوْتَ لاشَكَّ لاحِقِي

٢ تَمَنَّيْتُ أَنِّي ساكِنٌ في غَيابَةٍ   بِأَعْلَى مَهَبِّ الرِّيحِ في رَأْسِ شاهِقِ

٣ أُذِرُّ سَقِيطَ الحَبِّ في فَضْلِ عِيشَةٍ   وَحِيدًا، وَأَحْسُو الماءَ ثَنْيَ المَفالِقِ

٤ خَلِيلَيَّ مَنْ رامَ المَنِيَّةَ مَرَّةً   فقد رُمْتُها خَمْسِينَ، قَوْلَةَ صادِقِ

٥ كَأَنِّي، وقد حانَ ٱرْتِحالِيَ، لم أَفُزْ   قَدِيمًا مِنَ الدُّنْيَا بِلَمْحَةِ بارِقِ

٦ فَمَنْ مُبْلِغٌ عنِّي ٱبنَ حَزْمٍ وكان لي   يَدًا في مُلِمَّاتي وعند مَضايِقِي:

٧ عليكَ سَلامُ اللهِ إنِّي مُفارِقٌ   وَحَسْبُكَ زادًا مِن حَبيبٍ مُفارِقِ

٨ فلا تَنْسَ تَأْبِينِي إذا ما فَقَدتَنِي   وَتَذْكارَ أَيَّامِي وَفَضْلَ خَلائِقِي

٩ وَحَرِّكْ له بِاللهِ مَهْمَا ذَكَرْتَنِي   إذا غَيَّبُونِي كُلَّ شَهْمٍ غُرانِقِ

١٠ عَسَى هامَتِي في القَبْرِ تَسْمَعُ بَعْضَهُ   بِتَرْجِيعِ شادٍ أَوْ بِتَطْرِيبِ طارِقِ

١١ فَلِي في ٱدِّكارِي بعد مَوْتِيَ راحَةٌ   فلا تَمْنَعُونِيها عُلالَةَ زاهِقِ

١٢ وإِنِّي لَأَرْجُو اللهَ فيما تَقَدَّمَتْ   ذُنُوبِي بِهِ مِمَّا دَرَى مِن حَقائِقِي

8 Ibn Hazm

A

1 I love you with a love that knows no waning, whereas some of men's loves are midday mirages.
2 I bear for you a pure, sincere love, and in [my] heart there is a clear picture and an inscription [declaring] my love for you.
3 Moreover, if my soul were filled by anything but you, I would pluck it out, while any membrane [covering it] would be torn away from it by [my] hands.
4 I desire from you nothing but love, and that is all I request from you.
5 If I should come to possess it, then all the earth will [seem like] a senile camel and mankind like motes of dust, while the land's inhabitants will [seem like] insects.

B

1 My love for you, which is eternal by reason of its very nature, has reached its maximum proportions, hence it can neither decrease at all, nor increase.
2 Its only cause is the will, and no one knows any cause other than that!
3 When we discover that a thing is its own cause, then it is an existence that is unperishing,
4 But when we find that [its cause] is in something other than itself, its destruction will come about when we lack that which gave it existence.

C

1 Are you from the world of the angels, or are you a mortal? Explain this to me, for inability [to reach the truth] has made a mockery of my understanding.
2 I see a human shape, yet if I use my mind, then the body is [in reality] a celestial one.

---

8. SOURCES: Ibn Ḥazm, *Ṭauq al-ḥamāma*, ed. Ibrāhīm al Abyārī (Cairo, 1959), pp. 1–2; 6–7; 10; 13; 26–27; 37–38; 60; 101; ed. L. Bercher (Algiers, 1949).
METERS: **A**, **B**, **C**, **H**, *ṭawīl;* **D**, **G**, *basīṭ;* **E**, *khafīf;* **F**, *mutaqārib.*

٨

ابن حزم

A

١ أَوَدُّكَ وُدًّا لَيْسَ فيه غَضاضةٌ ... وبَعْضُ مَوَدّاتِ الرِّجالِ سَرابُ

٢ وأَمْحَضْتُكَ النُّصْحَ الصَّريحَ وفي الحَشَى ... لِوُدِّكَ نَقْشٌ ظاهِرٌ وكِتابُ

٣ فلو كانَ في رُوحي سِواكَ اقْتَلَعْتُهُ ... ومُزِّقَ بالكَفَّيْنِ عنه إهابُ

٤ وما لِيَ غَيْرُ الوُدِّ منك إرادةٌ ... ولا في سِواهُ لي إليك خِطابُ

٥ إذا حُزْتُه فالأَرْضُ جَمْعاءُ والوَرَى ... هَباءٌ وسُكّانُ البِلادِ ذُبابُ

B

١ وِدادي لكَ الباقي على حَسْبِ كَوْنِهِ ... تَناهَى فلم يَنْقُصْ بِشَيْءٍ ولم يَزِدْ

٢ ولَيْسَتْ له غَيْرُ الإرادةِ عِلَّةٌ ... ولا سَبَبٌ حاشاهُ يعلمه أَحَدْ

٣ إذا ما وَجَدْنا الشَّيْءَ عِلَّةَ نَفْسِهِ ... فذاكَ وُجودٌ لَيْسَ يَفْنى على الأَبَدْ

٤ وإمّا وَجَدْناهُ لِشَيْءٍ خِلافِه ... فإِعْدامُه في عُدْمِنا ما له وَجَدْ

C

١ أَمِنْ عالَمِ الأَمْلاكِ أَنْتَ أَمِ آنْسِيٌّ ... أَبِنْ لِي فَقَدْ أَزْرَى بِتَمْييزِيَ العِيُّ

٢ أَرَى هيئةً إنْسِيَّةً غَيْرَ أَنَّهُ ... إذا أُعْمِلَ التَّفْكيرَ فالجِرْمُ عُلْوِيٌّ

A. 1. "Midday mirages" flatten out objects in contrast with morning mirages which raise them vertically.

3. The original text reads *hawā-ka*, but *siwā-ka* has been proposed as a better reading.

3 Blessed be He who arranged the manner of being of His creation in such a way that you should be the [only] beautiful, natural light [in it].

4 I have no doubt but that you are that spirit which a resemblance joining one soul to another in close relationship has directed toward us.

5 We lacked any proof that would bear witness to your creation, which we could use in comparison, save only that you are visible.

6 Were it not that our eye contemplates [your] essence we could only declare that you are the Sublime, True Reason.

D

1 I enjoy conversation when, in it, he is mentioned to me and exhales a [scent] of sweet ambergris for me.

2 If he should speak, among those who sit in my company, I listen only to the words of that marvelous charmer.

3 Even if the Prince of the Faithful should be with me, I would not turn aside from [my love] for the former.

4 If I am compelled to leave him, I look back [at him] constantly and walk like [an animal] wounded in the hoof.

5 My eyes remain fixed firmly upon him though my body has departed, as the drowning man looks at the shore from the fathomless sea.

6 If I recall my distance from him, I choke as though with water, like the man who yawns in the midst of a dust storm and the sun's noonday heat.

7 And if you say: "It is possible to reach the sky," I reply: "Yes, and I know where the stairs may be found."

E

1 He who claims to love two lyingly commits perjury, just as Mānī is belied by his principles.

2 In the heart there is no room for two beloveds, nor is the most recent of things always the second.

3 Just as reason is one, not recognizing any creator other than the One, the Clement,

4 Likewise the heart is one and loves only one, though he should put you off or draw you to him.

E. 1. Mānī was the founder of Manichaeism, the dualist Persian heresy.

٣ تَبَارَكَ مَن سَوَّى مَذَاهِبَ خَلْقِهِ   على أَنَّكَ النُّورُ الأَنِيقُ الطَّبِيعِيُّ

٤ ولا شَكَّ عندي أَنَّكَ الرُّوحُ ساقَهُ   إِلَينا مِثالٌ في النُّفُوسِ اتِّصالِيُّ

٥ عَدِمْنَا دَلِيلًا في حُدُوثِكَ شاهِدًا   نَقِيسُ عَلَيْهِ غَيْرَ أَنَّكَ مَرْئِيُّ

٦ ولولا وُقوعُ العَيْنِ في الكَوْنِ لم نَقُلْ   سِوَى أَنَّكَ العَقْلُ الرَّفِيعُ الحَقِيقِيُّ

D

١ أَهْوَى الحَدِيثَ إِذا ما كانَ يُذْكَرُ لِي   فِيهِ ويَعْبَقُ لِي عَن عَنْبَرٍ أَرَجِ

٢ إِنْ قالَ لم أَسْتَمِعْ مِمَّنْ يُجالِسُنِي   إِلَّا سِوَى لَفْظَةِ المُسْتَطْرِفِ الغَنِجِ

٣ ولو يَكُونَ أَمِيرَ المُؤْمِنِينَ مَعِي   ما كُنْتُ مِن أَجْلِهِ عَنْهُ بِمُنْعَرِجِ

٤ فَإِنْ أَقُمْ عَنْهُ مُضْطَرًّا فَإِنِّي لا   أَزالُ مُلْتَفِتًا والمَشْيُ مَشْيُ وَجِي

٥ عَيْنَايَ فِيهِ وجِسْمِي عَنْهُ مُرْتَحِلٌ   مِثْلَ ارْتِقابِ الغَرِيقِ البَرَّ في اللُّجَجِ

٦ أَغَصُّ بالماءِ إِن أَذْكُرْ تَباعُدَهُ   كَمَنْ تَناءَبَ وَسْطَ النَّقْعِ والوَهَجِ

٧ وإِنْ تَقُلْ مُمْكِنٌ قَصْدُ السَّماءِ أَقُلْ   نَعَمْ وإِنِّي لَأَدْرِي مَوْضِعَ الدَّرَجِ

E

١ كَذَبَ المُدَّعِي هَوَى اثْنَيْنِ حَتْمًا   مِثْلَ ما في الأُصُولِ أَكْذَبَ مانِي

٢ لَيْسَ في القَلْبِ مَوْضِعٌ لِحَبِيبَيْنِ   ولا أَحْدَثُ الأُمُورِ بِثانِي

٣ فَكَمَا العَقْلُ واحِدٌ لَيْسَ يَدْرِي   خالِقًا غَيْرَ واحِدٍ رَحْمانِ

٤ فَكَذا القَلْبُ واحِدٌ لَيْسَ يَهْوَى   غَيْرَ فَرْدٍ مُباعِدٍ أَوْ مُدانِ

5 [He who claims to love two] is a suspect in the law of love; [he is] far from the true faith.

6 Likewise, religion is one and straight, while he who has two religions is a profound disbeliever.

F

1 Men have observed that I am a youth driven desperate by love; that I am brokenhearted, profoundly disturbed. And yet, by whom?

2 When they look at my condition they become certain [of it], yet if they inquire into the matter they are left in doubt.

3 [I am] like a handwriting whose trace is clear, but which, if they seek to interpret it, cannot be explained;

4 [I am] like the sound of a dove over a woody copse, cooing with its voice in every way,

5 Our ears delight in its melody, while its meaning remains obscure and unexplained.

6 They say: "By God, name the one whose love has driven sweet sleep from you!"

7 Yet I will never [name him]! Before they obtain what they seek, I will lose all my wits and face all misfortunes.

8 Thus will they ever remain prey to doubts, entertaining suspicion like certitude and certitude like suspicion.

G

1 Having seen the hoariness on my temples and sideburns, someone asked me how old I was.

2 I answered him: "I consider all my life to have been but a short moment and nothing else, when I think reasonably and exactly."

3 He replied to me: "How was that? Explain it to me, for you have given me the most grievous news and information."

4 So I said: "To the [girl] possessed of my heart I once gave one single kiss by surprise.

5 Hence, no matter how many years I live, I will not really consider any but that brief moment to have been my life."

٥ هو فى شِرْعةِ المَوَدَّةِ ذو شَكٍّ — بَعيدٌ مِن صِحَّةِ الإيمانِ
٦ وكذا الدِّينُ واحِدٌ مُسْتَقِيمٌ — وكَفُورٌ مَن عندَهُ دِينانِ

F

١ دَرَى النّاسُ أنّى فَتًى عاشِقٌ — كَئيبٌ مُعَنًّى، ولَكِنْ بِمَنْ
٢ إذا عايَنُوا حالتِى أيْقَنُوا — وإنْ فَتَّشُوا رَجَعُوا فى الظَّنَنْ
٣ كَخَطٍّ يُرَى رَسْمُهُ ظاهِرًا — وإنْ طَلَبُوا شَرْحَهُ لم يُبَنْ
٤ كَصَوتِ حَمامٍ على أيْكةٍ — يُرَجِّعُ بالصوتِ في كُلِّ فَنّ
٥ تَلَذُّ بفَحْواهُ أسْماعُنا — ومَعْناهُ مُسْتَعْجِمٌ لم يَبِنْ
٦ يَقولونَ باللّهِ سَمِّ الذى — نَفَى حُبُّهُ عنك طِيبَ الوَسَنْ
٧ وَهَيْهاتِ دونَ الذى حاوَلوا — ذَهابُ العُقُولِ وخوضُ الفِتَنْ
٨ فهم أبَدًا فى آخْتِلاجِ الشُّكوكِ — بظَنٍّ كَقَطْعٍ وقَطْعٍ كَظَنْ

G

١ وسائِلٍ لِىَ عَمّا لى مِن العُمْرِ — وقد رَأى الشَّيْبَ في الفَوْدَيْنِ والعُذُرِ
٢ أجبتُه ساعةً لا شيءَ أحْسِبُه — عُمْرًا سِواها بحُكْمِ العَقْلِ والنَّظَرِ
٣ فقالَ لى كَيْفَ ذا بَيِّنْهُ لى فَلَقَدْ — أخْبَرْتَنِى أشْنَعَ الأنباءِ والخَبَرِ
٤ فقُلْتُ إنَّ التى قَلْبِى بها عَلِقٌ — قَبَّلْتُها قُبْلَةً يَوْمًا على خَطَرِ
٥ فما أعُدُّ ولو طالَتْ سِنِّى سِوَى — تلك السُّوَيْعَةِ بالتَّحْقيقِ مِن عُمُرِى

H

1 They said: "He is far away." I replied: "It is enough for me that he is with me in the same age without being able to escape.
2 The sun passes over me just as it does over him every day that shines anew.
3 Furthermore, is one between whom and me there lies only the distance of a day's journey really far away,
4 When the wisdom of the God of creation joined us together? This mutual proximity is enough [for me]; I want nothing further."

H

١ وقالوا بَعِيدٌ قُلْتُ حَسْبِى بأَنَّهُ   مَعِى فى زَمانٍ لا يُطيقُ مَحِيدَا

٢ تَمُرُّ علىَّ الشَّمْسُ مِثْلَ مُرورِها   به كُلَّ يَومٍ يَسْتَنِيرُ جَديدَا

٣ فَمَنْ لَيْسَ بينِى فى المَسيرِ وبينَهُ   سِوَى قَطْعِ يومٍ هل يكونُ بَعيدَا

٤ وعِلْمُ إلٰهِ الخَلْقِ يَجْمَعُنا معًا   كَفَى ذا التَّدانِى ما أُرِيدُ مَزيدَا

9 Ibn Zaidūn

1 The morning hour of mutual separation has replaced that of mutual proximity and the moment of our mutual separation from the sweetness of our proximity has come.

2 Alas! While the morning of separation had drawn near, death greeted us at dawn so that the announcer of our death has stirred us because of death.

3 Who will be the bearer of a sorrow to those dressed in a robe of grief, a sorrow not worn out with time though it wears us out?

4 [Who will be the bearer of the message] that destiny, which had not ceased evoking our laughter in social enjoyment of their nearness, has now reverted to making us weep?

5 The enemies were angry by reason of the [cup of] love we were offered by one another [to drink] and they called [down upon us a curse] that we should choke, whereupon destiny said: "So be it!"

6 Thus was loosened what had been compacted by our souls and there was cut off that which had been joined by our hands.

7 Although we used to be such that our parting was never feared, but today we are such that we have no hope for our mutual encounter.

8 O would that I knew, seeing that we have not satisfied your enemies, whether our enemies have obtained any measure of satisfaction [from you].

9 We have believed firmly in nothing after you [have left] save in adopting faithfulness to you as our attitude, and other than it we have not embraced any religion.

10 It is no deserving of ours that you cool the eyes of one envious of us, or that you give pleasure to him who is hateful to us.

11 We used to observe despair whose obstacles would bring consolation to us; now indeed we are in despair, and yet why does despair make the heart grow fonder?

12 You have departed and we have departed but our ribs have never been restored to health because of yearning for you; nor have our tear ducts ever been dried up.

---

9. SOURCES: Ibn Zaidūn, *Dīwān*, ed. ᶜAlī ᶜAbd al-ᶜAẓīm (Cairo, 1957), pp. 141–148; ed. Karam al-Bustānī (Beirut, 1960), pp. 9–13.

METER: *basīṭ*.

One of the most famous of Hispano-Arabic poems, the Nūnīyya, or poem rhymed in Nūn, was sent by the poet to his beloved Wallāda, the daughter of

٩

ابن زيدون

١ أَضْحَى التَّنائِي بَدِيلاً مِنْ تَدانِينا ،   وَنابَ عَنْ طِيبِ لُقْيانا تَجافِينا

٢ أَلا ! وَقَدْ حانَ صُبْحُ البَيْنِ، صَبَّحَنا   حَيْنٌ، فَقامَ بِنا لِلْحَيْنِ ناعِينا

٣ مَنْ مُبْلِغُ المُلْبِسِينا ، بِٱنْتِزاحِهِمُ ،   حُزْنًا ، مَعَ الدَّهْرِ لايَبْلَى ويُبْلِينا

٤ أَنَّ الزَّمانَ الذى مازالَ يُضْحِكُنا ،   أُنْسًا بِقُرْبِهِمُ ، قَدْ عادَ يُبْكِينا

٥ غِيظَ العِدا مِنْ تَساقِينا الهَوَى فَدَعَوْا   بِأَنْ نَغَصَّ ، فَقالَ الدَّهْرُ آمِينا

٦ فَٱنْحَلَّ ما كانَ مَعْقُودًا بِأَنْفُسِنا ،   وٱنْبَتَّ ما كانَ مَوْصُولاً بِأَيْدِينا

٧ وَقَدْ نَكُونُ، وما يُخْشَى تَفَرُّقُنا ،   فَاليَوْمَ نَحْنُ، وما يُرْجَى تَلاقِينا

٨ يالَيْتَ شِعْرِى، وَلَمْ نُعْتِبْ أَعادِيَكُمْ ،   هَلْ نالَ حَظًّا مِنَ العُتْبَى أَعادِينا ؟

٩ لَمْ نَعْتَقِدْ بَعْدَكُمْ إِلاَّ الوَفاءَ لَكُمْ   رَأْيًا ، ولَمْ نَتَقَلَّدْ غَيْرَهُ دِينا

١٠ ما حَقُّنا أَنْ تُقِرُّوا عَيْنَ ذِى حَسَدٍ   بِنا ، وَلا أَنْ تَسُرُّوا كاشِحًا فِينا

١١ كُنَّا نَرَى اليَأْسَ تُسْلِينا عَوارِضُهُ ،   وَقَدْ يَئِسْنا فَما لِلْيَأْسِ يُغْرِينا

١٢ بِنْتُمْ وَبِنَّا ، فَما ٱبْتَلَّتْ جَوانِحُنا   شَوْقًا إِلَيْكُمْ ، وَلا جَفَّتْ مَآقِينا

---

al-Mustakfī (r. 1024–1025), after she had broken with him and he was forced to flee from Córdoba.

1. Note the repeated use of the sixth verbal form and the pronoun *nā* to suggest mutualness of feeling.

9. *Na*

13 When our intimate thoughts speak secretly in your ear we are nearly destroyed by sorrow, were it not that we constrain ourselves to patience.

14 Our days have been transformed by your absence so that they have become black-morned whereas with you our nights were white

15 When the side of life was joyous by reason of our friendship and the springtime habitation of joy was pure by our mutual purity [of friendship],

16 And when we bent the branches of [the tree of] love union offering their fruits, and then we plucked of them what pleased us.

17 May your days of friendship be given to drink of the gentle spring showers of joy, for you have been to our souls nothing save sweet-scented plants.

18 Do not think your distance from us will change us even though it has often happened that distance has changed those who love.

19 By God, our desires have not sought any substitute for you, and our hopes have not been turned aside from you.

20 O night traveling ray of lightning! Go to the palace in the morning and give to drink in it to one who gave us to drink of the pure drink of affection and love,

21 And ask therein whether frequent thoughts of us have distressed a friend, frequent thoughts of whom have come to disquiet us.

22 And O gentle Zephyr of the East, carry our greetings to the one who from a distance would restore our life if he were to greet us;

23 One who is never seen deciding to grant us assistance on his part, even though our demand for help be not made in error.

24 One who is fostered in royalty, as if God had created him of musk, whereas He decreed the creation of common men out of clay,

---

14. Because the faces of beautiful women are likened to full moons in Arabic poetry, it is implied that the poet's nights were white because they were illumined by the full moon of Wallāda's face.

17. *Rayaḥīn* may also mean "bounties."

١٣ نَكَادُ، حِينَ تُنَاجِيكُمْ ضَمَائِرُنَا،   يَقْضِي عَلَيْنَا الأَسَى لَوْلَا تَأَسِّينَا

١٤ حَالَتْ لِفَقْدِكُمُ أَيَّامُنَا، فَغَدَتْ   سُودًا، وَكَانَتْ بِكُمْ بِيضًا لَيَالِينَا

١٥ إِذْ جَانِبُ الْعَيْشِ طَلْقٌ مِنْ تَأَلُّفِنَا،   وَمَرْبَعُ اللَّهْوِ صَافٍ مِنْ تَصَافِينَا

١٦ وَإِذْ هَصَرْنَا فُنُونَ الْوَصْلِ دَانِيَةً   قِطَافُهَا، فَجَنَيْنَا مِنْهُ مَا شِينَا

١٧ لِيُسْقَ عَهْدُكُمُ عَهْدُ السُّرُورِ فَمَا   كُنْتُمْ لِأَرْوَاحِنَا إِلَّا رَيَاحِينَا

١٨ لَا تَحْسَبُوا نَأْيَكُمْ عَنَّا يُغَيِّرُنَا،   أَنْ طَالَمَا غَيَّرَ النَّأْيُ الْمُحِبِّينَا!

١٩ وَاللّٰهِ مَا طَلَبَتْ أَهْوَاؤُنَا بَدَلًا   مِنْكُمْ، وَلَا انْصَرَفَتْ عَنْكُمْ أَمَانِينَا

٢٠ يَا سَارِيَ الْبَرْقِ غَادِ الْقَصْرَ وَاسْقِ بِهِ   مَنْ كَانَ صِرْفَ الْهَوَى وَالْوُدِّ يَسْقِينَا

٢١ وَاسْأَلْ هُنَالِكَ: هَلْ عَنَّى تَذَكُّرُنَا   إِلْفًا، تَذَكُّرُهُ أَمْسَى يُعَنِّينَا؟

٢٢ وَيَا نَسِيمَ الصَّبَا بَلِّغْ تَحِيَّتَنَا   مَنْ لَوْ على الْبُعْدِ حَيًّا كَانَ يُحْيِينَا

٢٣ مَنْ لَا يُرَى الدَّهْرَ يَقْضِينَا مُسَاعَفَةً   مِنْهُ، وَإِنْ لَمْ يَكُنْ غَيًّا تَقَاضِينَا

٢٤ رَبِيبُ مُلْكٍ، كَأَنَّ اللّٰهَ أَنْشَأَهُ   مِسْكًا، وَقَدَّرَ إِنْشَاءَ الْوَرَى طِينَا

---

23. The editions of the *Dīwān* read *fa-hal ʾarā d-dahra* which makes little sense. The only likely reading is provided by al-Maqqarī, *Naḥf aṭ-ṭib: man lā yurā d-dahra*. The Arabic editions also prefer *ghibban* to the variant *ghaiyan*. The former would mean "on alternate days" rather than "in error."

25 Or as if He had fashioned him of silver unalloyed, and had crowned him with a crown of gleaming native gold [hair] in uniqueness of creation and embellishment of beauty.

26 When he bends over, the pearls of the necklace weigh him down by reason of his having been brought up in luxury, and the ankle rings make him bleed because of the tenderness of his skin.

27 The sun has been to him like a tender nurse in shading him and yet he has not shown himself in his splendor, to the sun, save for short moments.

28 It is as if the shining stars had been fixed upon the ball of his cheeks as an amulet against evil and as an ornament.

29 It has not been harmful that we should not have been his equal in nobility since in love there is a compensating equality from the fact of our mutual satisfaction.

30 O garden wherein long ago our glances plucked roses which youthful passion displayed in their freshness, as well as sweetbriar!

31 And O life [of this world] which made us enjoy by reason of its brilliance, desires of all sorts, and delights of all categories!

32 And O happy days by reason of whose richness we have walked [in enjoyment] [dressed] in the adorned silken robe of favors whose skirts we trailed for a time!

33 We do not name you [in our poem] by reason of our respect and honor [for you], moreover your elevated rank makes it unnecessary [to do] so,

34 Because you are peerless and you have no associate in any quality. Therefore a [mere] description [of you] suffices us by way of clarifying and distinguishing [the matter].

35 O garden of immortality in exchange for whose lotus drink and sweet tasting Kauthar we have been given the Zaqqūm and the drink made of sweat pouring off the bodies of the damned [given them to drink].

36 It is as if we had never passed a night while the love union was our third [partner] and good fortune lowered the eyelids of our denouncer.

---

35. *Kauthar,* i.e., the river of Paradise; Zaqqūm is a tree growing in Hell and producing a bitter, skull-shaped fruit.

٢٥ أَوْ صَاغَهُ وَرِقًا مَحْضًا وَتَوَّجَهُ   مِنْ نَاصِعِ التِّبْرِ إِبْدَاعًا وَتَحْسِينَا

٢٦ إِذَا تَأَوَّدَ آدَتْهُ ، رَفَاهِيَةً ،   تُومُ العُقُودِ ، وَأَدْمَتْهُ البُرَى لِينَا

٢٧ كَانَتْ لَهُ الشَّمْسُ ظِئْرًا فِي أَكِلَّتِهِ ،   بَلْ مَا تَجَلَّى لَهَا إِلَّا أَحَايِينَا

٢٨ كَأَنَّمَا أُنْبِتَتْ ، فِي صَحْنِ وَجْنَتِهِ ،   زُهْرُ الكَوَاكِبِ تَعْوِيذًا وَتَزْيِينَا

٢٩ مَا ضَرَّ أَنْ لَمْ نَكُنْ أَكْفَاءَهُ شَرَفًا ،   وَفِي المَوَدَّةِ كَافٍ مِنْ تَكَافِينَا

٣٠ يَا رَوْضَةً طَالَمَا أَجْنَتْ لَوَاحِظَنَا   وَرْدًا ، جَلَاهُ الصِّبَا غَضًّا ، وَنِسْرِينَا

٣١ وَيَا حَيَاةً تَمَلَّيْنَا ، بِزَهْرَتِهَا ،   مُنًى ضُرُوبًا ، وَلَذَّاتٍ أَفَانِينَا

٣٢ وَيَا نَعِيمًا خَطَرْنَا ، مِنْ غَضَارَتِهِ ،   فِي وَشْيِ نُعْمَى ، سَحَبْنَا ذَيْلَهُ حِينَا

٣٣ لَسْنَا نُسَمِّيكِ إِجْلَالًا وَتَكْرِمَةً ،   وَقَدْرُكِ المُعْتَلِي عَنْ ذَاكَ يُغْنِينَا

٣٤ إِذَا انْفَرَدْتِ وَمَا شُورِكْتِ فِي صِفَةٍ ،   فَحَسْبُنَا الوَصْفُ إِيضَاحًا وَتَبْيِينَا

٣٥ يَا جَنَّةَ الخُلْدِ أُبْدِلْنَا ، بِسِدْرَتِهَا   وَالكَوْثَرِ العَذْبِ ، زَقُّومًا وَغِسْلِينَا

٣٦ كَأَنَّنَا لَمْ نَبِتْ ، وَالوَصْلُ ثَالِثُنَا ،   وَالسَّعْدُ قَدْ غَضَّ مِنْ أَجْفَانِ وَاشِينَا

37 [We were] like two secrets in the heart of the gloom which was concealing us, until the tongue of the dawn was on the point of divulging us.

38 It is not astonishing that we should recall our sorrow when the interdiction of men forbids us [to visit] him, or [that we should] abandon the patience that has forgotten us.

39 Verily, we have recited [the lesson of] despair on the day of separation, since [it is composed of] suras written down for us [by divine decree], and we have taken patience as a lesson learned by heart.

40 As for your love, we cannot compare any drink equitably with a drink of it, for when we have been given to drink of it abundantly, then we are still made to thirst all the more.

41 We have not avoided any horizon of beauty of which you are the star, by consoling ourselves for [its loss], nor did we fly from it out of hate,

42 Nor out of choice did we remove away from it, while in proximity; however, in spite of ourselves the vicissitudes [of time] have made us depart.

43 We are unhappy because of you when a bubbling wine is passed from hand to hand among us, mingled with water, and our singers sing to us.

44 Neither the glasses of wine cause to appear from our nature any sign of cheerfulness, nor do the lute-strings amuse us.

45 Observe the promise which we observe zealously, for a wellborn person is one who treats equitably, as he is treated.

46 For we have sought no companion in substitution for you, for him to make us his inalienable property, nor have we had any lover to turn us from you.

47 Even if the moon [that lights up] the darkness inclined toward us from the high point of its rising, it would not excite us, I beg your pardon for mentioning it.

48 I weep out of loyalty even if you do not generously accord me a union; yet a dream image will satisfy us and a remembrance will suffice us.

---

37. After this verse the *Qalā'id* supplies another not found in the *Dīwān*: *in kāna qad ʿazza fī d-dunyā l-liqā'u fa-fī-mauqifi l-ḥashri nalqā-kum wa yakfīnā*, "If meeting in this world should be difficult, then at least will we meet you in the place of Resurrection, and this will suffice us."

٣٧ سِرَّانِ في خَاطِرِ الظَّلْمَاءِ يَكْتُمُنَا ، حَتَّى يَكَادُ لِسَانُ الصُّبْحِ يُفْشِينَا

٣٨ لا غَرْوَ في أَنْ ذَكَرْنَا الحُزْنَ حِينَ نَهَتْ عَنْهُ النُّهَى ، وَتَرَكْنَا الصَّبْرَ نَاسِينَا

٣٩ إِنَّا قَرَأْنَا الأَسَى ، يَوْمَ النَّوَى ، سُوَرًا مَكْتُوبَةً ، وَأَخَذْنَا الصَّبْرَ تَلْقِينَا

٤٠ أَمَّا هَوَاكِ ، فَلَمْ نَعْدِلْ بِمَنْهَلِهِ شُرْبًا وَإِنْ كَانَ يُرْوِينَا فَيُظْمِينَا

٤١ لَمْ نَجْفُ أُفْقَ جَمَالٍ أَنْتِ كَوْكَبُهُ سَالِينَ عَنْهُ ، وَلَمْ نَهْجُرْهُ قَالِينَا

٤٢ وَلا ٱخْتِيَارًا تَجَنَّبْنَاهُ عَنْ كَثَبٍ ، لَكِنْ عَدَتْنَا ، على كُرْهٍ ، عَوَادِينَا

٤٣ نَأْسَى عَلَيْكِ إِذَا حُثَّتْ ، مُشَعْشَعَةً ، فِينَا الشَّمُولُ ، وَغَنَّانَا مُغَنِّينَا

٤٤ لا أَكْؤُسُ الرَّاحِ تُبْدِي مِنْ شَمَائِلِنَا سِيمَا ٱرْتِيَاحٍ ، ولا الأَوْتَارُ تُلْهِينَا

٤٥ دُومِي على العَهْدِ ، مَا دُمْنَا ، مُحَافِظَةً ، فَالحُرُّ مَنْ دَانَ إِنْصَافًا كَمَا دِينَا

٤٦ فَمَا ٱسْتَعَضْنَا خَلِيلًا مِنْكِ يَحْبِسُنَا وَلا ٱسْتَفَدْنَا حَبِيبًا عَنْكِ يَثْنِينَا

٤٧ وَلَوْ صَبَا نَحْوَنَا ، مِنْ عُلْوِ مَطْلَعِهِ ، بَدْرُ الدُّجَى لَمْ يَكُنْ حَاشَاكِ يُصْبِينَا

٤٨ أَبْكِي وَفَاءً ، وَإِنْ لَمْ تَبْذُلِي صِلَةً ، فَالطَّيْفُ يُقْنِعُنَا ، وَالذِّكْرُ يَكْفِينَا

---

47. For *ḥāshā-ki*, "I beg your pardon for mentioning it," cf. Dozy, I 293, col. 1. This usage is peculiar to Western Arabic.

49 And in your answer there will be something positive [for us] if you add to it the unasked for benefactions which you have not ceased to confer upon us.

50 Upon you, from us, may the peace of God be, as long as an ardent love for you lasts, one which we try to conceal, but which reveals us openly [to the world].

٤٩ وَفي الجَوَابِ مَتَاعٌ، إنْ شَفَعْتِ بِهِ   بِيضَ الأَيادِي، التي ما زِلْتِ تُولِينَا

٥٠ عَلَيْكِ مِنَّا سَلامُ اللهِ ما بَقِيَتْ   صَبَابَةٌ بِكِ نَخْفِيهَا، فَتُخْفِينَا

10 Ibn ᶜAmmār

1 Pass round the glass for the breeze has arisen and the stars have slackened the reins of night travel;

2 The dawn has bestowed upon us its camphor after the night has claimed back [its] ambergris;

3 And the garden is like a fair woman dressed by its flowers in a robe of many hues; decked by its dew in a necklace of pearls,

4 Or like a boy who, when he blushes, turns red because of the roses of his cheeks, while he is proud of the myrtle-like down that has grown on them.

5 [It is] a garden such that the river in it seems like a limpid wrist on a green robe,

6 While the east wind makes it ripple so that you would think that it is the sword of Ibn ᶜAbbād scattering an army.

7 ᶜAbbād, the gifts of whose hands are bright green even when the sky has donned a dull grey robe,

8 The brightest jewel of time who gives us the most valuable, priceless jewel from his wealth,

9 Is a king such that, when kings throng to a water hole and he draws near to it, they do not go down for water until he has returned from it.

10 He is cooler to [men's] hearts than drops of dew, more delightful to [their] eyelids than deepest slumber.

11 When he gives gifts he chooses among maidens, the full-breasted one; among thoroughbred steeds, the short-haired one; among swords, the jewel-studded one.

12 He strikes sparks from the flint of glory, never leaving the fire of war save to [go to] the fire that will feast his guests.

13 No creature would read better than the edges of his sword, were you to compare [the enemy's] serried ranks to lines of handwriting.

14 I became certain that I was in a paradise consisting of his court when he gave me to drink a Kauthar consisting of the water of his generosity.

---

10. SOURCES: al-Maqqarī, *Analectes*, ed. R. Dozy, G. Dugat, L. Krehl, and W. Wright (Leiden, 1855–1861), I, 434–435; Ibn Khaqān, *Qalāʾid al-iqyān* (Bulaq, 1866), pp. 96–97.

METER: *kāmil.*

The poet first gained recognition as a young man by reciting this famous panegyric before al-Muᶜtaḍid ibn ᶜAbbād of Seville.

١٠

ابن عمّار

١ أَدِرِ الزُّجاجةَ فالنَّسيمُ قدِ ٱنبرى — والنَّجمُ قد صَرَفَ العِنانَ عن السُّرى

٢ والصُّبْحُ قد أَهْدى لنا كافورَهُ — لَمّا ٱسْتَرَدَّ اللَّيلُ مِنّا العَنْبَرا

٣ والرَّوْضُ كالحَسْنا كَساهُ زَهْرُهُ — وَشْيًا وقَلَّدَهُ نَداهُ جَوْهَرا

٤ أَوْ كالغُلامِ زَها بِوَرْدِ خُدودِهِ — خَجِلًا وتاهَ بآسِهِنَّ مُعَذَّرا

٥ رَوْضٌ كأَنَّ النَّهْرَ فيهِ مِعْصَمٌ — صافٍ أطلَّ على رِداءٍ أَخْضَرا

٦ وتَهُزُّهُ ريحُ الصَّبا فَتَخالُهُ — سَيْفَ ٱبنِ عَبّادٍ يُبَدِّدُ عَسْكَرا

٧ عَبّادٌ ٱلمُخْضَرُّ نائِلُ كَفِّهِ — والجَوُّ قد لَبِسَ الرِّداءَ الأَغْبَرا

٨ عِلْقُ الزَّمانِ الأَخْطَرُ المُهْدِي لَنا — مِنْ مالِهِ العِلْقَ النفيسَ الأَخْطَرا

٩ مَلِكٌ إذا ٱزْدَحَمَ المُلوكُ بِمَوْرِدٍ — ونَحاهُ لا يَرِدونَ حتى يَصْدُرا

١٠ أَنْدى على الأَكْبادِ مِن قَطْرِ النَّدى — وأَلَذُّ في الأَجْفانِ مِن سِنَةِ الكَرى

١١ يَخْتارُ إذْ يَهَبُ الخَريدةَ كاعِبًا — والطِّرْفَ أَجْرَدَ والحُسامَ مُجَوْهَرا

١٢ قَدّاحُ زَنْدِ المَجْدِ لا يَنْفَكُّ مِن — نارِ الوَغى إلّا إلى نارِ القِرى

١٣ لا خَلْقَ أَقْرأُ مِن شِفارِ حُسامِهِ — إنْ كُنْتَ شَبَّهْتَ المَواكِبَ أَسْطُرا

١٤ أَيْقَنْتُ أنّي مِن ذَراهُ بِجَنّةٍ — لَمّا سَقاني مِن نَداهُ الكَوْثَرا

---

2. Camphor when sublimated is white; ambergris, especially of inferior quality, is black.

4. *Qalāᵓid* reads *bi-wardi riyāḍihi.*

6. I.e., al-Muᶜtaḍid ibn ᶜAbbād of Seville.

8. This line is missing from *Analectes* but included in *Qalāᵓid.*

14. Kauthar is a river of paradise.

15 And I knew for sure that my field would be fertile when I appealed in it to him, the rainbearing cloud.

16 [He is] one whom mountains cannot equal when he sits upright, whom the winds do not outstrip when he advances.

17 He is effective in affairs, penetrating them deeply like a sharp sword, whereas the upper shaft of [the enemy] spears is blunted, [their] swords glance off without effect, and [their] horses' hooves stumble on the ground,

18 And lo, his cohorts, like the stars above them, with breastplates on them are like clouds in their huge proportions;

19 Each one of them being a white [warrior] who has girded on a sharp, white [sword] or a dark one who bears a dark [lance].

20 [He is] a king whose outward appearance and whose inner nature would amaze you just as a garden is beautiful both in its apparent and in its intrinsic qualities.

21 I used to swear by the name of "excellence" until I [actually] observed it and saw it made into an image contained inside his two cloaks.

22 And I did not know the real meaning of "generosity" until I visited him and read it with [the help of] the commentary provided by [the generosity of] his hands.

23 Perfumed with praise of him, the earth diffused a fragrance such that we thought all the ground to be made of ambergris,

24 While the baldness of its hillocks was crowned with flowers so that we thought each hill to be a Caesar.

25 My hand bent down the branch of his palm's wealth and gathered from it a garden of joy, while it was in bloom.

26 All I can do is my best, or else die and receive pardon, insofar as the favor he has conferred is concerned.

27 O king who has gained possession of the upper reaches [of glory] while his gift blossomed forth by means of my praise:

28 In war, the sword is more eloquent than Ziyād's preaching, when your right hand is its pulpit.

29 You have never ceased to enrich those who humbled themselves before you in expectation of a gift, nor to destroy those who were proud and insolent,

30 Until you have come to dwell within a broad expanse which you govern, while your government has achieved in you a clearness of vision.

---

15. *Analectes* reads *asāla* for *saʾaltu.*

19. *Qalāʾid* reads *taʾabbaṭa* for *taḥammala.*

١٥ وَعَلِمْتُ حَقًّا أَنَّ رَبْعِي مُخْصِب   لَمَّا سَأَلْتُ بِهِ الغَمَامَ المُمْطِرَا
١٦ مَنْ لا تُوازِنُه الجبالُ إذا ٱحْتَبَى   من لا تُسابِقُه الرِّياحُ إذا جَرَى
١٧ ماضٍ وصَدْرُ الرُّمْحِ يكهم والظُّبَى   تنبو وأَيْدِي الخَيْلِ تعثر فى البَرَى
١٨ فإذا الكَتائِبُ كالكَواكِبِ فَوْقَهم   مِن لَامِهِم مِثْلُ السَّحابِ كَنَهْوَرَا
١٩ مِنْ كُلِّ أَبْيَضَ قد تَقَلَّدَ أَبْيَضًا   عَضْبًا وأَسْمَرَ قد تَحَمَّلَ أَسْمَرَا
٢٠ مَلِكٌ يروقك خَلْقُه أَوْ خُلْقُه   كالرَّوْضِ يَحْسُنُ مَنْظَرًا أَوْ مَخْبَرَا
٢١ أَقْسَمْتُ بِٱسْمِ الفَضْلِ حتى شِمْتُه   فَرَأَيْتُهُ فى بُرْدَتَيْهِ مُصَوَّرَا
٢٢ وجَهِلْتُ مَعْنَى الجُودِ حتى زُرْتُه   فَقَرَأْتُه في رَاحَتَيْهِ مُفَسَّرَا
٢٣ فاحَ الثَّرَى مُتَعَطِّرًا بِثَنائِه   حتى حَسِبْنا كُلَّ تُرْبٍ عَنْبَرَا
٢٤ وتَتَوَّجَتْ بالزَّهْرِ صُلْعُ هِضابِه   حتى ظَنَنَّا كُلَّ هَضْبٍ قَيْصَرَا
٢٥ هَصَرَتْ يَدِي غُصْنَ الغِنَى مِنْ كَفِّه   وجَنَتْ به رَوْضَ السُّرورِ مُنَوَّرَا
٢٦ حَسْبِي على الصُّنْعِ الذى أَوْلاهُ أَنْ   أَسْعَى بِجِدٍّ أَوْ أَمُوتَ فَأُعْذَرَا
٢٧ يَأَيُّها المَلِكُ الذى حازَ العُلَا   وحَباهُ مِنْهُ بِمِثْلِ حَمْدِى أَنْوَرَا
٢٨ السيفُ أَفْصَحُ مِن زِيادٍ خُطْبَةً   في الحَرْبِ إنْ كانَتْ يَمِينُكَ مِنْبَرَا
٢٩ ما زِلْتَ تُغْنِي مَن عَنا لَكَ راجِيًا   نَيْلًا وتُفْنِي مَن عَتا وتَجَبَّرَا
٣٠ حتى حَلَلْتَ مِنَ الرِّياسَةِ مَحْجِرًا   رَحْبًا وضَمَّتْ منك طَرْفًا أَحْوَرَا

---

25. *Qalāʾid* reads *an-nadā* for *al-ghinā*.
27. *Qalāʾid* reads *al-munā* for *al-ᶜulā*.
28. On Ziyād, cf. *EI*[1], IV, 1232–1233.

31 A people who are considered to be nothing but Jews, though they are called Berbers, have been reduced to nothing by your sword.

32 You have caused your spear to bear the fruit of the heads of their brave warriors when you saw that the branch is prized for its ability to bear fruit,

33 And you have dyed your coat of mail in the blood of their kings when you learned that beauty is dressed in red.

34 Accept [this poem] as though it were a garden visited by the East wind, and which the dew has tenderly nursed until it has blossomed forth.

35 I have adorned it with a multicolored brocade gilded with an account of you, and have perfumed it with the musk that was pungent with your praise.

36 Who can surpass me when your account is like sandalwood which I have drawn from the fire of my thought while its coals were alive?

37 Hence, if you find the breeze of my praise to be fragrant, I have found the breeze of your favor to be even more fragrant!

---

31. A reference to the Zīrid dynasty of Granada, of Berber extraction, which ruled with the aid of Jewish viziers.

٣١ شقيتْ بِسَيْفِكَ أُمَّةٌ لَمْ تَعْتَقِدْ   إلَّا اليَهُودَ وإنْ تَسَمَّتْ بَرْبَرَا

٣٢ أَنْمَرْتَ رُمْحَكَ مِنْ رُؤُوسِ كُماتِهِم   لمّا رَأَيْتَ الغُصْنَ يُعْشَقُ مُثْمِرَا

٣٣ وصَبَّغْتَ دِرْعَكَ مِن دِمَاءِ مُلوكِهِم   لَمَّا عَلِمْتَ الحُسْنَ يُلْبَسُ أَحْمَرَا

٣٤ وَإِلَيْكَهَا كالرَّوْضِ زَارَتْهُ الصَبَى   وحنى عليه الطلُّ حتى نَوَّرَا

٣٥ نَمَّقْتُها وَشْيًا بِذِكْرِكَ مُذْهَبًا   وَفَتَقْتُها مِسْكًا بِحَمْدِكَ أَذْفَرَا

٣٦ مَنْ ذَا يُنَافِحُنِي وَذِكْرُكَ صَنْدَلٌ   أَوْرَدْتُهُ مِنْ نارِ فِكْرِي مِجْمَرَا

٣٧ فَلَئِنْ وَجَدتَّ نَسِيمَ حَمْدِي عاطِرًا   فَلَقَدْ وَجَدتُّ نَسِيمَ بِرِّكَ أَعْطَرَا

---

34. This line is placed at the end in *Qalāᵓid*.
36. *Analectes* reads *mandal* for *ṣandal*, a variant form.

11 al-Muʿtamid

1 Rest your heart; let your cares not overcome you. What good will grief and apprehension do you?

2 Control your eyelids; do not satisfy them with weeping. Be patient, for before now you have shown patience in adversity.

3 If an [evil] fate has hindered [your] purpose, there is no means of averting what fate decrees.

4 If one single defeat has taken place in the [present] age, how often have you not campaigned with victory as one of your supporters?

5 If in a moment of confusion caused by sin you have committed a fault, the purity of your apology will [shine like] a moon in the darkness of [that confusion].

6 How many a deep sigh rises from the bottom of [your] heart, and [how many a] tear rolls down because of the vicissitudes of fortune!

7 Trust in God when in fear, and rely on a certain Muʿtaḍid bi-llāh who will forgive.

8 Let no misfortunes frighten you, even if time is aggressive, for it is God who repels while the person aided [by Him] prevails.

9 Be patient for you are from a tribe possessed of patience who, when any misfortune assails them, remain steadfast.

10 Who is like your tribe? Who is like the valiant hero Abū ʿAmr, your father? He is endowed with glory and just titles for boasting.

11 He is a bountiful warrior who generously gives away thousands to start off with, yet he makes light of his gifts and excuses himself.

12 He has a hand which all proud tyrants kiss; were it not for its rainlike largesse we would say it is the Stone.

13 O lion that kills horsemen by crushing their necks: do not disable me, for I am [your] fang and [your] claw.

---

11. SOURCE: al-Muʿtamid, *Dīwān*, ed. Aḥmad Badawī and Ḥāmid ʿAbd al-Majīd (Cairo, 1951), pp. 36–40.

METER: *basīṭ*.

This ode was written by al-Muʿtamid during his youth after a disastrous campaign against Bādīs ibn Ḥabbūs of Granada at Málaga in 1064. "When Ismāʿīl, the eldest son, was killed by al-Muʿtaḍid himself because of rebellion when sent at the head of troops to attack Córdoba in 455/1063, Muḥammad [i.e., al-Muʿtamid] became the heir apparent. As such he was sent with an army against Bādīs' garrison at Málaga, where the Arabs were greatly dissatisfied with the Berber rule. He took the city itself by surprise, but the Berber garrison in the *al-qaṣaba* (fortress) refused to surrender. The Berber generals in Muḥammad's

١١

المعتمد

١ سَكِّنْ فُؤادَكَ، لا تَذهبْ بِكَ الفِكَرُ ماذا يُعيدُ عليك البَثُّ والحَذَرُ

٢ وٱزْجُرْ جُفُونَكَ، لاتُرْضِ البُكاءَ لَهَا وٱصْبِرْ، فَقَدْكُنْتَ عند الخَطبِ تَصْطَبِرُ

٣ وإن يَكُنْ قَدَرٌ قد عاقَ عن وَطَرٍ فلا مَرَدَّ لِمَا يَأْتِي به القَدَرُ

٤ وإنْ تَكُنْ خَيْبَةٌ في الدَّهْرِ واحِدَةٌ فكَمْ غَزَوْتَ ومِن أَشْيَاعِكَ الظَّفَرُ

٥ إنْ كُنْتَ في حَيْرَةٍ مِن جُرْمِ مُجْتَرِمٍ فإنَّ عُذْرَكَ فى ظَلْمَائِهَا قَمَرُ

٦ كَمْ زَفْرَةٍ فى شَغَافِ القَلْبِ صاعِدَةٍ وعَبْرَةٍ من شُؤُونِ الدَّهْرِ تَنْحَدِرُ

٧ فَوِّضْ إلى اللّٰهِ فِيما أَنْتَ خائِفُهُ وَثِقْ بِمُعْتَضِدٍ باللّٰهِ، يَغْتَفِرُ

٨ ولا تَرُعكَ خُطوبٌ، إنْ عَدَا زَمَنٌ فاللّٰهُ يَدْفَعُ والمَنْصُورُ يَنْتَصِرُ

٩ وَٱصْبِرْ، فإنَّكَ مِن قَوْمٍ أُولى جَلَدٍ إذا أَصابَتْهُمُ مَكْروهَةٌ، صَبَرُوا

١٠ مَن مِثْلُ قَوْمِكَ، مَن مِثْلُ الهُمَامِ أَبِى عَمْرٍو أَبِيكَ، لَهُ مَجْدٌ وَمُفْتَخَرُ

١١ سَمَيْذَعٌ يَهَبُ الآلافَ مُبْتَدِئًا وَيَسْتَقِلُّ عَطاياهُ ويَعْتَذِرُ

١٢ لَهُ يَدٌ، كلُّ جَبَّارٍ يُقَبِّلُهَا لَوْلا نَدَاها لَقُلْنَا إنَّها الحَجَرُ

١٣ يَا ضَيْغَمًا، يَقْتُلُ الفُرْسَانَ مُفْتَرِسًا لا تُوهِنَنِّى، فإنِّى النَّابُ والظُّفُرُ

---

army reassured the easy-going prince that he could allow his soldiers to celebrate their victory by copious libations of wine, because the garrison would surrender sooner or later. In the meantime word was sent by pigeons to Granada and Bādīs dispatched a large force to Málaga, surprising the Seville troops sound asleep. The prince succeeded in escaping, but Málaga was irretrievably lost. His father ordered him to stay at a castle until he should send further dispositions. The prince, knowing his father's violence, bethought himself of soothing him by flattering verses, and thus avoiding a more severe punishment . . ." (A. R. Nykl, *Hispano-Arabic Poetry* [Baltimore, 1941], p. 137).

10. I.e., Abū [c]Amr [c]Abbād al-Mu[c]taḍid bi-llāh, father of the poet.

12. I.e., the Black Stone of the Ka[c]ba which pilgrims kiss.

14 [O] horseman whose attack brave warriors fear: preserve the slave brought up in your own household for he is a sharp, cutting [sword].

15 He is the one whose blade your right hand does not sheath until it has attained [its] desire and [its] aim has been achieved.

16 Certain misfortunes which you know well have cast me into disgrace, and because of them muddiness has ruined the watering place of my hopes.

17 Therefore [my] soul is grieved, [my] eye is moistened with tears, [my] voice is lowered in humility, and [my] glance languishes.

18 My complexion has changed though there is no disease in [my] body, and my head has grown hoary though old age has not overtaken me.

19 I am dead—all but a last remnant of life in me that is withheld because I have observed you to pardon whenever you can.

20 Your slave has committed no sin for which he is deserving of punishment, yet lo, he has called out to you to offer his apologies.

21 The blame lies with none other than a people who nourish a hidden grudge, who when they betrayed [me] were enjoying the benefit of the treaty granted by you,

22 A people whose advice is false, whose love is [really] hatred, and whose only use, when they are employed to manage an affair, is to cause harm.

23 [Visible] hatred may be detected in [their] words when they speak, while hidden rancor may be recognized in [their] glances when they gaze.

24 If, when they speak, a breath burns the heart [with distress], [that breath] is none other than a spark from the fire of hatred.

25 My lord, to the plea of a slave painfully afflicted by thirst—though cool, fresh water lies in the palms of your hands—

26 Make answer by calling out to one whose heart is in power to despair and whose pupil has been captured by sleeplessness.

27 At this moment I have been given nothing to delight in, for I have known neither cup nor string[ed instrument].

28 No froward coquetry or shy modesty has overpowered me, nor has flirtation, or the intense blackness and whiteness [of bright eyes] captivated my soul.

---

21. A reference to the Berber generals who betrayed the prince.

١٤ وفارِسًا ، تَحْذرُ الأَبْطالُ صَوْلَتَهُ   صُنْ عَبْدَكَ القِنَّ، فَهْوَ الصّارِمُ الذَّكَرُ
١٥ هو الذى لَمْ تَشِمْ يُمْناكَ صَفْحَتَهُ   إلَّا تَأَتَّى مُرَادٌ ، وٱنقَضَى وَطَرُ
١٦ قَدْ أَخْلَقَتْنِى صُروفٌ ، أَنْتَ تَعْلَمُهَا   وغالَ مَوْرِدَ آمالِى بها كَدَرُ
١٧ فالنَّفْسُ جَازِعَةٌ ، والعَيْنُ دَامِعَةٌ   والصَّوتُ مُنْخَفِضٌ ، والطَّرْفُ مُنْكَسِرُ
١٨ وَحُلْتُ لَوْنًا ، وما بالجِسْمِ مِن سَقَمٍ   وشِبْتُ رَأْسًا ، ولَمْ يَبْلُغْنِيَ الكِبَرُ
١٩ ومُتُّ إلَّا ذَماءً فِيَّ، يُمْسِكُهُ   أَنِّى عَهِدتُّكَ تَعْفُو حِينَ تَقْتَدِرُ
٢٠ لَمْ يَأْتِ عَبْدُكَ ذَنبًا يَسْتَحِقُّ بِهِ   عَتْبًا ، وَهَا هُوَ قَدْ نادَاكَ يَعْتَذِرُ
٢١ ما الذَّنْبُ إلَّا على قَوْمٍ ذَوِى دَغَلٍ   وَفَى لهم عَهْدُكَ المَعْهودُ إذْ غَدَرُوا
٢٢ قَوْمٌ نَصيحَتُهُمْ غِشٌّ ، وحُبُّهُمْ   بُغْضٌ ، وَنَفْعُهُمْ – إنْ صَرَّفُوا – ضَرَرُ
٢٣ يُمَيِّزُ البُغْضَ في الأَلْفاظِ، إنْ نَطَقُوا   وَيُعْرَفُ الحِقْدُ فى الأَلْحاظِ، إنْ نَظَرُوا
٢٤ إنْ يُحْرِقُ القَلْبَ نفثٌ مِن مَقالِهِم   فإنَّمَا ذاك مِن نارِ القِلَى شَرَرُ
٢٥ مَوْلَاىَ ، دَعْوَةَ مَمْلُوكٍ به ظَمأٌ   بَرْحٌ ، وفى راحَتَيْكَ السَّلْسَلُ الخَصِرُ
٢٦ أَجِبْ نِداءَ أَخِى قَلْبٍ تَمَلَّكَهُ   أَسًى ، وذى مُقْلَةٍ أَوْدَى بها السَّهَرُ
٢٧ لَمْ أُوتَ مِن زَمَنِي شَيْئًا أَلَذُّ بِهِ   فَلَسْتُ أَعْهِدُ ما كَأْسٌ ولا وَتَرُ
٢٨ ولا تَمَلَّكَنِي دَلٌّ ولا خَفَرٌ   ولا سَبَى خَلَدِي غُنْجٌ ، ولا حَوَرُ

29 It is your pleasure—may I never be deprived of it—that constitutes the alleviation of my soul, for that is the weapon that bows to [the decrees] of fate.

30 It is the wine from which I derive consolation, for when I am deprived of it, cares sport in my heart.

31 Yes indeed, and I have another [source of] alleviation to which I have become much attached: [namely] that of stringing kidneys together on spears, while heads are being scattered.

32 My forsaking wine is not the result of asceticism or of godliness, for by my life, youth has not abandoned my years!

33 I hasten only [to earn] your approval; hence if I fail to get it, let life make no [further] room for me.

34 Apart from the time [when I enjoyed] your sympathy, no day, during which neglect has been careless of my person, has ever cheered me up.

35 How many a decisive encounter have I not had with the enemy, encounters that cause the stream of nights to pass away though the account of them does not perish.

36 [During those nights] the reddish pallor [of dawn] came to the horizons so that they were dispersed for in no creature but them could darkness be found.

37 May you ever remain in constant possession of a firm, lofty strength such that neither imagination nor sight can attain [even] to its nether areas.

38 May a shelter consisting of your good opinion about me never cease to exist, so that I may seek refuge in it. For what a splendid shelter and refuge that is!

39 Accept a garden of thoughts the plants of which the bounty of your right hand, not dew or rain, has generously watered.

40 Within its borders I have transformed the mention of you into flowers, while each moment in it is fruitful to the gatherer.

---

39. For the usage of *ilai-ka* with the meaning of *khudh*, *cf.* W. Wright, *A Grammar of the Arabic Language* (3d ed.; Cambridge, 1951), II, 78, ¶ A.

٢٩ رِضاكَ راحةُ نَفْسِي لا فُجِعْتُ بهِ   فهو العَتادُ الّذى لِلدَّهْرِ يُدَّخَرُ
٣٠ هُوَ المُدامُ الّتى أَسْلُو بها فإذا   عَدِمْتُها عَبِثَتْ فى قَلْبِيَ الفِكَرُ
٣١ أَجَلْ، وَلِي راحةٌ أُخْرَى كَلِفْتُ بها   نَظْمُ الكُلَى فى القَنَا والهَامُ تَنْتَثِرُ
٣٢ مَا تَرْكِيَ الخمْرَ مِن زُهْدٍ ولا وَرَعٍ   فَلَمْ يُفَارِقْ – لَعَمْرِي – سِنِّيَ الصِّغَرُ
٣٣ وإنَّما أنَا ساعٍ فى رِضاكَ، فَإنْ   أخفقتُ فيه، فلا يُفْسَحْ لِيَ العُمُرُ
٣٤ ما سَرَّنِي، وأُحاشِي عصرَ عطفِكُم   يَوْمٌ أخلّ به فى عَيْنِيَ القِصَرُ
٣٥ كَمْ وَقْعَةٍ لِيَ فى الأَعْداءِ وَاضِحةٍ   تُفْنِي اللّيَالِي، وما يَفْنى لها الخَبَرُ
٣٦ سارَتْ بها العَبَسُ فى الأفاقِ، فانْتَشَرَتْ   فلَيْسَ فى كُلِّ حَيٍّ غيرَها سَمَرُ
٣٧ لا زِلْتَ ذا عِزَّةٍ قَعْساءَ شامِخَةٍ   لا يبلُغ الوَهْمُ أدْناها ولا البَصَرُ
٣٨ ولا يَزَلْ وَزَرٌ مِن حُسْنِ رَأْيِكَ لي   آوِي إليه، نِعْمَ الكَهْفُ والوَزَرُ
٣٩ إلَيْكَ رَوْضَةَ فِكْرٍ جادَ مَنْبِتَها   نَدَى يَمِينِكَ، لا طَلٌّ، ولا مَطَرُ
٤٠ جَعَلْتُ ذِكْرَكَ فى أرْجائِها زَهَرًا   وكُلُّ أوْقاتِها لِلمُجْتَنِى ثَمَرُ

12 al-Muᶜtamid

1 A stranger, captive in the lands of the West, will be mourned by a certain pulpit and throne.
2 Should be come to naught, no caravan leader will hear of his sweet mention, or see that sporting of his again.
3 The white, sharp [swords] and also the spears will mourn for him and shed many a tear between them.
4 In his Zāhī and the Zāhir, largesse and its seekers will weep for him, as well as benefaction, [now] followed by refusal.
5 If it is said that his generosity has died in Aghmāt, it is because a flourishing state is not to be expected after death.
6 A time during which kingship was well used to his company has elapsed, while today he has been pushed aside from it.
7 Their fate has humbled the sons of Māᵓ as-Samāᵓ, so that the abasement of the sons of Māᵓ as-Samāᵓ is very great indeed!
8 [It has done so] in accordance with the corrupt decree of an erring destiny; yet when have the Fates ever been just to the just?
9 Hence their water is made of tears shed over them, of which oceans pour over men's hearts.
10 Would that I knew whether I shall ever again spend a night with a garden before me and a pool of water behind me.
11 In a grove of olive trees, the heritage of nobility, where doves coo and birds warble,
12 In its towering Zāhir, where the fine, soft rain refreshes it while the Thuraiyā points at us and we at it,
13 While the Zāhī glances at us with its Saᶜd as-Suᶜūd, both of them jealously, for the much devoted lover is ever jealous!
14 You will note that all this is [now] hard to attain rather than easy, yet what God wills is always easy [to bear]!

---

12. SOURCES: al-Muᶜtamid, *Dīwān*, ed. Aḥmad Badawī and Ḥāmid ᶜAbd al-Majīd (Cairo, 1951), pp. 98–99; Ibn Ḥamdīs, *Dīwān*, ed. Iḥsān ᶜAbbās (Beirut, 1960), pp. 267–268.

METER: *ṭawīl.*

Al-Muᶜtamid wrote this nostalgic poem to Ibn Ḥamdīs during his first year of captivity in Aghmāt.

2. This line is missing from al-Muᶜtamid's *Dīwān* but appears in that of Ibn Ḥamdīs.

4. The Zāhī was al-Muᶜtamid's favorite palace; the Zāhir was another.

5. Al-Muᶜtamid's *Dīwān* reads *li-l-jūdi baᶜdu nushūru* rather than *baᶜda l-mamāti nushūru.*

١٢

المعتمد

١ غَريبٌ بِأَرْضِ المَغْرِبَيْنِ أَسيرُ   سَيَبْكي عليه مِنْبَرٌ وسَريرُ

٢ إذا زالَ لَمْ يَسْمَعْ بِطيبِ ذِكْرِهِ   ولَمْ يَرَ ذاكَ اللَّهْوَ مِنه مُنيرُ

٣ وتَنْدُبُهُ البِيضُ الصَّوارِمُ والقَنَا   ويَنْهَلُّ دَمْعٌ بَيْنَهُنَّ غَزيرُ

٤ سَيَبْكيهِ في زاهِيهِ والزاهِرِ النَّدَى   وَ طُلَّابُهُ والعرفُ ثُمَّ نَكيرُ

٥ إذا قيلَ في أَغْماتَ قَدْ ماتَ جُودُهُ   فما يُرْتَجَى بعد المَماتِ نُشُورُ

٦ مَضَى زَمَنٌ والمُلْكُ مُسْتَأْنِسٌ بِهِ   وأَصْبَحَ عنه اليَوْمَ وَهْوَ نَفُورُ

٧ أَذَلَّ بَني ماءِ السَّماءِ زَمانُهُمْ   وَذُلُّ بَني ماءِ السماءِ كَثيرُ

٨ بِرَأْيٍ مِنَ الدَّهْرِ المُضَلِّلِ فاسِدٍ   مَتَى صلحَتْ للصالِحينَ دُهُورُ

٩ فَمَا ماؤُها إلَّا بُكاءٌ عليهِمُ   يفيضُ على الأَكْبادِ مِنْهُ بُحُورُ

١٠ فَيَا لَيْتَ شِعْري هَلْ أَبيتَنَّ لَيْلَةً   أَمامي وَخَلْفي رَوْضَةٌ وغَديرُ

١١ بِمَنْبِتَةِ الزَّيْتُونِ مَوْرُونَةِ العُلَى   تُغَنِّي حَمامٌ أَوْ تَرِنُّ طُيُورُ

١٢ بِزاهِرِها السَّامي الذُّرَى جادَهُ الحَيَا   تُشيرُ الثُّرَيَّا نَحْوَنا ونُشيرُ

١٣ ويَلْحَظُنا الزَّاهي وسَعْدُ سُعُودِهِ   غَيُورَيْنِ والصَّبُّ المُحِبُّ غَيُورُ

١٤ تُراهُ عَسيرًا لا يَسيرًا مَنالُهُ   أَلا كُلُّ ما شاءَ الإلٰهُ يَسيرُ

---

7. Māᵓ as-Samāᵓ was the mother of al-Mundhir and grandmother of Nuᶜmān III, king of Hira in pre-Islamic times, from whom the Sevillian dynasty claimed descent. This line and the next are inverted in the *Dīwān* of al-Muᶜtamid.

9. Māᵓ as-Samāᵓ means literally "the water of heaven," hence the pun in this line.

11. The *Dīwān* of Ibn Ḥamdīs reads *maurithati.*

12. The Thuraiyā, "the Pleiads," was another royal palace opposite the Zāhī.

13. The Saᶜd as-Suᶜūd, "the luckiest constellation," was the cupola of the Zāhī.

13 Ibn Ḥamdīs

1 A fortune that is wont to stumble often brought you honor, and a time in which you succored us has done you wrong.

2 The white blades have been sheathed in their scabbards such that from having ceased to strike they seem like women, though they are masculine.

3 Our affairs run counter to the decrees [of Fate], while Fate is at times just to man and at times unjust.

4 Do you despair of a day that will be the opposite of its eve, while the bright, shining [stars] still go around amid the signs of the zodiac?

5 Lords may well behave arrogantly after obscurity, while after an eclipse full moons may emerge.

6 If you are restricted to the abode you dwell in, [even] the lion is [sometimes] restricted though he is a crusher [of his prey].

7 It ennobles all captives that it should be said: "Muḥammad is a stranger, captive in the lands of the West!"

8 Brave men sighed because of its manacles in its captivity, and some of them are broken by misfortune in it,

9 While you were shrouded in a wall from among its prisons by the spears; indeed, prisons are tombs!

10 Until the present no full grown camels on whom a rider gallops at dawn have ever alarmed the night-flying sandgrouse,

11 Nor has a generous man ever rejoiced at the wealth that a poor man puts into his hands.

12 You have protected God's religion with the best of protections as though you were its heart, and it the thought.

13 And when you advanced with largesse in your hands, and Raḍwā and Thabīr were shaken because of you,

14 I raised my tongue for the sake of the approaching Resurrection—lo, look at those "mountains flying hither and thither."

---

13. Source: Ibn Ḥamdīs, *Dīwān*, ed. Iḥsān ᶜAbbās (Beirut, 1960), pp. 268–269. Meter: *ṭawīl.*

Ibn Ḥamdīs replied to the sorrowing monarch with the following words of consolation written in the same rhyme and meter as the preceding poem.

١٣

ابن حمديس

١ جَرَى بِكَ جَدٌّ بِالكِرامِ عَثُورُ   وجارَ زمانٌ كُنْتَ فيه تُجيرُ

٢ لقد أصْبَحَتْ بِيضُ الظُّبا في غُمودِها   إناثًا لِتَرْكِ الضَّرْبِ وَهْيَ ذُكورُ

٣ تَجيءُ خِلافًا لِلأُمورِ أُمورُنا   وَيَعْدِلُ دَهْرٌ في الوَرَى ويَجورُ

٤ أتَيْأَسُ في يَوْمٍ يُناقِضُ أمْسَهُ   وَزُهْرُ الدَّراري في البُروجِ تَدورُ

٥ وقد تَنْتَخِي الساداتُ بعد خمولِها   وتَخْرُجُ من بعد الكُسوفِ بُدورُ

٦ لَئِنْ كُنْتَ مَقْصورًا بِدارٍ عَمَرْتَها   فقد يُقْصَرُ الضِّرْغامُ وَهْوَ هَصُورُ

٧ أغَرَّ الأَسارَى أنْ يُقالَ مُحَمَّدٌ   غريبٌ بأَرْضِ المَغْرِبَيْنِ أَسيرُ

٨ تَنافَسَ من أغْلالِها في فِكاكِها   وَيُقْصَمُ منها بالمُصابِ ذُكورُ

٩ وكُنْتَ مسجًّى بالظُّبا مِن سُجونِها   بسورٍ لها إنَّ السُّجونَ قُبورُ

١٠ إلى اليَوْمِ لم تَذْعَرْ قَطا اللَّيْلِ قُرَّحٌ   يُغيرُ بها عند الصباحِ مُغيرُ

١١ ولا راحَ نادٍ بالمكارمِ لِلغِنَى   يقلبه في الرّاحتَيْنِ فَقيرُ

٢٢ لقد صُنْتَ دينَ اللّهِ خَيْرَ صيانةٍ   كأَنَّكَ قَلْبٌ فيه وَهْوَ ضَميرُ

١٣ ولمَّا رحلتُمْ بالنَّدَى في أكُفِّكم   وَقُلْقِلَ رَضْوَى منكمُ ونَبيرُ

١٤ رَفَعْتُ لِساني بالقِيامةِ قد أتَتْ   ألَا فانْظُروا هذي الجِبالَ تَسيرُ

---

7. Muḥammad Ibn ᶜAbbād, al-Muᶜtamid of Seville.

10. The sandgrouse is proverbial for its speed in Arabic poetry.

13. Raḍwā is a group of mountains near Medina. Thabir is a mountain outside Mecca.

14. An allusion to Koran 3:10.

14 Ibn Ḥamdīs

1 I remember a certain brook that offered the impiety of drunkenness to the topers [sitting] along its course, with [its] cups of golden [wine],

2 Each silver cup in it filled as though it contained the soul of the sun in the body of the full moon.

3 Whenever a glass reached anyone in our company of topers, he would grasp it gingerly with his ten fingers.

4 Then he drinks out of it a grape-induced intoxication which lulls his very senses without his realizing it.

5 He sends [the glass] back in the water, thus returning it to the hands of a cupbearer at whose will it had [originally] floated [to him].

6 Because of the wine bibbing we imagined our song to be melodies which the birds sang without verse,

7 While our cupbearer was the water which brought [us wine] without a hand, and our drink was a fire that shone without embers,

8 And which offered us delights of all kinds, while the only reward [of that cupbearer] for [giving us those delights] was that we offered him to the ocean to drink.

9 [It is] as if we were cities along the riverbank while the wine-laden ships sailed [the stretch] between us,

10 For life is excusable only when we walk along the shores of pleasure and abandon all restraint!

---

14. Source: Ibn Ḥamdis, *Dīwān*, ed. Iḥsān ʿAbbās (Beirut, 1960), p. 119.
Meter: *ṭawīl.*

This poem is a fine example of the Hispano-Arab "dolce vita." It is a description of a brook that circled around a garden and along which carousers were seated. A cupbearer was pouring wine out, filling each goblet and floating it down the brook to every drinker, who would take it from the water, drink its contents, and return the empty vessel via the water to its point of origin. There the cupbearer would refill it and send it off again.

١٤

ابن حمديس

١ وساقيةٍ تَسْقِي النَّدامى بِمَدِّها   كُؤُوسًا من الصَّهْباءِ طاغيةَ السُّكْرِ

٢ يُعَوِّمُ فيها كلُّ جامٍ كأنَّما   تَضَمَّنَ رُوحَ الشمسِ في جَسَدِ البَدْرِ

٣ إذا قَصَدَتْ مِنَّا نَديمًا زُجاجةٌ   تناولها رفقًا بأَنْمُلِهِ العشرِ

٤ فيشْرَبُ منها سَكْرَةً عِنَبِيَّةً   تُنَوِّمُ عَيْنَ الصَّحْوِ منه وما يَدْرِي

٥ وَيُرْسِلُهَا في مَائِها فيُعِيدُها   إلى راحتَيْ ساقٍ على حُكْمِهِ تَجْرِي

٦ جَعَلْنا على شُرْبِ العُقارِ سَماعَنا   لُحونًا تُغَنِّيها الطُّيورُ بلا شِعْرِ

٧ وسَاقِيَنا ماءٌ يَنيلُ بلا يَدٍ   ومَشْروبَنا نارًا تَضِيءُ بلا جَمْرِ

٨ سقانا مَسَرّاتٍ فكان جَزاؤُهُ   عليها لَدَيْنا أنْ سَقَيْناهُ لِلْبَحْرِ

٩ كأنَّ على شَطِّ الخَليجِ مَدائِنٌ   تسافرُ فيما بَيْنَنا سُفُنُ الخَمْرِ

١٠ وَما العَيْشُ إلّا في تَطَرُّفِ لَذَّةٍ   وَخَلْعِ عِذارٍ فيه مُسْتَحْسَنِ العُذْرِ

---

1. For this translation of *wau rubba*, "I remember," cf. W. Wright, *A Grammar of the Arabic Language* (3d ed.; Cambridge, 1951), II, 217*d*.

8 A daring conceit! The cupbearer is the water of the brook which is given to the ocean. The ocean is a symbol of generosity in Arabic poetry, therefore it is suggested that this cupbearer's services were generously requited. This reward was in turn derived by the drinkers from the fire of the wine; i.e., their intoxication moved them to feelings of generosity.

15 Abū Isḥāq

1 O say to all of the Ṣinhāja, the full moons of the time, and the lions of the thicket:

2 "Your lord has made a [fatal] slip whereby the enemy derive joy.

3 "He chose a nonbeliever to be his secretary, whereas had he so wished he could have chosen a Muslim.

4 "Thus the Jews have waxed arrogant because of [that secretary] and have behaved with insolence and pride, whereas before they were base.

5 "They obtained their desires going beyond the utmost limit, yet those living in misery have perished while [the Jews] have not noticed it.

6 "For how many a Muslim of noble origin has abased himself before a miserable monkey from among the nonbelievers!

7 "Nor was all this the result of their own efforts, but rather, their helper comes from us!

8 "Why did he not follow with regard to [the Jews] the example of those good and pious leaders of yore,

9 "And throw them down to the place they deserve, pushing them back to the [company of] the lowest of the low?

10 "Then would they go about among us with their poll taxes upon them; being demeaned, contemptible, and base,

11 "And they would rummage in the dung heaps for a coarse cloak variegated in color with which to cover their dead,

12 "Nor would they hold our noble ones in light esteem, nor would they scorn our pious men.

13 "Nor would they sit with them, since they are baseborn; nor would they ride with those near [to the King]!"

---

15. SOURCES: *Un alfaquí español, Abu Isḥāq de Elvira*, ed. E. García Gómez (Madrid and Granada, 1944), pp. 149–153; A. R. Nykl, *Mukhtarāt min ash-shiʿr al-Andalusī* (Beirut, 1949), pp. 141–143.

METER: *mutaqārib*.

Abū Isḥāq wrote this famous ode in 1066 to incite Bādīs ibn Ḥabbūs, the Zīrid king of Granada to kill his Jewish minister Yūsuf ibn Naghrīla and put an end to Jewish influence in Granadan government. The poem touched off a pogrom—one of the earliest in European history.

١٥

ابو اسحاق

١ أَلا قُلْ لِصِنْهاجَةٍ أَجْمَعِيـنْ ... بُدورِ الزمانِ وأُسْدِ العَرِيـنْ

٢ لَقَدْ زَلَّ سَيِّدُكُمْ زَلَّـةً ... تَقَرُّ بِها أَعْيُنُ الشامِتِيـنْ

٣ تَخَيَّرَ كاتِبَـهُ كافِـرًا ... ولو شاءَ كانَ مِنَ المُؤْمِنيـنْ

٤ فَعَزَّ اليَهـودُ بِه وٱنْتَخَـوْا ... وتاهُوا، وكانوا مِنَ الأَرْذَلِيـنْ

٥ ونالوا مُناهم وحازوا المَدَى ... فَحانَ الهَلاكُ وما يَشْعُرونْ

٦ فَكَمْ مُسْلِمٍ فاضِلٍ قانِتٍ ... لِأَرْذَلِ قِرْدٍ مِنَ المُشْرِكِيـنْ

٧ وما كانَ ذلكَ مِن سَعْيِهِمْ ... ولكِنَّ مِنّا يَقُومُ المُعِيـنْ

٨ فَهَلَّا ٱقْتَدى فيهِمُ بِٱلأُولى ... مِنَ القادةِ الخِيرَةِ المُتَّقِيـنْ

٩ وأَنْزَلَهُمْ حيثُ يَسْتَأْهِلُـونْ ... وَرَدَّهُمُ أَسْفَلَ السافِلِيـنْ

١٠ فَطافوا لَدَيْنا بِأَخْراجِهِمْ ... عليهم صَغارٌ وذُلٌّ وَهُـونْ

١١ وقَمُّوا المَزابِلَ عن خِرْقَةٍ ... مُلَوَّنَةٍ لِدِثارِ الدَّفيـنْ

١٢ ولم يستخِفُّوا بِأَعْلامِنا ... ولم يستطيلوا على الصالِحينْ

١٣ ولا جالَسوهم وهم هُجْنَةٌ ... ولا راكَبوهم مع الأَقْرَبيـنْ

---

1. The Ṣinhāja Berbers were the grouping to which the Zīrid dynasty belonged. García Gómez reads *budūri n-nadīya* for *budūri z-zamāni*. After this line Nykl has the following one, missing in García Gómez: *maqālata dhī miqatin mushfiqin—yaᶜuddu n-naṣīḥata zulfā wa dīn.*

5. Nykl reads: *wa qad kāna dhāka wa mā yashᶜurūn.*

6. Nykl reads: *musliman rāghibin rāḥibin.*

10. Nykl reads: *bi-afwāji-him*

11. This line is missing in Nykl.

14 O, Bādīs! You are an intelligent man whose thoughts attain the essence of certain truth,

15 Yet how have their evil deeds been concealed from you when their trumpets resound on this earth?

16 And how do you show partiality for these offshoots of adultery when they have made you appear loathsome in the eyes of all the worlds?

17 And how will you consolidate your ascent to power when they are tearing down what you have built?

18 How can you be generous in favoring a scoundrel and make him your boon companion when he is the worst of partners?

19 For God has revealed in His Revelation, warning us against the company of scoundrels!

20 Therefore do not choose any minister from among the [Jews], but rather hand them over to the curses of those who curse,

21 For the whole earth has cried out because of their evil and [soon] it will quake with all of us [and cause us to perish].

22 Contemplate with your own eyes [the earth's] different regions, and you will observe that [the Jews] are [treated] like dogs in them [all], being driven away with stones.

23 Why are you alone in favoring them when they are rejected throughout the land?

24 Over and above the fact that you are the King approved of [by God], offspring of glorious kings,

25 And that you have precedence among men, while you are a leader of great ones.

26 I myself arrived in Granada and saw that these [Jews] were meddling in its [affairs].

27 They had already divided up the city and its provinces [among themselves] and one of these cursed ones is in every place.

28 They collect its taxes, they eat in the enjoyment of a plentiful life, and they crunch with their teeth.

29 They don the high ranking robes while you [O Muslims] are dressed in their cast-off clothes.

---

14. I.e., Bādīs ibn Ḥabbūs the Berber king of Granada.
15. García Gómez reads: *fa-kaifa khtafat ʿan-ka ʾaʿyanu-hum*
16. García Gómez reads: *wa hum baghghadū-ka.*
22. García Gómez reads: *bi-ʿainai-ka.*

١٤ أَبَادِيسُ ، أَنْتَ ٱمْرُؤٌ حَاذِقٌ   تُصِيبُ بِظَنِّكَ نَفْسَ اليَقِينْ

١٥ فَكَيْفَ خَفِيَ عنك ما يَعْبَثُونْ   وفي الأَرْضِ تَضْرِبُ مِنها القُرُونْ

١٦ وَكَيْفَ تُحِبُّ فِراخَ الزِّنا   وقد بَغَّضُوكَ الى العالَمِينْ

١٧ وَكَيْفَ يَتِمُّ لَكَ المُرْتَقَى   إذا كُنْتَ تَبْنِي وهُمْ يُهْدِمُونْ

١٨ وَكَيْفَ آسْتَنَمْتَ إلى فاسِقٍ   وقارَنْتَهُ وهو بِئْسَ القَرِينْ

١٩ وقد أَنْزَلَ اللّٰهُ في وَحْيِهِ   يُحَذِّرُ عن صُحْبَةِ الفاسِقِينْ

٢٠ فلا تَتَّخِذْ مِنهم خادِمًا   وذَرْهُمْ إلى لَعْنَةِ اللاعِنِينْ

٢١ فقد ضَجَّتْ الأَرْضُ مِن فِسْقِهِمْ   وكادَتْ تَمِيدُ بِنا أَجْمَعِينْ

٢٢ تَأَمَّلْ بِعَيْنَيْكَ أَقْطارَها   تَجِدْهُمْ كِلابًا بها خاسِئِينْ

٢٣ وكَيْفَ آنْفَرَدْتَ بِتَقْرِيبِهِمْ   وهُمْ في البِلادِ مِن المُبْعَدِينْ

٢٤ على أَنَّكَ المَلِكُ المُرْتَضَى   سَلِيلُ المُلُوكِ مِن الماجِدِينْ

٢٥ وأَنَّ لَكَ السَّبْقَ بَيْنَ الوَرَى   كما أَنْتَ مِن جِلَّةِ السابِقِينْ

٢٦ وإنّي حَلَلْتُ بِغَرْناطَةٍ   فَكُنْتُ أَرَاهُمْ بها عابِثِينْ

٢٧ وقد قَسَموها وأَعْمالَها   فَمِنْهُم بِكُلِّ مَكانٍ لَعِينْ

٢٨ وهم يقبضون جِبايَاتِها   وهم يخضمون وهم يقضمون

٢٩ وهم يلبسون رَفِيعَ الكِسا   وأَنْتُمْ لِأَوْضَعِها لابِسُونْ

---

26. García Gómez reads: *wa innī ḥtalaltu.*

28. *khaḍama* means literally "to eat with the whole of the mouth, including the back teeth."

30 They are entrusted with your secrets [of state], yet how can traitors be trusted?

31 Others eat a dirham's worth of food and consider that a lot, yet they consider it insufficient when they eat.

32 They have struggled to supplant you in the favor of your lord, yet you do not forbid or disapprove [of this act].

33 They have obscured you by reason of [the noise] of their evening congregations, yet you neither listen nor see.

34 They slaughter [their animals] in our marketplaces, while you eat their non-kosher leftovers.

35 Their monkey has covered his house with marble ornaments and caused the purest springwater to flow to it.

36 Yet when we had need of him, we cooled our heels at his door,

37 And he mocks us as well as our religion. Verily it is to God that we will return!

38 Were I to say, regarding his wealth [O Bādīs], that it is like your wealth, I would say the truth.

39 So hasten to slaughter him as a good work whereby you will earn God's favor, and offer him up in sacrifice, for he is a [well] fattened ram,

40 And do not pardon his people for they have hoarded up all sorts of valuable treasures.

41 Distribute their property and seize their wealth, for you have a greater right to what they have collected.

42 Do not consider the slaying of them to be a breach of faith; nay, the real breach of faith would consist in leaving them to cause harm,

43 For they have already broken their pact with us; so how could you be blamed among pactbreakers?

---

31. During the Mulūk aṭ-Ṭawāʾif period, political division contributed to an economic crisis in which the dirham was devalued until, from being made of pure silver, it became almost pure copper. Therefore "a dirham's worth of food" here means "very little indeed."

33. Nykl reads: *bi-asḥāri-him.*

34. García Gómez reads: *li-aṭrāfi-hā* for *li-iṭrīfi-him.*

٣٠ وهم أُمَنَاكُمْ على سِرِّكُمْ ، وكيف يكون أَمينًا خَؤُونْ

٣١ ويَأْكُلُ غَيْرُهم دِرْهَمًا فيُقْصَى ويُدْنَوْنَ إذ يَأْكُلُونْ

٣٢ وقد ناهَضوكم إلى رَبِّكم فما يُمْنَعونَ وما يُنْكَرونْ

٣٣ وقد لابَسوكم بأَسْمارِهم فما تَسمعون ولا تُبْصِرونْ

٣٤ وهم يذبحون بأَسْواقِنا وأنتم لإِطْريفِهم آكِلونْ

٣٥ ورَخَّمَ قِرْدُهُمُ دارَهُ وأَجْرَى إليها نَميرَ العُيُونْ

٣٦ وصارَتْ حَوائِجُنا عِنْدَهُ ونحن على بابِه قائِمُونْ

٣٧ ويَضْحَكُ مِنَّا ومن دِينِنا فإِنَّا إلى رَبِّنا راجِعُونْ

٣٨ ولو قُلْتُ في مالِه إنَّه كَمالِكَ كُنْتُ مِنَ الصادِقينْ

٣٩ فبَادِرْ إلى ذَبْحِهِ قُرْبَةً وضَحِّ به فَهْوَ كَبْشٌ سَمِينْ

٤٠ ولا ترفع الضَغْطَ عن رَهْطِهِ فقد كنزوا كلَّ عِلْقٍ ثَمِينْ

٤١ وفَرِّقْ عُراهم وخُذْ مالَهم فأَنْتَ أَحَقُّ بِمَا يَجْمَعُونْ

٤٢ ولا تَحْسَبَنْ قَتْلَهم غَدْرَةً بَل الغَدْرُ في تَرْكِهم يَعْبَثُونْ

٤٣ فقد نَكَثوا عَهْدَنا عندهم ، فكَيْفَ تُلَامُ على الناكِثينْ

35. The reference is to the palace built by the Naghrīla family on the site now occupied by the Alhambra (cf. Frederick P. Bargebuhr, *El palacio de la Alhambra en el siglo XI* [Mexico, 1966]).

36. García Gómez reads: *fa-ṣārat*.

37. Interjection used to express misfortune.

44 How can they enjoy [the security of] the *dhimma* when we are abased and they are notorious?
45 We are downtrodden in comparison with them, as though we were the wrongdoers and they, the righteous.
46 Therefore do not permit what they are doing to us, for you are answerable for their deeds.
47 And fear your God insofar as his chosen people are concerned, for the elect of God are the ones who will enjoy eternal bliss!

---

44. The *dhimma* was a legal provision whereby non-Muslim subjects enjoyed protection, freedom of worship and property rights in Islamic states in exchange for the payment of a poll tax.

٤٤ وكَيْفَ تَكُونُ لَهُمْ ذِمَّةٌ   ونحن خُمُولٌ وهم ظاهِرونْ

٤٥ ونحن الأذِلَّةُ مِن بينهم   كأنَّا أسأنا وهم مُحْسِنونْ

٤٦ فلا تَرْضَ فينا بأفْعالِهِم   فأنْتَ رَهينٌ بما يَفْعَلونْ

٤٧ وَرَاقِبْ إلاهَكَ في حِزْبِهِ   فَحِزْبُ الإلهِ هُمُ المُفْلِحونْ

---

47. The "chosen people" are the Islamic community. García Gómez reads *humū l-ghālibūna*, "they are the ones who will be victorious."

16 Ibn al-Labbāna

1 The heavens weep with their morning and evening rain clouds over those excellent lords, the Banū ʿAbbād,

2 Over those [lofty] mountains whose very foundations have been demolished, though the earth was endowed with pegs thanks to them alone;

3 As for the plants on the hills, their flowers have faded and have appeared in the morning in the depressed vale [of Death].

4 They were a covert into which misfortunes intruded despite their snakes and lions in it,

5 And a Kaʿba which hopes once served, yet today no one dwells in it, nor does any nomad [visit it].

6 O guest, the home of generous deeds has become vacant so prepare to depart and gather together the remaining provisions for the journey;

7 And O you who hoped to settle in their vale; the inhabitants have fled and the crops have withered in the valley.

8 The road leading to generosity has misled the traveler, so journey to another goal, for no guide can guide you!

9 And you, O rider of horses which once proudly pranced in their harnesses, in countless numbers,

10 Put down your weapons and lay down your Mashrifī sword for you have come to find yourself in the maw of a hostile lion which seizes its prey unawares.

11 Those spears were spears of Khaṭṭ which the vicissitudes of Fate straightened in an unexpected manner,

12 While those swords were sharp-pointed blades whose edges were notched and turned away from their scabbards by the hands of Death.

13 When the appointed hour draws near no weapon can avert it, for everything is subject to an appointed hour and place.

---

16. SOURCES: Ibn Khaqān, *Qalāʾid al-iqyān* (Bulaq, 1866), p. 23; al-Marrakushī, *al-Muʿjib*, ed. Muhammad Saʿīd al-ʿAryān and Muḥammad al-ʿArabī (Cairo, 1949), pp. 148–149; E. García Gómez, *Qasidas de Andalucía* (Madrid, 1940), pp. 85–96.

METER: *baṣīt.*

This elegy was written over the fall of the ʿAbbādid dynasty of Seville after al-Muʿtamid had been taken in captivity to the Moroccan town of Aghmāt by the Almoravids.

1. Al-Marrakushī reads *bi-damʿin* instead of *bi-muẓnin.*

2. Mountains are referred to metaphorically as *autād al-arḍ*, "the pegs of the earth."

١٦

ابن اللبّانة

١ تَبْكِي السَّمَاءُ بِمُزْنٍ رائحٍ غادِ   على البَهالِيلِ مِن أَبْناءِ عَبّادِ

٢ على الجِبالِ التّى هُدَّتْ قَواعِدُها   وكانَتْ الأَرْضُ مِنهم ذاتَ أَوْتادِ

٣ والرابياتُ عليها اليانِعاتُ ذَوَتْ   أَنْوارُها فغَدَتْ في خَفْضِ أَوْهادِ

٤ عِرّيسةٌ دَخَلَتْها النائِباتُ على   أساوِدٍ لَهُمْ فيها وآسادِ

٥ وكَعبةٌ كانَتْ الآمالُ تَخْدِمُها   فاليَوْمَ لا عاكِفٌ فيها ولا بادِ

٦ يا ضَيْفُ أَقْفَرَ بَيْتُ المَكْرُماتِ فَخُذْ   في ضَمِّ رَحْلِكَ وآجْمَعْ فَضْلَةَ الزّادِ

٧ ويا مُؤَمِّلَ وَادِيهِم لِيَسْكُنَهُ   خَفَّ القَطِينُ وَجَفَّ الزَّرْعُ بالوَادِي

٨ ضَلَّتْ سَبيلُ النَدَى بِآبْنِ السَبيلِ فَسِرْ   لِغَيْرِ قَصْدٍ فما يُهْدِيكَ مِن هادِي

٩ وأَنْتَ يا فارِسَ الخَيْلِ التّى جَعَلَتْ   تَخْتالُ فى عُدَدٍ منهم وأَعْدادِ

١٠ أَلْقِ السِّلاحَ وخَلِّ المَشْرِفِيَّ فَقَدْ   أَصْبَحْتَ في لَهَواتِ الضَيْغَمِ العادِي

١١ تِلْكَ الرِّماحُ رِماحُ الخَطِّ ثَقَّفَها   خَطْبُ الزَّمانِ ثِقافًا غيرَ مُعْتادِ

١٢ والبِيضُ بِيضُ الظُّبا فَلَّتْ مَضارِبَها   أَيْدِى الرَّدَى وثَنَتْها دُونَ إغْمادِ

١٣ لَمَّا دَنا الوَقْتُ لَمْ تخلفْ لَهُ عُدَّةٌ   وكُلُّ شَيْءٍ لِمِيقاتٍ وَمِيعادِ

---

3. This line is extant only in al-Marrakushī's version.

5. Al-Marrakushī reads *taʿmuru-hā* for *takhdimu-hā.*

8. This line is supplied only by al-Marrakushī.

10. Mashrifī swords were considered to be of superior quality by pre-Islamic poets. The version of Ibn Khaqān reads *aṣ-ṣilāḥ* for *as-silāḥ.*

11. This line and the next appear only in al-Marrakushī. Spears of Khaṭṭ were highly prized in pre-Islamic Arabia and became proverbial for their excellence.

14 How many stars of good fortune have set, and how many pearls destined for unique glory have shattered!

15 If they were deposed, so were the Banū l-ᶜAbbās [before them], while before Seville, the land of Baghdad was likewise destroyed.

16 The ones were a light and the others a flower, yet the latter, after its prosperity, has withered away, while the former has been extinguished after being kindled.

17 They defended the privacy of their women's quarters until, when they were overpowered, they were driven off in single file, led along by a rope.

18 Once they were lodged on the backs of grey [steeds], but soon they were borne on [the surface of] black [ships] like unto those steeds.

19 Each collar of their coats of mail was destroyed and iron collars were fashioned out of them for [their] necks.

20 May I forget all but the sunrise on the river, when they, in the ships with sails unfurled [for the departure], were like corpses in their tombs,

21 While the people filled the two shores and sadly gazed at [those] pearls floating on the foamy crests of the waves.

22 The veil was lowered, for no secluded maiden concealed her face. Likewise faces were rent [in grief] as garments also were rent.

23 They separated, having once been neighbors, after each family had grown up with another family, and children with children.

24 The moment of farewell arrived and every woman and man cried out loudly, each one saying: "May I be thy ransom!"

25 Their ships set sail accompanied by mourning, as though they were camels urged on by the song of the caravan leader.

26 How many tears flowed into the water, and how many broken hearts did those galleys bear away!

27 Who will avail me of you, O Banū Māʾ as-Samāʾ when the water of heaven refuses to quench the heart of one who thirsts [for you]?

---

14. This line is supplied by al-Marrakushī.
16. This line is supplied by al-Marrakushī.
20. "The river," i.e., the Guadalquivir.

١٤ كَمْ مِن دَرارِيِّ سَعْدٍ قَدْ هَوَتْ ووَهَتْ　　هُناكَ مِن دُرَرٍ للمَجْدِ أَفْرادِ

١٥ إنْ يُخْلَعُوا فَبَنُو العَبَّاسِ قَدْ خُلِعُوا　　وقد خَلَتْ قَبْلَ حِمْصٍ أَرْضُ بَغْدادِ

١٦ نُورٌ ونَوْرٌ فهذا بعد نِعْمَتِهِ　　ذَوَى وذاك خَبَا مِن بعدِ إيقادِ

١٧ حَمَوْا حَرِيمَهم حتّى إذا غُلِبُوا　　سِيقُوا على نَسَقٍ فى حَبْلٍ مُقْتَادِ

١٨ وأُنْزِلُوا فى مُتُونِ الشُّهْبِ وآحْتُمِلوا　　فُوَيْقَ دُهْمٍ لِتِلْكَ الخَيْلِ أَنْدادِ

١٩ وعِيثَ فى كُلِّ طَوْقٍ مِن دُرُوعِهِمِ　　فَصِيغَ مِنْهُنَّ أَغْلَالٌ لِأَجْيادِ

٢٠ نَسِيتُ إلّا غَداةَ النَّهرِ كَوْنَهُمُ　　فى المُنْشِئَاتِ كأَمْواتٍ بأَلْحَادِ

٢١ والناسُ قَدْمَلَأُوا العَبْرَيْنِ وآعْتَبَرُوا　　مِن لُؤْلُؤٍ طافِيَاتٍ فَوْقَ أَزْبادِ

٢٢ حُطَّ القِنَاعُ فلم تُسْتَرْ مُخَدَّرَةٌ　　ومُزِّقَتْ أَوْجُهٌ تَمْزِيقَ أَبْرادِ

٢٣ تَفَرَّقُوا جِيرَةً مِن بعدِ ما نَشَئُوا　　أَهْلًا بأَهْلٍ وأَوْلَادًا بأَوْلَادِ

٢٤ حانَ الوَداعُ فضَجَّتْ كُلُّ صارِخَةٍ　　وصارِخٍ مِنْ مُفَدَّاةٍ وَمِنْ فادِ

٢٥ سارَتْ سَفائِنُهُمْ والنَّوْحُ يَصْحَبُها　　كأَنَّها إبْلٌ يَحْدُو بها الحَادِى

٢٦ كَمْ سالَ فى الماءِ مِن دَمْعٍ وكَمْ حَمَلَتْ　　تلك القَطَائِعُ مِنْ قِطَعاتِ أَكْبادِ

٢٧ مَنْ لِي بِكُمْ يا بَنِي ماءِ السَّماءِ إذا　　مَاءُ السماءِ أَبَى سُقْيَا حَشَا الصادِى

---

23. This line is recorded in al-Marrakushī's version.
25. Al-Marrakushī reads *yatbaʿu-hā* for *yaṣḥabu-hā*.
27. This verse is supplied by al-Marrakushī.

17 Ibn ᶜUbāda al-Qazzāz

1 I would give my father in ransom for a precious possession that clings to [my] soul!

2 I loved a new moon unique in its beauty borrowing from the gazelle its glances and [slender] neck.

3 A full moon that shone in shapely proportion was proud of its beauty, desiring no increase.

4 Grace had adorned him; his figure was graceful!

5 A full moon that conquered with evident charm, cheek down curling over a jasmine [complexion],

6 A lily placed in line with a well-guarded rose; when it appeared it [proudly] trailed the edges of beauty's robe.

7 Before me a creature appeared that was worthy of love!

8 My eyelids live only to find out about him; if my soul had but feathers, I would fly to him.

9 Beauty placed armies upon his pupils and [upon] the [arrow-like] glance feathered with licit charm.

10 He has a tall, graceful figure, hence [my] heart is in thrall to desire!

11 He has made it his aim to shun me ever since I have submitted to his love, yet have I squandered my patience despite the length of his shunning.

12 The water of beauty flows on his cheek's surface; his front teeth have put rows of pearls to shame;

13 His mouth is a receptacle for sweets worthy of being kissed!

14 When he donned a stylish robe as a costume, I wished to kiss his voluptuous, deep red lips,

15 So he said in verse, trying to act as one who refuses, and inclining coquettishly, with the sweetest of words:

16 "I say that you will not taste the tempting morsel, by God!"

---

17. Sources: Ibn Sanāᵓ al-Mulk, *Dār aṭ-ṭirāz fī ᶜamal al-muwashshaḥāt*, ed Jaudat ar-Rikābī (Damascus, 1949), pp. 52–53; S. M Stern, "Muḥammad ibn ᶜUbāda al-Qazzāz, un andaluz autor de 'muwashshaḥas,'" *Andalus*, XV (1950), 102–103.

Form: *muwashshaḥa*.

١٧

ابن عبادة القزّاز

١ بِأَبِي عِلْقُ — بالنَّفْسِ عَليقُ

٢ هَوِيتُ هِلالا في الحُسْنِ فَريدا — أَعارَ الغَزالا أَلْحاظًا وَجِيدا

٣ وَتاهَ جَمالا لَمْ يَبْغِ مَزيدا — بَدْرٌ يَتَلَأْلَأ في حُسْنِ ٱعْتِدالِ

٤ زانَهُ رَشْقُ — والقَدُّ رَشيقُ

٥ بَدْرٌ يَتَغَلَّبْ بالسِّحْرِ المُبينِ — عِذارٌ مُعَقْرَبْ على ياسَمينِ

٦ سَوْسانٌ مُكَتَّبْ بِوَرْدٍ مَصونِ — لَمّا لاحَ يَسْحَبْ ذُيولَ الجَمالِ

٧ عَنَّ لِي خَلْقُ — بالعِشْقِ خَليقُ

٨ جفانِي يَعيشْ لِوَقْفِي عَلَيْهِ — لَوْ بالنَّفْسِ ريشْ لَطِرْتُ إِلَيْهِ

٩ لِلْحُسْنِ جُيوشْ على مُقْلَتَيْهِ — واللَّحْظُ المَريشْ بالسِّحْرِ الحَلالِ

١٠ فَلَهُ مَشْقُ — والقَلْبُ مَشوقُ

١١ تَعَمَّدَ هَجْري مُذْ ذُبْتُ بِوُدِّهْ — وَبَدَدْتُ صَبْري على طُولِ صَدِّهْ

١٢ ماءُ الحُسْنِ يَجْري بِصَفْحَةِ خَدِّهْ — ثَنَاياهُ تُزْري بِنَظْمِ اللآلِي

١٣ فَمُهُ حُقُّ — باللَّثْمِ حَقيقُ

١٤ لَمّا أَنْ تَسَرْبَلْ ثَوْبَ الحُسْنِ زِيّا — أَرَدْتُ أُقَبِّلْ لَماهُ الشَّهِيّا

١٥ فَقالَ تَمَنَّلْ بالشِّعْرِ أَبِيّا — وَمالَ تَدَلَّلْ بِأَحْلى مَقالِ

١٦ أَنا قُولْ قُوقُو — لَيْسَ باللهْ تَذُوقُو

METRE: a–b–a–b–a–b–a–c *m–n*
6 6 6 6 6 6 6 6 5 6

RHYTHM: dactylic.

16. For *qūqū*, "tempting morsel," see. E. García Gómez, "Estudio del Dār aṭ-ṭirāz," *Andalus*, XXVII, (1962), 74. According to that author, this meaning of the word has survived to the present in colloquial Moroccan Arabic.

18 Ibn Ubāda al-Qazzāz

1 I would give my father in ransom for a gazelle of Ḥimā guarded by a lion of the thicket.

2 It is my custom to drink from deep red lips, the liquor of which is a Salsabīl.

3 There seduces my heart with [the waist] he sways when he bends down,

4 One well shaped, descended from a possessor of wealth from the [Banū] Thābit, one who spends the night in the shadows, under sweet dewdrops;

5 One gifted with languor, coquetry, and deep red lips for sipping;

6 He is a compounded perfume in his odor, beauty itself in his dress.

7 How much he arouses the passion of a sorrowing one afflicted with a prolonged illness.

8 One who offers excuses, if he but gave a second drink, would cause a mute to speak; while a certain gazelle, if he but looked, would restore the vision of one dazzled.

9 A bright one, to find his limit is to find the limit of love.

10 He is a Kauthar, the very essence of thirst when his own watering place is attained.

11 Gaze upon Muḥammad and walk slowly in his presence!

---

18. SOURCES: Ibn Sanāʾ al-Mulk, *Dār aṭ-ṭirāz fī ᶜamal al-muwashshaḥāt*, ed. Jaudat ar-Rikābī (Damascus, 1949), pp. 65–66; S. M. Stern, "Muḥammad ibn ᶜUbāda al-Qazzāz, un andaluz autor de 'muwashshaḥas,'" *Andalus*, XV (1950), 103–105.

FORM: *muwashshaḥa.*

١٨

ابن عبادة القزّاز

١ بِأَبِي ظَبْيٌ حِمَى تُكْنِفُهُ أُسْدُ غِيلْ

٢ مَذْهَبِي رَشْفُ لَمَا قَرْقَفُهُ سَلْسَبِيلْ

٣ يَسْتَبِي قَلْبِي بِمَا يَعْطِفُهُ إِذْ يَمِيلْ

٤ ذُو اعْتِدَالْ يُعْزَى إِلَى ذِي نِعْمَةٍ نَابِتِ

فِي ظِلَالْ تَحْتَ حُلَى قَطْرِ النَّدَى بَائِتِ

٥ ذُو فُتُورْ ذُو غُنُجِ ذُو مَرْشَفٍ أَلْعَسِ

٦ الْعَبِيرْ فِي أَرَجِ وَالْحُسْنُ فِي مَلْبَسِ

٧ كَمْ يُنِيرْ وَجْدَ شَجِي بِالدَّنَفِ مُكْتَسِ

٨ ذُو اعْتِلَالْ لَوْ عُلِّلَا انطق عن سَاكِتِ

وَغَزَالْ لَوْ مُقَلَا الحظ عن بَاهِتِ

٩ نَيِّرٌ حَدُّ الهَوَى إِنْ يَجِدُوا حَدَّهُ

١٠ كَوْثَرٌ سِرُّ الصَّدَى إِن يَرِدُوا وِرْدَهُ

١١ أُنْظُرُوا مُحَمَّدًا وَآتَئِدُوا عِنْدَهْ

METRE: a–b–c–d–a–b–c–d–a–b–c–d *m–n–o–m–n–o*
3 4 4 3 3 4 4 3 3 4 4 3 3 4 7 3 4 7

RHYTHM: dactylic.

2. *Salsabīl* is a fountain of Paradise mentioned in Koran 76:18.

10. *Kauthar* is a river in Paradise, generally used as a symbol of abundant water.

12 [He is] like a crescent moon such that when it is observed, it is beyond description, as well as pure water such that if it were generously given away, it would overcome the piety of the devout.
13 A full moon, a midday sun, a stem on a sand dune, fragrant musk;
14 None more full, none brighter, none more leafy, none more fragrant.
15 Of a truth, he who steals a glance, having become infatuated, is refused his desire.
16 Thus the love union is what has elapsed of the hope of a dying man, while the dream vision is what has arisen from the sighs of a speechless man on the verge of death.
17 My slayer, spare the blood of one who has become a heretic;
18 You used to tryst with me; what made you shun what once seemed good?
19 My questioner who seeks information: the cohorts of death have acted unjustly.
20 There is no point in enquiring after a tormented one who has wasted away in silence so that he can receive [the love] he hoped for, since the matter is in the hands of one who enjoys my discomfiture.
21 How proudly he treats me! How much so! And how much does passion refuse to change!
22 I am satisfied with him even though he has decreed the rule of love over [our] minds.
23 I said about him, since love could only be contented by what I say:
24 "Beauty is an inalienable bequest made over to the gazelle of the Banū Thābit. In love, there is no end, no indeed, to the bond firmly compacted with him!"

---

12. Rikābī reads *yartaqī*, which Stern corrects to *bazza tuqā*.

١٢ فِي هِلَالْ   لَوْ يُجْتَلَى   جَلَّ عن النَّاعِتِ
وَزُلَالْ   لَوْ بُذِلَا   بَزَّ تُقَى القَانِتِ

١٣ بَدْرُ تَمّْ   شَمْسُ ضُحَى   غُصْنُ نَقَى   مِسْكُ شَمّْ
١٤ مَا أَتَمّْ   مَا أَوْضَحَا   مَا أَوْرَقَا   مَا أَنَمّْ
١٥ لَا جَرَمْ   مَنْ لَمَحَا   قَدْ عَشِقَا   قَدْ حُرِمْ

١٦ فالوِصَالْ   مَا قَدْ خَلَا   في أَمَلِ فَائِتِ
والخَيَالْ   مَا قَدْ عَلَا   في نَفَسِ خَافِتِ

١٧ قَاتِلِي   اهن دَمَا   مَنْ قَدْ غَدَا   مُلْحِدًا
١٨ وَاصِلِي   كُنْتَ فَمَا   عَمَّا بَدَا   قَدْ عَدَا
١٩ سَائِلِي   مُسْتَفْهِمَا   جَيْش الرَّدَى   ٱعْتَدَى

٢٠ لَا سُؤَالْ   عن مُبْتَلَى   يُنْحَتُ في صَامِتِ
لِيَنَالْ   مَا أَمَلَا   والأَمْرُ لِلشَّامِتِ

٢١ كَمْ يَتِيهْ   كَمْ وَكَمْ   يَا بِي الجَوَى   أَن يَحُولْ
٢٢ أَرْتَضِيهْ   وَإِنْ حَكَمْ   حُكْمَ الهَوَى   في العُقُولْ
٢٣ قُلْتُ فِيهْ   وَالحُبُّ لَمْ   يَرْضِ سِوَى   مَا أَقُولْ

٢٤ الجَمَالْ   وَقْفٌ عَلَى   ظَبْيِ بَنِي نَابِتِ
لَا زَوَالْ   فِي الحُبِّ لَا   عن عَهْدِهِ النَّابِتِ

19 Ibn Arfaᶜ Raᵓsuh

1 The lute trills the most wondrous melodies
2 And the watercourses cut through the flower beds of the gardens.
3 The birds sing on the branches of the *bān*,
4 And joy enlivens the lions of the battlefield.
5 Every one of us is an Emir and a sultan because of the wine.
6 The lute-strings speak with eloquent charm
7 While the birds respond to them from the myrtle branches.
8 Come, give me wine to drink for the garden exudes fragrance;
9 The Pleiads have set and it is sweet to take the morning drink
10 Offered to me by a lovely gazelle
11 Who is like a tender branch enveloped in a cloak of eglantine,
12 Whose sides are covered in embroidered silks, who almost breaks because he is so tender.

---

19. SOURCE: S. M. Stern, "Four Famous Muwashshaḥas from Ibn Bushrā's Anthology," *Andalus*, XXIII (1958), 344–346.
FORM: *muwashshaḥa.*
METER: a–b–a–b–a–c *m–n–o–p*
7 7 7 7 7 7 7 7 7 7
RHYTHM: iambic.

١٩

ابن ارفع رأسه

١ الْعُودُ قَدْ تَرَنَّمْ — بِأَبْدَعِ تَرْنِينْ
٢ وَشَقَّتِ الْمَذَانِبْ — رِيَاضَ الْبَسَاتِينْ
٣ وَغَنَّتْ الطُّيُورُ — عَلَى قُضُبِ الْبَانْ
٤ وَأَضْمَرَ السُّرُورُ — أُسُودَ الْمَيَدَانْ
٥ فَكُلُّنَا أَمِيرُ — بِالرَّاحِ وَسُلْطَانْ
٦ مِنْ وَتَرٍ تَكَلَّمْ — بِالسِّحْرِ الْمُبِينْ
٧ وَطَائِرٍ تَجَاوَبْ — مِنْ قُضْبِ الرَّيَاحِينْ
٨ هَاتِ ٱسْقِنِي الْحُمَيَّا — فَالرَّوْضُ يَفُوحُ
٩ قَدْ مَالَتِ الثُّرَيَّا — وَطَابَ الصَّبُوحُ
١٠ يَحُثُّهَا عَلَيَّا — غَزَالٌ مَلِيحُ
١١ كَالْغُصْنِ الْمُنَعَّمْ — فِي حُلَّةِ نِسْرِينْ
١٢ مُطَرَّزِ الْجَوَانِبْ — يَنْقَدُّ مِنَ اللِّينْ

This poem is a panegyric in praise of the poet's patron, al-Ma^ɔmūn ibn Dhī n-Nūn of Toledo, the Berber ruler descended from the Huwwāra family [r. 1037–1075].

12. For *nisrīn*, "eglantine," cf. Dozy, II, 667.

13 Hold fast to the love and drink to the health of the Possessor
of Dual Glory,
14 Who supports the lands of the East and the West,
15 And who gives succor to believers, a descendant of Yaʿrub,
16 The lofty king, who humbles sultans,
17 Who leads cavalcades, and is the lion of the battlefields.
18 He is a king whose heart is braver than the lion's,
19 Just as his finger is more generous than the rain clouds.
20 Should Time ever appear frowning or with a severe face
21 He meets it smiling like the flowers in the gardens.
22 His deeds are stars [shining out over] this world and religion.
23 The beloved refuses to return the greeting
24 While the heart is aflame from the excess of love.
25 Thus the sorrowing one sings the song of one confused by love:
26 "You go by, yet you give no greeting as though you were
al-Maʾmūn,
27 The terrorizer of armies, Yaḥya ibn Dhī n-Nūn."

---

13. "The Possessor of Dual Glory" is the poet's patron, Maʾmūn ibn Dhī n-Nūn of Toledo.

١٣ أَقِمْ عَلَى وِدَادِ   ذِي الْمَجْدَيْنِ وَ آشْرَبْ

١٤ مُمَهِّدِ الْبِلَادِ   مِنْ شَرْقٍ وَمَغْرِبْ

١٥ وَنَاصِرِ الْعِبَادِ   سُلَالَةِ يَعْرُبْ

١٦ الْمَلِكِ الْمُعَظَّمْ   مُذِلِّ السَّلَاطِينْ

١٧ مُرَتِّبِ الْمَوَاكِبْ   هِزَبْرِ الْمَيَادِينْ

١٨ مَلْكٌ لَهُ جَنَانُ   مِنَ اللَّيْثِ أَقْدَمْ

١٩ كَمَا لَهُ بَنَانُ   مِنَ الْغَيْثِ أَكْرَمْ

٢٠ إِنْ عَبَّسَ الزَّمَانُ   يَوْمًا أَوْ تَجَهَّمْ

٢١ يَلْقَاهُ يَتَبَسَّمْ   كَنَوْرِ الْبَسَاتِينْ

٢٢ أَفْعَالُهُ كَوَاكِبْ   لِلدُّنْيَا وَلِلدِّينْ

٢٣ تَرَجَّعَ الْحَبِيبُ   عَن رَدِّ السَّلَامِ

٢٤ وَفِي الْحَشَا لَهِيبُ   مِنْ فَرْطِ الْغَرَامِ

٢٥ حَتَّى شَدَا الْكَئِيبُ   شَدْوَ الْمُسْتَهَامِ

٢٦ تَخْطَرْ وَلَسْ تَسَلَّمْ   كَأَنَّكَ الْمَأْمُونْ

٢٧ مُرَوِّعُ الْكَتَائِبْ   يَحْيَى بْنُ ذِي النُّونْ

---

15. Yaʿrub ibn Qaḥṭān was the legendary ancestor of the South Arabians from whom the Berbers claimed descent by a genealogical fiction.

20 Ibn ᶜAbdūn

1 It is Fate [alone] that causes us distress, first by the blow itself and then by the traces it leaves; so what is the use of weeping over illusions and vain imaginings?

2 I warn you, I warn you; I unceasingly warn you against dozing between the fangs and claws of the lion!

3 For Fate is [like] wartime even though it manifests peace, while men of pure honor and chiefs of noble rank are like white swords and tawny lances;

4 Nor is any peace to be found between the pommel held in the hand of the smiting warrior and the sharp steel blade.

5 Therefore be not deceived by the [apparent] slumber of your world, for the [real] occupation of both its eyes is none other than to be ever vigilant.

6 What thing of Time's—may God forgive our lapse!—belongs to Time, when the hand of fortune's vicissitudes has betrayed it?

7 In each of its moments, in each of our members, it leaves wounds, even though they are hidden from sight;

8 It causes us to enjoy a thing, yet [only] that it may deceive us by means of it, just like the viper that rushes from the flower upon the [unsuspecting] gatherer.

9 How many a state that has ruled for its duration with divine aid is such that no trace remains of it—consult your memory!

10 [Time] hurled Darius down [from power] and notched the edge of [Alexander] his slayer's sword; though the latter was a sharp, lustrous sword drawn against kings,

11 It reclaimed from the Banū Sāsān what it had given them, and left no trace of the Banū Yūnān.

12 It joined Ṭasm to its sister tribe [Jadīs], while [Fate], the undoer of all powers, turned against ᶜĀd and Jurhum.

13 Nor did it spare the fair Yemenites, nor did it protect the lofty-goaled Muḍarites.

---

20. Source: al-Marrakushī, *al-Muᶜjib fī talkhīṣ akhbār al-Maghrib*, ed. Muḥammad Saᶜīd al-ᶜAryān and Muḥammad al-ᶜArabī al-ᶜIlmī (Cairo, 1949), pp. 76–87.

Meter: *basīṭ*.

This ode was written to lament the fall of the Afṭasid dynasty of Badajoz, the Banū Muẓaffar, who had patronized the poet and were deposed and murdered by the Almoravids. The erudite historical references are explained by Ibn Badrūn,

٢٠

ابن عبدون

١ الدهرُ يُفجع بعد العَينِ بالأثَرِ   فما البُكاءُ على الأشباحِ والصورِ؟

٢ أنهاكَ أنهاك لا آلوك موعظةً   عن نَومةٍ بين نابِ الليثِ والظُّفُرِ

٣ فالدهرُ حربٌ وإن أبدَى مُسالَمَةً   والبِيضُ والسُّودُ مثلُ البيضِ والسُّمُرِ

٤ ولا هَوادَةَ بينَ الرأسِ تأخذُه   يدُ الضِّرابِ وبين الصارمِ الذَّكَرِ

٥ فلا تَغُرَّنْكَ مِن دُنْيَاك نَوْمَتُها   فما صِناعةُ عينَيْها سِوَى السَّهَرِ

٦ ما لِلّيالي أقالَ اللهُ عثرَتَنا   مِن الليالي وخانَتْها يَدُ الغِيَرِ

٧ فى كلّ حِينٍ لها في كلّ جارِحةٍ   مِنّا جِراحٌ وإن زاغَتْ عن النَّظَرِ

٨ تُسِرُّ بالشيءِ لكِنْ كَيْ تُغِرَّ بِهِ   كالإيمِ ثارَ إلى الجانِي من الزَّهَرِ

٩ كَم دَولةٍ وَلِيَتْ بالنصرِ خدْمَتَها   لم تُبْقِ مِنْها وسَلْ ذِكراكَ مِن خَبَرِ

١٠ هَوَتْ بِدارا وفَلَّتْ غَرْبَ قاتِلِهِ   وكان عَضْبًا على الأملاكِ ذا أُثُرِ

١١ وآسترجَعَتْ مِن بنى ساسانَ ما وَهَبَتْ   ولم تَدَعْ لبنى يُونانَ من أَثَرِ

١٢ وألحقَتْ أُخْتَها طَسْمًا، وعادَ على   عادٍ وجُرْهُمَ منها ناقِضُ المِرَرِ

١٣ وما أقالت ذوى الهَيْئاتِ مِن يَمَنٍ   ولا أجارَتْ ذوى الغاياتِ مِن مُضَرِ

Sharḥ qasīdat ibn ᶜAbdūn: Commentaire historique de poème d'Ibn ᶜAbdoun, ed. R. Dozy (Leiden, 1846).

11. Banū Sāsān: the Sassanians of Persia; Banū Yūnān: the Ptolemies of Egypt.

12. Legendary pre-Islamic peoples of Arabia. On the people of ᶜĀd cf. Koran 69:6.

13. The two great subgroups into which the Arabs were divided.

14 It scattered the Sabaeans in every land so that no evening traveler of theirs ever encountered a morning traveler.

15 It carried out its sentence against Kulaib and struck down Muhalhil in a lonely place.

16 It did not restore the wandering king [Imruʾ al-Qais] to a sound state nor prevent the tribe of Asad from [killing] its lord Ḥujr.

17 It humbled the Dhubyān and their brethren the ᶜAbs, and overwhelmed the Banū Badr near the reservoir [of al-Habāʾa].

18 In ᶜIrāq, it added the red-eyed, red-haired [Nuᶜmān III] to [the dead] ᶜAdī [ibn Zaid], at the hand of the latter's son.

19 It caused Parwīz to perish by means of his own son and chased Yazdajird to Marw from whence he never returned.

20 It chased Yazdajird to China and cut off all the Turks and Khazars from him [so that he remained with none but his] Persians.

21 Neither the swords of Rustum nor the spears of the royal chamberlain [Kharzad] were able to keep Saᶜd [ibn Abī Waqqās] from him during that unfortunate hour.

22 On the battle day of the ditch it was [the victims of the battle of] Badr who perished, while the ditch of Badr delivered all those it contained to hellfire.

23 It destroyed Jaᶜfar [ibn Abī Ṭālib] by the sword and snatched Ḥamza, the generous slaughterer of camels, from his lair.

24 It raised Khubaib aloft on a tall [pole], and caused Ṭalḥa the bouṇtiful to bite the dust.

---

14. The Sabaeans fled from the Yemen after the legendary bursting of the dam of Mārib.

15. Kulaib Wāʾil and Muhalhil were chiefs of the Banū Taghlib who died during the war of Basūs in pre-Islamic times.

16. Imruʾ al-Qais, the famous Muᶜallaqa poet, was the son of Ḥujr, king of Kinda, whom the Banū Asad killed. The poet died from wearing a poisoned tunic.

17. An allusion to an episode of the war of Dāhis between the ᶜAbs and the Dhubyān, during which a subgroup of the latter, the Banū Badr, were destroyed.

18. Nuᶜmān III, Arab king of Hira, won the throne with the help of ᶜAdī ibn Zaid whom he later killed. The latter's son, Zaid ibn ᶜAdī, avenged his father's death by persuading the Persian emperor Parwīz to destroy Nuᶜmān.

19. Parwīz came to power by putting to death his father Hormūz, after which his own son Shīrawaih murdered him.

20. Yazdajird III son of Shahrayar was the last Sassanian to rule Persia. After suffering defeat at the hand of the Arabs in Nihawand (A.H. 14), he fled

١٤ وَمَزَّقَتْ سَبَأً فِي كُلِّ قَاصِيَةٍ   فَمَا الْتَقَى رَائِحٌ مِنهم بِمُبْتَكِرِ

١٥ وَأَنْفَذَتْ في كُلَيْبٍ حُكْمَهَا ، وَرَمَتْ   مُهَلْهِلًا بين سَمْعِ الأرضِ والبَصَرِ

١٦ ولم تَرُدَّ على الضِّلِّيلِ صِحَّتَهُ   ولا ثَنَتْ أَسَدًا عن ربِّها حُجُرِ

١٧ ودَوَّخَتْ آلَ ذُبْيَانٍ وإِخْوَتَهُمْ   عَبْسًا ، وغَصَّتْ بني بَدْرٍ على النَّهَرِ

١٨ وأَلْحَقَتْ بِعَدِيٍّ بالعِرَاقِ على   يَدِ ٱبنِهِ أَحمرَ العينَيْنِ والشَّعَرِ

١٩ وأَهلَكَتْ إِبْرَوِيزًا بِٱبنِهِ ورَمَتْ   بِيَزْدَجِرْدَ إلى مَرْوٍ فلم يَحُرِ

٢٠ وبَلَّغَتْ يَزْدَجِرْدَ الصِّينَ وٱختزَلَتْ   عنه سِوَى الفُرْسِ جمعَ التُّرْكِ والخَزَرِ

٢١ ولم تَرُدَّ مَوَاضِي رُسْتُمٍ وَقَنَا   ذِي حاجِبٍ عنه سعدًا في ٱبنةِ الغِيَرِ

٢٢ يومَ القَلِيبِ بَنُو بَدْرٍ فَنَوْا وسعَى   قَلِيبُ بَدْرٍ بِمَنْ فيه إلى سَقَرِ

٢٣ ومزَّقَتْ جَعْفَرًا بالبِيضِ وٱختلَسَتْ   مِن غِيلِهِ حَمْزَةَ الظَّلَّامَ لِلجُزُرِ

٢٤ وأَشرفَتْ بِخُبَيْبٍ فوق فَارِعَةٍ   وأَلصقَتْ طَلْحَةَ الفَيَّاضَ بالعفرِ

---

to Marw where he was eventually deserted by his troops and murdered.

21. During the battle of Qādisiyya the Persian army was led by Rustum the Armenian and the chamberlain Kharzād. Saᶜd was the commander of the victorious Arab forces.

22. Allusion to the battle of Badr where Muhammad constructed a ditch to impede the movements of the enemy Quaraishites. After the battle, twenty-four bodies of the enemy were flung into the ditch.

23. Jaᶜfar was martyred at the battle of Muᵓta after having both his arms cut off and receiving fifty wounds. Ḥamza ibn ᶜAbd al-Muṭṭalib, uncle of Muhammad, was martyred at the battle of Uḥud. He was nicknamed "the lion of God" which explains the reference to the "lair" in this line.

24. Khubaib ibn ᶜAdī, one of the Anṣār, was captured at the battle of Rajīᶜ (A.H. 3) and sold to the Quraishites in Mecca, who crucified him. Ṭalḥa ibn ᶜUbaid Allāh at-Tamīmī was another partisan of the Prophet martyred at the battle of the Camel. He was one of the ten people to whom Muhammad guaranteed entry into Paradise.

25 It dyed the white hair of ᶜUthmān with blood and made for az-Zubair; nor did it abstain from ᶜUmar.

26 It was unmindful of Abū l-Yaqẓān's friendship, offering him only watered milk to drink in a small bowl.

27 It incited the sword of "the most wretched of men" to slaughter Abū Ḥasan [ᶜAlī ibn Abī Ṭālib] and empowered the hands of Shāmir [Ibn al-Jaushan] [to kill] Ḥusain.

28 Since it accepted Khārija as ransom for ᶜAmr, would that it had accepted any other human being as ransom for ᶜAlī.

29 Moreover, upon [Muᶜāwiya] the son of Hind, and Ḥasan the son of [ᶜAlī], the chosen of God, it brought a misfortune distressing to minds and to thoughts,

30 For some of us speak of the treachery done to him by a certain person, while others hold their peace about the attack to which he fell victim.

31 It destroyed [ᶜUbaid Allāh] Ibn Zīyād because of Ḥusain [ibn ᶜAlī], though the former was not even worth a broken sandal thong or fingernail of the latter.

32 It wound a turban of sword's edges about the temples of Abū Anas, while the spear of Zufar was unable to avert death from him.

33 It brought Muᶜṣab down from the height of a lofty place [Kufa] wherein the blood of al-Mukhtār had found refuge [i.e., "had been shed"].

34 It was unmindful of the station of Ibn az-Zubair, and showed no regard for [the fact that] he had invoked the protection of the Holy Sanctuary and the [Black] Stone [of the Kaᶜba].

---

25. ᶜUthmān, the third Caliph, was assassinated at the age of eighty-two in A.H. 35. Zubair ibn al-ᶜAuwām, an early convert to Islam, died during the battle of the Camel at the age of seventy-five. ᶜUmar, the second Caliph, was assassinated by a Christian slave, Abū Luᵓluᵓa at the age of sixty-three (A.H. 23).

26. Abū l-Yaqẓān ᶜAmmār ibn Yāsir, standard-bearer of the Caliph ᶜAlī, was killed at the battle of Ṣiffīn by Muᶜāwiya's partisans (A.H. 36). He is said to have called for a drink of water before the battle and upon receiving instead a bowl of milk, to have exclaimed: "The Prophet of God—may God bless and keep him—told me that milk was the last thing I would drink in this world."

27. ᶜAlī was assassinated by ᶜAbd ar-Raḥmān ibn Muljam at-Tujībī. According to a *ḥadith*, the Prophet said: "O ᶜAlī, the most wretched of [men] is the one who will dye this with this" pointing to ᶜAlī's beard and head. Ḥusain, son of ᶜAlī, was killed at Karbalāᵓ on the banks of the Euphrates where Shāmir led the victorious forces.

28. ᶜAmr ibn al-ᶜĀṣ was governor of Egypt. In a plot to kill ᶜAlī, Muᶜāwiya and ᶜAmr, the Persian Zādawaih was deputed to assassinate the latter, but by mistake murdered one of his followers, the qadi Khārija ibn Ghānim.

٢٥ وخَضَّبَتْ شَيْبَ عُثْمانٍ دمًا وخَطَتْ   إلى الزُّبَيْرِ ولم تَسْتَحْيِ مِن عُمَرِ

٢٦ ولا رَعَتْ لِأَبي اليَقْظانِ صُحْبَتَهُ   ولم تُزَوِّدْهُ إلّا الضَّيْحَ في الغُمَرِ

٢٧ وأَجْزَرَتْ سيفَ أشقاها أبا حَسَنٍ   وأَمْكَنَتْ مِن حُسَيْنٍ راحَتَيْ شَمِرِ

٢٨ ولَيْتَها إذ فَدَتْ عَمْرًا بِخارِجةٍ   فَدَتْ عَلِيًّا بِمَن شاءَتْ مِنَ البَشَرِ

٢٩ وفي ابنِ هِنْدٍ وفي ابنِ المُصْطَفَى حَسَنٍ   أَتَتْ بِمُعْضِلَةِ الألبابِ والفِكَرِ

٣٠ فبعضُنا قائلٌ ما اغتالَهُ أَحَدٌ   وبعضُنا ساكتٌ لم يُؤْتَ مِن حَصَرِ

٣١ وأَرْدَتْ ابنَ زِيادٍ بالحُسَيْنِ فلم   يَبُؤْ بِشِسْعٍ له قد طاحَ أو ظُفُرِ

٣٢ وعَمَّمَتْ بالظُّبَى فَوْدَيْ أبي أَنَسٍ   ولم تَرُدَّ الرَّدَى عنه قَنا زُفَرِ

٣٣ وأَنْزَلَتْ مُصْعَبًا مِن رأسِ شاهقةٍ   كانت بها مُهْجَةُ المُخْتارِ في وَزَرِ

٣٤ ولم تُراقِبْ مكانَ ابنِ الزُّبَيْرِ ولا   راعَتْ عِياذَتَهُ بالبَيْتِ والحَجَرِ

---

29. Ḥasan ibn ᶜAlī seems to have been poisoned in doubtful circumstances. Some Muslims claim that it was Ḥasan's wife Jaᶜda bint al-Ashᶜath who poisoned him in collusion with Muᶜāwiya in order to secure the throne for the latter's son Yazīd.

31. ᶜUbaid Allāh ibn Ziyād ibn Marjāna, the Umayyad governor of Kufa, gave orders to ᶜAmr ibn Saᶜd to attack Ḥusain who perished at Karbalāᵓ. In retaliation, ᶜUbaid was killed by the ᶜAlids at the battle of Khāzir.

32. Allusion to the battle of Marj Rāhit near Damascus where in A.H. 64 Abū Anas aḍ-Ḍaḥḥāk ibn Qais al-Fihrī, a follower of ᶜAbd Allāh ibn az-Zubair, along with Zufar ibn al-Ḥārith al-Kilābī, fought against the Umayyad Caliph ᶜAbd al-Mālik ibn Marwān and was killed, while Zufar was forced to flee.

33. Muṣᶜab ibn az-Zubair, brother of ᶜAbdullāh ibn az-Zubair was governor of Kufa. The Caliph ᶜAbd al-Malik defeated him at the battle of Jathulīq (A.H. 71–72) and he was killed in battle. Earlier, in Kufa, al-Mukhtār ibn ᶜUbaid ath-Thaqafī had been killed by Muᶜṣab (A.H. 67).

34. ᶜAbdullāh ibn az-Zubair was besieged in Mecca by the Umayyad governor al-Ḥajjāj ibn Yūsuf and fell in the Kaᶜba itself, in A.H. 73.

35 It exercised its cunning against the gaping-mouthed man and flocked to the foul-breathed, fly-ridden man.

36 Yet it left not even his sharp sword to the fly-ridden one, nor has ʿAmr of the gaping mouth been aided by it.

37 It burned the remains of Zaid [ibn ʿAlī ibn al-Ḥusain] after the very innermost portions of the [Koran's] verses and chapters had burned in anger against him.

38 It seized al-Walīd ibn al-Yazīd in its clutches, not allowing the Caliphate to remain [in the company] of wine cup or stringed [instrument].

39 As for Ḥabāba, a pomegranate seed was preordained [to cause her death], along with a red [wine] perfumed by the aroma of aloeswood.

40 It did not avert the swords of [Abū l-ʿAbbās ʿAbdullāh] as-Saffāḥ from the head of Marwān [II] or his wicked partisans.

41 It shed the tear of the angel Gabriel over a blood pertaining to the family of God's elect that was shed in Fakhkh with no retaliation.

42 It gave Jaʿfar [al-Barmakī] a taste of the bright, sharp, steel blade, while al-Faḍl [his brother] and the venerable Yaḥya [his father] were still in expectation of it.

43 It treacherously broke the oath of inheritance sworn in favor of al-Amīn [ibn Hārūn ar-Rashīd] and aroused Jaʿfar [ibn al-Muʿtaṣim al-Mutawakkil's] own son and treacherous slaves against him.

44 It did not respect the oaths sworn in favor of al-Mustaʿīn nor the rope strands firmly twisted in favor of al-Muʿtazz.

---

35. ʿAmr ibn Saʿd the Umayyad was called "the man slapped by the jinn" because of his gaping mouth, or possibly because of his eloquence. The Umayyad Caliph ʿAbd al-Malik ibn Marwān was nicknamed the "fly-ridden man" because it is said that his foul breath attracted flies. ʿAmr had aspired to the Caliphate, and ʿAbd al-Malik assassinated him in A.H. 70 to ensure his own accession.

37. Zaid, a descendant of the Caliph ʿAlī, died in A.H. 122 while fighting against the Umayyad Caliph Hishām. His body was crucified and burned while his head was sent to Damascus.

38. Walīd II was notorious for his addiction to wine, women, and song. He was killed in A.H. 126.

39. Ḥabāba was a singing girl to whom the Caliph Yazīd was deeply attached and who is said to have died choked by a pomegranate seed tossed to her by her own royal lover. A few days later, in A.H. 105, Yazīd also died, reportedly out of grief at her loss.

40. As-Saffāḥ was the first Abbasid Caliph. He killed the last Eastern Umayyad, Marwān II, at Būsīr in Egypt, in A.H. 132.

٣٥ وأعملتْ فى لَطِيمِ الجنِّ حِيلتَها   واستوسقتْ لِأَبِى الذِّبَّانِ ذى البَخَرِ

٣٦ ولم تَدَعْ لِأَبِى الذِّبَّانِ قاضِبَه   ليس اللَّطيمُ لها عمْرٌو بمنتصرِ

٣٧ وأحرقتْ شِلْوَ زَيْدٍ بعد ما احترقتْ   عليه وجدًا قلوبُ الآى والسُّوَرِ

٣٨ وأظفرَتْ بالوَلِيدِ بن اليَزِيدِ ولم   تُبْقِ الخِلافةَ بين الكأسِ والوَتَرِ

٣٩ حَبَابةٌ حَبُّ رُمَّانٍ أُتِيحَ لها   وأحمرٌ قطَّرَتْه نفحةُ القطرِ

٤٠ ولم تعدْ قُضُبُ السَّفَّاحِ نائيةً   عن رأسِ مَرْوانَ أو أشياعِه الفُجُرِ

٤١ وأسبلَتْ دمعةَ الروحِ الأَمينِ على   دمٍ بفخٍّ لآلِ المُصْطَفَى هَدَرِ

٤٢ وأشرقَتْ جَعْفَرًا والفضلُ يَنظُرُه   والشيخُ يَحْيَى بريقَ الصارم الذَّكَرِ

٤٣ وأخفرَتْ فى الأَمينِ العهدَ، وانتدبَتْ   لِجَعْفَرٍ بابْنِهِ والأَعْبُدِ الغُدرِ

٤٤ وما وَفَتْ بعُهُودِ المُسْتَعِينِ ولا   بما تأكَّدَ لِلمُعْتَزِّ مِن مِرَرِ

41. In A.H. 169, under the Abbasid Caliph al-Hādī, several ʿAlid descendants were put to death at Fakhkh near Mecca, among them Ḥusain ibn ʿAlī, six generations removed from the Caliph ʿAlī ibn Abī Ṭālib.

42. Jaʿfar the vizier of Hārūn ar-Rashīd was executed by order of the latter while his brother and father were poisoned to death at Raqqa.

43. Hārūn ar-Rashīd appointed his son al-Amīn as his immediate successor, to be followed by his other son Maʾmūn. The two brothers swore to abide by this decision, the text of which was hung on the Kaʿba and otherwise publicized. Maʾmūn, however, ousted his weaker brother from power. Al-Mutawakkil, the tenth Abbasid Caliph, attempted to reserve the succession for his son al-Muʿtazz, but another son, al-Muntaṣir, killed his father with the aid of Turkish mercenaries.

44. Al-Mustaʿīn ruled after al-Muntaṣir, coming to power in A.H. 248. But a civil war broke out between him and al-Muʿtazz. He was deposed in A.H. 252 and assassinated soon after. Al-Muʿtazz succeeded him but was confined to a prison by the Turks and died there in A.H. 255.

45 It has bound every Muᶜtamid in its noose and irritated the eye of every Muqtadir with its mote.

46 It has terrified every Ma'mūn and Muᶜtamin, and betrayed every Manṣūr and Muntaṣir.

47 It has tripped up the family of ᶜAbbād—may they rise up once more!—with the train of a great misfortune [which, unlike] a hairy-faced camel, [is so stubborn that] it does not shy away in panic [at the shadow cast by its own beard].

48 O Banū Muẓaffar! Since Time—may it not be inhabited!—is made up of road stations one day's journey apart, and men are ever journeying because of it,

49 May the day [of your death] be accursed among days, and may no night bear its equal in time to come!

50 Who will [sit on] thrones and [manage] the reins [of government] and who will guide the lances to the frontier?

51 [Who will wield] sword edges and spearpoints now that the tips of their tongues have been bound by speechlessness,

52 And [Time] has caused the black Fates to encircle their white helmets to oppress them? Therefore wonder at it all, for only memory of them survives!

53 [Who will ply] the pen? Who will be accomplished in every excellence? Who will be generous? Who will reward or punish?

54 [Who will] repel a blow of misfortune, avert an impending doom, prevent an evil accident that renders even Fate powerless?

55 Woe to generosity; woe to courage—should they still be sound—for the mourning of religion and the world [is poured out] over [Abū Muḥammad] ᶜUmar [al-Mutawakkil ibn al-Muẓaffar of Badajoz]!

56 May the fresh graves of al-Faḍl and al-ᶜAbbās [his sons] be watered by a flowing [rain cloud] which, insofar as generosity is concerned, is related to them rather than to rain.

---

45. There are two Muᶜtamids: Aḥmad ibn Mutawakkil the Abbasid who was poisoned to death in A.H. 279, and Muḥammad ibn ᶜAbbād of Seville who was imprisoned in Aghmāt by the Almoravids and died in A.H. 488. Likewise there are two Muqtadirs: Jaᶜfar ibn Muᶜtaḍid the Abbasid [d. 320] and Aḥmad ibn Sulaimān ibn Hūd of Saragossa (d. A.H 475). In this way the poet makes a transition from the East to the situation in Muslim Spain.

46. There are several Ma'mūn's, among them the Abbasid, the son of Muᶜtamid of Seville, and Yaḥya ibn Dhī n-Nūn of Toledo. ᶜAbd al-Azīz ibn Abī ᶜĀmir took the title of Muᶜtamin, and among the Manṣūrs, in Spain the most famous was Muḥammad ibn Abī ᶜĀmir ("Almanzor") followed by several

٤٥ وأَونَقَتْ فى عُراها كلَّ مُعْتَمِدٍ   وأَشرقَتْ بِقَذاها كلَّ مُقْتَدِرِ
٤٦ وروَّعَتْ كلَّ مَأْمُونٍ ومُؤْتَمِنٍ   وأَسلَمَتْ كلَّ مَنْصُورٍ ومُنْتَصِرِ
٤٧ وأَعثرَتْ آلَ عَبَّادٍ لَعًا لَهُمُ   بِذَيْلِ زَبَّاءَ لم تَنْفِرْ مِن الذُّعُرِ
٤٨ بَنِى المُظَفَّرِ والأيّامُ ـ لا نُزِلتْ ـ   مَراحِلٌ، والوَرَى منها على سَفَرِ
٤٩ سُحْقًا لِيَومِكُمُ يَومًا ولا حملتْ   بمثلِهِ لَيلةٌ فى غابِرِ العُمُرِ
٥٠ مَن لِلأَسِرَّةِ، أو مَن لِلأَعِنَّةِ، أو   مَن لِلأَسِنَّةِ يُهْدِيها إلى الثُّغَرِ
٥١ مَن لِلظُّبَى وعَوالِى الخطِّ قد عُقِدَتْ   أَطرافُ أَلْسُنِها بالعِىِّ والحَصَرِ
٥٢ وطَوَّقتْ بالمَنايا السُّودِ بَيْضَهُمُ   فأعجبْ لذاك وما منها سِوَى الذِكَرِ
٥٣ مَن لِلْيَراعةِ أو مَن لِلْبَراعةِ أو   مَن لِلسَّماحةِ أو للنَّفْعِ والضَّرَرِ
٥٤ أو دَفْعِ كارثةٍ أو ردعِ آزِفةٍ   أو قَمْعِ حادثةٍ تَعْيَا على القُدَرِ
٥٥ وَيْبَ السَّماحِ ووَيْبَ البَأْسِ لو سَلِمَا   وحسرةُ الدينِ والدنيا على عُمَرِ
٥٦ سَقَتْ ثَرَى الفضلِ والعباس هاميةٌ   تُعْزَى إليهم سَماحًا لا إلى المَطَرِ

Ṭawāᵓif rulers who adopted his title, including Muḥammad ibn Maslama ibn al-Afṭas of Badajoz. There was an Abbasid Muntaṣir (Abu Jaᶜfar Muḥammad ibn Mutawakkil).

47. Allusion to the ᶜAbbādids of Seville. A variant of this line reads: "It has tripped up the family of ᶜAbbās—may they rise up once more!—with the train of a dire misfortune consisting of white [swords] and tawny [lances]" (*bi-dhaili riyāᵓi min biḍin wa min sumurī*).

48. The Banū Muẓaffar were the Afṭasid dynasty of Badajoz to whom the present elegy is dedicated.

57 Those three: never did Venus or Jupiter see their equal in nobility even though they should both be reinforced by the sun and the moon.

58 Those three: neither the Eagle nor Lyra nor any of the eagles that fly have ascended or flown as high as they.

59 Those three are like the passing of Time itself; since they have become separated from me, Time has passed without stopping or turning back,

60 While the sweetest part of everything in it is gone, even enjoyment of the evening and morning hours.

61 Where is the majesty before which our hearts were awed and the radiant stars lowered their eyes in respect?

62 Where is the heroic, disdainful pride whose pillars they set firmly upon foundations of power and victory?

63 Where is the loyalty whose laws they purified so that no one ever drew turbid waters from them?

64 They were the stabilizers of God's earth; since they have departed, it, along with its inhabitants, is sundered and unsteady.

65 They were its shining lamps, yet since they have been extinguished all these creatures have stumbled about, by God, as if overcome by giddiness.

66 They obstructed the throat of Fate and therefore its deceits beguiled them with vain delusions like those of the people of ᶜĀd, delusions that came running at a fast pace.

67 Woe to the mother of him who seeks blood revenge taking it from them in retaliation for brave, lionlike warriors steadfast in battle!

68 Who will avail me—if he has not availed them—when [we] are oppressed by dire misfortunes whose nighttime will never see the dawn?

69 Who will avail me—if he has not availed them—when all laws have been forsaken and the tongues of traditions and histories have been silenced?

70 Who will avail me—if he has not availed them—when trials flock in great numbers and their flow will never return whence it came?

71 To those noble virtues—even if patience [cannot console us] after their [loss]—let there be greetings from an onlooker waiting for the [eternal] Reward,

---

67. Variant to the second hemistich: *law kāna dainan ᶜalā l-aiyāmi dhī ᶜasarī*, 'even though it is a debt owed by the hard times.'

٥٧ ثلاثةٌ ما رأى السعدانُ مثلَهُمُ   فضلًا ولو عُزِّزَا بالشمسِ والقمرِ
٥٨ ثلاثةٌ ما ارتقى النَّسْرانُ حيثُ رَقوا   وكلُّ ما طارَ مِن نَسْرٍ ولم يَطِرِ
٥٩ ثلاثةٌ كذواتِ الدهرِ منذ نَأَوْا   عنّي، مضى الدهرُ لم يَرْبَعْ ولم يَحُرِ
٦٠ ومَرَّ مِن كلِّ شيءٍ فيه أطيَبُهُ   حتى التمتُّعُ بالآصالِ والبُكَرِ
٦١ أَيْنَ الجلالُ الذي غضَّتْ مَهابَتُهُ   قُلوبَنا وعُيونُ الأَنْجُمِ الزُّهُرِ
٦٢ أَيْنَ الإباءُ الذي أَرْسَوْا قَواعِدَهُ   على دَعائِمَ مِن عِزٍّ ومِن ظَفَرِ
٦٣ أين الوَفاءُ الذي أصْفَوْا شَرائِعَهُ   فلم يَرِدْ أحدٌ منها على كَدَرِ
٦٤ كانوا رَواسِيَ أرضِ اللهِ منذ مَضَوْا   عنها استطارَتْ بِمَن فيها ولم تَقِرِ
٦٥ كانوا مَصابِيحَها فمُذْ خَبَوْا عَثَرَتْ   هذي الخَليقةُ يا لَلّهِ في سَدَرِ
٦٦ كانوا شَجَى الدهرِ فاستهوتْهُمُ خُدَعٌ   منه بأحلامِ عادٍ في خُطَى الحضرِ
٦٧ وَيْلُمِّهِ مِن طَلُوبِ الثأرِ مُدْرِكِهِ   منهم بأُسْدٍ سُرَاةٍ في الوَغَى صُبُرِ
٦٨ مَن لي ولا مَن بِهِمْ إنْ أظْلَمَتْ نُوَبٌ   ولم يكن لَيلُها يُفْضِي إلى سَحَرِ
٦٩ مَن لي ولا مَن بِهِمْ إنْ عُطِّلَتْ سُنَنٌ   وأُخْفِيَتْ أَلْسُنُ الآثارِ والسِّيَرِ
٧٠ مَنْ لي ولا مَنْ بِهِمْ إنْ أطبقتْ مِحَنٌ   ولم يكنْ وِرْدُها يَدعو إلى صَدَرِ
٧١ على الفضائلِ إلا الصبرَ بَعدَهُمُ   سَلامُ مُرْتَقِبٍ للأَجْرِ مُنْتَظِرِ

72 One hoping for "perhaps" and even for its sister "it may be," for Fate has many different revolutions and vicissitudes.

73 I have adorned the ears of those [who constitute the subject] of this [poem] with [an earring] which will cause lovely women to despise rubies and pearls,

74 [A poem] which will travel to the furthest ends of the earth and interrupt the vain chatter uselessly poured forth in the desert and in the towns,

75 [A poem] whose authority will be respected by [men's] minds while it will satisfy ears that have never been satisfied by anything else.

٧٢ يَرْجُو عَسَى ولـه فى أُخْتِهـا أَمَـلٌ   والدهرُ ذو عُقَبٍ شَتَّى وذو غِيَـرِ

٧٣ قَرَّطتُ آذانَ مَن فيهـا بفاضِحَـةٍ   على الحسانِ حَصَى الياقوتِ والدُّرَرِ

٧٤ سَيَّارةٍ فى أَقاصِى الأَرضِ قاطِعـةٍ   شَقاشِقًا هَدَرَتْ فى البَدْوِ والحَضَرِ

٧٥ مُطاعَةِ الأَمْـرِ في الأَلْبابِ قاضيـةٍ   مِن المَسامِعِ ما لم يُقْضَ مِن وَطَرِ

21 Ibn Khafāja

1 By your life, do you know whether it is the violence of the south winds dashing against my saddle, or the backs of excellent camels?

2 For hardly had I observed a certain star in the early dawn, when I set off at sunrise [and traveled on] until the very end of the sunset

3 Alone, while the waterless deserts led me on from one to another. Thus I see the faces of the fates [hidden] under the veil of deepest gloom,

4 For there is no refuge save in a keen blade, nor is there any home save in the wooden saddle frames of the riders.

5 And there is no human companionship save in my sporting for a [short] hour with the mouths which are the objects of my desire, contained in the faces from which I seek the satisfaction of my wants,

6 And many a night which passed as I said: "It has finally come to an end," has revealed a promise that belies conjecture.

7 On such a night I dragged the [edges of the mantle] of a darkness black of locks, that I might embrace [the goal of my] hopes, white of breasts.

8 Then I tore the collar of the nights off the form of a grayish [wolf] which appeared bright of front teeth, grinning.

9 I observed with him a fragment of the dawn during the last part of the night, contemplating a certain star that had lighted up, a shining one.

10 [I also observed] a mountain with a sharp peak, lofty of summit, grandiose, vying in height with the [uppermost] regions of the sky, having a [crest] like the upper part of a camel's hump,

11 Stopping the blowing of the wind from all directions and at night, pressing against the stars above it with its shoulders,

12 Rising gravely over the surface of the waterless plain, as if through the long nights it were one reflecting on the consequences of [all] things.

13 The clouds wind black turbans around its [head] in such a way that the flashes of lightning make it appear to have red locks.

---

21. Sources: Ibn Khafāja, *Dīwān*, ed. Karam al-Bustānī (Beirut, 1961), pp. 42–44; Jaudat ar-Rikābī, *Fī l-adab al-Andalusī* (Cairo, 1960), pp. 139–142.

Meter: *ṭawīl.*

٢١

ابن خفاجة

١ بِعَيْنَيْكَ هل تدري، أَهُوجُ الجَنائِبِ،   تَخُبُّ بِرَحْلي، أَمْ ظُهورُ النَّجائِبِ؟

٢ فما لُحْتُ في أُولَى المَشارِقِ كَوْكَبًا   فأَشْرَقْتُه، حتى جِئْتُ أُخْرَى المَغارِبِ

٣ وَحيدًا تَهاداني الفَيافي، فأَجْتَلي   وُجوهَ المَنايا، في قِناعِ الغَياهِبِ

٤ ولا جارَ إلاّ مِن حُسامٍ مُصَمِّمٍ،   ولا دارَ إلاّ في قُتُودِ الرَّكائِبِ

٥ ولا أُنْسَ إلاّ أَنْ أُضاحِكَ، ساعَةً،   ثُغورَ الأَماني في وُجوهِ المَطالِبِ

٦ ولَيْلٍ، إذا ما قُلْتُ قَدْ بادَ، فانْقَضَى،   تَكَشَّفَ عن وَعْدٍ مِنَ الظَّنِّ كاذِبِ

٧ سَحَبْتُ الدَّياجي فيهِ سُودَ ذَوائِبٍ،   لِأَعْتَنِقَ الآمالَ بِيضَ تَرائِبِ

٨ فمَزَّقْتُ جَيْبَ اللَّيْلِ عن شَخْصِ أَطْلَسٍ   تَطَلَّعَ وَضّاحِ المَضاحِكِ قاطِبِ

٩ رَأَيْتُ بهِ قِطْعًا مِنَ الفَجْرِ أَغْبَشًا،   تَأَمَّلَ عن نَجْمٍ، تَوَقَّدَ، ثاقِبِ

١٠ وأَرْعَنَ طَمّاحِ الذُّؤابَةِ باذِخٍ،   يُطاوِلُ أَعْنانَ السَّماءِ بِغارِبِ

١١ يَسُدُّ مَهَبَّ الرِّيحِ عن كلِّ وُجْهَةٍ،   ويَزْحَمُ، لَيْلًا، شُهْبَهُ بالمَناكِبِ

١٢ وَقورٍ، على ظَهْرِ الفَلاةِ، كأَنَّهُ،   طِوالَ اللَّيالي، مُفْكِرٌ في العَواقِبِ

١٣ يَلُوثُ عليهِ الغَيْمُ سُودَ عَمائِمٍ،   لَها، مِن وَمِيضِ البَرْقِ، حُمْرُ ذَوائِبِ

14 I listened to it even though it was dumb and silent, yet during the nights of journeying it informed me of marvels,

15 Saying: "Lo, for how long will I be the shelter of murderers and the abode of sorrowing penitents devoted to God's service?

16 And how many times have travelers going off at night and returning [by day] passed by me, while riding beasts and riders have taken their siesta in my shade,

17 And contrary winds have lashed out at my flanks while the green seas have dashed against my sides!

18 And all this took place only in order that the hand of death might enfold them and so that the wind of separation and misfortune might carry them off in its flight!

19 The quivering of my groves is but the panting of a [feverish] chest [struggling for breath], while the mourning of my doves is but the wail of one lamenting the dead.

20 Nor has consolation restrained my tears; rather I have exhausted my tears in separation from my companions.

21 Until when will I remain behind when a dear one travels away, saying farewell to him when he departs never to return?

22 Until when will I watch the stars [like a shepherd watches his flock], remaining awake all night long, for they will rise and set to the end of the nights?

23 Hence show merciful compassion, O my lord, for the plea of a humble entreater, who extends a supplicating hand toward your blessing."

24 In this way it caused me to listen, in its exhortation, to every useful example which the tongue of trials interpreted for it;

25 Moreover it gave consolation by moving to tears, and joy by causing grief, when it was the best of companions during the night journey,

26 So I said, having turned away from it to reach a [certain] goal: "Farewell, for some of us must remain while others must depart."

١٤ أَصَخْتُ إليهِ، وهوَ أَخْرَسُ صَامِتٌ، فحدَّثني لَيْلَ السُّرى بالعَجائِبِ
١٥ وقالَ: أَلا كَمْ كُنْتُ مَلْجأَ قاتِلٍ، ومَوْطِنَ أَوَّاهٍ، تَبَتَّلَ، تائِبِ
١٦ وكَمْ مَرَّ بي مِن مُدْلِجٍ ومُؤَوِّبٍ، وقالَ بِظِلِّي مِن مَطِيٍّ وراكِبِ
١٧ ولاطَمَ، مِن نُكبِ الرِّياحِ، مَعاطِفِي، وزاحَمَ، مِن خُضْرِ البِحارِ، غَوارِبِي
١٨ فَما كانَ إلاّ أَنْ طَوَتْهُمْ يَدُ الرَّدَى، وطارَتْ بِهِم ريحُ النَّوَى والنَّوائِبِ
١٩ فَما خَفْقُ أَيْكِي غَيْرَ رَجْفَةِ أَضْلُعٍ، ولا نَوْحُ وُرْقِي غَيْرَ صَرْخَةِ نادِبِ
٢٠ وما غَيَّضَ السُّلْوانُ دَمْعِي، وإنَّما نَزَفْتُ دُمُوعِي في فِراقِ الصَّواحِبِ
٢١ فحتى متى أَبْقَى، ويَظْعَنُ صاحِبٌ، أُوَدِّعُ مِنْهُ راحِلاً غَيْرَ آيِبِ؟
٢٢ وحتى متى أَرْعَى الكَواكِبَ ساهِرًا، فَمِنْ طالِعٍ، أُخْرَى اللَّيالي، وغارِبِ؟
٢٣ فَرُحْماكَ يا مَوْلايَ، دَعْوَةَ ضارِعٍ، يَمُدُّ إلى نُعْماكَ راحَةَ راغِبِ
٢٤ فأَسْمَعَني، مِن وَعْظِهِ، كلَّ عِبْرَةٍ، يُتَرْجِمُها عَنْهُ لِسانُ التَّجارِبِ
٢٥ فَسَلَّى بِمَا أَبْكَى، وسَرَّى بِما شَجَا، وكانَ، على عَهْدِ السُّرَى، خَيْرَ صاحِبِ
٢٦ وقُلْتُ، وقَدْ نَكَّبْتُ عنه لِطِيَّةٍ: سَلامٌ، فَإنَّا مِنْ مُقِيمٍ وذاهِبِ

22 Ibn az-Zaqqāq

1 My two friends, the love of one's two sons is not heresy, so surely you will both establish my innocence concerning the matter.

2 My heart is divided between two children: one of its halves belongs to the one while the other has clung to the other half.

3 [They are] both small, yet my life is not diminished because of them, nor is my luck scant or paltry.

4 Moreover, one man says: "In secret you prefer Muḥammad," and another: "Ibrāhīm is preferred in secret."

5 Yet I reply: "They are two offshoots which I treat as equal raindrops, though the father of two children may [at times be] unjust.

6 They are unequal in years, yet they are equal in the fondness and love [concealed] in [my] ribs and [my] breast.

7 Their place in the lodging of the heart is one, so that wherever Abū Bakr is, there too is Abū ᶜAmr.

8 I love the goodness of Time in their company, and were it not for them I would pay no attention to Time.

9 For anyone may seek to enjoy life, yet I enjoy my life only in their good health.

---

22. SOURCE: Ibn az-Zaqqāq, *Dīwān*, ed. ᶜAfīfa Dairānī (Beirut, 1964), pp. 176–177.
METER: *ṭawīl.*

٢٢

ابن الزّقّاق

١ خليليّ ما حُبُّ البُنَيَّيْنِ بِبِدْعَةٍ فهل أَنْتُمَا فيه مُقِيمانِ مِن عُذْرِي

٢ تَقَسَّمَ قَلْبِي بَيْنَ طِفْلَيْنِ شَطْرُهُ لِهذا، وهذا قد تَعَلَّقَ بالشَّطْرِ

٣ صَغِيرَيْنِ لم تَصْغُرْ حَياتي عليهما ولا كانَ حَظِّي باليَسيرِ ولا النَّزْرِ

٤ فَمِنْ قائلٍ آثرْتَ سِرًّا مُحَمَّدًا وآخرُ إبْراهِيمَ تُؤْثِرُ في السِّرِ

٥ فَقُلْتُ : هُمَا غُصْنانِ أَعْدِلُ فيهِمَا إذا جارَ ذو النجلين،عَدْلَ نَدَى القَطْرِ

٦ وما آسْتَوَيَا سِنًّا ولٰكِنْ تَساوَيا وَلوعًا وحُبًّا في الجَوانِحِ والصَّدْرِ

٧ مَحَلُّهما في مَنْزِلِ القَلْبِ واحِدٌ فَحَيْثُ أَبُو بَكْرٍ فَثَمَّ أَبُو عَمْرِو

٨ أُحِبُّ صَلاحَ الدَّهْرِ في جانِبَيْهِما ولولاهما ما كُنْتُ أَحْفَلُ بالدَّهْرِ

٩ فَمَنْ كانَ يَبْغِي العمرَ مستمتعًا به فلا أَبْغِ إلاّ في صَلاحِهِما عُمْرِي

23 Al Aʿmā at-Tuṭīlī

1 Tears that are shed and a breast that is burned
Water and fire!
Things never joined save for matters of moment!
2 By my life, it is harsh, what the censor has said,
For life is but short while love's toils are long.
3 O, for the sighs that betray one who loves!
And O, for the tears that flow like a stream!

4 Sleep is taboo, visitation is far;
No peace and quiet!
I would fly, yet I find no place to take flight!
5 O Kaʿba to which all hearts journey forth
Torn by passion that calls and answering love,
6 You called on a sinner returning to you;
Here I am! I heed not the words of the spy!

7 Allow me to travel and worship therein;
Make no excuse!
My heart is the gift and my tears are the stones.
8 Welcome is he, though he expose me to death;
One supple of waist and languid of eye.
9 O hardness of heart which love sees as soft,
You have caused me to learn that thoughts can think ill!

10 Since he made off from those nights which were short
My tears gush forth
As though in my lids were sharp-pointed swords!
11 I've chosen a lord who unjustly condemns;
To him I allude not revealing his name;
12 My justice is wondrous in view of his wrong!
Him you may ask for the tryst and refusal.

13 He tore from a passion well proven my share
Of obedience,
Though shunned. Joy after him may choose whom it wills.

---

23. SOURCES: al-Aʿmā at-Tuṭīlī, *Dīwān*, ed. Iḥsān ʿAbbās (Beirut, 1963), pp. 261–262; E. García Gómez, *Las jarchas romances de la serie árabe en su marco* (Madrid, 1965), pp. 103–107.

FORM: *muwashshaḥa*.

METER: a—a—a—a *m—m—m*
11 11 11 11 11 4 11

RHYTHM: dactytic.

1. García Gómez reads *damʿun safūḥun.*
3. García Gómez reads *ʿan ʿalīl;* also *qad aṣābat masīl.*

٢٣

الاعمى التطيلي

١ دَمْعٌ مَسْفوحْ وضُلوعٌ حِرارْ ماءٌ ونارْ ما ٱجْتَمَعا إلّا لِأَمْرٍ كُبارْ

٢ بِئسَ لَعَمْرِي ما أَرادَ العَذولْ عُمْرٌ قَصيرٌ وعِناءٌ طَويلْ

٣ يا زَفَراتٍ نَطَقَتْ عن غَليلْ ويا دُموعًا قد أَعانَتْ مَسيلْ

٤ إِمْتَنَعَ النَّومُ وشَطَّ المَزارْ ولا قَرارْ طِرْتُ ولٰكِنْ لم أعدهٔ مَطارْ

٥ يا كعبةً حَجَّتْ إليها القُلوبْ بَيْنَ هَوًى داعٍ وشَوْقٍ مُجيبْ

٦ حَنَّة أَوّاهٍ إليها مُنيبْ لَبَّيْكَ لا أَلْوِ لِقَوْلِ الرَّقيبْ

٧ جُذْلي بِحَجٍّ عندها وٱعْتِمارْ ولا ٱعْتِذارْ قَلْبِيَ هَدْيٌ ودُموعِي جِمارْ

٨ أَهْلًا وإنّ عرض بي لِلمَنُونْ بِمائِسِ الأَعْطافِ ساجِي الجُفُونْ

٩ يا قَسْوَةً يَحْسِبُها الصَّبُّ لِينْ عَلَّمْتِني كَيْفَ تَسُوءُ الظُّنُونْ

١٠ مُذْ بانَ عن تلك الليالي القِصارْ نَوْمي غِرارْ كأَنَّما بَيْنَ جُفوني غِرارْ

١١ حَكَّمْتُ مَوْلًى جارَ في حُكْمِهِ أَكْنِي به لا مُفْصِحًا بِٱسْمِهِ

١٢ فٱعْجَبْ لِإنْصافِي على ظُلْمِهِ وٱسْأَلْهُ عن وَصْلِي وعن حُرْمِهِ

١٣ أَلْوَى بِحَقِّي عن هَوًى وٱخْتِيارْ طوعَ النِّفارْ فكلُّ أُنْسٍ بَعْدَهُ بالخِيارْ

---

4. García Gómez reads *lam uṣādif maṭār.*

6. The *Dīwān* reads *la alhū wa qul li-r-raqīb.*

7. The *Dīwān* reads *mur-nī bi ḥajjin.*

8. *Bi-māʾisi l-aᶜṭāfi* is missing in the *Dīwān,* but is supplied by García Gómez.

9. The *Dīwān* reads *kaifa ʾusīʾu.*

12. García Gómez reads *ᶜan ṣarmi-hi.*

13. García Gómez reads *alwā bi-ḥaẓẓī.*

14 I cannot resist him on any condition;
A lord who accuses, treats harshly, delays;
15 Who left me in pledge to despair and disease,
Then sang with an air between boldness and love:

16 "Meu l-ḥabīb enfermo de meu amar.
¿Que no ha d'estar?
¿Non ves a mibe que s'ha de no llegar?"

---

16. The Romance words mean: 'My beloved is sick for love of me. How can he not be so? Do you not see that he is not allowed near me?'

١٤ لا بُدَّ لي مِنه على كلّ حالْ　　مَوْلًى تَجَنَّى وجَفَا وٱسْتَطالْ

١٥ غادَرَني رَهْنَ أَسًى وٱعْتِلالْ　　ثُمَّ شَدَا بَيْنَ الهَوَى والدَّلالْ:

١٦ مَوْ أَلْحَبِيبْ أَنْفَرْمُ ذِي مَوْأَمَرْ، كَنَ دَشْتَرْ، نُنْفِيسْ أَمِيبِ كَسَدِ نُولْيِغَرْ

24 Al-Aʿmā at-Tuṭīlī

1	Laughing out of pearls,	A full moon appears
	Surpassing all Time	Though held in my heart;
2	Alas for my woe!	I pine in distress!
3	I danced to her tune;	A gentle assailant.
4	If I say: "At last,"	"How d'you know?" says she.
5	She sways like a willow	Green, supple, and fresh
	Which is teased by the hands	Of the breeze and the rain.
6	I cannot resist you:	Take my heart in abasement.
7	A fresh spring of honey	Puts an end to the patience
8	Which I try to maintain;	My yearning bears witness
9	To the daughter of jugs	And to that sweet mouth.
	What's the face of all Time	To the flush of that wine?
10	All my love I conceal,	Would my efforts could end it!
11	When it starts to arise,	Its horizon's my heart.
12	That beautiful vision	Leaves my passion unhealed
13	O, why, by my father,	Did a pearly bright star
	Shine forth and reveal	Her excuse and my plea?
14	Is there no way to you?	Must I always despair?
15	I wept not a little;	Tears flowed and I sighed;
16	I thought what to say;	"Perhaps" makes me sad,

---

24. SOURCES: al-Aʿmā at-Tuṭīlī, *Dīwān*, ed. Iḥsān ʿAbbās (Beirut, 1963), pp. 253–254; Jaudat ar-Rikābī, *Fī l-adab al-Andalusī* (Cairo, 1960), pp. 315–316.

FORM: *muwashshaḥa*

METER: a–a–a–a–a–a *m–n–m–n*
6 7 6 7 6 7 7 6 7 6

RHYTHM: mixed (óooóoó).

٢٤

الاعمى التطيلي

١ ضاحِكٌ عن جُمانْ سافِرٌ عن بَدْرِ ضَاقَ عنه الزَّمانْ وَحَواهُ صَدْرِي

٢ آهْ مِمَّا أَجِدْ شَفَّنِي ما أَجِدُ

٣ قامَ بِي وقَعَدْ باطِشٌ مُتَّئِدُ

٤ كُلَّمَا قُلْتُ قَدْ قالَ لى أَيْنَ قَدُ

٥ وَٱنْثَنَىخُوطَ بَانْ ذا مَهَزٍّ نَضْرِ عابَثَتْهُ يَدانْ لِلصَّبَا والقَطْرِ

٦ لَيْسَ لي مِنْكَ بُدْ خُذْ فُؤادِي عَنْ يَدْ

٧ لم تَدَعْ لي جَلَدْ غير أَنِّي أَجْهَدْ

٨ مَكْرَعٌ مِن شُهُدْ وٱشْتِياقِي يَشْهَدْ

٩ مالِبِنْتِ الدِّنانْ ولِذاكَ الثَّغْرِ أَيْنَ مُحَيَّا الزَّمانْ مِن حُمَيَّا الخَمْرِ

١٠ بي هَوًى مُضْمَرُ لَيْتَ جَهْدِي وَفْقُهْ

١١ كُلَّما يَظْهَرُ فَفُؤادِي أُفْقُهْ

١٢ ذلك المَنْظَرُ لا يُداوِى عِشْقُهْ

١٣ بِأَبِي كَيْفَ كانْ فَلَكِيٌّ دُرِّي راقَ حتى ٱسْتَبانْ عُذْرُهُ وَعُذْرِي

١٤ هَلْ إلَيْكَ سَبيلْ أَوْ إلى أَنْ أَيْأَسا

١٥ ذُبْتُ إلَّا قَليلْ عَبْرَةً أَوْ نَفَسا

١٦ ما عَسَى أَنْ أَقولْ ساءَ ظَنِّي بِعَسَى

---

9. The *Dīwān* reads *muḥaiyā l-jamrī.*

17 Since all comes to nought. Yet am I headstrong;
I gallop loose reined, Unbridling restraint.
18 It harms not my blamer That she keeps avoiding,
19 Yet for the love of a doe Whose habit's accusing
20 I'm possessed by despair, While she sings this ditty:
21 "I see that you're pining; I say, what's with you man;
You know Time will pass And you will forget me."

21. The variant *laisa ʿalai-ka sa-tadrī* is recorded in the *Dīwān*, but García Gómez has corrected the reading to *aish ʿalai-ka* (see: "Estudio del Dār aṭ-ṭirāz," *Andalus*, XVII [1962], 21–104).

١٧ وَٱنْقَضَى كُلُّ شَانْ   وأَنَا أَسْتَشْرِي   خالِعًا مِن عِنانْ   جَزَعِي أَوْ صَبْرِي
١٨ ما على مَنْ يَلُومْ   لَوْ تَناهَى عَنِّي
١٩ هَلْ سِوَى حُبِّ رِيمْ   دِينُهُ التَّجَنِّي
٢٠ أَنا فيهِ أَهِيمْ   وَهْوَ بي يُغَنِّي :
٢١ قَدْ رَأَيْتُكْ عيانْ   أَيْشْ عليكْ سَتَدْرِي   سَيَطُولُ الزَّمَانْ   وَسَتَنْسَى ذِكْرِي

25 Ibn Baqī

1 I have no wine other than sorrows mixed in the cup with flowing tears.
2 To God be attributed the tears dispersed
3 By a lover who wept out of deepest emotion,
4 Whom a wild fawn destroyed on the day of al-Baqīʿ.
5 Thus he lies slain, nay—pierced through and through; his moment of death lies twixt hope and despair.
6 I have been wounded to death; I wring my hands,
7 For [the love] between me and my friend has been changed.
8 There is no doubt that from separation my death will ensue.
9 The time of departure is at hand, even though there are rights in my favor such that if al-ʿAbbās were to repudiate them, then would he be al-Amīn.
10 Do you not behold the full moon—the full moon of good augury?
11 It has donned a green robe
12 While it bent in its supple freshness, among the [svelte] figures,
13 It declared in broad daylight: "Die, O mournful one: The jasmine [of my cheeks] has been clad with the myrtle [of my beard]."

---

25. SOURCE: Ibn Sanāʾ al-Mulk, *Dār aṭ-ṭirāz fī ʿamal al-muwashshaḥāt*, ed. Jaudat ar-Rikābī (Damascus, 1949), pp. 67–68.
FORM: *muwashshaḥa.*
METER: a–b–a–b–a–b *m–n–o–n*
6 5 6 5 6 5 5 5 7 5
RHYTHM: mixed (óooó/óooó/oóoóoó/óooó/oóooóo/óooóo).
4. Al-Baqīʿ is one of the "battle days" of pre-Islamic Arabia.

٢٥

ابن بقي

١ مالي شَمولْ إلاَّ شُجونْ مِزاجُها في الكاسْ دَمْعٌ هَتونْ

٢ لِلّهِ ما بَذَرْ مِنَ الدُّموعِ

٣ صَبٌّ قدِ ٱسْتَعْبَرْ مِنَ الوَلوعِ

٤ أَوْدَى بهِ جُؤْذَرْ يَوْمَ البَقيعِ

٥ فَهْوَ قَتيلْ لا بَلْ طَعينْ بَيْنَ الرَّجاوالياسْ لَهُ مَنونْ

٦ جُرِحْتُ لِلحَيْنِ كَفِّي بِكَفِّي

٧ وحِيلَ ما بَيْني وبَيْنَ إلْفي

٨ لا شَكَّ بالبَيْنِ يَكونُ حَتْفي

٩ حانَ الرَّحيلْ ولي دُيُونْ إنْ رَدَّها العَبّاسْ فَهْوَ الأَمينْ

١٠ أَما تَرَى البَدْرَا بَدْرَ السُّعودِ

١١ قَدِ ٱكْتَسَى خُضْرَا مِنَ البُرودِ

١٢ إذا ٱنْثَنَى نَضْرَا بَيْنَ القُدودِ

١٣ أَضْحَى يَقولْ مُتْ يا حَزينْ قَدِ ٱكْتَسَى بِالآسْ أَلْيَاسَمينْ

---

9. Al-Amīn and Maʾmūn were the two sons of the Abbasid Caliph Hārūn ar-Rashīd. Upon the death of the latter al-Amīn produced a will written by his father which provided for a dual succession. Soon after, he produced a second document in direct contravention to his father's will and designed to oust his brother from the throne. Al-Amīn reigned from A.D. 808 to 813 and was eventually ousted by his more capable brother Maʾmūn (*cf.* W. Muir, *The Caliphate* [reprint ed.; Beirut, 1963], p. 489). Al-ʿAbbās is presumably the name of the person panegyrized in this poem).

14 I said, after he had caused sleep to flee from me,
15 And had caused my visitors to despair of my ailment:
16 "Leave [me]!" Yet, when he left [me] I gnashed my teeth!
17 My body is emaciated; beyond recognition. [My] companions seek it where the sobbing is [heard].
18 My heart in its passion has exceeded all limits,
19 And imposed insomnia on me. Would that I could bear it!
20 I said, after night had spread over me like a canopy:
21 "[It is] a long night, with none to help me. O heart of a certain person, will you not soften?"

١٤ قُلْتُ وَقَدْ شَرَّدْ   أَلنَّوْمَ عَنّي

١٥ وأَيْأَسَ العُوَّدْ   لِلسُّقْمِ مِنّي

١٦ صَدٌّ فَلَمَّا صَدّْ   قَرَعْتُ سِنّي

١٧ جِسْمي نَحِيلْ   لا يَسْتَبِينْ   تَطْلُبُهُ الجُلّاسْ   حَيْثُ الأَنِينْ

١٨ تُجاوِزُ الحَدّا   قَلْبي آشْتِياقا

١٩ وكَلَّفَ السُّهْدا   مَن لو أَطاقا

٢٠ قُلْتُ وَقَدْ مَدّا   لَيْلي رِواقا

٢١ لَيْلٌ طَوِيلْ   ولا مُعِينْ   يا قَلْبَ بَعْضِ النَّاسْ   أَمَا تَلِينْ؟

26 Ibn Quzmān

My life is spent in dissipation and wantonness!
O joy, I have begun to be a real profligate!
Indeed, it is absurd for me to repent
When my survival without a wee drink would be certain death.
Vino, vino! And spare me what is said;
Verily, I go mad when I lose my restraint!
My slave will be freed, my money irretrievably lost
On the day I am deprived of the cup.
Should I be poured a double measure or a fivefold one,
I would most certainly empty it; if not, fill then the *jarrón*!
Ho! Clink the glasses with us!
Drunkenness, drunkenness! What care we for proper conduct?

---

26. SOURCES: A. R. Nykl, *El cancionero de Abén Guzmán* (Madrid and Granada, 1933), pp. 214–218; O. J. Tuulio, *Ibn Quzmān poète hispano-arabe bilingue* (Helsinki, 1941), pp. 114–125.

FORM: *zajal* in colloquial Hispano-Arabic, interspersed with Romance words.

METER: *m*—*m* a—a—a *m*
12 12 12 12 12 12

RHYTHM: mixed (óoóooóoóoooó).

1. Nykl reads *nafnī*, but *fanā* is not a transitive verb.

2. The exact meaning of *bayāḍ* in colloquial Hispano-Arabic is not known. The present translation 'joy' is based on *bayaḍu l-qalb*, 'candor, purity of soul' (cf. Dozy, I, 135).

3. Nykl reads *in natūb*. In colloquial Spanish Arabic the first person

٢٦

ابن قزمان

١ نَفْنِ عُمْرِي فِالْخَنْكَرَهْ وَالْمُجُونْ

٢ يا بَيَاضِ خَلِيعْ بَدِيتْ أَنْ نَكُونْ

٣ إِنَّمَا أَنْ نَتُوبَ آنَا فَمُحَالْ

٤ وَبَقَاي بِلَا شُرَيْبَهْ ضَلَالْ

٥ بِينْ بِينْ وَدَعْنِ مِمَّا يُقَالْ

٦ إِنَّ تَرْكِ الْخَلَاعَهْ عِنْدِي جُنُونْ

٧ خَادِمِي حُرّْ مَا لِي لِلْأَحْبَاسْ

٨ النَّهَارْ الَّذِى نُعَطِّلَ آلْكَاسْ

٩ وَإِنْ أُسْقِيتْ بِعَلَّالْ أَوْ خَمَّاسْ

١٠ إِنْ نَضِيتُهْ إِلَّا آحْلِقْ الْجَرُّونْ

١١ أَيْ آلْطَمْ بِنَا بِذَا الْأَقْدَاحْ

١٢ سُكْرَ سُكْرَ أَيْ مَعْنَى فِينَا صِحَاحْ

---

singular of the imperfect was based on the pattern *naktub*, hence *natūb*.

4. Note the colloquial usage of the diminutive.

5. *Vino*: Spanish for 'wine.'

8. Nykl reads: *na*ᶜ*ṭal al-kās*; Tuulio: *nu*ᶜ*aṭṭal kās*; MS: *n*ᶜ*ṭl al-kās*.

9. ᶜ*Allāl*, 'a bottle of double measure'; *khammās*, 'a fivefold measure.' Tuulio translates ᶜ*ullāl* as the Spanish *olla*, 'pot,' but this is impossible.

10. *Jarrón*: Spanish for 'jug.' Nykl reads *in asqait . . . in naḍḍait ilā ḥalqi li-l-jurūn*. *In*: a colloquial form for *innī*.

11. For *laṭama*, 'to clink glasses,' *cf.* Dozy, II, 533. In the colloquial language the quality of *a* (*alṭam*) appears at the beginning of the imperative of I (cf. G. S. Colin, "Spanish Arabic," *EI*², I, 501–503).

13 And when you wish to quaff a morning drink,
14 Awaken me before the *volcón*!
15 Take my money and squander it on drink;
16 My clothes, too, and divide them up among the whores,
17 And assure me that my reasoning is correct.
18 I am never deceived in this occupation!
19 And when I die, let me be buried thus:
20 Let me sleep in a vineyard, among the vinestocks;
21 Spread [its] leaves over me in lieu of a shroud,
22 And let there be a turban of vine tendrils on my head!
23 Let my companion persevere in immorality, to be followed by every beloved one.
24 And remember me continuously as you go about it.
25 As for the grapes, let whomsoever eats a bunch,
26 Plant the [leftover] stalk on my grave!
27 I will offer a toast to your health with the large cup;
28 Take your bottle, lift it high and empty it!

---

14. *Volcón*: Spanish for 'the emptying of cups.'

15. *Khudhu* = *khudhū*.

20. *Jifan* is a colloquial form of *jifān*, 'vinestocks.' This theme brings to mind the poetry of Eastern poets such as Abū Miḥjān.

١٣ وَمَتَى مَا أَرَدتُّمْ أَلْإِصْطِبَاحْ

١٤ أَنْبِهُونِي مِنْ أَوَّلْ أَلْبُلْقُونْ

١٥ خُذْ مَالِي وَبَدَّدُوهْ فِي شَرَابْ

١٦ وَنِيَابِي فَفَصَّلُوا لِلْقِحَابْ

١٧ وَاحْلِفُوا لِي بِأَنَّ رَآيِ صَوَابْ

١٨ لَمْ نَكُنْ قَطُّ فِي ذَا الْعَمَلْ مَغْبُونْ

١٩ وَإِذَا مُتُّ مَذْهَبِي فِالدَّفَنْ

٢٠ أَنِّي نَرْقُدْ فِي كَرْمَ بَيْنَ الْجِفَنْ

٢١ وَتَطُمُّوا الْوَرَقْ عَلَيَّ كَفَنْ

٢٢ وفي رَاسِي عَمَامَ مِنْ زَرَجُونْ

٢٣ وَيُقِيمْ صَاحِي سَوْ ثُمَّ كُلّْ وَدُودْ

٢٤ وَانْذُكُرُونِي عليهْ قِيامْ وَقُعُودْ

٢٥ وَالْعِنَبْ كُلُّ مَنْ أَكَلْ عَنْقُودْ

٢٦ فَيَغَرَّسْ فِي قَبْرِيَ الْعَرْجُونْ

٢٧ سِرُّكَ الْعَالِي بِالْكَبِيرْ نَسْقِيهْ

٢٨ خُذْ قَطِيعَكْ وَآرْفَعْ لَفَوقْ وَآمْحِيهْ

21. Nykl reads *taẓummū*.
23. Tuulio reads *wa thumma*. *Ṣāḥī* is poetic license for *ṣāḥibī*, 'my friend.'
27. For *al-kabīr*, 'large cup,' cf. Dozy, II, 438.
28. For *qatī*[c], 'bottle,' cf. Dozy, II, 372. *La-fauq* is equivalent to *ilā-fauq*.

29 What a wonderful toast you have been honored by.
30 Let whatever you decree against me come to pass!
31 By God, were it not for a trick done to me in a matter concerning a woman,
32 I would have won bliss. She said [to me]: "There is a certain desire which
33 I will not grant you, it being a question of my honor."
34 Alas! The price of that was paid out later!
35 I, by God, was seated, when there came to me with a garland on her head,
36 A Berber girl; what a beauty of a *conejo*!
37 "Whoa!" [Said I, "she] is not a *sera* of *cardacho*,
38 But don't pounce [on her] for neither is she a *grañón*!"
39 "Milady, say, are you fine, white flour or what?"
40 "I am going to bed." "By God; you do well!"
41 I said: "Enter." She replied: "No, you enter first, by God."
42 (Let us cuckold the man who is her husband.)

---

29. Tuulio reads *bīh.*
30. *at* is a colloquial form of *anta.*
31. Nykl reads *aḥtāla.*
32. Nykl reads *narbaḥū ḥir*; Tuulio: *narbaḥū khair*; MS: *nrbaḥu/w/a/ḥir.*
33. *isi* is colloquial for *laisa* (*cf.* Colin, *op. cit.* Tuulio translates *isi* as the Spanish *así*, 'thus,' which makes no sense and is impossible since Spanish *s* > Arabic *shīn*, not *sīn*. Nykl reads *ᶜirḍi.*
35. For *tāj*, 'garland of flowers,' *cf.* Dozy, I, 154.
36. *Conejo* is Spanish for 'rabbit.' Nykl reads *fi-berberīyya.*

٢٩ وَنِعْمَ سِرُّ مَا تَفَضَّلْتَ فِيهْ

٣٠ كُلْمَا تَحْكُمْ أَنْتْ عَلِيَّ يَكُونْ

٣١ بِاللّٰهِ إِلَّا ٱحْتَيَالْ بِنَا فِي مَرَا

٣٢ نَرْبَحُوا جِرْ قَالْ يَكُونْ وَطَرَا

٣٣ إِسِ أَجُودْ لَكُمْ فِي عِرْضِ جَرَى

٣٤ أَوْ ذَاكَ ٱلثَّمَنْ بَعَدْ مَوْزُونْ

٣٥ نَحْنُ وَاللّٰهْ جُلُوسْ وَجَاتْنَا بِتَاجْ

٣٦ بَرْبَرِيَّ وَأَيْ حُسَنْ مِنْ قُنَاجْ

٣٧ أَرَّ بَعَدْ لَسْ شِيرَ مِنْ قَرْطَاشْ

٣٨ وَلَا تَهْجَمْ فَلَسْ إِغْرَنُّونْ

٣٩ مَوْلَتِي قُلْ دَرْمَكْ أَنْتْ أَوْ أَشْنَتْ

٤٠ لِلْمَبِيتْ جِيتْ وَاللّٰهْ لَقَدْ أَحْسَنْتَ

٤١ قُلْتْ قُومْ أَنْتَ قَالْ لَا وَاللّٰهْ إِلَّا أَنْتَ

٤٢ نَجْعَلْ لِلرَّجُلْ مَتَعْهَا قُرُونْ

---

37. An obscure line that Nykl takes to be in Berber. Tuulio renders it *Arra! baᶜd* [*vos*] *lexo assayarme en cortejo* (Whoa! later will I allow you to test me in courtship). The line that follows is not any clearer, and the proposed translation is conjectural and based on Colin. *Sera* 'basket,' *cardacho* 'thistle,' *grañón* 'boiled wheat-porridge.'

39. Tuulio reads: *qul lī. Darmak* is a fine, soft flour of high quality to which the smooth skin of the girl is compared in popular poetry.

42. *Matāᶜ* is a colloquial possessive used in cases where a normal *iḍāfa* would be awkward (cf. Dozy, II, 567; Colin *op. cit.*). The Arabic literally reads 'let us put horns on her husband.'

43 Hardly had I beheld that leg
44 And those two lively, lively eyes,
45 When my penis arose in my trousers like a pavilion,
46 And made a tent out of my clothes.
47 And since I observed that a certain "son of Adam" was dilated,
48 The chick wished to hide in the nest.
49 "Where are you taking that *pollo*, for an immoral purpose?
50 Here we have a man to whom they say: 'O what shamelessness!'"
51 I, by God, immediately set to work:
52 Either it came out, or it went in,
53 While I thrust away sweetly, sweet as honey,
54 And [my] breath came out hotly between her legs.
55 It would have been wonderful, had it not been for the insults that were exchanged next day,
56 For they began to squabble and to brawl:
57 "Remove your hand from my beard, O ass!"

---

46. Nykl reads *qaiṭurūn* which is a scribal error. *Qaiṭūn* in colloquial Spanish Arabic signifies 'a tent' (cf. Dozy, II, 378. *Ba-ḥāl*, 'as,' is a grammatical link word peculiar to Hispano-Arabic (cf. Colin, *op. cit.*).

47. In Hispano-Arabic, between an indefinite noun and its qualifying adjective there is an indeclinable participle *-an*, as here in *ibn Adam-an mafrūsh* (cf. *ibid.*).

48. *ʿūsh* is the classical *ʿushsh*, 'nest.'

49. *Bullūsh* appears to be the Latin *pullus*, Spanish *pollo*, 'chicken,' which appears elsewhere in Ibn Quzmān's poetry in the form *fullūs* (Dozy, II,

إنَّمَا هُ مَا رَايْتُ ذَاكَ الشَّاقْ
وَذِكْ أَلْعَيْنَيْن أَلرَّشَاقْ الرَّشَاقْ
وَرَفَعْ أَيْرِي فِالسَّرَاوِيلْ رِوَاقْ
وَعَمَلْ فِي الثِّيَابِ بِحَالْ قَيْطُونْ
فَكَمَا رَيْتُ آبْنَادَمًا مَفْرُوشْ
أَرَادَ الفَرْخْ أَنْ يَنْطَمَرْ فِي العُوشْ
أَيْ تَجِي زَيْغَ بِهَذَكَ الْبُلُّوشْ
أَهَنَا إِنْسَانْ يُقَلْ لُهْ أَ مُجُونْ
أَنَا وَاللَّهْ قَدِ ٱبْتَدَيْتْ فِي الْعَمَلْ
أَوْ ذَاهُ قَدْ خَرَجْ أَوْ ذَاهُ قَدْ دَخَلْ
وَأَنَا نَدْفَعْ حُلُو حُلُو كَالْعَسَلْ
وَخَرَجْ رُوحِ بَيْنْ سَقَيْهَا سُخُونْ
جِيدْ هُ لَوْ لَا مَا اَشَّاتَمُوا بِالنَّهَارْ
ثُمَّ قَامُوا لِلْعَرْبَطَهْ وَالنَّقَّارْ
خَلِّ يَدَّكْ مِنْ لِحْيَتِي يَا حِمَارْ

---

278). The *fa* and *ba* are easily confused in Maghribī calligraphy. These words and those of the following line are presumably spoken by the woman. *Pollo* here appears to have an obscene meaning. *Ai* is the classical *ain*. For the disappearance of the final *n*, cf. Colin, *op. cit.*

55. For the shortened pronoun *hu* for *huwa*, cf. *ibid. Aṣhshātamū* is the colloquial sixth form of *shatama* (cf. Tuulio, *op. cit.*, p. 130 n. 14), based on the pattern *atfā*ʿ*al* with assimilation of *tā*ʾ to *shīn* (cf. Colin, *op. cit.*).

56. 'They,' i.e., presumably the Berber woman and her family. ʿ*Arbaṭa* is the classical ʿ*arbada*.

58 "You, throw the frying pan for the *tostón*!"
59 One claws at an eyelid, the other slaps;
60 One tears clothes to shreds, the other floors his adversary;
61 No matter where I throw green quinces,
62 I get hit only on the head by the *bastón*!
63 That is the way the world is! Not that it is my style,
64 Yet in this way they managed to humiliate me.
65 As for me, O people, although it was a light [punishment],
66 Never have I suffered such shame as at present.
67 Indeed, my opinion is as follows: You are viewed by the eye of reproof;
68 No place in this city is big enough for you to hide.
69 Where are the means [of departure] for one such as Ibn Quzmān?
70 In my opinion nothing is more certain than that [I shall get them].
71 O my hope and my well-watched star;
72 My life and my beloved one:

---

58. *Matā* is a colloquial possessive found between two nouns (cf. *ibid.*). *Tostón* is a Spanish word meaning 'a piece of toast fried in olive oil.'

60. Tuulio corrects the MS reading to *yartazam*.

61. *Ai-mā* is the classical *aina-ma* (cf. *ibid.* for the disappearance of final *n* in *ain*. *Bastón* is Spanish for 'cudgel.'

٥٨ أَرْمِي أَنتْ الطَّابِقْ مَتَى الطُّشْتُونْ
٥٩ هذا يَقْلَعْ جِفَنْ وَذا يَلْطَمْ
٦٠ ذا يُقَطِّعْ ثِيَابْ وَذا يَرْزَمْ
٦١ أَيْ مَا أُرْمِي سَفَرْجَلْ حَصْرَمْ
٦٢ لَمْ يَجِينِ غَيرْ لِرَاسِي الْبَشْطُونْ
٦٣ هذا عَالَمْ لَسَّنْهُ مِنْ شَكْلِي
٦٤ وَكذا يَبْلُغُوا إلى ذُلِّ
٦٥ أَنَا بِاللّٰهْ يَا قَومْ وَبِالسَّهْلِ
٦٦ لَسْ أَنَا عِنْدَ ذَكْ بِهذا الهُونْ
٦٧ إِنَّ رَايِّ تُنْظَرْ بِعَيَنْ الْهَوَانْ
٦٨ لَسْ يَسْعَكُمْ في ذِي المَدِينَهْ مَكَانْ
٦٩ أَيْ طَرِيقَهْ لِمِثْلَ آبَنْ قُزْمَانْ
٧٠ لَسْ يَكُنْ عِنْدِي مِثْلْ هذَاكْ مَكِينْ
٧١ يَا رَجَآيِ وَنَجْمِيَ الْمَرْقُوبْ
٧٢ وَحَيَاتِي وَشَخْصِيَ الْمَحْبُوبْ

---

63. *lassanhu* is a contraction of *laisa anna-hu.*
66. *las* is the classical *laisa.*
67. Nykl reads: *in ra'a tunẓar.*
69. All the editions read *wa-mithl.* The proposed emendation seems to improve the meaning of the line.

73 I desire largesse and it is from you that it is desired!
74 I am your guarantor for your glory will be guaranteed!
75 Your hands have an eminent right to dispose of me,
76 And in your honor do I go and stop,
77 While your virtues are too excellent for me to describe.
78 Drops of water are not to be compared with bursting rain clouds.
79 You have shown me a path to prosperity;
80 You have adorned me before my enemy and my friend;
81 For in you my hand has been attached to a firm rope;
82 You who are such that all others are withheld from me.
83 O, Abū Isḥāq, O lord among viziers,
84 Bright flower of this world and lord among emirs!
85 The like of you gives new life to poetry for poets,
86 While you make public a generosity that was hidden [before your arrival]!
87 May you remain happy, achieving your aspirations,

---

73. *Hu* is an abbreviated form of the classical *huwa* (cf. *ibid.*).

75. Note the indeclinable particle *-an* of *ḥaqq-an*.

77. Tuulio reads *ḥasanātu-k* correcting the MS reading (which has been preferred). *Naqīf* and *naṣīf* are colloquial forms of *naqīfu* and *naṣīfu*.

78. The original should have been: *bi-ghaith-an hatūn*. The error is prob-

أَنَا رَاغِبْ وَأَنْتَ ، الْمَرْغُوبْ
وَأَنَا ضَامِنْ وَمَجْدُكْ اَلْمَضْمُونْ
لِأَيَادِيكْ عَلَيَّ حَقًّا شَرِيفْ
وَلِفَضْلِكْ نَجِي أَنَا وَنَقِيفْ
وَمَحَاسِنُكْ أَجَلّْ مِمَّا نَصِيفْ
لَيْسْ تُقَاسْ اَلنُّقَطْ بِغَيْثٍ هَتُونْ
عَرَضْتَنِي إِلَى السَّعَادَهْ طَرِيقْ
زَيَّنْتَنِي بَيْنَ الْعَدُو وَالصَّدِيقْ
وَظَفَرْ يَدِّي مِنْكْ بِحَبْلًا وَثِيقْ
اَلَّذِي كُلّْ مَنْ سِوَاهْ مَحْقُونْ
يَا أَبُو إِسْحَقْ يَا سَيِّدْ اَلْوُزَرَا
زَهْرَةْ اَلدُّنْيَا وَسَيِّدْ اَلْأُمَرَا
مِثْلُكْ أَحْيَا الشِّعْرَ لِلشُّعَرَا
وَنَشَرْتَ النَّدَى وَكَانَ مَدْفُونْ
دُمْتَ مَسْرُورْ مُبَلَّغْ الْآمَالْ

---

ably attributable to the Eastern scribe who did not know the dialect of al-Andalus.

81. Note the conjunctive particle *-an* in *ḥabl-an wathīq* (cf. n. 47).

83. Possibly Abū Isḥāq Ibrāhīm ibn Aḥmad al-Washkī, a friend of the poet (cf. Nykl, *op. cit.*, p. 341).

88 And may you witness high rank and nobility with affability,
89 As long as darkness changes [to light] and the new moon shines,
90 And as long as a plant still grows green and branches rise high!

90. Nykl reads *akhḍar*.

٨٨ وَتَرَى جَاهْ وَعِزَّ في إقْبَالْ

٨٩ مَا آسْتَحَالْ الظَّلَامْ وَلَاحْ الْهِلَالْ

٩٠ وَمَا إخْضَرَّ نَبَاتْ وَقَامَتْ غُصُونْ

27 Ibn Quzmān

1 I am madly in love despite the angry behavior of one who finds fault [with me]!
2 I am the lover of my time:
3 I fear no one in matters of love!
4 Love has made me thin, it has turned me pale:
5 Look, and see how my color has changed!
6 Yet I can still say "Ah!" O dark-skinned one!
7 As for my clothes, there is no flesh inside them.
8 You would not see me
9 Were it not that I still moan!
10 By God, I am a man enmeshed in love's snares
11 And my condition proves that I speak the truth.
12 Moreover, I excel in composing this *zajal*;

---

27. SOURCE: A. R. Nykl, *El cancionero de Abén Guzmán* (Madrid and Granada, 1933), pp. 283–284.

FORM: *zajal* in colloquial Hispano-Arabic.

METER: a—a—a *m–n–m*
10 10 10 11 5 7

RHYTHM: dactylic.

In this *ars poetica* the poet ridicules the classical tradition and courtly love.

5. *Atghayyara* is the colloquial form of *taghayyara* which in Hispano-Arabic was changed to the pattern *atfa*^{cc}*al* (cf. G. S. Colin, "Spanish Arabic," EI^2, I, 503.

٢٧

ابن قزمان

أَنَا ُ عَاشِقْ لِغَيْظِ مَنْ فَنَّدْ
عَاشِقْ زَمَانِي
لَسْ نَخَافْ فِي عِشْقْ أَحَدْ
قَدْ رَدَّنِي ٱلْعِشْقْ نَاحِلْ أَصْفَرْ
أُنْظُرْ تَرَى لَوْنِي أَشْ أَتْغَيَّرْ
لَقَدْ نَقُلْهَا بَعَدْ يَا ٱلْأَسْمَرْ
أَمَّا نِيَابِي فَلَسْ فِيهَا جَسَدْ
لَسْ كِن تَّرَانِي
لَوْ لَا مَا نَانُ بَعَدْ
وَاللّٰهْ لَانِّي رَجُلًا عَاشِقْ
وَحَالِي يَشْهَدْ بِأَنِّي صَادِقْ
وَنُمَّ أَنَا فِي ذَا الزَّجَلْ فَايِقْ

---

6. *Hā* is an exclamation of wonder or surprise. The poet means he can still marvel at his beloved's beauty.

8. "Spanish Arabic evolved a contingent tense . . . (after a protasis with *lau*). . . It is formed by the imperfect preceded by *kān* (Ibn Quzmān = *kīn*), which is constant and of which the final *-n* is normally assimilated by the preformatives *t-* and *y-*" (Colin, *op. cit.*).

10. Note the indeclinable particle *-an* peculiar to Hispano-Arabic, in *rajul-an ʿāshiq* (cf. *ibid.*).

Poetry passes through my mind whenever [its sword] is drawn;
As for the sword of my tongue,
No coat of mail can stop it!
Spare me the method of Jamīl and ʿUrwa,
Since people have a model in al-Ḥasan.
And say to one who does not follow the method of al-ʿUrwa:
"O you who honor a certain person even more than Ḥātim,
What is the method used by a certain debauched fellow
Who is ostracized throughout the land?"
Throw off your restraint in loving the youthful,
And as for the beloved, if you see that his sash is hard to undo,
Give him to drink, and do it again, as often as needed.
Then, if he drinks from the large cup and endures,
Pour him out a second:
He will collapse though he be a lion!
When my beloved drank his cup for you,

---

13. Nykl's edition records *yajbad*, a misprint.

16. Jamīl al-ʿUdhrī and ʿUrwat ibn Ḥizām were two early Umayyad poets reputed to have developed the love lyric which sang of a languishing, hopeless sentiment later called ʿUdhrite love.

17. Al-Ḥasan is Abū Nuwās.

١٣ يَشُقّ زِهْنِيَ ٱلشِّعْرْ إنّ يُجْبَدْ

١٤ وَ سَيفْ لِسَانِي

١٥ لَمْ يَقِفْ لُ قَطْ زَرَدْ

١٦ خَلِّينِ مِنْ دِينْ جَمِيلْ وَعُرْوَهْ

١٧ وَفِالْحَسَنْ لَهُمْ النَّاسْ أُسْوَهْ

١٨ وَقُلْ لِمَنْ لا يَدِينْ بِٱلعُرْوَهْ

١٩ يَا مَنْ يَفَضَّلْ على حَاتِمْ أَحَدْ

٢٠ أَشْ فَنّ زَانِي

٢١ يُهْزَ بِهْ فِي كُلّ بَلَدْ

٢٢ أَخْلَعْ عِذَارَكْ فِي عِشْقِ آلصِّبْيَانْ

٢٣ وَالْمَعْشُوقْ إنْ رَايْتُهْ صَعبْ الهِمْيَانْ

٢٤ أَسْقِيهْ وَثْنِي عَلَيهْ كَيفْ مَا كَانْ

٢٥ فَإنْ شَرَبْ ٱلْكَبِيرْ وَأَجَّلَّدْ

٢٦ أَسْقِ لُ ثَانِي

٢٧ يَنْطَرَحْ لَوْ كَانْ أَسَدْ

٢٨ لَمَّا شَرَبْ لَكْ حَبِيبِ كَاسُهْ

19. Ḥātim Ṭā'ī was a pre-Islamic hero proverbial for his generosity. Thus, the poet compliments his protector by saying he is more generous than Ḥātim.

25. *Ajjallad* is the colloquial form of *tajallada* with assimilation of *ta* to *jīm* (*cf.* n. 5).

27. Nykl reads *wa lau kān*, but *lau kān* fits the meter perfectly.

29 And drunkenness made him droop among his seated companions,
30 I redoubled my efforts whenever he raised his head;
31 My beloved drank; he drank until he keeled over.
32 There is no safety from me
33 For one who gets drunk and then falls asleep!

٢٩ وَ مَالْ بِهِ السُّكَرْ بَيْنَ جُلَّاسُهْ

٣٠ أَشْتَدُّتْ لُ عِنْدَ تَقْوِيمْ رَاسُهْ

٣١ شَرَبْ حَبِيبِ شَرَبْ حَتَّى سَجَدْ

٣٢ فِي غَيْرْ ضَمَانِي

٣٣ كُلّْ مَنْ سَكَرْ وَ رَقَدْ

28 al-Abyaḍ

1 The drinking of wine is not pleasing to me
2 Upon the camomile flower beds
3 Without [the company] of one who is slender waisted
4 Who when he grows dizzy from wine in the morning
5 Or in the evening, begins to say: "Why does the fresh wine thus slap my cheek,
6 And why does the North wind blow so that the shapely branch contained in [my] cloak sways?"
7 After he wastes our hearts
8 He appears before us full of suspicions.
9 O for his glance! Add to our sins!
10 O for his fresh lips!
11 The cool refreshment of the thirst of a sick lover who will not change in his faithful vows with you
12 And will not cease hoping for the love tryst under any circumstance, though he is rejected.
13 You have divided the grieved one's heart
14 Between hopes and laments
15 Just as al-Ḥaḍramī is sundered

---

28. SOURCE: S. M. Stern, "Four Famous Muwashshaḥas from Ibn Bushrā's Anthology," *Andalus*, XXIII (1958), 352–353.
FORM: *muwashshaḥa*.

٢٨

الابيض

١ مَا لَذَّ لِي شَرْبُ رَاحِ

٢ عَلَى رِيَاضِ الأَقَاحِ

٣ لَوْلَا هَضِيمُ الوِشَاحِ

٤ إِذا آنْتَشَى فِي الصَّبَاحِ

٥ أَوْ فِي الأَصِيلْ   أَضْحَى يَقُولْ   مَا لِلشَّمُولْ   لَطَّمَتْ خَدِّ

٦ وَلِلشَّمَالْ   هَبَّتْ فَمَالْ   غُصْنُ آعْتِدَالْ   ضَمَّهُ بُرْدِ

٧ لَمَّا أَبَادَ القُلُوبَا

٨ بَدَا لَنَا مُسْتَرِيبَا

٩ يَا لَحْظَهُ زِدْ ذُنُوبَا

١٠ وَيَا لَمَاهُ الشَّنِيبَا

١١ بَرْدُ غَلِيلْ   صَبٍّ عَلِيلْ   لَا يَسْتَحِيلْ   فِيكَ عَنْ عَهْدِ

١٢ وَلَا يَزَالْ   يَرْجُو الوِصَالْ   فِي كُلِّ حَالْ   وَهْوَ فِي الصَّدِّ

١٣ قَسَمْتَ قَلْبَ الشَّجِيِّ

١٤ بَيْنَ المُنَا وَالنَّعِيِّ

١٥ تَقَسُّمَ الحَضْرَمِيِّ

METER: a–a–a–a *m–m–m–n* *m–m–m–n*
8 8 8 8 4 4 4 5 4 4 4 5

RHYTHM: dactylic.

The poem is a panegyric to a certain Mālik al-Ḥaḍramī.

16 Between battle cry and liberality.

17 He is a fierce lion, a pouring rain cloud, a polished sword of resplendent fame;

18 Sweet in friendship, having qualities like pure water mixed with honey.

19 Leave aside those who aspire to kingdoms

20 But are not like Mālik!

21 How many of your followers has . . .

22 And how much of your wealth have you given away

23 In more than abundance, to seekers of your largesse who by the swords of your bounty are slain?

24 [You are] an ocean of gifts such that its pearls can only be reached by means of praise.

25 How lovable is the merry lass

26 Who sent the messenger of slumber

27 To the frightened gazelle,

28 Reciting in humble tones:

29 "By God, messenger, explain to the lover, how to find his way so that he may come and spend the night with me.

30 I shall grant him [my] locks, behind the curtains, by way of torment, and shall add my breasts!"

---

21. Obscure word in the manuscript.

١٦ بَيْنَ النَّدَا وَالنَّدِى

١٧ لَيْثٌ بَصُولْ غَيْثٌ يَسِيلْ سَيْفٌ صَقِيلْ بَيِّنُ المَجْدِ

١٨ حُلْوٌ حَلاَلْ لَهُ خِلاَلْ مِثْلُ الزُّلاَلْ شِيبَ بِالشُّهْدِ

١٩ دَعْ مَنْ سَمَا بِالمَمَالِكْ

٢٠ فَتًى وَلَيْسَ كَمَالِكْ

٢١ كَمْ قَدْ ... مِنْ رِجَالِكْ

٢٢ فَكَمْ وَهَبْتَ مِنْ مَالِكْ

٢٣ فَوْقَ الجَزِيلْ لِمُسْتَنِيلْ أَضْحَى قَتِيلْ بِظُبَى الرِّفْدِ

٢٤ بَحْرُ النَّوَالْ لَيْسَ يُنَالْ مِنْهُ اللآلْ بِسِوَى الحَمْدِ

٢٥ أَحْبِبْ بِخَوْدٍ شَمُوعِ

٢٦ دَسَّتْ رَسُولَ الهُجُوعِ

٢٧ إِلَى الغَزَالِ المَرُوعِ

٢٨ فَأَنْشَدَتْ عن خُضُوعِ

٢٩ بِاللّٰهِ رَسُولْ قُلْ لِلْخَلِيلْ كَيْفَ السَّبِيلْ وَيَبِيتُ عِنْدِى

٣٠ نُعْطِيهِ دَلاَلْ خَلْفَ الحِجَالْ عَلَى النَّكَالْ وَنَزِيدُ نَهْدِى

29 Ibn Bājja(?)

1 Trail the edge of your robe wherever it pleases, and add more drunkenness to your intoxication.
2 And light your tinder with a flame
3 Of silver contained in gold,
4 Crowned by a string of the pearls of froth,
5 In the company of a bright-eyed, shining, fresh-lipped one
6 Whose cup has been filled with wine—a frozen water, a liquid ember.
7 There the light of dawn has already shone,
8 While the wind among the flower beds has exuded its fragrance already.
9 Do not light a lantern in the dark;
10 Leave it aside and uncover the wine instead
11 While the tears of the dew flow, and you see the flowers of the garden smiling.
12 The pearls of nobility have been gathered into a strand
13 By the hand of the king who is an ornament to kingship.
14 God has created no other king like him.

---

29. Source: S. M Stern, "Four Famous Muwashshaḥas from Ibn Bushrā's Anthology," *Andalus*, XXIII (1958), 360–361.

Form: *muwashshaḥa*.

Meter: a—a—a—a *m—m* Rhythm: mixed (óooóoóoooóo).
10 10 10 10 10 10

This famous poem is attributed by one source to Ibn aṣ-Ṣairafī, although the editor tends to think that it was actually composed by the philosopher Ibn

٢٩

ابن باجّة

١ جَرِّرِ الذَّيْلَ أَيَّمَا جَرِّ وَصِلِ السُّكْرَ مِنْكَ بِالسُّكْرِ

٢ وَٱخْضِبِ الزَّنْدَ مِنْكَ بِاللَّهَبْ

٣ مِنْ لُجَيْنٍ قَدْ حُفَّ بِالذَّهَبْ

٤ تَحْتَ سِلْكٍ مِنْ جَوْهَرِ الحَبَبْ

٥ مَعْ أَحْوَرٍ أَغَرٍّ ذِي شَنَبْ

٦ أُودِعَتْ كَأْسُهُ مِنَ الخَمْرِ جَامِدَ المَاءِ ذَائِبَ الجَمْرِ

٧ هَاكَ ضَوْءُ الصَّبَاحِ قَدْ لَاحَا

٨ وَنَسِيمُ الرِّيَاضِ قَدْ فَاحَا

٩ لَا تَقِدِّ فِي الظَّلَامِ مِصْبَاحَا

١٠ خَلِّ عَنْكَ وَشَعْشِعِ الرَّاحَا

١١ حَيْثُ تَنْهَلُّ أَدْمُعُ القَطْرِ وَتَرَى الرَّوْضَ بَاسِمَ الزَّهْرِ

١٢ نَظَمَتْ جَوْهَرَ العُلَا سِلْكَا

١٣ كَفُّ مَلِكٍ يَزِينُ المُلْكَا

١٤ مَا بَرَى اللَّهُ مِثْلَهُ مَلْكَا

Bājja. It was recited in praise of the Almoravid governor of Saragossa Ibn Tīfalwīt who upon hearing it exclaimed: "'What a joy!,' tearing his clothes and saying: 'How beautifully you began and how beautifully you finished!' He swore an irrevocable oath that Ibn Bājja would walk home over gold. The philosopher feared, however, that the matter would not end well, and for this reason sought a way out: he put some gold into his shoe and so 'walked over it.'" (Ibn Khaldūn, *Muqaddima*, *apud* Stern, *op. cit.*, pp. 357–358).

15 He shines like a full moon while his perfume for me is like musk.
16 He is like the rain, like the dawn, like the ocean; like ᶜAlī in battles, or like ᶜAmr.
17 What a lion, what a lion-like warrior,
18 What a spear, what a sword,
19 Piercing the chest, cutting off heads.
20 When he wheels and returns to the fray,
21 He gives his white [sword] a red cloak, and pastures his spear in [the enemy's] throat.
22 Whenever he appears, his face veiled
23 Like the crescent moon covered by clouds
24 While a banner flutters above his head,
25 Arabs and non-Arabs sing about him:
26 "May God raise the standard of victory for Abū Bakr, the prince of excellence!"

---

16. I.e., ᶜAlī ibn Abī Ṭālib and ᶜAmr ibn al-ᶜĀṣ who fought in the battle of Ṣiffīn.

لَاحَ بَدْرًا أَوْ فَاحَ لِي مِسْكَا
كَالحَيَا كَالصَّبَاحِ كَالبَحْرِ   كَعَلِي فِي الحُرُوبِ أَوْ عَمْرِو
أَيُّ لَيْثٍ وَأَيُّ ضِرْغَامِ
أَيُّ رُمْحٍ وَأَيُّ صَمْصَامِ
طَاعِنِ الصَّدْرِ ضَارِبِ الهَامِ
بَيْنَ كَرٍّ وَبَيْنَ إِقْدَامِ
يَلْحَفُ البِيضَ بِالحلَاءِ الحُمْرِ   وَيُرَوِّي القَنَاةَ فِي النَّحْرِ
كُلَّمَا لَاحَ وَهْوَ مُلْتَثَمْ
كَهِلَالٍ تَحُفُّهُ دِيَمْ
خَافِقًا فَوْقَ رَأْسِهِ عَلَمْ
غَنَّتِ العُرْبُ فِيهِ وَالعَجَمْ
عَقَدَ اللّٰهُ رَايَةَ النَّصْرِ   لِأَمِيرِ العُلَا أَبِي بَكْرِ

22. The Almoravids adhered to the custom of veiling their faces with the *lithām*.

30 Ibn Zuhr

1 O cupbearer, our complaints are addressed to you; we have called upon you even though you do not listen!
2 Many a drinking partner have I loved for his bright face,
3 And from his hands have I drunk wine!
4 Whenever he was aroused from his drunkenness
5 He drew the wineskin toward him, sat back on his heels, and gave me to drink four [drinks] from four [cups].
6 What is wrong with my eye that it is blinded by a glance?
7 After you, it has rejected the light of the moon!
8 If you so desire, listen to my tale:
9 My eyes have been blinded from prolonged weeping, since one part of me wept with me over another part of me.
10 A willow branch bent from its upright position;
11 The one who loved it died from excess of passion,
12 Quivering in his heart, weakened in his strength.
13 Whenever he thought of separation he wept; woe to him who weeps over what never took place!
14 I have no patience or any firmness!

---

30. SOURCE: Ibn Sanā' al-Mulk, *Dār aṭ-ṭirāz fī ʿamal al-muwashshaḥāt*, ed. Jaudat ar-Rikābī (Damascus, 1949), pp. 73–74.

METER: *ramal.* Rhyme: a—a—a *m—n*
12 12 12 12 12

RHYTHM: mixed (óooóooóoóoó).

٣٠

ابن زهر

١ أَيُّها السَّاقي إِلَيْكَ المُشْتَكَى   قَدْ دَعَوْنَاكَ وَإِنْ لَمْ تَسْمَعِ
٢ وَنَدِيمٍ هِمْتُ في غُرَّتِهِ
٣ وَشَرِبْتُ الراحَ مِنْ رَاحَتِهِ
٤ كُلَّمَا آسْتَيْقَظَ مِنْ سَكْرَتِهِ
٥ جَذَبَ الزِّقَّ إِلَيْهِ وَآتَّكَا   وَسَقَانِي أَرْبَعًا في أَرْبَعِ
٦ مَا لِعَيْنِي عَشِيَتْ بِالنَّظَرِ
٧ أَنْكَرَتْ بَعْدَكَ ضَوْءَ القَمَرِ
٨ وَإِذَا مَا شِئْتَ فَآسْمَعْ خَبَرِي
٩ عَشِيَتْ عَيْنَايَ مِن طُولِ البُكَا   وَبَكَى بَعْضِي على بَعْضِي مَعِي
١٠ غُصْنُ بَانٍ مَالَ مِن حَيْثُ آسْتَوَى
١١ مَاتَ مَنْ يَهْوَاهُ مِنْ فَرْطِ الجَوَى
١٢ خَفِقَ الأَحْشَاءِ مَوْهُونَ القُوَى
١٣ كُلَّمَا فَكَّرَ في البَيْنِ بَكَى   وَيْحَهُ يَبْكِي لِمَا لَمْ يَقَعِ
١٤ لَيْسَ لِي صَبْرٌ وَلَا لِي جَلَدُ

---

5. I.e., two cups of wine plus the "wine" of the glances from his two eyes.
9. I.e., my eyes wept over my broken heart.

15 What is wrong with my people that they have upbraided me and exerted themselves in so doing?

16 They have denied my complaint whereby I am moved to passion.

17 The like of my state is deserving of complaint: [namely] the weakness of despair and the humility of passion.

18 A heart that burned and tears that flow

19 Acknowledge the fault, yet are not acknowledged!

20 O you who disclaim what I describe:

21 My love for you has grown and increased. Do not proclaim in matters of love: "I am a claimant!"

١٥ مَالِقَوْمِي عَذَلُوا وَٱجْتَهَدُوا

١٦ أنْكَرُوا شَكْوَايَ مِمَّا أَجِدُ

١٧ مِثْلُ حَالِي حَقُّها أَنْ تُشْتَكَى كَمَدُ اليَأْسِ وَذُلُّ الطَّمَعِ

١٨ كَبِدٌ حَرَّى وَدَمْعٌ يَكِفُ

١٩ يَعْرِفُ الذَّنْبَ ولا يَعْتَرِفُ

٢٠ أَيُّهَا المُعْرِضُ عَمَّا أَصِفُ

٢١ قَدْ نَمَا حُبُّكَ عِنْدِي وَزَكَا لَا تَقُلْ فِي الحُبِّ إِنِّي مُدَّعِي

31 Ar-Ruṣāfī of Valencia

1 Were you to go to the fire of the Guidance on the side of Mount Sinai, you could take all the knowledge and light you wish

2 From every brightly glowing [fire] whose flame neither is visible from afar at night to a traveler, nor does it blaze [to warm] those suffering from the cold.

3 The abundance of fire from the light of Prophecy or of Guidance dispels the gloom of idolatry.

4 A man fasting at midday, rising frequently to pray during the night, has not ceased to feed piety to [the fire] on its hearth

5 Until it shone with the Faith after being kindled by a firebrand which was concealed beneath the ashes of unbelief:

6 A light such that God concealed the flint that would bring it into being, from the spark, storing them up until the age of the Mahdi,

7 As well as a miraculous sign [bright as] the light of the sun, before an expedition destined to be fulfilled by the Qaisite king.

8 O abode, which is the abode of the Prince of the Faithful at the foot of the lofty peak which is the peak of the Guidance: May you be blessed among abodes!

9 [You are] endowed with the two columns of power and kingship superimposed on the two bases of holiness and purity.

10 Your builder was not lacking in regard [when he constructed] a fortress enclosed above the meeting place of the two seas!

11 For it is the stepping place of a prophet, while a long time has passed since the two footsteps of praising and magnifying God have been joined to it.

12 Wherever his two sandals held him upright they were blessed, while every stepping and crossing place [of his] was rendered pure.

---

31. SOURCE: Ar-Ruṣāfī, *Dīwān*, ed. Iḥsān ᶜAbbās (Beirut, 1960), pp. 77–86. METER: *basīṭ*.

When ᶜAbd al-Muᵓmin, the leader of the Almohads, landed at Gibraltar in 1161 on his way to conquer Arab Spain, a poetic contest was held at which the leading poets of al-Andalus vied with one another in eulogizing the conqueror. Ar-Ruṣāfī, who had not yet reached the age of twenty, created this often quoted panegyric at that time. It is remarkable for its description of Gibraltar.

1. Cf. Koran 20:9–10: "Has the story of Moses reached you? Behold, he saw a fire: so he said to his family, 'Tarry ye; I perceive a fire: perhaps I can bring you some burning brand therefrom, or find some guidance at the fire.'"

٣١

الرّصافي

١ لَوْ جِئتَ نارَ الهُدَى مِنْ جانِبِ الطُّورِ   قَبَسْتَ ما شِئتَ مِنْ عِلْمٍ و مِنْ نُورِ
٢ مِنْ كُلِّ زَهْرَاءَ لَمْ تُرْفَعْ ذُؤابَتُها   لَيْلاً لِسارٍ ولَمْ تُشْبَبْ لِمَقْرُورِ
٣ فَيْضِيَّةُ القَدْحِ مِنْ نُورِ النُّبُوَّةِ أَوْ   نُورِ الهِدايَةِ تَجْلُو ظُلْمَةَ الزُّورِ
٤ ما زالَ يُقْضِمُها التَّقْوَى بِمَوْقِدِها   صَوَّامُ هاجِرَةٍ قَوّامُ دَيْجُورِ
٥ حتى أَضاءَتْ مِن الإِيمانِ عَنْ قَبَسٍ   قد كانَ تَحْتَ رَمادِ الكُفْرِ، مَكْفُورِ
٦ نُورٌ طَوَى اللهُ زَنْدَ الكَوْنِ مِنه على   سِقْطٍ إِلَى زَمَنِ المَهْدِيِّ مَذْخُورِ
٧ وَآيَةٌ كَإِيَاةِ الشمْسِ بَيْنَ يَدَيْ   غَزْوٍ على المَلِكِ القَيْسِيِّ مَنْذُورِ
٨ يا دارُ دارَ أَمِيرِ المُؤْمِنِينَ بِسَفْـ   ـحِ الطَّوْدِ، طَوْدِ الهُدَى، بُورِكْتِ في الدُّورِ
٩ ذاتَ العِمادَيْنِ مِن عِزٍّ وَمَمْلَكَةٍ   على الأَساسَيْنِ مِن قُدْسٍ وَتَطْهِيرِ
١٠ ما كانَ بانِيكِ بِالْوانِي الكَرامةِ عن   قَصْرٍ على مَجْمَعِ البَحْرَيْنِ مَقْصُورِ
١١ مَواطِئٌ مِن نَبِيٍّ طالَ ما وُصِلَتْ   فيها الخُطَى بَيْنَ تَسْبِيحٍ وَتَكْبِيرِ
١٢ حَيْثُ ٱسْتَقَلَّتْ بِه نَعْلاهُ بُورِكَتا   فَطَيَّبَتْ كُلَّ مَوْطُوءٍ ومَعْبُورِ

---

2. I.e., it is the *spiritual* fire of the Almohad propaganda, not a material fire.

4. The man is ᶜAbd al-Muʾmin.

6. I.e., the Mahdi of the Almohads, Ibn Tūmart, who initiated the movement and was succeeded by ᶜAbd al-Muʾmin.

7. Although the Mahdi was a Berber, his descent was connected by pious genealogists to the family of the Prophet, who was of Qaisite, that is, northern Arab ancestry.

8. The "lofty peak" is Gibraltar.

13 And wherever the spear of religion rose aloft it drags along behind it the banner of victory which is clearly displayed over the two continents.

14 [It is held] in the hand of one tucking up his two mantles; possessed of godliness; one who has broken his fast on fear of God and purity of soul,

15 [One who] conjoined you to the world of holiness; both esoteric and exoteric [after you had been] in a state of absence from his favor.

16 He embarked upon the ships on the shore of the Straits [of Gibraltar] when they had been summoned together [with the call]: "O best of the ships of glory, set sail!"

17 So they set sail bearing the command of God, from a king seeking victory in God and made victorious through God.

18 On their part every top offers recognition to him by bowing before him, and every rope confers praise upon him.

19 When they outraced one another in the Straits with him, they left its two shores in doubt and perplexity

20 [As to whether] the sea was trembling in its swell because it was overpowered by joy, or whether its waves heaved with a heart full of fear.

21 It was as if he were crossing over a pool on the earth stained with the heart's blood of armed men,

22 [Blood drawn by] the swords which melted at his assault when he cast his ardor at the fire of their warring.

23 He possesses full-sailed vessels the ropes of which are like braids of hair in the way they hang and are plaited.

24 The softness and fragrance of his nature charmed the waters and the gusts of the winds on them.

25 Each one consisted of a pregnant virgin in whose ribs there were two perfumes, namely rose ambergris and camphor.

26 You would think that they were submerged, between the arms which were their oars, in rosewater from Jūr.

27 And many a time did they plow through the dashing waves, flying as if with the wings of eagles soaring [in the air].

28 When they crossed you would think they were like swimmers in a bountiful sea of generosity wrung out from his right hand.

---

14. I.e., "tucking up his two mantles" to wage war, referring to ʿAbd al-Muʾmin.

١٣ وحَيْثُ قامَتْ قَناةُ الدينِ تَرْفُلُ في   لِواءِ نَصْرٍ على البَرَّيْنِ مَنْشُورِ
١٤ في كَفِّ مُنْشَمِرِ البُرْدَيْنِ ذي وَرَعٍ   على التُّقَى وصَفاءِ النَّفْسِ مَفْطُورِ
١٥ يَلْقاكَ في حالِ غَيْبٍ مِن سَريرَتِهِ   بِعَالَمِ القُدْسِ مَشْهُورٍ ومَحْضُورِ
١٦ تَسَنَّمَ الفُلْكَ مِن شَطِّ المَجازِ وقد   نُودِينَ يا خَيْرَ أَفْلاكِ العُلا سِيرِي
١٧ فَسِرْنَ يَحْمِلْنَ أَمْرَ اللهِ مِن مَلِكٍ   باللهِ مُسْتَنْصِرٍ في اللهِ مَنْصُورِ
١٨ يُومِي لَهُ بِسُجودٍ كُلُّ مَحْرَكَةٍ   مِنها ويُولِيهِ حَمْدًا كُلَّ تَصْدِيرِ
١٩ لَمَّا تَسابَقْنَ في بَحْرِ الزُّقاقِ بِهِ   تَرَكْنَ شَطَّيْهِ في شَكٍّ وتَحْبِيرِ
٢٠ أَهَزَّ مِن مَوْجِهِ أَثْناءَ مَسْرُورِ   أَمْ خاضَ مِن لُجِّهِ أَحْشاءَ مَذْعُورِ
٢١ كأَنَّهُ سالِكٌ مِنه على وَشَلٍ   في الأَرْضِ مِن مُهَجِ الأَسْيافِ مَقْطُورِ
٢٢ مِن السُّيوفِ التي ذابَتْ لِسَطْوَتِهِ   وقد رَمَى نارَ هَيْجاها بِتَسْعِيرِ
٢٣ ذُو المُنْشَآتِ الجَوارِي في أَجِرَّتِها   شَكْلُ الغَدائِرِ في سَدْلٍ وتَضْفِيرِ
٢٤ أَغْرَى المِياهَ وأَنْفاسَ الرِّياحَ بِها   ما في سَجاياهُ مِن لِينٍ وتَعْطِيرِ
٢٥ مِنْ كُلِّ عَذْراءَ حُبْلَى في تَرائِبِها   رَدْعانِ مِن عَنْبَرٍ وَرْدٍ وَكافُورِ
٢٦ تَخالُها بَيْنَ أَيْدٍ مِن مَجاذِفِها   يَغْرَقْنَ في مِثْلِ ماءِ الوَرْدِ مِنْ جُورِ
٢٧ وَرُبَّما خاضَتِ التيَّارَ طائِرَةً   بِمِثْلِ أَجْنِحَةِ الفُتْخِ الكَواسِيرِ
٢٨ كأَنَّما عَبَرَتْ تَخْتالُ عائِمَةً   في زاخِرٍ مِنْ نَدَى يُمْناهُ مَعْصُورِ

---

25. The rose ambergris is the reddish water seen at dawn. The camphor, which is black, refers to the pitch on the hulls of the ships.
26. Jūr is a city in Persia famous for its bright *red* rosewater.

29 Until they directed against the Mount of the two Conquests, which was within their reach, the ray of his unobscured lightning bolt.

30 To God belongs the Mount of the two Conquests among all mountains, elevated in height, famous among mountains!

31 Rising high in aloof pride, in its color there is a dusty grayness; it has a collar made of clouds which is not buttoned up.

32 By reason of the protection it offers, it conveys information about the protection given by a king, the generosity and protection of whose hand and shoulders are [eagerly] sought; one showered with abundance.

33 The stars appear at night over the crown of its head, in the air, hovering above like gold dinars,

34 And many a time do they brush it with their tails on every part jutting out which is dragged across its two temples.

35 It has lost tooth after tooth of its central incisors by reason of what has been taken from it through biting the sticks of bygone eras.

36 Taught by experience, it has experienced the faces of the days and has driven them as the caravan leader drives his file of camels.

37 It is impeded in its movement, [yet] a great wanderer in its fancy [when thinking of] the wonder of its two conditions, namely the past and the future.

38 It has attained silence and has cast down its eyes in meditation; it is manifest as to its calmness, concealed as to its secrets,

39 As if it were distressed by that which humiliates it, namely the fear of the two threats: the "flying hither and thither" and the "leveling."

40 How deserving it will be, when the mountains of the earth quake, to enjoy quiet on the morrow, [freedom] from all danger.

41 It is enough for it insofar as nobility is concerned, that the two sandals of a sovereign excellent in his endeavor, worthy of gratitude, have stepped in its stepping places,

42 [The Mount] snuffs, thanks to them, the wind of intercession proceeding from the grave of an Imam buried in the farthest West.

---

29. The "Mount of the two Conquests" is Gibraltar, first conquered by the Arabs in A.D. 711, and now again by ʿAbd al-Muʾmin.

36. "The faces of the days," i.e., good and evil.

٢٩ حتى رَمَتْ جَبَلُ الفَتْحَيْنِ مِن كَثَبٍ　　بِسَاطِعٍ مِن سَناهُ غَيْرَ مَبْهُورِ
٣٠ لِلّهِ ما جَبَلُ الفَتْحَيْنِ مِنْ جَبَلٍ　　مُعَظَّمِ القَدْرِ في الأَجْبَالِ مَذْكُورِ
٣١ مِن شَامِخِ الأَنْفِ في سَحْنائِهِ طَلَسٌ　　لَهُ مِنَ الغَيْمِ جَيْبٌ غَيْرُ مَزْرُورِ
٣٢ مُعْتَبِّرًا بِذُرَاهُ عن ذُرَى مَلِكٍ　　مُسْتَمْطَرِ الكَفِّ والأَكْنَافِ مَمْطُورِ
٣٣ تُمْسِي النُّجُومُ على إِكْلِيلِ مَفْرِقِهِ　　في الجَوِّ حائمةً مِثْلَ الدَّنانِيرِ
٣٤ ورُبَّمَا مَسَحَتْهُ مِنْ ذَوائِبِهَا　　بِكُلِّ فَضْلٍ على فَوْدَيْهِ مَجْرُورِ
٣٥ وَأَدْرَدٍ مِن ثَنَايَاهُ بِمَا أَخَذَتْ　　مِنهُ معاجِمُ أَعْوَادِ الدَّهارِيرِ
٣٦ مُحَنَّكٍ حَلَبَ الأَيَّامَ أَشْطُرَهَا　　وساقَها سَوْقَ حادِي العِيرِ لِلْعِيرِ
٣٧ مُقَيَّدُ الخَطْوِ جَوَّالُ الخَواطِرِ في　　عَجِيبِ أَمْرَيْهِ مِن ماضٍ ومَنْظُورِ
٣٨ قد وَاصَلَ الصَّمْتَ والإِطْراقَ مُفْتَكِرًا　　بادِي السَّكِينَةِ مُغْفَرَّ الأَسارِيرِ
٣٩ كأَنَّهُ مُكْمَدٌ مِمَّا تَعَبَّدَهُ　　خَوْفَ الوَعِيدَيْنِ مِن دَكٍّ وتَسْيِيرِ
٤٠ أَخْلِقْ بِهِ وجِبالُ الأَرْضِ راجِفَةٌ　　أَنْ يَطْمَئِنَّ غَدًا مِن كُلِّ مَحْذُورِ
٤١ كَفاهُ فَضْلًا أَنِ انْتابَتْ مَواطِئَهُ　　نَعْلَا مَلِيكٍ كَرِيمِ السَّعْيِ مَشْكُورِ
٤٢ مُسْتَنْشِئًا بِهِما رِيحَ الشَّفاعَةِ مِنْ　　ثَرَى إِمامٍ بِأَقْصَى الغَرْبِ مَقْبُورِ

---

39. Cf. Koran 51:9–10: "On the day when the firmament will be in dreadful commotion, and the mountains will *fly hither and thither*"; Koran 89:21: "Nay when the earth is *leveled*" (or: "pounded to powder").

42. The "Imam buried in the farthest West" is Ibn Tūmart.

43 It has not given up hope of something positive from him, when facing the day of Resurrection, irreversible and predetermined.

44 Until it perish from this world upon a last gasp, it will seek fulfillment of the promise, before the blast of the trumpet.

45 Overlooking the Western side, as if it were one spending the night in a very dark region of the air, it is watching out

46 For the flasher of a sword who drew it, after the predetermined decree [of God], in the West, one of the lands famous for their white swords;

47 When it flashed, he being a Qaisite, it incited him to the very brink of neglecting religion since he was in need of seeking his blood vengeance.

48 It was a king who came lording it over the age for nothing had been brought forth in it which had not been worthy of scorn.

49 No aim has occurred to him in religion or this world, but that it has redounded in his favor without any reservations.

50 Nor did he direct his desires toward any goal, but that the attainment of things predestined guided his arrow,

51 To the point that it seems as if he possesses the power of enslaving and governing the [whole] world at all times.

52 His army is distinguished, for his retinues consist of [men] each one of whom is overthrown from the throne of kingship, conquered.

53 At first they submitted to him under constraint and became obedient to his command [to practice a distinction] between what is forbidden and what is commanded,

54 After they had disobeyed an order, hence they left no state of ease to one in difficulty when pardon became possible.

55 The remainder of the war they gave up, yet there was no sign of lagging behind in them insofar as striking and thrusting were concerned.

56 The fighting men do not deny what they hold in their hands in the way of white notched swords or tawny broken lances.

57 When you worked out God's command while striving in holy war, you cut off, by yourself alone, the heads of multitudes.

58 He who [seeks to establish] a cause for matters should most certainly not be surprised because of any scarcity in numbers, nor should he rely upon large numbers.

---

45. I.e., "The western side" of the peninsula of Algeciras.
47. The one in "need of vengeance" is ʿAbd al-Muʾmin.

٤٣ ما انْفَكَّ آمِلَ أَمْرٍ مِنه بَيْنَ يَدَيْ — يَوْمِ القِيامةِ مَحْتُومٍ ومَقْدُورِ

٤٤ حتى تَصَدَّى مِن الدُّنْيا على رَمَقٍ — يَسْتَنْجِزُ الوَعْدَ قَبْلَ النَّفْخِ في الصُّورِ

٤٥ مُسْتَقْبِلَ الجانِبِ الغَرْبِيِّ مُرْتَقِبًا — كأَنَّهُ بائِتٌ في جَوِّ أَسْمِيرِ

٤٦ لِبارِقٍ مِن حُسامٍ سَلَّهُ قَدَرًا — بالغَرْبِ مِنْ أُفُقِ البِيضِ المَناهِيرِ

٤٧ إذا تَأَلَّقَ قَبْسًا أَهابَ بِهِ — إلى شَفا مِن مَضاعِ الدِينِ مَوْتُورِ

٤٨ مَلْكٌ أَتَى عِظَمًا فَوْقَ الزَّمانِ فَما — يُمَرُّ فيه بِشَيْءٍ غَيْرِ مَحْقُورِ

٤٩ ما عَنَّ في الدينِ والدنيا له أَرَبٌ — إلا تَأَتَّى لهُ مِن غَيْرِ تَعْذِيرِ

٥٠ ولا رَمَى مِن أَمانِيهِ إلى غَرَضٍ — إلا هَدَى سَهْمَهُ نُجْحُ المَقادِيرِ

٥١ حتى كأَنَّ له في كُلِّ آوِنَةٍ — سُلْطانَ رِقٍّ على الدُّنْيا وتَسْخِيرُ

٥٢ مُمَيَّزُ الجَيْشِ مُلْتَفًّا مَواكِبُهُ — مِنْ كُلِّ مَنْلُولِ عَرْشِ المُلْكِ مَقْهُورِ

٥٣ مِن الأُولَى خَضَعُوا قَسْرًا له وَعَنَوْا — لِأَمْرِهِ بَيْنَ مَنْهِيٍّ ومَأْمُورِ

٥٤ مِن بَعْدِ ما عانَدُوا أَمْرًا فما تَرَكُوا — إذْ أَمْكَنَ العَفْوُ مَيْسُورًا لِمَعْسُورِ

٥٥ بَقِيَّةُ الحَرْبِ فاتُوها وما بِهِمُ — في الضَّرْبِ والطَّعْنِ سِيماءُ لِتَقْصِيرِ

٥٦ لا يُنْكِرُ القَوْمُ مِمَّا في أَكُفِّهِمُ — بِيضٍ مَفالِيلَ أَوْ سُمْرٍ مَكاسِيرِ

٥٧ إذا صَدَعْتَ بأَمْرِ اللهِ مُجْتَهِدًا — ضَرَبْتَ وَحْدَكَ أَعْناقَ الجَماهِيرِ

٥٨ لا يَذْهَلَنَّ لِتَقْلِيلٍ أَخُو سَبَبٍ — مِن الأُمُورِ ولا يَرْكَنْ لِتَكْثِيرِ

59 For the sea became dry by reason of the blow of the staff [of Moses] and the earth was flooded by reason of the gushing forth of the fountains of the earth.

60 Here we have the sword of God, indeed, which He girded on the most powerful of those guiding [along the path of salvation] as a means of repelling a much feared calamity.

61 Therefore, if its hilt is in the hand of the Mahdi, the place where its sword point lies is very glorious.

62 While the sun, were it to remember Moses, would not forget his successor Joshua, the subduer of tyrants.

---

59. Cf. Koran 11:40: "At length, behold! There came Our Command, and the fountains of the earth gushed forth!"

61. I.e., Ibn Tūmart.

62. Cf. Joshua 10:14: "So the sun stood still in the midst of heaven, and hastened not to go down about a whole day. . . ." *Fatā* in classical Arabic is a

٥٩ فالبَحْرُ قَدْ عادَ مِنْ ضَرْبِ العَصَا يَبَسًا   والأَرْضُ قد غَرِقَتْ مِن فَوْرِ تَنُّورِ
٦٠ وإِنَّمَا هُوَ سَيْفُ اللّٰهِ قَلَّدَهُ   أَقْوَى الهُدَاةِ يَدًا في دَفْعِ مَحْذُورِ
٦١ فَإِنْ يَكُنْ بِيَدِ المَهْدِيِّ قَائِمُهُ   فَمَوْضِعُ الحَدِّ مِنْهُ حَدُّ مَشْهُورِ
٦٢ والشَّمْسُ إِنْ ذَكَرَتْ مُوسَى فما نَسِيَتْ   فَتَاهُ يُوشَعَ قَمَّاعَ الجَبَابِيرِ

'brave young warrior,' a concept somewhat akin to the Greek *hero*. The word came to mean 'servant,' 'novice,' and even 'eunuch' (cf. Dozy, II, 241). What is implied in this line is that ʿAbd al-Muʾmin is the servant or successor of Ibn Tūmart as Joshua was that of Moses, and it is further implied that ʿAbd al-Muʾmin's exploits will make the sun stand still.

32 Ḥātim ibn Saʿīd

1 A sun drew near to a full moon: wine and a drinking companion!
2 Pass round the wine cups scented with ambergris; the garden is truly joyous.
3 The blowing of the breeze has decked the river in a coat of mail,
4 And the hand of the West and of the East has unsheathed lightning swords against the horizon,
5 While the weeping of the clouds has brought laughter to the flowers.
6 Lo, I have a lord who exercised his power and became my master. Were it not
7 For the tears which disclose the secret [of my love] I would have guarded it very carefully.
8 Where can I find [strength] to guard [that secret] when my tears are a flood in which fires burn the brighter?
9 Moreover, who has ever seen burning embers floating on waves?
10 When one who saw [him] accuse me falsely blamed me [for loving] him, I sang to him in rhythmic melody:
11 "Perhaps he deserves to be excused, even though you blame him!"

---

32. Source: Ibn Sanāʾ al-Mulk, *Dār aṭ-ṭirāz fī ʿamal al-muwashshaḥāt*, ed. Jaudat ar-Rikābī (Damascus, 1949), pp. 45–46.
Form: *muwashshaḥa*.

٣٢

حاتم بن سعيد

شَمْسٌ قارَنَتْ بَدْرا   راحٌ وَنَدِيمْ
أَدِرْ أَكْؤُسَ الخَمْرِ   عَنْبَرِيَّةَ النَّشْرِ   إِنَّ الرَّوْضَ ذو بِشْرِ
وَقَدْ دَرَّعَ النَّهْرا   هُبُوبُ النَّسِيمْ
وَسَلَّتْ على الأُفْقِ   يَدُ الغَرْبِ وَالشَّرْقِ   سُيُوفًا مِن البَرْقِ
وَقَدْ أَضْحَكَ الزَّهْرا   بُكاءُ الغُيُومْ
أَلا إِنَّ لِي مَوْلَى   تَحَكَّمَ فَاسْتَوْلَى   أَما إِنَّهُ لَوْلا
دُمُوعٌ تَفْضَحُ السِّرّا   لَكُنْتُ كَتُومْ
أَنَّى لِيَ كِتْمانْ   وَدَمْعِي طُوفانْ   شَبَّتْ فيه نِيرانْ
فَمَنْ أَبْصَرَ الجَمْرا   في لُجٍّ يَعُومْ
إِذا لامَنِي فِيهِ   مَنْ رَأَى تَجَنِّيهِ   شَدَوْتُ أُغَنِّيهِ
لَعَلَّ لَهُ عُذْرا   وَأَنْتَ تَلُومْ

METER: a–a–a *m–n*
7 7 7 7 6
RHYTHM: mixed (óoóooóo/oóooó).

33 Ibn Sahl of Seville

1 Does the fawn of al-Ḥimā know that he has kindled the heart of a lover in which he dwelt

2 So that it is burning and throbbing, just as the firebrand teased by the east wind?

3 O full moons which arose on the day of departure, bright countenanced, going forth on the path of peril:

4 My heart bears no sin in loving; instead it is from you that beauty comes, while from my eye comes the glance.

5 I gather pleasures while wounded by my passion, although I take pleasure in my beloved [only] with my thoughts.

6 Whenever I complain of my love to him, he smiles like the hills at the [cloud] crossing [the horizon] abundant [in its gushing rain],

7 When it brings the rain to them as if it were a funeral gathering, whereas they, in their joy seem as though they are at a wedding reception,

8 I am overcome by a conqueror who conquers through the languor of his gait, one in whose ransom I would give my father, for he is a harsh yet gentle creature.

9 We have never seen the likes of the mouth he displays, the camomile flowers of which are arranged in rows, flowers from which a heady wine is pressed,

10 From which his two eyes drew their warring while insofar as my heart is concerned, its intoxication will never sober up.

11 Black of tresses, honey sweet of red lips, dark eyed of glance, desirable of red lips,

12 His face resembles Ḍuḥā in smiling whereas in his shunning he is ᶜAbasa.

---

33. SOURCES: Ibn Sahl, *Dīwān*, ed. Aḥmad Ḥusain al-Qarnī (Cairo, 1926), pp. 53–55; Jaudat ar-Rikābī, *Fī l-adab al-Andalusī* (Cairo, 1960), pp. 328–330.

FORM *muwashshaḥa*.

METER: *ramal*. *Rhyme*: a–b–a–b–a–b *m–n–m–n*

1. Al-Ḥimā: a place-name in Arabia mentioned in pre-Islamic poetry.

3. The *Dīwān* reads *budūran ashraqat*.

٣٣

ابن سهل

١ هَلْ دَرَى ظَبْيُ الحِمَى أَن قَدْ حَمَى   قَلْبَ صَبٍّ حَلَّهُ عن مَكْنِسِ
٢ فَهْوَ فى حَرٍّ وخَفْقٍ مثلما   لَعِبَتْ رِيحُ الصَّبا بالقَبَسِ
٣ يا بُدورًا أَطلعَتْ يومَ النوَى   غُرَرًا تسلك فى نَهْجِ الغَرَرْ
٤ ما لِقَلْبِي فى الهَوَى ذَنْبٌ سِوَى   مِنكم الحُسْنُ ومِن عيني النَظَرْ
٥ أَجْتَنِي اللذّاتِ مَكْلومَ الجَوَى   وٱلتِذاذِي مِن حبيبي بِالفِكَرْ
٦ كُلَّمَا أَشْكُوهُ وَجْدِي بَسِمَا   كالرُّبَى بالعارِضِ المُنْبَجِسِ
٧ إِذْ يقيمُ القَطْرَ فيها مَأْتَمَا   وَهْيَ مِن بَهْجَتِها فى عُرُسِ
٨ غالِبٌ لى غالبٌ بالتُّؤَدَهْ   بِأَبِى أَفْدِيهِ مِن جافٍ رَقيقْ
٩ ما رَأَيْنا مثلَ ثَغْرٍ نَضَّدَهْ   أُقْحُوانًا عُصِرَتْ منه رَحيقْ
١٠ أَخذَتْ عيناهُ مِنه العَرْبَدَهْ   وفُؤادِي سُكْرُهُ ما إِنْ يُفِيقْ
١١ فاحِمُ الجُمَّةِ مَعْسولُ اللَّمَى   أَكْحَلُ اللَّحْظِ شَهِيُّ اللَّعَسِ
١٢ وَجْهُهُ يَتْلُو الضُّحَى مُبْتَسِمَا   وَهْوَ فى إِعْراضِهِ فى عَبَسِ

---

4. The *Dīwān* reads *mā li-nafsī.*
5. The *Dīwān* reads *wa-ltadānī.*
9. The *Dīwān* reads *mā ᶜalimnā*
11. The *Dīwān* reads *fāḥimu l-limmati*, and *sāḥiru l-ghanji* for *akḥalu l-lahẓi.*
12. Ḍuḥa, 'the forenoon,' is the name of Sura 92. ᶜAbasa, 'He frowned,' is the name of Sura 80.

13 O you who ask about my humility toward him: to me belongs the penalty for the sin, yet he is the sinner.

14 The noonday sun took from the ball of his cheeks a place of rising for the sun which set in him.

15 The tears of my eyelids came forth because of him while he had a cheek made ruddy-gold by my glance.

16 The rose blooms by reason of my planting it, whenever my eye steals a furtive glance from him.

17 Would that I knew what thing has made that rose unlawful to its planter.

18 Whenever I complain to him of my ardors, his eyes leave me abandoned and seriously ill.

19 Of my last breath of life, his glances have left the track of the ant upon the hard rock.

20 Yet I thank him with what is left [of that last breath]; I do not blame him for what he has destroyed,

21 For he, in my opinion, is just, in spite of his tyranny, but as for my severe censor, his speech is like dumbness.

22 I have had no authority in my love ever since he has been lodged in my soul in the place of my breathing.

23 From him there comes a kindling of the fire in my heart, which burns what it wills at all moments.

24 Yet [that fire] in his cheeks is a cooling and peace-giving agent, though it produces harm and a conflagration in the heart.

25 I fear and revere in him, being under the authority of passion, the lion of the thicket, yet I love him since he is a young fawn.

26 I said [to him] when he appeared wearing a mark to distinguish him in combat while he was guarded by his glances:

27 "O you who have taken my heart as booty lawfully won in battle, grant the love union in exchange for the *khums*!"

---

13. The *Dīwān* reads *ʿan jurmī*, 'my crime.'

14. The "noonday sun" is the golden wine, the flush of which "arose" from his cheeks. The "sun which set in him" is the wine he drank.

15. The *Dīwān* reads *dhahabat ad-damʿu bi-ashwāqi ilai-hi*. The poet suggests that the girl's cheek turns red with shame at his glance.

16. The *Dīwān* reads *bi-gharsin*.

١٣ أَيُّها السائِلُ عن ذُلّي لَدَيْه ‏‏ لِي جَزاءُ الذَّنْبِ وهو المُذْنِبُ

١٤ أَخَذَتْ شَمْسُ الضُّحى مِن وَجْنَتَيْه ‏‏ مَشْرِقًا لِلشَّمْسِ فيه مَغْرِبُ

١٥ ذَهَبَتْ أَدْمُعُ أَجفانِي عَلَيْه ‏‏ ولـه خَدٌّ بِلَحْظِي مُذْهَبُ

١٦ يَنْبُتُ الوَرْدُ بِغَرْسِي كُلَّما ‏‏ لاحَظَتْهُ مُقْلَتِي فى الخَلَسِ

١٧ لَيْتَ شِعْرى أَىُّ شيءٍ حَرَّمَا ‏‏ ذلك الوَرْدَ على المُغْتَرِسِ؟

١٨ كُلَّما أَشْكُو إليه حُرَقِي ‏‏ غادَرَتْني مُقْلَتاهُ دَنِفَا

١٩ تَرَكَتْ أَلْحاظُهُ مِن رَمَقِي ‏‏ أَثَرَ النَّمْلِ على صُمِّ الصَّفَا

٢٠ وأَنا أَشْكُرُهُ فيما بَقِي ‏‏ لَسْتُ أَلْحاهُ على ما أَتْلَفَا

٢١ فَهْوَ عِنْدِي عادِلٌ إنْ ظَلَمَا ‏‏ وعَذُولِي نُطْقُهُ كالخَرَسِ

٢٢ لَيْسَ لي فى الحُبِّ حُكْمٌ بَعْدَما ‏‏ حَلَّ مِن نَفْسِي مَحَلَّ النَّفَسِ

٢٣ مِنْهُ لِلنّارِ بِأَحْشائِي اضْطِرام ‏‏ يَلْتَظِي فى كُلِّ حِينٍ ما يَشا

٢٤ وَهْيَ فى خَدَّيْهِ بَرْدٌ وسَلام ‏‏ وَهْيَ ضُرٌّ وحَرِيقٌ فى الحَشَا

٢٥ أَتَّقِي مِنه على حُكْمِ الغَرام ‏‏ أَسَدَ الغابِ وأَهْواهُ رَشَا

٢٦ قُلْتُ لَمّا أَنْ تَبَدَّى مُعْلَمَا ‏‏ وَهْوَ مِن أَلْحاظِهِ فى حَرَسِ

٢٧ أَيُّها الآخِذُ قَلْبِي مَغْنَمَا ‏‏ اجعل الوَصْلَ مَكانَ الخُمُسِ

---

19. I.e., the glances have left almost *nothing* of his last breath of life.
22. The *Dīwān* reads *laisa lī fī l-amri*.
25. The *Dīwān* reads *asadan wardan*, 'a russet-hued lion.'
27. The *khums*, 'fifth,' is the fifth part of the booty taken in battle, which according to Islamic law reverts to the community of Muslims.

34 Shushtarī

1 A little shaikh from the land of Meknès sings in the middle of the marketplaces:
2 "What have I to do with men, and what have men to do with me?
3 What, O friend, have I to do with any creature
4 [When] He whom I love is a Creator, a Provider?
5 Unless you are sincere, my son, say not a word.
6 Take down my words on paper and write them like an amulet on my authority.
7 What have I to do with men, and what have men to do with me?"
8 Here is a clear statement that needs no explanation:
9 "What has anyone to do with anyone? Grasp this allusion well,
10 And observe my old age, my staff, and my begging wallet.
11 Thus did I live in Fez and thus do I live here too.
12 What have I to do with men, and what have men to do with me?"
13 How beautiful are his words when he struts through the marketplaces

---

34. Source: Shushtarī, *Dīwān*, ed. ᶜAlī Sāmī an-Nashshār (Alexandria, 1960), pp. 272–275.
Form: *zajal.*
Meter: a–b–c–b–d–b   *m–n–m–n*
7 7 7 7 7 7   7 7 7 7
Rhythm: mixed (oóoóooó/óooóoóo).

This *zajal* is a good example of how the profane songs of Ibn Quzmān

٣٤

ششتري

١ شُوَيخْ مِن أَرْضِ مِكْنَاسْ   وَسْطَ الأَسْواقْ يُغَنِّي

٢ أَشْ عَلَيَّا مِن النَّاسْ   وَآشْ على النّاسِ مِنِّي

٣ أَشْ عليَّا يا صاحِبْ   مِن جَمِيعِ الخَلايِقْ

٤ الذى هُوَ نَهْوَاهْ   هُوَ خَالِقْ وَرَازِقْ

٥ لا تَقُلْ يَاَ بْنِى كِلْمَهْ   إِلَّا إِنْ كُنْتَ صَادِقْ

٦ خُذْ كَلامِي فى قِرْطاسْ   وآكْتُبُوا حِرْزَ عَنِّي

٧ أَشْ عَليَّا مِن النَّاسْ   وَآشْ على النَّاسِ مِنِّي

٨ ثَمَّ قَولْ مُبِينْ   ولا يَحْتَاجْ عِبَارَهْ

٩ أَشْ علَى حَدّْ مِن حَدْ   إِفْهَمُوا ذِى الإِشَارَهْ

١٠ وآنْظُرُوا كِبْرَ سِنِّي   والعَصَى والغَرَارَهْ

١١ هكذا عِشْتُ فى فَاسْ   وكَذاكَ هُونْ هُونِي

١٢ أَشْ عليَّا مِن النَّاسْ   وَآشْ على النَّاسِ مِنِّي

١٣ وَمَا أَحْسَنْ كَلامُو   إِذْ يَخْطُرْ فى الأَسْوَاقْ

---

were transformed into mystic poetry. Its refrain was adopted by Raymond Lull who rendered it as "What care I/What will men say" (cf. L. Massignon, "Investigaciones sobre Shushtarī," *Andalus*, XIV, (1949), 3 and v. 1).

1. "Shaikh" in the vocabulary of Sufi mystics means a 'master' as opposed to the *murīd* or 'disciple.' Meknès is a city in Morocco, near Fez.

4. Var. *if*ᶜ*al ul-khaira tanjū*/*wa-itba*ᶜ *ahla l-ḥaqā*ʾ*iq*.

14 And you see the shopkeepers turn their necks in his direction.
15 With his begging wallet hanging from his neck, a short staff and cork sandals,
16 He is a well-built little shaikh, built as God created him.
17 "What have I to do with men, and what have men to do with me?"
18 Were you to see this little shaikh, how elegant he is in the true sense of the word!
19 He turned to me and said to me: "Do I see you follow me?
20 I set down my begging bowl—and may He who has mercy on us have mercy on it."
21 And he placed it among different kinds [of people] saying: "Leave me alone, leave me alone.
22 What have I to do with men, and what have men to do with me?
23 He who does good, O my son, receives only good in return;
24 He will look to his faults and reprove his own deeds,
25 While he who is close to my state will remain innocent and free."
26 He whose soul is good will grasp the innocence of the singer;
27 "What have I to do with men, and what have men to do with me?"
28 And in this way he busies himself in blessing Muhammad,
29 And [requesting God's] pleasure for his minister the glorious Abū Bakr,
30 And for the truthful ʿUmar and for the martyr of every place of martyrdom,
31 And for ʿAlī the grand judge over iniquities who, when he struck out, did not repeat the blow.

---

15. For *aqrāq*, 'cork sandals,' cf. Dozy, II, 334. It is the Spanish *alcorque*.
20. The *zanbīl* is a basket of palm leaves.

١٤ وتَرَى أَهْلَ الحَوانِتْ   تَلْتَفِتْ لُو بالأَعْنَاقْ

١٥ بِغَرَارَهْ فِى عُنْقُو   وَعْكَيْكِزْ وَأَقْرَاقْ

١٦ شُوَيخْ مَبْنِي عَلَى آسَاسْ   كَمَا آنْشَا آللّٰهُ مَبْنِي

١٧ أَشْ عَلَيَّا مِنَ النَّاسْ   وآشْ على النَّاسِ مِنِّي

١٨ لَوْ تَرَى ذا الشُوَيِّخْ   ما أَرَقُّوا بِمَعْنَى

١٩ إِلْتَفَتْ لِي وَقَالْ لِي   أَشْ نَراكَ تَتْبَعْنَا

٢٠ أَنَا نَنْصِبْ لِي زَنْبِيلْ   يَرْحَمُوا مَنْ رَحِمْنَا

٢١ وَأَقامُوا بَينْ أَجْنَاسْ   وَيَقُولْ دَعْنِي دَعْنِي

٢٢ أَشْ عليَّا مِنَ النَّاسْ   وآشْ على النَّاسِ مِنِّي

٢٣ مَنْ عَمِلْ يَا بْنِى طَيِّبْ   مَا يُصِيبْ إِلَّا طَيِّبْ

٢٤ لِعُيُوبُوا سَيَنْظُرْ   وَفِعَالُوا يُعَيِّبْ

٢٥ وَالْمُقَارِبْ بِحَالِي   يَبْقَى بَرًّا مُسَيَّبْ

٢٦ مَنْ مَعُوا طِيبَةَ أَنفَاسْ   يَدْرِى عُذْرَ المُغَنِّي

٢٧ أَشْ عليَّا مِنَ النَّاسْ   وَآشْ على النَّاسِ مِنِّي

٢٨ وَكَذاكْ إِشْتِغَالُوا   بالصَّلاه عَلَى مُحَمَّدْ

٢٩ وَالرِّضَا عَنْ وَزِيرُوا   أَبِى بَكْرِ المُمَجَّدْ

٣٠ وَعُمَرْ قائِلَ الحَقّْ   وَشَهِيدْ كُلِّ مَشْهَدْ

٣١ وَعَلِي مُفْتِي الأَرْجَاسْ   إِذَا يَضْرِبْ ما يَثْنِي

32 "What have I to do with men, and what have men to do with me?
33 O my Lord, I have put my hope in you; be generous to me in granting me repentance.
34 I have asked you in the name of the Prophet and [his] noble friends.
35 The devil has distracted me and I am involved with him.
36 Evil suggestions have filled my heart, namely what he seeks from me.
37 What have I to do with men, and what have men to do with me?"
38 Here ends the description of the little shaikh as I have set it down.
39 I am a basket weaver and I send my compliments to those of my profession.
40 When they test me the first words I say are:
41 "A little shaikh from the land of Meknès sings in the middle of the marketplaces:
42 'What have I to do with men, and what have men to do with me?'"

٣٢ أَشْ عليَّا مِن النَّاسْ   وَآشْ على النَّاسِ مِنِّي

٣٣ يَا إِلٰهِي رَجَوْتُكْ   جُدْ عليَّا بِتَوْبَهْ

٣٤ بِالنَّبِي قَدْ سَأَلْتُكْ   وَالكِرَامِ الأَحِبَّهْ

٣٥ الرَّجِيمْ قَدْ شَغَلْنِي   وَآنَا مَعُوا فى نُشْبَهْ

٣٦ قَدْ مَلَا قَلْبِي وَسْوَاسْ   مِمَّا هُ يَبْغِي مِنِّي

٣٧ أَشْ عليَّا مِن النَّاسْ   وَآشْ على النَّاسِ مِنِّي

٣٨ تَمَّ وَصْفُ الشُّوَيِّخْ   فى مَعَانِي نِظَامِي

٣٩ وِآنِّي خَوَّاصْ وَنُقْرِى   لأَهْلِ فَنِّي سَلامِي

٤٠ وَإِذا جَوَّزُونِي   نَقُلْ أَوَّلْ كَلامِي

٤١ شُوَيخْ مِن أَرْضِ مِكْنَاسْ   وَسْطَ الأَسْوَاقْ يُغَنِّي

٤٢ أَشْ عليَّا مِن النَّاسْ   وآشْ على النَّاسِ مِنِّي

35 Shushtarī

1 My beloved has visited me and my moments have become sweet. My beloved listened to me
2 And forgave all my sins, despite the spy's wrath.
3 The goal of my hopes visited me and [all] harm ceased. He gave news of the union,
4 And was present in my presence while the cup went round and I achieved my hopes.
5 We drank and our breaths were sweetened with a permitted wine.
6 Fill my cup, for in it are my lofty pleasures, so that I may drink it up, O you who understand!
7 My beloved is my [sole] joy and the niche [holding a lamp], ever present with me, close at hand.
8 O for his liquor! O for his wine! O for the wine seller! O for the joy! O for the song
9 Among gardens in which flowers have opened and shone for us,
10 While the birds in the tree pulpits deliver sermons among us!
11 And he filled my glasses and cups, but not with [the juice] of grapes or of raisins!
12 O fellow drinkers, understand well my allusions; my hour is wondrous indeed!
13 How fine was that wine, how clear that drink in a happy place!

---

35. SOURCE: Shushtarī, *Dīwān*, ed. ᶜAlī Sāmī an-Nashshār (Alexandria, 1960), pp. 89–91.
FORM: *zajal*.
METER: a—b—a—b—a—b *m—n—m—n*
11 7 11 7 11 7 11 7 11 7
RHYTHM: mixed (óooóooóooóo/ooóooó).

This Sufi poem has reminiscences of Ibn Quzmān, particularly in lines

٣٥

ششترى

١ زَارَنِـي حِبّي وَطَابَتْ آوقَاتِـي   وَسَمِعْ لِـي آلْحَبِيبْ

٢ وَعَفَـا عَـن جَمِيـعِ زَلَّاتِـي   عَلَى غَيْظِ الرَّقِيبْ

٣ زَارَنِـي مُنْيَتِي وَزَالَ البَاسْ   وَسَمِعْ بِالوِصَالْ

٤ وَحَضَرْ حَضْرَتِي وَدَارَ الكَاسْ   وَبَلَغْتُ الآمَالْ

٥ وَشَرِبْنَا وَطَابَتِ الأَنْفَاسْ   مِنْ مُدَامٍ حَلَالْ

٦ إِمْلَا كَاسِي فَفِيهِ مُزَاتِي   نَشْرُبُوا يا لَبِيبْ

٧ وَحَبِيبِي أُنْسِي وَمِشْكَاتِي   مَعِي حَاضِرْ قَرِيب

٨ أَىْ مُدَامَهْ وَآىْ خَمْرُهْ وَآىْ خَمَّارْ   وَآىْ طَرَبْ وَآىْ غِنَا

٩ فى رِيَاضٍ تَفَتَّحَتْ أَزْهَارْ   وَأَنَارَتْ لَنَا

١٠ وَالطُّيُورْ فى مَنَابِرِ آلأَشْجَارْ   تَخْتَطِبْ بَيْنَنَا

١١ وَزُجَاجَاتِي مَلَا وْطَاسَاتِي   دُونْ عِنَبْ دُونْ زَبِيبْ

١٢ يا نَدَامَى آفْهَمُوا إِشَارَاتِي   إِنَّ وَقْتِي عَجِيبْ

١٣ رَقَّ ذا الخَمْرُ رَاقَ ذا المَشْرُوبْ   فى مَحَلٍّ سَعِيدْ

2, 18, 19. It touches upon the theme of the "dark night of the soul" as expressed by Islamic mystics.

4. "In my presence." In the language of the Sufis *al-ḥaḍrat al-ᶜamāʾiyya* is the highest degree in the scale of divine manifestations (cf. Dozy, I, 298).

7. Cf. Koran 24:35: "God is the light of the heavens and the earth. The parable of this light is as if there were a *niche and within it a lamp*: the lamp enclosed in glass. . . ."

14 Let me drink and love my beloved every new day!

15 It is the fool who tells me to repent when I am most certainly on the right path.

16 I say to the censor when he appears: "My hour is wondrous indeed!"

17 My knowledge is about what has passed and what is to come; he who makes me sick is himself the physician.

18 In this love I am the prince of my time and the lover of ribaldry.

19 In loving beauties I have wasted my life and exhausted all branches of knowledge.

20 My full moon visited me in the pitch-black darkness of night and no eye saw him.

21 He so illuminated my lodging and my courtyards that I almost lost my mind.

22 He rested in my rest and in my movements, ever present, never absent.

23 In my sect, I give my soul to him whom I love desperately

24 And who was present in my presence, present in my joy while the hour was illuminated by him.

25 And I say to him: "O my full moon, O my sun," when I meet him,

26 "My beloved has visited me and my moments have become sweet. My beloved has been generous to me

27 Since he forgave all my sins, despite the spy's wrath!"

١٤ دَعْنِي نَشْرُبْ وَنَعْشَقْ المَحْبُوبْ   كُلَّ يَوْمٍ جَدِيدْ
١٥ السَّفِيهُ الذى يَقُولْ لِّي تُوبْ   إِنَّمَا آنا رَشِيدْ
١٦ وَنَقُولْ لِلْعَذُولِ إِنْ يَأْتِي   إِنَّ وَقْتِى عَجِيبْ
١٧ عِلْمِي في مَا مَضَى وَمَا يَأْتِي   مُمْرِضِي هُ الطَّبِيبْ
١٨ أَنَا فى ذَا الهَوَى إِمَامْ عَصْرِى   وَمُحِبُّ المُجُونْ
١٩ وَفى عِشْقِ المِلَاحْ فَنِيتْ عُمْرِى   وَفَنَيْتُ الفُنُونْ
٢٠ فى دُجَى اللَّيلِ زَارَنِي بَدْرِى   لا تَرَاهُ العُيُونْ
٢١ وَأَضَا مَنْزِلِي وَسَاحَاتِي   كَادَ عَقْلِي يَغِيب
٢٢ فى سُكُونِي سَكَنْ وَحَرَكَاتِي   حَاضِرٍ لا يَغِيبْ
٢٣ أَنَا فى مَذْهَبِي نَهَبْ نَفْسِي   لِلَّذى هِمْتُ فِيهْ
٢٤ وَحَضَرْ حَضْرَتِي حَضَرْ أُنْسِي   وَأَضَا آلوَقْتُ بِيهْ
٢٥ وَنَقُلْ لُو يَا بَدْرِى يَا شَمْسِي   عِنْدَمَا نَلْتَقِيهْ
٢٦ زَارْنِي حِبِّي وَطَابَتَ آوْقَاتِي   وَسَمَحْ لِى آلْحَبِيبْ
٢٧ مُذْ عَفَا عن جَمِيعِ زَلَّاتِي   عَلَى غَيْظِ الرَّقِيبْ

36 Ibn al-ᶜArabī

1 O doves of the *arāk* and the *bān* trees; take pity; to not redouble my sorrows with [your] mourning.

2 Take pity; do not reveal my hidden affections and secret sorrows with your sad cooing.

3 I respond to her in the evening and in the latter part of the forenoon with the mournful lament of one deeply moved by passion and the moaning of one madly in love.

4 The spirits faced each other from opposite sides in the *ghaḍā* thicket [like winds blowing from contrary directions] so that they bent their branches over me, thus annihilating me.

5 And they brought me different kinds of tormenting desire and passion as well as novel forms of affliction.

6 Hence, who will give me the assurance of [attaining] Jamᶜ, who of al-Muḥaṣṣab of Minā, who of Dhāt al-Athl, and who of Naᶜmān?

7 They walk around my heart moment after moment for the sake of a certain love and affliction [of mine], and they kiss my pillars,

8 Just as the best of mankind walked around the Kaᶜba, which the evidence of reason proclaims to be imperfect,

9 And kissed some stones in it, though he was a Nāṭiq; yet what is the rank of the Holy Sanctuary in comparison with the dignity of one human being?

---

36. SOURCES: Ibn al-ᶜArabī, *The Tarjumān al-Ashwāq*, ed. R. A. Nicholson (London, 1911), pp. 19, 66–70; *Tarjumān al-ashwāq* (Beirut: Dār Sader, 1961), pp. 40–44.

METER: *ṭawīl.*

1. The "doves" are the influences of holiness and purity; the *arāk* is a thorny tree used for making toothpicks; the *bān* is a type of *moringa* producing a fragrant oil. These trees symbolize purity and holiness.

3. "I respond to her," i.e., I repeat to her what she says to me, as God said to the soul when he created it, "Who am I?" and it answered, "Who am I?" referring to its qualities, whereupon He caused it to dwell four thousand years in the sea of despair and indigence and abasement until it said to Him, "Thou art my Lord."

4. *Arwāḥ* is the plural of *rūḥ*, "spirit," as well as of *rīḥ*, "wind," hence the pun in this line. "Faced one another" because love entails the union of two opposites. The *ghaḍā* is a species of tamarisk whose wood produces a hard and long-burning charcoal. Here it stands for the fires of love. The "branches" are flames. "Annihilated me," in order that He alone might exist, not I, through jealousy that the lover should have any existence in himself apart from his beloved.

٣٦

ابن العربى

١ ألا يا حمامات الأراكة والبان   ترفقن لا تضعفن بالشجو أشجاني

٢ ترفقن لا تظهرن بالنوح والبكا   خفي صباباتي ومكنون أحزاني

٣ أطارحها عند الأصيل وبالضحى   بحنة مشتاق وأنة هيمان

٤ تناوحت الأرواح في غيضة الغضا   فمالت بأفنان علي، فأفناني

٥ وجاءت من الشوق المبرح والجوى،   ومن طرف البلوى إلي بأفنان

٦ فمن لي بجمع والمحصب من منى   ومن لي بذات الأثل من لي بنعمان

٧ تطوف بقلبى ساعة بعد ساعة،   لوجد وتبريح وتلثم أركاني

٨ كما طاف خير الخلق بالكعبة التي   يقول دليل العقل فيها بنقصان

٩ وقبل أحجارا بها، وهو ناطق   وأين مقام البيت من قدر إنسان

---

6. "Jamᶜ," i.e., union with the loved one in the station of proximity, which is al-Muzdalifa, a station of the pilgrimage between Mecca and Minā. "Al-Muḥaṣṣab," the place where the thoughts that prevent lovers from attaining their object of desire are cast out. "Dhāt al-Athl," referring to the principle (*aṣl*), for it is the principle in love that thou shouldst be the very essence of thy Beloved and shouldst disappear in Him from thyself. "Naᶜmān," the place of Divine and holy bliss (*naᶜīm*).

7. "For the sake of a certain love and affliction," i.e., in order to inspire me with passion. "And they kiss my pillars" (properly, kiss over the *lithām* or veil covering the mouth), i.e., he is veiled and unable to behold them except through a medium (*wāṣiṭa*). The "pillars" are the four elements on which the human constitution is based.

8. The Beirut edition records *khairu r-rusli*. The "best of mankind" is the Prophet Muhammad.

9. In the Ismāᶜīlī system Muhammad, regarded as an incarnation of Universal Reason, is the Nāṭiq of the sixth prophetic cycle (cf. E. W. Browne, *Literary History of Persia*, [Cambridge, 1956], I, 408 ff.).

10 How often did they not swear and solemnly vow that they would not change, yet one dyed with henna does not keep faith.

11 Yet one of the most wondrous things is a young veiled gazelle who points with fingertips dyed red like the jujube and winks with [its] eyelids,

12 While its pasture is [the region] lying between [my] breastbones and my abdomen. Lo, how wondrous is a garden in the midst of fires!

13 My heart has adopted every shape; it has become a pasture for gazelles and a convent for Christian monks,

14 A temple for idols and a Pilgrim's Kaᶜba, the tables of a Torah and the pages of a Koran.

15 I follow the religion of Love; wherever Love's camels turn, there Love is my religion and my faith.

16 We have an example in Bishr, the lover of Hind and her sister, and in Qais and Laila, also in Maiya and Ghailān.

---

10. The Beirut edition reads *fa-kam*. "One dyed with henna": he refers to sensual influences (*wāridātu nafsiyya*), such as descended on the soul when God addressed it and said, "Am I not your Lord?" (Koran, VII, 171), and received from it a promise and covenant. Then it did not faithfully keep the station of unification (*at-tauḥīd*), but followed other gods. No one was exempt from this polytheism, for everyone said, "I did" and "I said," at the time when he forgot to contemplate the Divine Agent and Speaker within him.

11. "A veiled gazelle," i.e., a Divine subtlety (*laṭīfa*) veiled by a sensual state (*ḥālatun nafsiyya*), in reference to the unknown spiritual feelings (*aḥwāl*) of gnostics, who cannot explain their feelings to other men; they can only indicate them symbolically to those who have begun to experience the like. "With fingertips dyed red like the jujube": he means the same thing as he meant by "One dyed with henna" in the last line. "And winks with [its] eyelids," i.e., the speculative proofs concerning the principles of gnostics are valid only for those who have already been imbued with the rudiments of this experience. Gnostics, though they resemble the vulgar outwardly, are Divines (*rabbanīyyūna*) inwardly. The Beirut edition reads *wa min ᶜajabi*.

12. "While its pasture," etc., as ᶜAlī said, striking his breast, "Here are sciences in plenty, could I but find people to carry them [in their minds]." "A garden in the midst of fires," i.e., manifold sciences that, strange to say, are not consumed by the flames of love in his breast. The reason is that these sciences are produced by the fires of seeking and longing, and therefore, like the salamander, are not destroyed by them.

13. "My heart has adopted every shape," as another has said, "The heart (*al-qalb*) is so called from its changing (*taqallubu-hu*)," for it varies according to the various influences by which it is affected in consequence of the variety

١٠ وَكَمْ عَهِدَتْ أَنْ لا تَحُولَ وَأَقْسَمَتْ   وَلَيْسَ لِمَخْضُوبٍ وَفَاءٌ بِأَيْمَانِ

١١ وَمِنْ أَعْجَبِ الأَشْيَاءِ ظَبْيٌ مُبَرْقَعٌ   يُشِيرُ بِعُنَّابٍ ، وَيُومِي بِأَجْفَانِ

١٢ وَمَرْعَاهُ ما بَيْنَ التَّرائِبِ والحَشَا   ويا عَجَبًا مِن رَوْضَةٍ وَسْطَ نِيرانِ

١٣ لَقَدْ صارَ قَلْبِي قابِلًا كُلَّ صُورَةٍ   فَمَرْعًى لِغِزْلانٍ وَدَيْرٌ لِرُهْبانِ

١٤ وَبَيْتٌ لِأَوْثانٍ وكَعْبَةُ طائِفٍ   وأَلْواحُ تَوْراةٍ ومُصْحَفُ قُرْآنِ

١٥ أَدِينُ بِدِينِ الحُبِّ أَنَّى تَوَجَّهَتْ   رَكائِبُهُ فالحُبُّ دِينِي وإِيمانِي

١٦ لَنا أُسْوَةٌ في بِشْرِ هِنْدٍ وَأُخْتِها   وقَيْسٍ ولَيْلَى ، ثُمَّ مَيٍّ وغَيْلانِ

---

of its states of feeling (*aḥwāl*); and the variety of its feelings is due to the variety of the Divine manifestations that appear to its inmost ground (*sirr*). The religious law gives to this phenomenon the name of "transformation" (*at-taḥawwul wa t-tabaddul fī ṣ-ṣuwar*). "A pasture for gazelles," i.e., for the objects of his love. "A convent for Christian monks": inasmuch as he makes the loved ones to be monks, he calls the heart a convent.

14. "A temple for idols," i.e., for the Divine Realities that men seek and for whose sake they worship God. "A Pilgrim's Kaᶜba," because his heart is encompassed by exalted spirits. "The tables of a Torah," i.e., his heart is a table on which are inscribed the Mosaic sciences that have accrued to him. "The pages of a Koran," because his heart has received an inheritance of the perfect Muhammadan knowledge.

15. "I follow the religion of Love," in reference to the verse "Follow me, then God will love you" (Koran 3:29). "Wherever Love's camels turn. . . ," i.e., "I accept willingly and gladly whatever burden He lays on me. No religion is more sublime than a religion based on love and longing for Him whom I worship and in whom I have faith." This is a peculiar prerogative of Muslims, for the station of perfect love is appropriated to Muhammad beyond any other prophet, since God took him as His beloved (*ḥabīban*).

16. He says, "Love, qua love, is one and the same reality to those Arab lovers and to me, but the objects of our love are different, for they loved a phenomenon, whereas I love the Essential." "We have an example in them," because God only afflicted them with love for human beings like themselves in order that he might show, by means of them, the falseness of those who pretend to love Him and yet feel no such transport and rapture in loving Him as deprived those enamored men of their reason and made them unconscious of themselves.

37 Ḥāzim al-Qarṭājannī

1 Dawn for you is night and darkness is light; [now] the girls of enjoyable company shy away, contrary to the days of youth.

2 You have enjoyed the company of a certain light during the nights of your youth, yet it no longer enjoys your company; the presence of its darkness constituted that light.

3 Therefore would that no white [hairs] had arisen like rays on my temple, and that those black [hairs] had not forsaken it.

4 Yet they departed and because of them misfortune overtook my youth; because of them my eyelid is sleepless and [my] heart is constricted.

5 I have caused my heart to tremble on account of the farewells said by the girls to me, just as a herd of gazelles when it is scattered takes you by surprise.

6 O pearl of the oystershell floating on the waves of the morning mirage; in her both bright flowers and shining light are drowned out!

7 A leafy green branch swayed by the wind, pelted by the rain, namely you, has caused [this] love prelude to flow like a breeze and [my] tears to flow like rain.

8 A rising star, namely you, has behaved with pride toward other stars in the place where necklaces and neckstrands are caused to shine,

9 [As has also] a string of pearls, as if your throat against it were a dawn against its pearly stars.

10 What beauty there is in the arrival and departure [of those whom] women's riding saddles and curtained canopies contained!

11 It is as though blue cloaks had appeared in the morning mirage, in which the herds of wild cows were pictures.

12 It is despair enough that after their [departure] the springtime abode of human companionship has come to be inhabited by a herd of wild gazelles in place of the tame.

---

37. SOURCE: Ḥāzim al-Qarṭājannī, *Dīwān*, ed. ʿUthmān al-Kaʿāʿk (Beirut, 1964), pp. 59–62.

METER: *basīṭ*.

After the conquest of Cartagena by the Christians in 1241, al-Qarṭājannī fled to North Africa where he resided at the court of the Ḥafṣid ruler of Tunis,

٣٧

حازم القرطاجنّي

١ الصُّبْحُ عندكَ لَيْلٌ والدُّجَى نُورُ   إنَّ الأَوانِسَ عن ضِدِّ الصِّبا نُورُ

٢ آنَسْتَ نُورًا على لَيْلِ الشبابِ فلم   يُؤْنِسْكَ أُنْسُ دُجَاه ذلك النُورُ

٣ فَلَيْتَ فَوْدِيَ لم تُشْرِقْ به شُهُبٌ   ولا ٱنجلتْ عنه هاتيكَ الدَّياجِيرُ

٤ نَأَتْ فنابَ شَبابي عندَها نُوَبٌ   جَفْني بها ساهِرٌ والقلبُ مَصْبُورُ

٥ ذعرتُ سربي بتَوْدِيعِ الأَوَانِسِ لي   كَمَا يُفاجِيكَ سِرْبٌ وَهْوَ مَذْعُورُ

٦ يا دُرَّةَ الصَّدَفِ الطَّافِي على لُجَجٍ   لِلآلِ يُغْرَقُ فيها النَّوْرُ والنُّورُ

٧ أَجْرَى النَسيبَ نَسيمًا والدموعَ حَيَا   غُصْنٌ يَرُوحُ مَرُوحٌ منكِ مَمْطُورُ

٨ تاهَتْ على الشهبِ شُهْبٌ منكِ طالعةٌ   حَيْثُ القَلائِدُ تُزْهى والتَقاصِيرُ

٩ وعِقْدُ دُرٍّ كأَنَّ النَّحْرَ منكِ به   صُبْحٌ بِكَوْكَبِهِ الدُّرِّيِّ مَنْحُورُ

١٠ ماذا مِن الحُسْنِ في حَلٍّ ومُرْتَحَلٍ   حَوَتْهُ تلك الحَوايا والمَقاصِيرُ

١١ كأَنَّما الآلُ تَبْدُو فيه أَرْدِيَةٌ   زُرْقٌ صِوارُ المَهَا فيها تَصاوِيرُ

١٢ كَفَى أَسًى أَنَّ رَبْعَ الأُنْسِ بعدهمُ   بِرَبْرَبِ الوَحْشِ بعد الأُنْسِ مَعْمُورُ

Abū Zakariyāʾ Yaḥya. The latter had inherited the power of the Almohad empire and was looked to by Spanish Muslims for deliverance from the Christian attacks. In this ode the poet congratulates the ruler for the conquest of Ceuta and inspires him to invade al-Andalus in defense of Islam.

13 A certain springtime abode such that every rain cloud renews for my eye, of its trace, what the pillars of dust raised by whirlwinds have effaced,

14 (Each [cloud] shining in the sky, pure white of sides, with its contours glistening in the rain,

15 Such that when its lightening encircles it, you would think it to be gold from which bracelets are made that encircle a wrist,

16 As if, when it passed by, white, secluded women had rattled and exposed to view the ornaments of their wrists):

17 [Such a springtime abode] is the home in which sleep is ever at hand; in it the offense of the nights is forgiven in the hour of separation!

18 So wonder at the clemency whereby one whose homeland is Tunisia spent the night in the company of one whose homeland is Todmir.

19 In this way those abodes, homelands, and dwelling places reunited us as they once used to join us.

20 [He is] a bough of the *bān* tree when a hand bends it down, yet he is bent down [only] in the inner recesses of the mind,

21 For I was not ungrateful for the favors I received from him when the [black] musk of darkness had become morning and he was covered with the [white] camphor [of dawn].

22 And a bird sang sweetly in the upper reaches of the dawn when he appeared in the blackness of night like a blaze on a horse's head.

23 O, would that no daylight would spread from the whiteness of dawn into the furthermost recesses of darkness,

24 For in the face of the Emir Abū Yaḥya there is brilliance enough for us, were the whiteness of dawn not to shine at all!

25 [It is] a face like the noonday sun; the light of dawn is dazzled by that part of his light that has spread over the earth.

26 [He is] a sea of generosity when his gifts pour out so that land and sea are flooded by their [endless] flow.

27 [He is] a king possessed of the loftiest ambitions (and these have sought to emulate him), while everything held in great esteem is despicable in comparison with them.

---

18. "One whose homeland is Tunisia," i.e., Abū Zakariyāʾ Yaḥya, the first Ḥafṣid ruler of Tunis from 1229 to 1249, to whom this panegyric is directed (cf. André Julien, *Histoire de l'Afrique du Nord* [Paris, 1964], pp. 135–137). Al-Qarṭājannī was himself from the eastern Andalusian province of Todmir

١٣ رَبْعٌ تُجِدُّ لِعَيْنِي كُلَّ مُعْصِرَةٍ   مِن رَسْمِهِ ما تُعَفِّيهِ الأعاصِيرُ

١٤ مِنْ كُلِّ غَرّاءَ مُبْيَضٍّ جَوانِبُها   بالوَدْقِ مشرقةٌ منها الأَسارِيرُ

١٥ إذا اسْتَدارَ سَنَاها خِلْتَه ذَهَبًا   دارَتْ على مِعْصَمٍ منه أَساوِيرُ

١٦ كأَنَّما قَعْقَعَتْ في جَوْزِهِ وجَلَتْ   حُلَى مَعَاصِمِها البِيضُ المَقاصِيرُ

١٧ دارُ التي لم تَزَلْ تَدْنُو بِها سِنَةٌ   ذَنْبُ الليالي بها في البُعْدِ مَغْفُورُ

١٨ فَاْعْجَبْ لِحلْمٍ به قَدْ باتَ يُؤْنِسُ مَنْ   مَثْواهُ تُونِسَ مَنْ مَثْواهُ تُدْمِيرُ

١٩ فَجَمَّعَتْنا كَمَا كانَتْ تُجَمِّعُنا   تِلك المَنَازِلُ والأَوْطانُ والدُّورُ

٢٠ غُصْنٌ مِن البَانِ لَمَّا تَهْتَصِرْهُ يَدٌ   لٰكِنَّهُ بِضَمِيرِ النفسِ مَهْصُورُ

٢١ فَلَسْتُ كافِرَ نُعْمَى مِنه حِينَ غدَا   مِسْكُ الدُّجَى وهو بالكَافُورِ مَكْفُورُ

٢٢ وَقَدْ شَدَا في فُرُوعِ الصُّبْحِ حِينَ بَدَا   في دُهْمَةِ الليْلِ كالعُصْفُورِ عُصْفُورُ

٢٣ يَالَيْتَ أن بَيَاضَ الصُّبْحِ ما سَطَعَتْ   في أُخْرِيَاتِ الدُّجَى مِنه تَبَاشِيرُ

٢٤ فَفِي مُحَيَّا أَبِي يَحْيَى الأَمِيرِ لَنَا   إنْ لم يُنَوِّرْ بَيَاضُ الصُّبْحِ تَنْوِيرُ

٢٥ وَجْهٌ كَشَمْسِ الضُّحَى نُورُ الصَّبَاحِ بِمَا   قَدْ فَاضَ مِن نُورِهِ في الأَرْضِ مَبْهُورُ

٢٦ وَبَحْرُ جُودٍ إذا فَاضَتْ مَوَاهِبُهُ   فالبَرُّ مِن فَيْضِها والبَحْرُ مَغْمُورُ

٢٧ مَلْكٌ لَهُ الهِمَمُ العُلْيَا إليه عَطَتْ   وكلُّ مُسْتَعْظَمٍ فيهِنَّ مَحْقُورُ

(Murcia) and had fled from Cartagena when it fell to the Christians in 1241, being then thirty years old.

24. I.e., the Ḥafṣid ruler Abū Zakariyāʾ Yaḥya.

28 He is divided in joining the two portions of gift-giving and prudence; goodness and nobility were engendered with him and engendered him.

29 Therefore the mark of his hand is abundance and generosity, while the mark of his soul is holiness and purity.

30 For the clouds are naturally disposed to be as generous as he, and the breezes are perfumed with his fragrance.

31 It is his fortunate advance that has betrayed the advancing enemy indeed, wheresoever thought has controlled his point of view.

32 His sword has made the religious and the secular powers secure during the time of the Guidance's message so that a wolf and a gazelle have been conjoined.

33 He received a covenant of succession from a leader who was the rightful heir to the Guidance, whose nature it is to observe the virtues of reverence toward God and well doing [toward those men to whom well doing was owed as a duty].

34 Therefore the organization of hopes and safety became excellent at the same time, while the organization of the enemy came to be scattered,

35 For in his right hand raised aloft there is a ray of [the light of] the Guidance, as well as a thin, sharp blade from among the swords of God.

36 Whenever the squadrons of the latter proudly trail their robes' ends, he is a king tucking up [his garment] to bare [a man] of illustrious ancestry.

37 So the sharp-edged swords are quenched of their thirst by the palm of his hand wherever courage is kindled and blazes forth.

38 How excellent is the family of Abū Ḥafṣ, for each of its members has become famous in the age on account of his brilliance!

39 [They are] seas of knowledge and the means of kindling the fire of every battle, heated by the keen blades and the ardor of war.

40 For knowledge is always chosen from their council chamber, wherein the tradition handed down by an uninterrupted chain of authorities is preferred.

41 A hoped-for generosity and a much feared courage of yours have revived the seekers of largesse, having at the same time destroyed the enemy.

---

38. Abū Ḥafṣ was the ancestor of the Ḥafṣid dynasty (*ibid.*, p. 100).

٢٨ مُفَرِّقٌ جَامِعٌ شَمْلَيْ لُهًى وَنُهًى   نَمَا بِهِ وَنَمَاهُ الخَيْرُ والخِيرُ
٢٩ فَشِيمَةُ الكَفِّ مِنهُ سَطْوَةٌ ونَدًى   وَشِيمَةُ النفْسِ تَقْدِيسٌ وتَطْهِيرُ
٣٠ فَفِي الغَمَائِمِ خِيمٌ مِن مَكارِمِهِ   وفي النَّواسِمِ مِن رَيَّاهُ تَعْطِيرُ
٣١ إِقْبَالُهُ غَادَرَ الأَعْدَاءَ مُقْبِلَةً   أَيَّانَ أَحْكَمَ مِنهُ الرأىَ تَدْبِيرُ
٣٢ قد أَمَّنَ الدينَ والدُّنيا مُقَلِّدُهُ   عَهْدَ الهُدَى فآلتَقَى سِيدٌ ويَعْفُورُ
٣٣ عَهْدٌ تَلَقَّاهُ مِن هادٍ وَليِّ هُدًى   على سَجَايا التُّقَى والبِرِّ مَفْطُورُ
٣٤ فَرَاقَ نَظْمُ الأَمانِي والأَمانِ مَعًا   وظَلَّ نَظْمُ الأَعَادِى وَهْوَ مَنْثُورُ
٣٥ فَفِي يَمِينِ العُلَا مِنه شِهابُ هُدًى   وَمُرْهَفٌ مِن سُيُوفِ اللّٰهِ مَطْرُورُ
٣٦ مَلْكٌ لَهُ كُلَّمَا جَرَّتْ كَتائِبُهَا   أَذْيالَهَا عن صَرِيحِ الجِدِّ تَشْمِيرُ
٣٧ فَلِلصَّوَارِمِ إِرْوَاءٌ بِرَاحَتِهِ   في حيث لِلْبَأْسِ إِيرَاءٌ وتَسْعِيرُ
٣٨ لِلّٰهِ آلُ أَبِي حَفْصٍ فكُلُّهُمُ   غَدَا بِلألائِهِ في الدَّهْرِ مَشْهُورُ
٣٩ بِحَارُ عِلْمٍ ومَذْكَى نارِ كُلِّ وَغًى   بالمُرْهَفَاتِ وحَرُّ الحَرْبِ مَسْجُورُ
٤٠ فالعِلْمُ يُؤْثَرُ مِنْ نَادِيهِمُ أَبَدًا   حيثُ الحَديثُ عن المَأْثُورِ مَأْثُورُ
٤١ أَحْيَا العُفَاةَ وقَدْ أَرْدَى العُدَاةَ معًا   جُودٌ مرَجّى وبَأْسٌ منك مَحْذُورُ

40. For *nādin*, 'council chamber,' cf. Dozy, II, 654, col. 1.

42 A graciousness and a sword: the one is the collar of the obedient while the other is a collar buttoned on the neck of him who disobeys you.

43 For no death or life is ever decreed to him who disobeys you or seeks your largesse, without [one of] these two.

44 O rightful heir to the Guidance; conquests all belong to you; the rapidly approaching future one of them as well as the past one that has already been observed.

45 While the Conquest of Ceuta came to you leading [Ceuta] as the caravan follows the footsteps of its leader.

46 So congratulations for the brilliant conquests [like an opening up of enemy territory] that have accrued to you, just as flowers open up in the garden's bed.

47 What an auspicious investiture [of your rule] they have constituted; on account of them the party of error is in grief, while the party of the Guidance is cheerful and happy!

48 How much good news and congratulations does the peninsula enjoy on account of them; the eyes of [all] hopes are inclined in their direction,

49 For they have renewed certain traces that had become effaced here, for the Guidance; traces along [the path of] which both Christians and Moors gallop,

50 On every deep black [steed] dragging its feet, clattering over stones, lofty of stature so that the hillocks and knolls humble themselves in its presence,

51 And [on] lean [horses] such that the goals [they hoped to reach] kept them all one-eyed, after the training places where steeds are made lean had reduced their fat.

52 The Imam of a Guidance seeking victory from God, victorious through God, attacks the enemy by means of the necks [of those steeds].

53 [He is also] an offshoot of glory, pure in respect of goodness, and there is no wondering at the goodness of an offshoot whose constituent elements are pure.

54 A [poem like a] virgin [in that its like has never been attempted before], in which all beauty is confined, has come to you, falling short of the generosity there is in you.

---

49. "The peninsula," i.e., al-Andalus, where the Muslim cities expected help and relief from the Tunisian dynasty in their struggle for survival against Christendom.

٤٢ سَيْبٌ وسَيْفٌ فذا طَوْقُ المُطِيعِ وذا طَوْقٌ على جِيدِ مَنْ يَعْصِيكَ مَزْرُورُ

٤٣ فلا مَمَاتَ ولا مَحْيَا بِغَيْرِهِمَا يومًا لِعاصِيكَ أَوْ عافيك مَقْدُورُ

٤٤ وَلِيَّ عَهْدِ الهُدَى إنَّ الفُتُوحَ لَكُمْ مُعَجَّلٌ قادِمٌ مِنها ومَنْظُورُ

٤٥ وفَتْحُ سِبْتَةَ قَدْ وَافَاكَ يُقْدِمُها كما ٱقْتَفَتْ أَثَرَ الحادي بها العِيرُ

٤٦ فاهنأْ بِغُرِّ فُتُوحٍ طالَعَتْكَ كما تَفَتَّحَتْ في ذُرَى الرَّوضِ الأَزاهِيرُ

٤٧ أَيْمِنْ بِهَا بَيْعَةً حِزْبُ الضَّلالِ شَجٍ بها وحِزْبُ الهُدَى جَذْلانُ مَسْرُورُ

٤٨ كَمْ لِلْجَزِيرَةِ مِن بُشْرَى وتَهْنِئَةٍ عنها عُيونُ الأَماني نَحْوَها صُورُ

٤٩ فَجَدَّدُوا مِنْ رُسومٍ لِلهُدَى دَرَسَتْ هُنَاكَ يَسْتَنُّ فيها الرُّومُ والمُورُ

٥٠ بِكُلِّ جَوْنٍ زَحُوفٍ بالحَصَى زَجِلٍ سامٍ تُخاشِعُ فيه الأُكْمُ والقُورُ

٥١ وشُزَّبٍ أَبْقَتِ الغاياتُ أَعْيُنَها عُورًا وقد أَضْمَرَتْ منها المَضامِيرُ

٥٢ يَرْمِي العِدَا بِهَوَادِيها إمَامُ هُدًى لِلّٰهِ مُسْتَنْصِرٌ، باللّٰهِ مَنْصُورُ

٥٣ وَفَرْعُ مَجْدٍ زَكا طِيبًا ولا عَجَبٌ مِن طِيبِ فَرْعٍ زَكَتْ مِنه العَناصِيرُ

٥٤ جاءَتْكَ تَقْصُرُ عَمَّا فيك مِن كَرَمٍ بِكْرٌ عليها جَمِيعُ الحُسْنِ مَقْصُورُ

55 Were it to be written down on paper, its blackness on the whiteness of the page would be given the blackness of [dark] eyes in dowry.

56 I abandoned my sleep when I fled toward you, in whom was the resting place in exchange for which midday journeying has been given.

57 In every trackless desert in which the gusts of the winds became still, while the humming of the jinn could be heard like a roar,

58 Its chameleon remained watching the sun as if it were cooled by the blazing heat.

59 How many countries have we not crossed, and how many a hope since the crossing has remained ever verdant!

60 In whatsoever the changing winds [of fortune] forbid or command, may you never desist from that which the Fates love!

٥٥ سَوَادُها في بَيَاضِ الطِّرْسِ إنْ سُطِرَتْ ... في مُهْرَقٍ بِسَوَادِ الطَّرْفِ مَمْهُورُ
٥٦ هَجَّرْتُ نَوْمِيَ إذْ هَاجَرْتُ نَحْوَكُمْ ... حَيْثُ المَقِيلُ بَدِيلٌ مِنْه تَهْجِيرُ
٥٧ بِكُلِّ بَيْداءَ أَنْفاسُ الرِّياحِ بها ... خَوافِتٌ ، وعَزِيفُ الجِنِّ مَجْهُورُ
٥٨ يَظَلُّ حِرْباؤُها لِلشَّمْسِ مُرْتَقِبًا ... كأَنَّه في آحْتِدامِ الحَرِّ مَقْرُورُ
٥٩ فكَمْ بِلادٍ طَوَيْناها وكَمْ أَمَلٍ ... قَدْ ظَلَّ منذ طواها وَهْوَ مَنْشُورُ
٦٠ لا زِلْتَ في كلِّ ما تَنْهَى وتَأْمُرُهُ ... مُصَرَّفاتٌ بِمَا تَهْوى المَقادِيرُ

38 ar-Rundī

1 Everything declines after reaching perfection, therefore let no man be beguiled by the sweetness of a pleasant life.

2 As you have observed, these are the decrees that are inconstant: he whom a single moment has made happy, has been harmed by many other moments;

3 And this is the abode that will show pity for no man, nor will any condition remain in its state for it.

4 Fate irrevocably destroys every ample coat of mail when Mashrifī swords and spears glance off without effect;

5 It unsheaths each sword only to destroy it even if it be an Ibn dhī Yazan and the scabbard Ghumdān.

6 Where are the crowned kings of Yemen and where are their jewel-studded diadems and crowns?

7 Where are [the buildings] Shaddād raised in Iram and where [the empire] the Sassanians ruled in Persia?

8 Where is the gold Qārūn once possessed; where are ʿĀd and Shaddād and Qaḥṭān?

9 An irrevocable decree overcame them all so that they passed away and the people came to be as though they had never existed.

10 The kingdoms and kings that had been came to be like what a sleeper has told about [his] dream vision.

11 Fate turned against Darius as well as his slayer, and as for Chosroes, no vaulted palace offered him protection.

12 It is as if no cause had ever made the hard easy to bear, and as if Solomon had never ruled the world.

13 The misfortunes brought on by Fate are of many different kinds, while Time has causes of joy and of sorrow.

14 For the accidents [of fortune] there is a consolation that makes them easy to bear, yet there is no consolation for what has befallen Islam.

---

38. Sources: al-Maqqarī, *Nafḥ aṭ-ṭib*, ed. Muḥammad Muḥyī d-Dīn ʿAbd al-Ḥamīd (Cairo, 1949), VI, 232–234; al-Maqqarī, *Analectes* (Leiden, 1855–1861), II, 780–782; A. R. Nykl, *Mukhtarāt min ash-shiʿr al-Andalusī* (Beirut, 1949), pp. 200–202.

Meter: *basīṭ*.

Although ar-Rundī's exact dates are not known, this elegy on the fall of Andalusian cities into Christian hands can be dated approximately, since it was inspired by the capture of Seville which took place in December, 1248. The purpose of the poem was to appeal to the North Africans for help in stemming the onrush of the Reconquista.

٣٨

الرّندى

١ لِكُلِّ شَيءٍ إذا ما تَمَّ نُقْصَانُ ... فلا يُغَرَّ بِطِيبِ العَيْشِ إنْسانُ

٢ هِيَ الأُمُورُ كَما شاهَدْتَها دُوَلٌ ... مَنْ سَرَّهُ زَمَنٌ ساءَتْهُ أزْمانُ

٣ وهذه الدارُ لا تُبْقِي على أَحَدٍ ... ولا يَدُومُ على حالٍ لها شانُ

٤ يُمَزِّقُ الدهرُ حَتْمًا كُلَّ سابِغَةٍ ... إذا نَبَتْ مَشْرَفِيّاتٌ وخِرْصانُ

٥ ويَنْتَضِي كُلَّ سَيْفٍ لِلْفَناءِ ولَوْ ... كانَ ابْنَ ذِي يَزَنٍ والغِمْدُ غُمْدانُ

٦ أَيْنَ المُلوكُ ذَوُو التِّيجانِ مِنْ يَمَنٍ ... وأَيْنَ مِنهم أكالِيلٌ وتِيجانُ

٧ وأيْنَ ما شادَهُ شَدّادُ في إرَمٍ ... وَأَيْنَ ما ساسَهُ في الفُرْسِ ساسانُ

٨ وأَيْنَ ما حازَهُ قارُونُ مِنْ ذَهَبٍ ... وأَيْنَ عادٌ وشَدّادٌ وقَحْطانُ

٩ أَتَى على الكُلِّ أَمْرٌ لا مَرَدَّ لَهُ ... حتى قَضَوْا فكأنَّ القَوْمَ ما كانوا

١٠ وصارَ ما كانَ مِن مُلْكٍ ومِن مَلِكٍ ... كَما حَكَى عن خَيالِ الطَّيْفِ وَسْنانُ

١١ دارَ الزَّمانُ على دارا وقاتِلِهِ ... وأَمَّ كِسْرَى فما آواهُ إيوانُ

١٢ كأنَّما الصَّعْبُ لم يَسْهُلْ لَهُ سَبَبٌ ... يومًا ولا مَلَكَ الدنيا سُلَيْمانُ

١٣ فَجائِعُ الدَّهْرِ أَنْواعٌ مُنَوَّعَةٌ ... ولِلزَّمانِ مَسَرّاتٌ وأَحْزانُ

١٤ ولِلْحَوادِثِ سُلْوانٌ يُسَهِّلُها ... وما لِمَا حَلَّ بالإسلامِ سُلْوانُ

---

4. For *khirṣān*, 'spears,' cf. Dozy, I, 362, col. 2. Mashrifī swords were proverbial for their excellence.

5. Saif Ibn Dhī Yazan was a pre-Islamic Yemenite king. Note the pun on his name *Saif*, 'sword.' Ghumdān was his castle.

7. Shaddād was a king of the legendary people of ʿĀd of Ḥaḍramaut, who built a city called "many-columned Iram" (cf. Koran 89:6).

8. Qaḥṭān was the ancestor of the South Arabians. Qārūn: cf. Koran 28:76.

11. The slayer of Darius was Alexander the Great.

15 An event which cannot be endured has overtaken the peninsula; one such that Uḥud has collapsed because of it and Thahlān has crumbled!

16 The evil eye has struck [the peninsula] in its Islam so that [the land] decreased until whole regions and districts were despoiled of [the faith]

17 Therefore ask Valencia what is the state of Murcia; and where is Játiva, and where is Jaén?

18 Where is Córdoba, the home of the sciences, and many a scholar whose rank was once lofty in it?

19 Where is Seville and the pleasures it contains, as well as its sweet river overflowing and brimming full?

20 [They are] capitals which were the pillars of the land, yet when the pillars are gone, it may no longer endure!

21 The tap of the white ablution fount weeps in despair, like a passionate lover weeping at the departure of the beloved,

22 Over dwellings emptied of Islam that were first vacated and are now inhabited by unbelief;

23 In which the mosques have become churches wherein only bells and crosses may be found.

24 Even the mihrabs weep though they are solid; even the pulpits mourn though they are wooden!

25 O you who remain heedless though you have a warning in Fate: if you are asleep, Fate is always awake!

26 And you who walk forth cheerfully while your homeland diverts you [from cares], can a homeland beguile any man after [the loss of] Seville?

27 This misfortune has caused those that preceded it to be forgotten, nor can it ever be forgotten for the length of all time!

28 O you who ride lean, thoroughbred steeds which seem like eagles in the racecourse;

29 And you who carry slender, Indian blades which seem like fires in the darkness caused by the dust cloud [of war],

30 And you who are living in luxury beyond the sea enjoying life, you who have strength and power in your homelands,

31 Have you no news of the people of Andalus, for riders have carried forth what men have said [about them]?

---

15. "The peninsula," i.e., al-Andalus. Uḥud and Thahlān are mountains near Mecca.

16. *Analectes* reads *fa-mtaḥanat* for *fa-rtazaʾat*.

١٥ دهى الجزيرةَ أمرٌ لا عزاءَ له   هوى له أُحُدٌ وانهدّ ثهلانُ

١٦ أصابها العينُ فى الإسلامِ فارتزأتْ   حتى خلتْ منه أقطارٌ وبلدانُ

١٧ فاسألْ بلنسيةَ ما شأنُ مرسيةَ   وأينَ شاطبةٌ أمْ أينَ جيّانُ

١٨ وأينَ قرطبةٌ دارُ العلومِ، فكمْ   من عالمٍ قد سما فيها له شانُ

١٩ وأينَ حمصُ وما تحويه من نزهٍ   ونهرُها العذبُ فيّاضٌ وملآنُ

٢٠ قواعدٌ كنّ أركانَ البلادِ فما   عسى البقاءُ إذا لم تبقَ أركانُ

٢١ تبكى الحنيفيةُ البيضاءُ من أسفٍ   كما بكى لفراقِ الإلفِ هيمانُ

٢٢ على ديارٍ من الإسلامِ خاليةٍ   قد أقفرتْ ولها بالكفرِ عُمرانُ

٢٣ حيثُ المساجدُ قد صارتْ كنائسَ ما   فيهنّ إلّا نواقيسٌ وصلبانُ

٢٤ حتى المحاريبُ تبكى وهى جامدةٌ   حتى المنابرُ ترثى وهى عيدانُ

٢٥ يا غافلاً ولهُ فى الدهرِ موعظةٌ   إنْ كنتَ فى سنةٍ فالدهرُ يقظانُ

٢٦ وماشيًا مرحًا يُلهيهِ موطنُه   أبعدَ حمصٍ تغرُّ المرءَ أوطانُ

٢٧ تلك المصيبةُ أنستْ ما تقدّمها   وما لها مع طولِ الدهرِ نسيانُ

٢٨ يا راكبينَ عتاقَ الخيلِ ضامرةً   كأنّها فى مجالِ السبقِ عقبانُ

٢٩ وحاملينَ سيوفَ الهندِ مرهفةً   كأنّها فى ظلامِ النقعِ نيرانُ

٣٠ وراتعينَ وراءَ البحرِ فى دعةٍ   لهمْ بأوطانِهم عزٌّ وسلطانُ

٣١ أعندكمْ نبأٌ من أهلِ أندلسٍ   فقد سرى بحديثِ القومِ رُكبانُ

---

19. Seville was called Ḥimṣ, 'Emessa,' after that Syrian town by the Arabs from that city who were settled there.

26. Seville was conquered in December, 1248, by Fernando III of Castile.

32 How often have the weak, who were being killed and captured while no man stirred, asked our help?

33 What means this severing of the bonds of Islam on your behalf, when you, O worshipers of God, are [our] brethren?

34 Are there no heroic souls with lofty ambitions; are there no helpers and defenders of righteousness?

35 O, who will redress the humiliation of a people who were once powerful, a people whose condition injustice and tyrants have changed?

36 Yesterday they were kings in their own homes, but today they are slaves in the land of the infidel!

37 Thus, were you to see them perplexed, with no one to guide them, wearing the cloth of shame in its different shades,

38 And were you to behold their weeping when they are sold, the matter would strike fear into your heart, and sorrow would seize you.

39 Alas, many a mother and child have been parted as souls and bodies are separated!

40 And many a maiden fair as the sun when it rises, as though she were rubies and pearls,

41 Is led off to abomination by a barbarian against her will, while her eye is in tears and her heart is stunned.

42 The heart melts with sorrow at such [sights], if there is any Islam or belief in that heart!

---

32. Nykl reads *kam yastaghīthu sanādīdu r-rijāl wa hum . . .*; *Analectes* prefers *banū* for *bi-nā*.

٣٢ كَمْ يَسْتَغِيثُ بِنَا الْمُسْتَضْعَفُونَ وَهُمْ   قَتْلَى وأَسْرَى فما يَهْتَزُّ إِنْسانُ

٣٣ ماذا التَّقاطُعُ فى الإسلامِ بَيْنَكُمْ   وأَنْتُمُ يا عِبادَ اللّهِ إِخْوانُ

٣٤ أَلا نُفُوسٌ أَبِيَّاتٌ لَها هِمَمٌ   أَما على الخَيْرِ أَنْصارٌ وأَعْوانُ

٣٥ يا مَن لِذُلَّةِ قَوْمٍ بعدَ عِزِّهِم   أَحالَ حالَهُم حَوْرٌ وطُغْيَانُ

٣٦ بِالأَمْسِ كانوا مُلوكًا فى مَنازِلِهِم   واليومَ هم فى بِلادِ الكُفْرِ عَبْدانُ

٣٧ فَلَوْ تَراهم حَيارَى لا دَليلَ لهم   عليهِمْ مِن ثِيابِ الذُّلِّ أَلْوانُ

٣٨ ولَوْ رَأَيْتَ بُكاهُمْ عندَ بَيْعِهِم   لَهالَكَ الأَمْرُ واسْتَهْوَتْكَ أَحْزانُ

٣٩ يا رُبَّ أُمٍّ وطِفْلٍ حِيلَ بَيْنَهُما   كَما تُفَرَّقُ أَرْواحٌ وأَبْدانُ

٤٠ وطِفْلَةٍ مثلِ حُسْنِ الشمسِ إذ طَلَعَتْ   كأَنَّما هِىَ يَاقُوتٌ ومَرْجَانُ

٤١ يَقودُها العِلْجُ لِلْمَكْرُوهِ مُكْرَهَةً   والعَيْنُ باكِيَةٌ والقَلْبُ حَيْرانُ

٤٢ لِمِثْلِ هذا يَذُوبُ القَلْبُ مِن كَمَدٍ   إِنْ كانَ فى القَلْبِ إِسْلامٌ وإِيمانُ

---

35. Al-Maqqarī reads *kufrun* for *ḥaurun*.
41. Nykl reads *yaqūdu-hā l-ʿilju ʿinda s-sabyi.*

39 Ibn al-Khaṭīb

1 May the rain cloud be bountiful to you when the rain cloud pours, O time of love union in al-Andalus!

2 Union with you is now but a dream during drowsiness, or the deceit perpetrated by a deceiver.

3 When Time leads to the dispersion of hopes we transcribe the writing as they have traced it,

4 Being dispersed alone and in pairs [answering a call] like as the Meccan places of pilgrimage beckon the pilgrims.

5 Yet the rain once filled the garden with radiance so that the mouths of the flowers smiled in it.

6 And an-Nuᶜmān related traditions on the authority of Māᵓ as-Samāᵓ, as Mālik related traditions on the authority of Anas.

7 For beauty clothed [the anemone] in a varicolored garment whereby it glories in the most splendid clothing.

8 On certain nights which would have concealed love's secret with [their] darkness, were it not for the suns of brightness,

9 During which the star of the cup set and then rose again straight on its journey, good omened in its path,

10 There was a desirable situation whose only defect was that it passed by [swift as] a glance.

11 When sleep had been pleasant awhile, or as dawn intrudes upon [one] with the intrusion of police officers,

12 The bright stars carried us away or perhaps the eyes of the narcissus left an impression on us.

13 What thing of man's has ever been pure that the garden should have been empowered [to possess purity]?

14 In it the flowers seize the opportune moments that are safe from the hated thing they fear;

---

39. SOURCE: Jaudat ar-Rikābī, *Fī l-adab al-Andalusī* (Cairo, 1960), pp. 333–337.
FORM: *muwashshaḥa*.
METER: *ramal* Rhyme: a–b–a–b–a–b *m–n–m–n*

This *muwashshaḥa* was composed in imitation of the one by Ibn Sahl, the first two lines of which it uses as a *kharja*. It was addressed to Muḥammad V of Granada.

6. An-Nuᶜmān III was king of Hira in pre-Islamic times. Also, *shaqīqat an-nuᶜmān*, 'the red anemone, peony.' Māᵓ as-Samāᵓ was the mother of al-

٣٩

ابن الخطيب

١ جادَكَ الغَيْثُ إذا الغَيْثُ هَمَى   يا زَمانَ الوَصْلِ بِالأَنْدَلُسِ
٢ لم يَكُنْ وَصْلُكَ إلّا حُلُمَا   فى الكَرَى أَوْ خَلْسَةَ المُخْتَلِسِ
٣ إذْ يَقودُ الدَّهْرُ أَشْتاتَ المُنَى   نَنْقُلُ الخَطْوَ على ما تَرْسُمُ
٤ زُمَرًا بَيْنَ فُرادَى وَثُنَا   مِثْلَما يَدْعُو الحَجِيجَ المَوْسِمُ
٥ والحَيَا قَدْ جَلَّلَ الرَّوْضَ سَنَا   فَثُغُورُ الزَهْرِ فيهِ تَبْسِمُ
٦ ورَوَى النُّعْمانُ عن مَاءِ السَّمَا   كَيْفَ يَرْوِى مالِكٌ عَنْ أَنَسِ
٧ فَكَسَاهُ الحُسْنُ ثَوْبًا مُعْلَمَا   يَزْدَهِى مِنْهُ بِأَبْهَى مَلْبَسِ
٨ فى لَيالٍ كَتَمَتْ سِرَّ الهَوَى   بالدُّجَى لَوْلا شُمُوسُ الغُرَرِ
٩ مالَ نَجْمُ الكَأْسِ فيها وهَوَى   مُسْتَقِيمَ السَّيْرِ سَعْدَ الأَثَرِ
١٠ وَطَرٌ ما فيه مِن عَيْبٍ سِوَى   أَنَّهُ مَرَّ كَلَمْحِ البَصَرِ
١١ حِينَ لَذَّ النَّوْمُ شَيْئًا أَوْ كَمَا   هَجَمَ الصُّبْحُ هُجُومَ الحَرَسِ
١٢ غارَتِ الشُّهْبُ بِنَا أَوْ رُبَّمَا   أَثَّرَتْ فينا عُيونُ النَّرْجِسِ
١٣ أَىُّ شَىْءٍ لِامْرِئٍ قَدْ خَلَصَا   فَيَكُونَ الرَّوْضُ قد مُكِّنَ فِيهْ
١٤ تَنْهَبُ الأَزْهارُ فيهِ الفُرَصَا   أَمِنَتْ مِنْ مَكْرِهِ ما تَتَّقِيهْ

Mundhir and grandmother of Nuʿmān. Māʾ as-Samāʾ literally means 'the water of heaven.' Mālik ibn Anas was a Medinese doctor and the founder of the Mālikite rite. Thus the secondary meaning of the verse is: 'the red anemone derived its beauty from the rain with the same assurance as the traditions handed down from father to son.'

8. The "suns" are beautiful faces.

11. For *ḥaras*, 'police officers,' cf. Dozy, I, 270.

15 So, when the water and the pebbles murmured to one another and every sincere friend spoke in confidence with his friend,

16 You would observe that the rose, being annoyed out of jealousy had clad itself with that wherewith it is clad, out of anger;

17 And you would see that the myrtle, understanding well because of its sound judgment, was stealthily listening with the two sharp ears of a horse.

18 O beloved members of the tribe of Wādī l-Ghadā, in my heart there is a place where you may be found!

19 An ample breadth has been all too narrow to contain my love for you, hence I do not mind its rising from the place in which it has set.

20 So restore the bond of a friendship that has passed, that you may free your slave from his grief,

21 And fear God by reviving a passion-torn man whose soul has been reduced to nought in its sighs,

22 One who has devoted his heart exclusively to you out of nobility of soul. Surely you are not pleased by the perishing of those things devoted exclusively [to love]?

23 Yet in my heart there is something that draws near to you by ever renewed hopes, though it is far;

24 There is a moon whose place of setting causes the pining misery in it to rise, although he [the moon] is happy.

25 A well doer or an evildoer are equally exposed to a promise or a threat in loving him.

26 Intensely white and black of eye; honey sweet of deep red lips, he passed through the soul like a life-giving breath;

27 He aimed the arrow, and killed [his game] on the spot, when he shot at my heart the arrow of a lion crushing its prey.

28 Even though he was unjust and hope was deceived, the heart of the lover still melts with desire,

29 For he is the first beloved of the soul; there is no offense attaching to any beloved in [true] love.

30 His order is executed in all its strength, fully obeyed in chests and hearts which he has first worn out.

---

16. I.e., its *red* color.

17. I.e., its leaves are likened to horses ears.

18. Wādī l-Ghadā, the 'vale of the tamarisks,' is a place in northern Arabia called Buwaira (cf. Yāqūt, *Muʿjam al-buldān* [Cairo, 1906–1907], I, 765). Here it appears to represent the Genil, the river of Granada.

١٥ فَإذا المَاءُ تَنَاجَى والحَصَا   وخَلَا كُلُّ خليلٍ بِأَخِيهْ

١٦ تُبْصِرُ الوَرْدَ غَيُورًا بَرِمَا   يَكْتَسِى مِن غَيْظِهِ ما يَكْتَسِى

١٧ وتَرَى الآسَ لَبِيبًا فَهِمَا   يَسْرِقُ السَّمْعَ بِأُذْنَيْ فَرَسِ

١٨ يا أُهَيْلَ الحَيِّ مِن وَادِى الغَضَا   وبِقَلْبِى مَسْكَنٌ أَنْتُمْ بِهِ

١٩ ضَاقَ عن وَجْدِى بِكُمْ رَحْبُ الفَضَا   لا أُبَالِى شَرْقَهُ مِن غَرْبِهِ

٢٠ فَأَعِيدُوا عَهْدَ أُنْسٍ قد مَضَى   تُعْتِقُوا عَبْدَكُمُ مِن كَرْبِهِ

٢١ وَٱتَّقُوا اللّٰهَ، وأَحْيُوا مُغْرَمَا   يَتَلَاشَى نَفَسًا فى نَفَسِ

٢٢ حَبَسَ القَلْبَ عليكُمْ كَرَمَا   أَفَتَرْضَوْنَ عَفَاءَ الحُبُسِ

٢٣ وبِقَلْبِى مِنْكُمُ مُقْتَرِبُ   بِأَحَادِيثِ المُنَى وَهْوَ بَعِيدْ

٢٤ قَمَرٌ أَطْلَعَ مِنْهُ المَغْرِبُ   شِقْوَةَ المُضْنَى به وَهْوَ سَعِيدْ

٢٥ قَدْ تَسَاوَى مُحْسِنٌ أَوْ مُذْنِبُ   فى هَوَاهُ بَيْنَ وَعْدٍ ووَعِيدْ

٢٦ أَحْوَرُ المُقْلَةِ مَعْسُولُ اللَّمَى   جَالَ فى النَّفْسِ مَجَالَ النَّفَسِ

٢٧ سَدَّدَ السَّهْمَ فَأَصْمَى إذْ رَمَى   بِفُؤَادِى نَبْلَةَ المُفْتَرِسِ

٢٨ إنْ يَكُنْ جَارَ وخَابَ الأَمَلُ   فَفُؤَادُ الصَّبِّ بالشَّوْقِ يَذُوبْ

٢٩ فَهْوَ لِلنَّفْسِ حَبِيبٌ أَوَّلُ   لَيْسَ فى الحُبِّ لِمَحْبُوبٍ ذُنُوبْ

٣٠ أَمْرُهُ مُعْتَمَلٌ مُمْتَثَلُ   فى ضُلُوعٍ قد بَرَاهَا وقُلُوبْ

---

24. The "moon" is the beloved.

25. I.e., love for this "moon" is so strong that it voids the distinction between the virtuous and the sinful.

31 He has made the glance be his judge, so it judged with authority, showing no fear, [by having no mercy on] weak souls, of Him who

32 Exacts justice for the wronged from him who has committed the wrong, and requites both the just and the oppressor.

33 What is wrong with my heart? Whenever the East wind blows, a renewed feast of yearning returns to it;

34 [A feast] bringing on anxiety for [my heart] as well as exhaustion, yet it is eager for more torments.

35 God's words regarding it were inscribed in [His] Register: "Truly my punishment is terrible indeed."

36 It is a burning inside my ribs that has been stirred up [burning like] a fire among dry stubble.

37 It leaves none but the last remnants of life in my soul, like as the dawn lingers on after the last remnants of the night.

38 Submit, O soul, to the dictates of Fate, and live now in repentance and contrition,

39 And put aside all remembrance of a time that was spent in the granting of a favor now finished as well as in reproof.

40 And shift your speech to the benevolent lord, who is inspired by the succor in the prototype of the Book,

41 The noble in issue and in origin, the lion of the saddle and the full moon of the assembly,

42 To whom victory has been revealed as the Revelation was revealed by the Blessed Spirit,

43 The elect of God, the namesake of the Elect, al-Ghanī bi-llāh "the satisfied with God" to the exclusion of everyone else.

44 He who, when he has sworn an oath, fulfills it; and when he has embarked upon an enterprise, concludes it successfully.

45 It suffices him to descend from Qais ibn Saᶜd, in a place where the Naṣrid house is lofty in its columns;

46 Where the Naṣrid house is rendered inaccessible in its protected places, harvested in its excellence; pure in its source of origin.

47 And affection constitutes a heavy shadow pitched like a [protecting tent], while moisture speeds toward the thing that was planted.

---

32. The Arabic source reads *yunṣifu* which makes no sense in this context.
35. Cf. Koran 14:7.
40. I.e., the heavenly prototype of the Koran.
42. The "Blessed Spirit" is the Angel Gabriel.

٣١ حَكَّمَ اللَّحْظَ بِهِ فَٱحْتَكَمَا لَمْ يُراقِبْ فى ضِعافِ الأَنْفُسِ
٣٢ مُنْصِفَ المَظْلُومِ مِمَّنْ ظَلَمَا ومُجازِى البَرِّ مِنها والمُسِى
٣٣ مَا لِقَلْبِى كُلَّمَا هَبَّتْ صَبَا عادَهُ عِيدٌ مِن الشَّوْقِ جَدِيدْ
٣٤ جَلَبَ الهَمَّ لَهُ والوَصَبَا فَهْوَ لِلأَشْجانِ فى جَهْدٍ جَهِيدْ
٣٥ كانَ فى اللَّوْحِ لَهُ مُكْتَتَبَا قَوْلُهُ : إنَّ عَذابِى لَشَدِيدْ
٣٦ لاعِجٌ فى أَضْلُعِى قد أُضْرِمَا فَهْىَ نارٌ فى هَشِيمِ اليَبَسِ
٣٧ لَمْ يَدَعْ فى مُهْجَتِى إلَّا ذِمَا كَبَقاءِ الصُّبْحِ بعد الغَلَسِ
٣٨ سَلِّمِي يا نَفْسُ فى حُكْمِ القَضَا وٱعْمُرِي الوَقْتَ بِرُجْعَى وَمَتابْ
٣٩ وَدَعِي ذِكْرَ زَمانٍ قَدْ مَضَى بَيْنَ عُتْبَى قَدْ تَقَضَّتْ وعِتابْ
٤٠ وَٱصْرِفِي القَوْلَ إلَى مَوْلَى الرِّضَى مُلْهَمِ التَّوْفِيقِ فى أُمِّ الكِتابْ
٤١ الكَرِيمِ المُنْتَهَى والمُنْتَمَى أَسَدِ السَّرْجِ وبَدْرِ المَجْلِسِ
٤٢ يُنْزَلُ النَّصْرُ عليه مِثْلُما يُنْزَلُ الوَحْيُ بِرُوحِ القُدُسِ
٤٣ مُصْطَفَى اللهِ سَمِيُّ المُصْطَفَى الغَنِي باللهِ عن كُلِّ أَحَدْ
٤٤ مَنْ إذا ما عَقَدَ العَهْدَ وَفَى وإذا ما فَتَحَ الخَطْبُ عَقَدْ
٤٥ مِن بَنِى قَيْسِ بْنِ سَعْدٍ وكَفَى حَيْثُ بَيْتُ النَّصْرِ مَرْفُوعُ العَمَدْ
٤٦ حَيْثُ بَيْتُ النَّصْرِ مَحْمِيُّ الحِمَى وَجَنِيُّ الفَضْلِ زَكِيُّ المَغْرِسِ
٤٧ والهَوَى ظِلٌّ ظَلِيلٌ خَيَّمَا والنَّدَى هَبَّ إلَى المُغْتَرَسِ

43. "The namesake of the Elect," i.e., Muḥammad V, namesake of Muhammad the Prophet.

45. The Naṣrid house was the dynasty ruling Granada. It claimed Qaisite ancestry.

48 Lo, in this wise, O descendant of the eminent Anṣār who, if you stumble, it is Time itself that forgives your lapse,
49 A young woman whom beauty had clothed as in a *mulā*ʾ, dazzling the eye with her brightness and sheen,
50 Imitated in words, meaning, and literary adornments the composition of one whom love had caused to speak so that he declared:
51 "Does the fawn of al-Ḥimā know that he has kindled the heart of a lover in which he dwelt?
52 So that it is burning and throbbing, just like the firebrand teased by the east wind?"

48. The Anṣār were the "helpers" of the Prophet, i.e., his Medinan collaborators.

49. The *mulā*ʾ was a blue and white striped cotten garment worn by women of low social status (cf. Dozy, II, 609–610).

هَاكَهَا يا سِبطَ أَنْصارِ العُلَى   والذى إن عَثَرَ الدَّهْرُ أَقَالْ ٤٨

غادةً أَلْبَسَها الحُسْنُ مُلَا   تَبْهَرُ العَيْنَ جَلَاءً وَصِقالْ ٤٩

عَارَضَتْ لَفْظًا وَمَعْنًى وَحِلَى   قَوْلَ مَنْ أَنْطَقَهُ الحُبُّ فَقَالْ: ٥٠

"هَلْ دَرَى ظَبْيُ الحِمَى أَنْ قَدْ حَمَى   قَلْبَ صَبٍّ حَلَّهُ عن مَكْنِسِ" ٥١

"فَهْوَ فى حَرٍّ وخَفْقٍ مثلما   لَعِبَتْ رِيحُ الصَّبَا بالقَبَسِ" ٥٢

---

51. This line and the following constitute the *kharja* quoted from the *muwashshaḥa* by Ibn Sahl (**33**).

40 Ibn Zamrak

1 Question the horizon adorned by the bright stars, for I have entrusted a description of my condition to it.

2 And I have caused the languor of the breeze to bear a trust such that my hopes have traversed the duration of time with it.

3 So, O you who observe souls—and they are weak!—: I lay upon them that which makes mountains to be light.

4 The evil suggestions of many have become accredited whereas with me only love is so; therefore my upset heart was thought to be dying.

5 While one who is submissive to glances when entangled in the snare of love, will certainly rebel against a disinterested adviser as well as against a person who reproaches him.

6 I have turned my heart from the governance of his judgment on the morn it was pleased with the tyranny of the glance as a ruler.

7 For love is but a glance which arouses passion and occasions something which not even the healing physician is able to cure.

8 So, wonder at an eye which is allowed to travel freely so that the heart is laden with sorrow because of it.

9 Lo, there is no dear soul striving in God's path, but that love cheapens of it the price that once was high.

10 O, many an affection did I satisfy during my youth, while I was generous in seeking mutual satisfaction in the relationship of love.

11 I have been alone, unobserved, with the one I love; yet I was not devoid of my chastity.

12 And many a day have I spent in the company of shy gazelles quick to take flight; striving for a love union and wearing out in it my mind.

13 I have not recovered from [the intoxication caused by] the wine of the glance with which one of bright countenance kindled my passion in the forenoon.

---

40. SOURCES: al-Maqqarī, *Nafḥ aṭ-ṭīb*, ed. Muḥammad Muḥyī d-Dīn ʿAbd al-Ḥamīd (Cairo, 1949), X, 49–56; inscription in Sala de las Dos Hermanas, Alhambra, Granada.

METER: *ṭawīl.*

This panegyric written in praise of Muḥammad V of Granada is extra-

٤٠

ابن زمرك

١ سَلِ الأُفْقَ بالزُّهْرِ الكَواكِبِ حالِيا   فإنّى قد أوْدَعْتُهُ شرحَ حالِيا

٢ وحَمَّلْتُ مُعْتَلَّ النَّسيمِ أمانةً   قطعْتُ بها عُمْرَ الزّمانِ أمانِيا

٣ فيا مَنْ رأى الأرْواحَ وهْيَ ضعيفةٌ   أُحَمِّلُها ما يَسْتَخِفُّ الرَّواسيا

٤ ومَاوِىَّ كم جَدَّتْ وجَدَّ بِيَ الهوى   فَعُدَّ بِهِ القلْبُ المُقَلَّبُ هازِيا

٥ ومَنْ يَطَّعِ الألحاظَ فى شِرْعةِ الهوى   فلا بُدَّ أنْ يَعْصى نصيحًا ولاحِيا

٦ عَدَلْتُ بِقلبى عن ولايةِ حُكْمِهِ   غداةَ ارْتَضى من جائرِ اللَّحْظِ والِيا

٧ وما الحُبُّ إلّا نظرةٌ تَبْعَثُ الهوى   وتُعْقِبُ ما يُعْيِى الطَّبيبَ المُداوِيا

٨ فيا عجبًا لِلْعَيْنِ تُمْشى طليقةً   ويُصْبِحُ مِن جرّائِها القلْبُ عانِيا

٩ ألا فى سبيلِ اللهِ نفسٌ نفيسةٌ   يُرَخِّصُ منها الحُبُّ ما كانَ غالِيا

١٠ ويا رُبَّ عَهْدٍ للشّبابِ قضيْتُهُ   وأحْسَنْتُ من دَيْنِ الوصالِ التَّقاضِيا

١١ خَلَوْتُ بِمَنْ أهْواهُ مِن غيرِ رِقْبَةٍ   ولكِنْ عفافِى لَمْ أكُنْ عنه خالِيا

١٢ ويَوْمٍ بِمُسْتَنِّ الظِّباءِ شَهِدْتُهُ   أجِدُّ وِصالًا بالِيًا فيه بالِيا

١٣ ولم أصْحُ مِنْ خَمْرِ اللِّحاظِ توقُّدا   به الجَوَّةَ وَضّاحُ الأسِرَّةِ ضاحِيا

---

ordinary in its description of the Alhambra. Parts of it were slightly modified by the poet himself, and carved on the walls of the Sala de las Dos Hermanas in that palace, where they may still be admired today. Lines 60–70, 87–89, 92–93, 103–105, 123 are inscribed in the Sala.

11. I.e., "Chastity" was the third partner in the love union.

14 He unsheathed from the scabbard of the clouds a keen sword consisting of a ray of lightning, polished on its flat surface, pure [white].

15 He smiled, and moved my eyelids to weeping great amounts of liquid which filled my cloak with the pearls of its tears.

16 And he reminded me of a mouth from which I eagerly desired to drink, which, by ʿUdhrite love, I have never forgotten.

17 And one whose heart throbbed with sorrow, took comfort like me, as though in the bolt of lightning in the wilderness there were the love pangs that I felt.

18 [He also reminded me] of a night the full moon spent as my bedfellow while the eyes of the stars spent it gazing at me.

19 That night I sipped from the drinking place of a mouth embellished with pearls, between sweet [lips] and flashing [teeth].

20 I drank from it the honey of lip dew which seemed as though it were a choice wine, and I kissed camomile blossoms set in a blissful liquor.

21 O for the coolness of that mouth with which you quenched my burning thirst, and O for the heat of my breath with which you caused my heart to melt!

22 And many a garden of beauty in the freshness of youth is such that I have gazed on a willow branch in it, ready for plucking.

23 I have spent the night watering the rose of the cheek with my tears so that the violets of the glance appeared withered in the morning because of them.

24 And [girls] whose shape was languorous stole my heart; so what is the matter with those languorous shapes and with me?

25 May God reward that affection by restoring it, for a long time has passed since He has brought back rewards to the springtime pasture of the gazelles.

26 And say to those nights which I enjoyed during my youth when I spent them in companionship: "May you be watered, O my nights!"

27 And O my oasis, whose shadow spread over me when we passed round [the cup of] love, may you be ransomed, O my oasis!

28 In it the eyes of gazelles aimed at me; nay, they aimed at the targets of love with my heart.

---

16. ʿUdhrite love was the hopeless, languishing love expressed in the poetry of early Islamic Bedouin artists such as Jamīl. It was characterized by the death of the ʿUdhrī, when enamored, from the violence of his passion.

١٤ وجَرَّدَ مِن غِمْدِ الغَمَامَةِ صارِمًا   مِنَ البَرْقِ مَصْقُولَ الصَّفِيحَةِ صافِيَا

١٥ تَبَسَّمَ فٱسْتَبْكَى جُفونِيَ غَمْرَةً   مَلَأَتْ بِدُرِّ الدَّمْعِ منها رِدائِيا

١٦ وأَذْكَرَنِى ثَغْرًا ظَمِئْتُ لِوِرْدِهِ   ولا وَالهَوَى العُذْرِيِ ماكُنْتُ ناسِيَا

١٧ وَراحَ خُفُوقُ القَلْبِ مِثْلِى كأَنَّما   بِبَرْقِ الحِمَى مِن لوعةِ الحُبِّ مابِيَا

١٨ وَلَيْلَةَ بَاتَ البَدْرُ فيها مُضاجِعِى   وباتَتْ عُيونُ الشُّهْبِ نَحْوِى رَوانِيَا

١٩ كَرَعْتُ بِها بَيْنَ العَذيبِ وبَارِقٍ   بِمَوْرِدِ ثَغْرٍ باتَ بالدُّرِّ حالِيَا

٢٠ رَشَفْتُ بهِ شُهْدَ الرُّضابِ سُلافةً   وَقَبَّلْتُ فى ماءِ النَعيمِ الأَقاحِيَا

٢١ فَيَا بَرْدَ ذاك الثَّغْرِ رَوَّيْتَ غِلَّتِى   ويَا حَرَّ أَنْفَاسِى أَذَبْتَ فُؤادِيَا

٢٢ ورَوْضَةِ حُسْنٍ لِلشَّبابِ نَضِيرَة   بَصُرْتُ بِغُصْنِ البانِ فيها المَجانِيَا

٢٣ وَبِتُّ أُسَقِّى وَرْدَةَ الخَدِّ أَدْمُعِى   فأَصْبَحَ فيها نَرْجِسُ اللَّحْظِ ذاوِيَا

٢٤ ومالَتْ بِقَلْبِى مائِلاتٌ قُدودُها   فَمَا لِلقُدودِ المائِلاتِ وَمالِيَا

٢٥ جَزَى اللّٰهُ ذاك العَهْدَ عَوْدًا فَطالَمَا   أَعادَ على رَبْعِ الظِبَاءِ الجَوازِيَا

٢٦ وقُلْ لِلَيالٍ فى الشَّبابِ نَعِمْتُها   وَقَضَيْتُها أُنْسًا : سُقِيتِ لَيالِيَا

٢٧ وَيَا وَادِيًا رَقَّتْ علَىَّ ظِلالُهِ   ونَحْنُ نُديرُ الوَصْلَ فُدِّيتَ وَادِيَا

٢٨ رَمَتْنِى عُيونُ السِّرْبِ فيهِ وإنَّمَا   رَمَيْنَ بِقَلْبِى فى الغَرامِ المَرامِيَا

20. The beloved's teeth are compared with camomile blossoms.
22. The lithe figure of the beloved is described as a "willow bough."

29 Thus, were it not for my seeking the protection of the Emir Muḥammad I would never have been saved from the assault of those glances.

30 Therefore, say to him whose poetry is constructed according to [the canons of] beauty: "According to [those canons] may you never cease to construct it because of his favor."

31 How many a complaint of love have you soothed and lifted up in praise, when praise followed!

32 And how many a night have I spent awake eulogizing him, contending against the bright stars with the pearls of poetry composed about him!

33 While the pillar of dawn shone bright as his lineage upon which I raised up my construction in order to praise him.

34 [He is] an Imam whose age has benefited from noble qualities and has lodged him above the very highest stars.

35 He has surpassed the light and loftiness of the full moon since he is unsatisfied by the pursuit of any other than perfections.

36 He is the sun spreading his usefulness over the broad expanse of the earth while his light guides both the near one and the far.

37 He is the [salt] ocean whose waves swell with generosity, yet he is sweet [water] to the person seeking his favor.

38 He is the one cloud that pours whereas [other] clouds receive his downpour; he quenches the thirsty with the downpour of his generosity.

39 [He possesses] good qualities beautiful as gardens; never do their fresh flowers become withered.

40 So, O son of the proud-necked kings of the family of Khazraj, possessing a genealogy like the dawn that has arisen high,

41 Are you not the person in whom those seeking favor place their hopes since your gifts put the early morning clouds to shame?

42 Are you not the person whose assault is feared by the unjust, since your elevated rank scares away recurring difficulties?

43 Whereas, whenever the stars err in wandering, they make for your guidance and follow it, being guided under the wing of gloom.

44 While your firm resolve is more penetrating than your sword in battle, no matter how penetrating the latter is since it is polished on both its flat edges.

---

29. Muḥammad V of Granada, to whom the panegyric is directed.

٢٩ فَلَوْ لا آعْتِصامِى بِالأَمِيرِ مُحَمَّدٍ   لَمَا كُنْتُ مِن فَتْكِ اللَّواحِظِ ناجِيَا
٣٠ فَقُلْ لِلَّذِى يُبْنَى على الحُسْنِ شِعْرُهُ   عليهِ مع الإحْسانِ لا زِلْتَ بانِيَا
٣١ فَكَمْ مِن شَكاةٍ فى الهَوَى قد رَفَأْتُها   ورَقَّعْتَها بِالمَدْحِ إذْ جاءَ تالِيَا
٣٢ وكَمْ لَيْلَةٍ فى مَدْحِهِ قد سَهِرْتُها   أُباهِى بِدُرِّ النَّظْمِ فيه الدَّرارِيَا
٣٣ ولاحَ عَمودُ الصُّبْحِ مِثْلَ آنْتِسابِهِ   رَفَعْتُ عليهِ لِلْمَدِيحِ المَبانِيَا
٣٤ إمامٌ أفادَ المكرماتِ زَمانُهُ   وساكَنَهُ فَوْقَ النُّجومِ العَوالِيَا
٣٥ وجاوَزَ قَدْرَ البَدْرِ نُورًا ورِفْعَةً   ولم يَرْضَ إلَّا بالكَمالِ مُوالِيَا
٣٦ هُوَ الشَّمْسُ بَثَّتْ فى البَسيطَةِ نَفْعَها   وأَنْوارُها أَهْدَتْ قَرِيبًا وقاصِيَا
٣٧ هُوَ البَحْرُ بِالإحْسانِ يَزْخَرُ مَوْجُهُ   ولٰكِنَّهُ عَذْبٌ لِمَنْ جاءَ عافِيَا
٣٨ هُوَ الغَيْثُ يَهْمِى يَمْسِكُ الغَيْثُ سُحْبَهُ   يُرَوِّى بِسُحْبِ الجُودِ مَن كانَ صادِيَا
٣٩ شَمائِلُ لَوْ أَنَّ الرِّياضَ بِحُسْنِها   لَمَا صارَ فيها زَهْرُها الغَضُّ ذاوِيَا
٤٠ فَيا آبْنَ المُلوكِ الصِّيدِ مِن آلِ خَزْرَجٍ   وذا نَسَبٌ كالصُّبْحِ عَزَّ مُسامِيَا
٤١ أَلَسْتَ الذى تَرْجُو العُفاةُ نَوالَهُ   فَتُخْجِلُ جَدْواهُ السَّحابَ الغَوادِيَا
٤٢ أَلَسْتَ الذى تَخْشَى البُغاةُ صِيالَهُ   فَتُوجِلُ عَلْياهُ الصِّعابَ العَوادِيَا
٤٣ وهَدْيُكَ مَهْما ضَلَّتِ الشُّهْبُ قَصْدَها   تَوَلَّتْهُ فى جُنْحِ الدُّجُنَّةِ هادِيَا
٤٤ وعَزْمُكَ أَمْضَى مِن حُسامِكَ فى الوَغَى   وَإنْ كانَ مَصْقولَ الغِرارَيْنِ ماضِيَا

---

33. "The pillar of dawn," i.e., the light or gleam of dawn.

45 Against how many a striker of religion, ungrateful to his Lord, have you struck the flint stick of [your] zealous defense [of religion], kindling it!

46 And [such a one] was immediately scared away by a certain sword and a firm resolve, both of which illuminated the surrounding darkness on the nights of Fate.

47 Thus, were it not for you, O sun of the Caliphate, the concealed path leading to holy war would never have been revealed.

48 And were it not for you, there would have risen up no pall of dust wherein the [spears] white as to their heads appeared shining brightly like stars.

49 And were it not for you the branches of the lances would not have taken even their first drink though they were thirsting to drink blood.

50 For the spearhead enjoyed in [that blood] the fruits of a strong victory, gathering the fruits of conquest which were fresh and within close reach.

51 And whenever your blood-spilling sword edge appeared naked, leaving the face of the earth clothed with blood,

52 God, from above the heavens, pronounced in judgment that it was [that sword] which should judge against whomsoever on earth refused Islam.

53 Thus, how many a people defending a stronghold of unbelief have you not visited in the morning in the company of an army that turned dawn into darkest gloom!

54 You mounted toward [that stronghold] while the swords were drawn and those souls in it reached the point where they competed in rising [to heaven].

55 And you conquered its fortified upper region by violent means, and monotheism that night rose up to announce [itself].

56 But its church bell was in disuse in the evening because of the constraint [exercised against it] though its pulpit was embellished in the morning through invocation [of God's name].

57 [These are] wonders that are not easily grasped by the mind, for we can only derive them from an ambition which is what it is.

58 Hence it was from you that Time derived every wonder such that kings will boast about it to the end of the nights.

59 While it is about you that the people relate every strange deed whose dictations are written on the page of Time.

---

57. I.e., which is well known.

٤٥ فكَمْ قادِحٍ فى الدِينِ يَكْفُرُ رَبَّهُ   قَدَحْتَ لـه زَنْدَ الحَفيظةِ وَارِيَا
٤٦ وما راعَهُ إلَّا حُسامٌ وعَزْمَةٌ   يُضِيآنِ فى لَيْلِ الخُطوبِ الدَواجِيَا
٤٧ فلَوْلاكَ يَا شَمْسَ الخِلافَةِ لم يَبِنْ   سَبِيلُ جِهادٍ كانَ مِن قَبْل خافِيَا
٤٨ وَلَوْلاكَ لم تُرْفَعْ سَمَاءُ عَجاجةٍ   تَلُوحُ بها بِيضُ النُّصولِ دَرارِيَا
٤٩ وَلَوْلاكَ لم تنهل غُصونٌ مِن القَنَا   وكانَتْ إلى وِرْدِ الدِّماءِ صَوادِيَا
٥٠ فَأَثْمَرَ فيها النَّصْلُ نَصْرًا مُوَزَّرًا   وأَجْنَى قِطافَ الفَتْحِ غَضًّا ودَانِيَا
٥١ ومَهْمَا غَدَا سَفَّاحُ سَيْفِكَ عارِيَا   يُغَادِرُ وَجْهَ الأَرْضِ بالدَّمِ كاسِيَا
٥٢ قَضَى اللّٰهُ مِن فوق السَّمَوَاتِ أَنَّهُ   على من أَبَى الإسْلامَ فى الأَرْضِ قاضِيَا
٥٣ فَكَمْ مَعْقِلٍ لِلْكُفْرِ صَبَّحْتَ أَهْلَهُ   بِجَيْشٍ أَعادَ الصُّبْحَ أَظْلَمَ داجِيَا
٥٤ رَقَيْتَ إليه والسُّيُوفُ مُشِيحَةٌ   وقَدْ بَلَغَتْ فيه النُّفوسُ التَراقِيَا
٥٥ فَفَتَحْتَ مَرْقَاهُ المُمَنَّعَ عَنْوَةً   وَبَاتَ به التَوْحِيدُ يَعْلُو مُنادِيَا
٥٦ وَنَاقُوسُهُ بالقَسْرِ أَمْسَى مُعَطَّلًا   وَمِنْبَرُهُ بالذِّكْرِ أَصْبَحَ حالِيَا
٥٧ عَجائِبُ لم تُخْطَرْ بِبالٍ وإنَّمَا   ظَفَرْنَا بها عن هِمَّةٍ هِىَ ماهِيَا
٥٨ فَمِنْكَ ٱسْتَفَادَ الدَّهْرُ كُلَّ عَجِيبَةٍ   يُبَاهِى بها الأَمْلَاكُ أُخْرَى لَيَالِيَا
٥٩ وَعَنْكَ يُرَوِّى الناسُ كُلَّ غَرِيبَةٍ   تُخَطُّ على صَفْحِ الزَّمانِ الأَمالِيَا

60 How excellent is your beautiful building, for it certainly surpasses all others by the decree of the stars!

61 How many joyful solaces for the eyes are to be found in it; in it even the dreamer will renew the objects of his desire!

62 And the bright stars would like to establish themselves firmly in it rather than to continue wandering about in the vault of the sky.

63 Were they to remain in its antechambers they would outstrip the handmaidens in serving you in such a way as to cause you to be pleased with them.

64 In it the portico has exceeded [the utmost limits] of beauty, while thanks to it the palace has come to compete in beauty with the vault of heaven.

65 With how many a decoration have you clothed it in order to embellish it, one consisting of multicolored figured work which causes the brocades of Yemen to be forgotten!

66 And how many arches rise up in its vault supported by columns which at night are embellished by light.

67 You would think that they are the heavenly spheres whose orbits revolve, overshadowing the pillar of dawn when it barely begins to appear after having passed through the night.

68 The capitals [of the columns] contain all sorts of rare wonders so that proverbs [about them] fly in all directions and become generally known.

69 In it there is burnished marble whose light has shone and thus illuminated the darkest shadows remaining in the gloom.

70 When they are illuminated by the rays of the sun you would think that they are made of pearls by reason of the quantity of celestial bodies in them.

71 In it the fountain pours out its excess of water so that when the breeze advances you would think [the pool] to be vying [with the wind].

72 When the hands of the breeze stirred its surface, they caused us to see coats of mail which could win great powers for us,

73 And a dancing girl, obedient to her bridle, in the fountain, responded to the melodies of the singing girls.

---

62. The order of this line has been changed in the Sala and it has been altered to *thabitat bi-hā*.

63. The Sala records *saḥatai-hā wa sābaqat*.

65. The Sala records *as-sarīra l-yamāniyā*.

67. I.e., who revolve in their orbits. This "inverted" way of expressing

٦٠ وَلِلّهِ مَبْنَاكَ الجَمِيلُ فَإِنَّهُ يَفُوقُ على حُكْمِ السُّعودِ المَبَانِيَا
٦١ فَكَمْ فِيهِ لِلأَبْصارِ مِن مُتَنَزَّهٍ تُجِدُّ بِهِ نَفْسُ الحَلِيمِ الأَمانِيَا
٦٢ وتَهْوى النُّجومُ الزُّهْرُ لَوْ ثَبَتَتْ بِهِ ولَمْ تَكُ فى أُفْقِ السَّماءِ جَوارِيَا
٦٣ وَلَوْ مَثُلَتْ فى سابِقِيهِ لَسابَقَتْ إلى خِدْمَةٍ تَرْضِيكَ مِنها الجَوارِيَا
٦٤ بِهِ البَهْوُ قد حازَ البَهاءَ وقد غَدَا بِهِ القَصْرُ آفاقَ السَّماءِ مُباهِيَا
٦٥ وكَمْ حُلَّةٍ جَلَّلْتَهُ بِحَلِيِّها مِنَ الوَشْيِ تُنْسِى السَّابِرِيَّ اليَمانِيَا
٦٦ وكَمْ مِن قِسِيٍّ فى ذُراهُ تَرَفَّعَتْ على عُمُدٍ بالنُّورِ باتَتْ حَوالِيَا
٦٧ فَتَحْسَبُها الأَفْلاكَ دارَتْ قِسِيُّها تُظِلُّ عَمُودَ الصُّبْحِ إذ باتَ بادِيَا
٦٨ سَوارِى قَدْ جاءَتْ بِكُلِّ غَرِيبَةٍ فطارَتْ بها الأَمْثالُ تَجْرِى سَوارِيَا
٦٩ بهِ المَرْمَرُ المَجْلُوُّ قد شَفَّ نُورُهُ فيَجْلُو مِنَ الظَّلْماءِ ما كانَ داجِيَا
٧٠ إذا ما أَضاءَتْ بالشُّعاعِ تَخالُها على عِظَمِ الأَجْرامِ مِنها لآلِيَا
٧١ بهِ البَحْرُ دَفّاعُ العُبابِ تَخالُهُ إذا ما انْبَرَى وَفْدُ النَّسِيمِ مُبارِيَا
٧٢ إذا ما جَلَتْ أَيْدِى الصَّبا مَتْنَ صَفْحِهِ أَرَتْنا دُرُوعًا أَكْسَبَتْنا الأَيادِيَا
٧٣ وَراقِصَةٍ فى البَحْرِ طَوْعَ عِنانِها تُراجِعُ أَلْحانَ القِيانِ الأَغانِيَا

---

the planetary movements is due to the Ptolemaic notion that the spheres rotated around the earth.

68. The Sala records *fa-sawāriyā qad jāʾat.*

73. The "dancing girl" is the jet of water rhythmically rising and falling in the fountain.

74 When she rose into the air and then sank again she decorated the surrounding spectators by scattering pearls.

75 A silver [substance] melts and flows among jewels appearing pure white like her in beauty.

76 A flowing [substance] appears to the eyes like a solid one so that I cannot discern which of the two is flowing.

77 Hence if you really wish to compare it concretely so as to hit the mark and be praised as a good marksman,

78 Then say, that the pool causes the side of her back to dance just as one playing with a child causes it to dance.

79 She manifested her generous nature to us while she was still small, yet she has not derived satisfaction save from growing in generosity.

80 She watered the mouths of the flowers of the garden with the sweetness of her cooling waters, having arisen to convey a stream of water forever.

81 As if she had seen the river of the Milky Way flowing and had arisen to cause the streams to flow in its direction.

82 The "daughters of the lofty trees" stand about [the pool] singly while some of them follow in pairs.

83 Sipping from the lap of passion they flourished and became inflamed; then kindled a love for them in my heart.

84 In [the garden] there are all sorts of [trees] with [branches like] plaited locks hanging down, such that the hands of the breeze cause them to sway in whirling about.

85 And in it the slender neck of the branch rose high, being devoid of ornaments, until finally its upper portions were decked in its blossoms like a necklace.

86 While its twigs were adorned by the pearls of the flowers, the wild thyme spent the night slandering them with its fragrance.

87 [The garden] gives double satisfaction for the amount which the judge of beauty imposed on it [as a fine].

88 For if the hand of the breeze fills it with [silver] dirhams of light, he is satisfied by its [payment].

89 Yet [in surplus] the [gold] dinars of the sun fill the enclosure of the garden filtering through its branches, leaving it embellished.

---

74. "Pearls," i.e., drops of water.

75. "Silver:" water; "jewels:" flowers.

76. I.e., the poet has inverted the image of water and that of the stone statue pouring it out into the pool. He says that the "liquid" statue is pouring into the "solid" water.

٧٤ إذا ما علت فى الجو ثم تحدرت ... تحلى بمرفض الجمان النواحيا

٧٥ يذوب لجين سال بين جواهر ... غدا مثلها فى الحسن أبيض صافيا

٧٦ تشابه جار للعيون بجامد ... فلم أدر أيا منهما كان جاريا

٧٧ فإن شئت تشبيها له عن حقيقة ... تصيب بها المرمى وبوركت راميا

٧٨ فقل أرقصت منها البحيرة متنها ... كما يرقص المولود من كان لاهيا

٧٩ أرتنا طباع الجود وهى وليدة ... ولم ترض فى الإحسان إلا تغاليا

٨٠ سقت ثغر زهر الروض عذب برودها ... وقامت لكى تهدى إلى الدهر ساقيا

٨١ كأن قد رأت نهر المجرة ناضبا ... فقامت بأن تجرى إليه السواقيا

٨٢ وقامت بنات الدوح فيه موائلا ... فرادى ويتلو بعضهن مثانيا

٨٣ رواضع فى حجر الغرام ترعرعت ... وشبت فشبت حبها فى فؤاديا

٨٤ بها كل ملتف الغدائر مسبل ... تجيل به أيدى النسيم مداريا

٨٥ وأشرف جيد الغصن فيها معطلا ... فقلدت النوار منه التراقيا

٨٦ إذا ما تحلت در زهر عروسة ... يبيت لها النمام بالطيب واشيا

٨٧ مصارفة نقدين فيه بمثلها ... أجاز بها قاضى الجمال التقاضيا

٨٨ فإن ملأت كف النسيم بمثلها ... دراهم نور ظل عنها مكافيا

٨٩ فتملأ حجر الروض حول غصونها ... دنانير شمس تترك الروض حاليا

---

82. The "daughters of the lofty trees" are the pigeons.

87. al-Maqqarī reads: *muṣāfaratu n-naqdaini fī-hā bi-mithli-hā / ajāza bi-hā an-naqdaini min-hā kamā hiyā.*

88. The Sala records *an-nasīm ma*ᶜ *ḍ-ḍuḥā.*

90 The birds come to nest in its branches whenever the hands of the singing girls play [their instruments] in it.

91 [The birds] answer them in rhythmic modulation, so that you would think from their voices that songs were being dictated to them.

92 Moreover we do not know of any other garden more pleasant in its freshness, more fragrant in its surroundings, or sweeter in the gathering of its fruits.

93 Nor have we observed any palace higher in its lookout spots, clearer in its horizons, or ampler in its halls of assembly.

94 You selected the innermost qualities of perfections themselves, and with them you adorned all the halls with beauty.

95 And you undertook to build it on a holiday you declared, in which you sent forth announcements both east and west.

96 And when you called on the people to construct it they answered the one who called them from as far off as the Ghaur.

97 And they directed their steps toward it drawing near from the furthest countries, nor has [your] good fortune ceased bringing the most distant ones near to you.

98 You called to mind the Day of Judgment in your generosity and your fortitude when you sat in judgment, rewarding [those who deserved it].

99 Then you rewarded each according to the state of his endeavor so that he came to gather what his own right hand had planted.

100 And you caused howdahs to appear, built out of bundles of sticks which remind the heedless of the day of departure from Mīna to Mecca [during the Pilgrimage].

101 And when [the palace] enters the morning, it blazes up serving as beacons to the surrounding villages, so it is no wonder that you cause streams of water to flow about it.

102 And it contains [a vault] rising up high in the air, unreachable, such that its furthest limits exhaust and weaken the glance.

103 The constellation of Gemini extends a ready hand [to help it] and the full moon of the heavens draws near to whisper secretly to it.

104 It is no wonder that it surpasses the stars in the heavens, and passes beyond their furthest limits.

105 For it is before your dwelling that it has arisen to perform its service, since he who serves the highest, acquires merits thereby.

---

96. The Ghaur is in Arabia.

103. The Sala records *kaffa muṣāfiḥin.*

٩٠ تَعوَّدَ فى أفنانِها الطَّيْرُ كُلَّمَا   تَجَسَّ بِهِ أَيْدى القِيانِ المَلاهِيَا

٩١ تُراجِعُها سَجْعًا فَتَحْسُبُ أَنَّها   بِأَصْواتِها تُمْلِى عليها الأغانِيَا

٩٢ فَلَمْ نَدْرِ رَوْضًا مِنه أَنْعَمَ نَضْرَةٍ   وأَعْطَرَ أَرْجَاءٍ وأَحْلَى مُجانِيَا

٩٣ وَلَمْ نَرَ قَصْرًا منه أَعْلَى مَظاهِرًا   وأَرْفَعَ آفاقًا وأَفْسَحَ نادِيَا

٩٤ مَعانِىَ مِن نَفْسِ الكَمالِ ٱنْتَقَيْتَها   وَزَيَّنْتَ مِنها بالجَمالِ المَغانِيَا

٩٥ وفاتَحْتَ مَبْناهُ بِعِيدٍ شَرَعْتَهُ   تَبَثُّ بِهِ فى الخافِقَيْنِ التَهانِيَا

٩٦ ولَمَّا دَعَوْتَ الناسَ نَحْوَ صَنِيعِهِ   أَجابوا لَهُمْ مِن جانِبِ الغَوْرِ داعِيَا

٩٧ وَأَمُّوهُ مِن أَقْصَى البِلادِ تَقَرُّبًا   وما زالَ منك السَعْدُ يُدْنِى الأَقاصِيَا

٩٨ وأَذْكَرْتَ يَوْمَ العَرْضِ جُودًا ومَنْعَةً   بِمَوْقِفِ عَرْضٍ كُنْتَ فيه المُجازِيَا

٩٩ جَزَيْتَ بِهِ كُلًّا على حالِ سَعْيِهِ   فما غَرَسَتْ يُمْناهُ أَصْبَحَ جانِيَا

١٠٠ وأَطْلَعْتَ مِن جَزْلِ الوُقُودِ هَوادِجًا   تُذْكِرُ يَوْمَ النَّفْرِ مَن كانَ ساهِيَا

١٠١ وحِينَ غَدَا يَذْكِى مَنائِرَ لِلْقُرَى   فَلَا غَرْوَ أَنْ أَجْرَيْتَ فيه المُذاكِيَا

١٠٢ وطَامِحَةٍ فى الجَوِّ غَيْرِ مُطالَةٍ   يَرُدُّ مَداها الطَّرْفَ أَحْسَرَ عارِيَا

١٠٣ تَمُدُّ لَها الجَوْزاءُ كَفَّ مُسارِعٍ   ويَدْنُو لَها بَدْرُ السَّماءِ مُناجِيَا

١٠٤ ولا عَجَبٌ أَنْ فاتَتِ الشُّهْبَ بالعُلَا   وأَنْ جاوَزَتْ منها المَدَى المُتَناهِيَا

١٠٥ فَبَيْنَ يَدَىْ مَثْواكَ قامَتْ لِخِدْمَةٍ   ومَنْ خَدَمَ الأَعْلَى ٱسْتَفادَ المَعالِيَا

104. The Sala records *fī l-ʿulā*.
105. The Sala records *fa-baina yadai mautayā*.

106 And the proof of this lies in the fact that I am standing at your court, while the bright stars have envied my position.

107 And [flowers like those stars] had suckled the breasts of the clouds before [the stars came out], in the expanse of the flower beds wherein they grow.

108 For as soon as they could be distinguished from the abode of their roots they desired to rise up to the level of the clouds,

109 Since they considered that meeting the clouds would be a feast and a joyous occasion; for this reason they rose early in the morning to the sound of the flute diverting early risers.

110 During the [revelry] the flowers caused the quivering bolt of lightning to laugh and spend the night giving [drink] to their brilliant cups.

111 The flowers saw that they had grown tall so they thought that they could surpass their goal, in spite of their lagging behind.

112 Then [the stars] which had ceased [to shine] returned promptly like birds which had delayed long on their way to the nest falling upon one another in confusion.

113 They resembled bees by way of comparison, since the swarm of bees about whom a stick [is shaken] aimed at their abode, fall upon one another as they rise.

114 Some of their targets are fixed, so that they reach them; while some of them travel in the upper regions circling about slowly.

115 While a strongly defended fortress has ascended as high as the abode [of the stars], soaring far up into the empty regions of the air.

116 It is as if the lightning bolts of the upper atmosphere were descending to the plains, revealing the towers of the palaces you built to rise high.

117 For you built a tower rising straight up, bringing a revelation to [the bolts of lightning], to be a prophet who would bring them together.

118 [The palace] enters into different sorts of stages, appearing in different kinds of ornaments which tempt chaste women who wear no ornaments.

119 For it has silver anklets on its feet, a sash on its waist, and a crown in the direction where the highest parts are located.

---

119. The "feet" are the river Darro; the sash, the green expanse of the mountain; and the "crown," the Alhambra on its summit.

١٠٦ وَشَاهِدُ ذا أَنّى بِبَابِكَ واقِفٌ   وَقَدْ حَسَدَتْ زُهْرُ النُّجُومِ مَكانِيَا

١٠٧ وَقَدْ أَرْضَعَتْ نَدْىَ الغَمائِمِ قبلها   بِحِجْرِ رِيَاضٍ كُنَّ فيه نَواشِيَا

١٠٨ فَلَمَّا أُبِينَتْ عن قَرارَةِ أَصْلِها   أَرادَتْ إلى مَرْقَى الغَمامِ تَعالِيَا

١٠٩ وعَدَّتْ لِقَاءَ السَّحْبِ عِيدًا ومَوْسِمًا   لِذاكَ آغْتَدَتْ بالزَّمْرِ تُلْهِى الغَوادِيَا

١١٠ فَأَضْحَكَتِ البَرْقَ الطَّرُوبَ خَلالَها   وباتَ لِأَكْوَاسِ الدَّرارِى مُعاطِيَا

١١١ رَأَتْ نَفْسَها طالَتْ فَظَنَّتْ بِأَنَّها   تَفُوتُ على رَغْمِ اللَّحاقِ المَرامِيَا

١١٢ فَخَفَّتْ إِلَيْها الزَّائِلاتُ كأَنَّها   طُيُورٌ إلى وَكْرٍ أَطَلْنَ تهاوِيَا

١١٣ حَكَتْ شَبَهًا لِلنَّحلِ والنَّحْلُ حَوْلَهُ   عَصَى إلى مَنْوَاهُ تَهْوِى عَوالِيَا

١١٤ فَمِنْ مُنْبِتٍ مِنْها الرَّمِيَّةِ مُدْرِكٍ   وَمِنْ طائِشٍ فى الجَوِّ حَلَّقَ وَانِيَا

١١٥ وَحِصْنٌ مَنِيعٌ فى ذَراها قَدِ آرْتَقَى   فَأَبْعَدَ فى الجَوِّ الفَضاءِ المَراقِيَا

١١٦ كأَنَّ بُرُوقَ الجَوِّ غارَتْ وقَدْ أَرَتْ   بُرُوجَ قُصُورٍ شَدْتَهُنَّ سَوامِيَا

١١٧ فَأَنْشَأَتْ بُرْجًا صاعِدًا مُتَنَزِّلاً   يَكُونُ رَسولاً بَيْنَهُن مُدارِيَا

١١٨ تَصَوَّرَ حالاتٌ أَتَى فى ضُرُوبِها   بأَنْواعِ حَلْىٍ تَسْتَفِزُّ الغَوانِيَا

١١٩ فَحَجْلٌ بِرِجْلَيْها وِشاحٌ بِخَصْرِها   وَتَاجٌ إلى ما حَلَّ منها الأَعالِيَا

120 And [that crown] is none other than a bird of good omen placed at the summit, which in the early morning, begins to scare away the russet-colored hawk of the rosy dawn, in order to infer an omen from its flight.

121 Ah, my lord; O pride of kings, in whom God's religion will most certainly attain what is hoped for!

122 According to the decree of a happy fortune, your children are five, and that is a number which does not cease to guard against the evil eye!

123 The hand of the Pleiads will spend the night invoking God's protection in their favor and they will awaken to the gentle blowing of the breeze.

124 Names were bestowed upon them upon which marks of good fortune were impressed; names in which you will observe strength, both permanent and apparent.

125 You made Abū l-Ḥajjāj to open the list of them, while conquests that open up one after another are recognized thanks to you.

126 May you be satisfied by Saᶜd and then by Naṣr, followed by Muḥammad al-Arḍā ["The Very Satisfied"] since you continue to be al-Rāḍī ["The Satisfied"].

127 By means of him you set up a law out of your natural inclination for the religion of Islam, while you also restored the erased traces of the Holy Guidance.

128 He appeared full of as much comeliness as the eyes can behold; the face of the earth kisses a bright and resplendent one.

129 Therefore, O detractor who arouses his like, not even the like of you can shed the blood of ferocious lions.

130 Greetings came to you from Egypt to honor you for the hands of the merchants did not tear open the precious goods.

131 And an amulet reached you from the land of al-Ḥijāz, one which perfected God's creation; may it not cease to be clearly manifested!

132 And the Sultan of Ṭaiba called you "the dreadful"; so, O how fragrant was that [name] which he bestowed upon you in calling.

---

120. Russet hawks were considered to be of the best quality. Presumably a *good* omen is implied.

122. A reference to the "hand of Fatima" carved on the gate of the Alhambra. It represents the five pillars of Islam, and was used as a talisman against the evil eye.

123. The Sala records *khamsu th-thurayā; muᶜtalu n-nawāsimi rāqiyā.*

124. In this line and the next the poet mentions the names of four out of Muḥammad V's five children. Presumably the fifth was a daughter whose name

١٢٠ وَمَا هُوَ إِلَّا طَيْرُ سَعْدٍ بِذَرْوَةٍ   غَدَا زَاجِرًا مِنْ أَشْهَبِ الصُّبْحِ بَازِيَا

١٢١ أَمَوْلَاىَ يَا فَخْرَ الْمُلُوكِ وَمَنْ بِهِ   سَيَبْلُغُ دِينُ اللّٰهِ مَا كَانَ رَاجِيَا

١٢٢ بَنُوكَ على حُكْمِ السَّعَادَةِ خَمْسَةٌ   وذا عَدَدٌ لِلْعَيْنِ مَازَالَ وَاقِيَا

١٢٣ تَبِيتُ لَهُمْ كَفُّ الثُّرَيَّا مُعِيذَةً   وَيُصْبِحُ مُعْتَلُّ النَّسِيمِ رَوَاقِيَا

١٢٤ أَسَامٍ عليها لِلسَّعَادَةِ مَيْسَمٌ   تَرَى العِزَّ فيها مُسْتَكِنًّا وَبَادِيَا

١٢٥ جَعَلْتَ أَبَا الحَجَّاجِ فَاتِحَ طِرْسِهِمْ   وَقَدْ عُرِفَتْ منكَ الفُتُوحُ التَوَالِيَا

١٢٦ وَحَسْبُكَ سَعْدٌ ثُمَّ نَصْرٌ يَلِيهِمْ   مُحَمَّدٌ الأَرْضَى، فَمَا زِلْتَ رَاضِيَا

١٢٧ أَقَمْتَ بِهِ مِن فِطْرَةِ الدِّينِ سُنَّةً   وَجَدَّدْتَ مِن رَسْمِ الهِدَايَةِ عَافِيَا

١٢٨ وَجَاؤُا بِهِ مِلْءَ العُيُونِ وَسَامَةً   يُقَبِّلُ وَجْهُ الأَرْضِ أَزْهَرَ بَاهِيَا

١٢٩ فَيَا عَاذِلًا مَا كَانَ أَجْرَأَ مِثْلَهُ   فَمِثْلُكَ لا يُدْمِى الأُسُودَ الضَوَارِيَا

١٣٠ وجاءَتْكَ مِن مِصْرَ التَّحَايَا كَرَائِمًا   فَمَا فَتَّقَتْ أَيْدِى التُّجَارِ الغَوَالِيَا

١٣١ ووَافَتْكَ مِن أَرْضِ الحِجَازِ تَمِيمَةٌ   تُتَمِّمُ صُنْعَ اللّٰهِ لا زَالَ بَادِيَا

١٣٢ ونَادَاكَ بِالتَّهْوِيلِ سُلْطَانُ طَيْبَةٍ   فَيَا طِيبَ مَا أَهْدَى إِليك مُنَادِيَا

Ibn Zamrak omits in accordance with the rules of Muslim politeness, since it is considered bad form to mention womenfolk in public.

131. These are allusions to gifts presented to the sovereign by Eastern powers. A *tamīmat* is either a head ornament or an amulet (cf. Dozy, I, 152). 152).

132. Ṭaiba, 'the fragrant,' is a name of Medina, so called because it contains the Prophet's tomb.

133 He stood, while visiting the tomb of Muḥammad, praying there for your exalted majesty.

134 Your heart is mercy; may you be rewarded for its endeavor by a God who requites endeavors with a compensation.

135 For, by God, were it not for a certain Prophetic Law in which we have accepted him, he being guided toward it, and guiding us,

136 And an exemption whose authority was decreed to you from the Divine Law by lofty events,

137 The horrors of a [battle] place which causes the uppers shafts of spears to turn hoary headed by reason of the white spearheads, would have frightened [your heart] into being butchered.

138 To you belongs praise thereby, for a good deed you reckon [as yours], while its third in glory will glorify a second.

139 Gemini fasten tight the knot of their Orion belt for [the battleground], so that they may serve thereby to attain the highest rank.

140 I have congratulated [you] for it with praises, and your essence has come to overflow thereby with generosity,

141 Since you have before you some jewels from the sea of rhetoric which are to be held in great esteem for they are not sold save at a high price.

142 I have attempted in them the description of every rare wonder, and in this way I have baffled all those who are to come as well as those who have departed.

143 So, O heir to the Anṣār, and not on the basis of a remote kinship: the inheritance of a lofty majesty finds mountains to be light!

144 The composition is interspersed with praises of him; he who recites it will chant it when invoking [God's] name.

145 Islam has recognized from what I have declared, both the noble deeds of the Naṣrids and their power.

146 The peace of God be upon you, so may you ever remain in peace, renewing holidays while wearing out your enemies!

---

143. The Naṣrids of Granada claimed descent from the Anṣār, the Prophet's "helpers" in Medina.

143. Note the allusion to line 3 of this same poem. By use of the phrase

١٣٣ وقامَ وقد وَافَى ضَرِيحَ مُحَمَّدٍ   لِسُلْطانِكَ الأَعْلَى هُنالِكَ داعِيا
١٣٤ سَرِيرَتُكَ الرُّحْمَى جَزَاكَ بِسَعْيِهِا   إلٰهٌ يُوفِي فى الجَزَاءِ المَساعِيَا
١٣٥ فَوَاللّٰهِ لَوْلا سُنَّةٌ نَبَوِيَّةٌ   عَهِدْنَاهُ مَهْدِيًّا إليها وهَادِيَا
١٣٦ وعُذْرٌ مِنَ الأَعْذارِ قَرَّرَ حُكْمَهُ   مِن الشَّرْعِ أَخْبارٌ رَفَعنَ عَوالِيَا
١٣٧ تَرَاءَتْ بِها لِلْجَزْرِ أَهْوَالُ مَوْقِفٍ   تُشِيبُ بِمُبْيَضِّ النُّصولِ العَوالِيَا
١٣٨ لَكَ الحَمْدُ فيه مِن صَنِيعٍ تَعُدُّهُ   فَنالِتُهُ فى الفَخْرِ عَزَّزَ ثانِيَا
١٣٩ تَشُدُّ لَهُ الجَوْزَاءُ عِقْدَ نِطاقِها   لِتَخْدِمَ فيه كَىْ تَنالَ المَعالِيَا
١٤٠ وَهَنَّيْتُ بالأَمْداحِ فيه وقد غَدَا   وُجُودُكَ فيه بالإجَادَةِ وَافِيَا
١٤١ وَدُونَكَ مِن بَحْرِ البَيَانِ جَواهِرَا   كُرِمْنَ فَمَا يُشْرَيْنَ إلَّا غَوالِيَا
١٤٢ وَطَارَدتُّ فيها وَصْفَ كُلِّ غَريبَةٍ   فأَعْجَزْتُ مَن يَأْتِى ومَن كانَ ماضِيَا
١٤٣ فَيَا وَارِثَ الأَنْصارِ لا عن كَلالَةٍ   تُرَاثُ جَلالٍ يَسْتَخِفُّ الرَّواسِيَا
١٤٤ بأَمْدَاحِهِ جاءَ الكِتابُ مُفَصَّلًا   يُرَتِّلُهُ فى الذِّكْرِ مَن كانَ تالِيَا
١٤٥ لَقَدْ عَرَفَ الإسْلامُ مِمَّا أَفَدتَّهُ   مَكارِمَ أَنْصارِيَّةً وأَيادِيَا
١٤٦ عليكَ سَلامُ اللّٰهِ فَاسْلَمْ مُخَلَّدًا   تُجَدِّدُ أَعْيَادًا وتُبْلِى أعادِيَا

"do not *consider mountains to be light*" at the beginning, and "the inheritance of a lofty majesty *finds mountains to be light*," the poem progresses from initial despair to final consolation found in the glory of the sovereign.

41 Yūsuf III

1 My friend go gently, for Time is as you know it to be, since there is no avoiding an easy life in spite of the [present] trace of hardship,

2 For whenever a bright cloudless day becomes overcast there is no avoiding rain, and whenever a calamity becomes dark there is no avoiding daybreak,

3 Since the blessings of God's beneficence are marvellous in appearance.

4 His judgment and sentence are carried out according to [the principles of] justice, and His [peculiar] gift is to gain submission to whatsoever He wills.

5 Yet whoever has followed the right path according to the clear and certain truth, has witnessed the banner of victory fluttering over himself.

6 As for an oppressor who has turned away from the banner of victory, may [God] estrange him [from prosperity]!

7 O for the victory of one who has unsheathed the blade of his untiring effort, without knowing at night what the softness of his bed was like!

8 One applying God's Law in many ways when among His worshipers and repelling His enemies when far from His homeland;

9 For he is constrained by his purity and sincerity toward God in his prayers.

10 And O, wonder at one who has forsaken the [respect] due his Lord, one from the manner of whose love hatred is recognized,

11 For he does not sniff the breeze of [God's] approval from its windward side, and whenever the invoker of the right path calls out, he does not answer him;

12 Thus how can he boast when victory [is granted] as a reward [for virtue]?

---

41. SOURCE: Yūsuf III, *Dīwān*, ed. ʿAbd Allāh Kanūn (Cairo, 1965), pp. 70–72.
METER: *ṭawīl*. Rhyme: b–b–b–b–*a* c–c–c–c–*a*
FORM: *mukhammasa*.

The king of Granada records in his *Dīwān* that "during the hour of need when the enemy descended upon the frontier town of Antequera, we composed the following poem, beseeching help and explaining our situation" (p. 70). There are several Christian accounts of the conquest of Antequera, among them the Spanish ballad "De Antequera partió el moro—tres horas antes del día"

٤١

يوسف الثالث

١ خَلِيلَيَّ مَهْلًا فالزَّمانُ كَمَا تَدْرِى   ولا بُدَّ مِن يُسْرٍ على أَثَرِ العُسْرِ
٢ فَمَهْمَا دَهَى صَحْوٌ فَلابُدَّ مِن قَطْرِ   ومَهْمَا دَجَا خَطْبٌ فلابُدَّ مِن فَجْرِ
٣ وَأَلْطَافُ صُنْعِ اللّٰهِ رائعةُ البَشْرِ
٤ على العَدْلِ يَجْرِى حُكْمُهُ وقَضَاؤُهُ   وَمَنالُهُ التَّسْلِيمُ فيما يَشاؤُهُ
٥ ومَن كانَ بالحَقِّ اليَقِينِ آهْتِداؤُهُ   رَأَى النَّصْرَ خفاقًا عليهِ لِوَاؤُهُ
٦ وسُحْقًا لِباغٍ حادَ عن عَلَمِ النَّصْرِ
٧ ويَا فَوْزَ مَن أَنْضَى حُسامَ آجْتِهادِهِ   ولم يَذْرِ لَيْلًا ما وَنيرُ مهادِهِ
٨ يُصَرِّفُ حُكْمَ اللّٰهِ بَيْنَ عِبادِهِ   وتُثْنِى عِداهُ نَزَّعًا عن بِلادِهِ
٩ بإخْلاصِهِ لِلّٰهِ دَعْوُهُ مُضْطَرٌّ
١٠ وَيَا عَجَبًا مِن تَارِكِ حَقَّ رَبِّهِ   تَعَرَّفَتِ البَغْضاءُ مِن كُنْهِ حُبِّهِ
١١ فلم يَنْتَشِقْ رَوْحَ الرِّضَا مِن مَهَبِّهِ   ومَهْمَا دَعَا دَاعِى الهُدَى لم يُلَبِّهِ
١٢ فأَنَّى لَهُ بالفَخْرِ والفَوْزُ بالأَجْرِ

(*Romancero español*, ed. L. Santullano [Madrid, 1946], pp. 611–617). With the recent publication of Yusūf's *Dīwān*, a new literary account in Arabic of the loss of Antequera is made available. The city fell in A.D. 1410.

6. The "oppressor" is Ferdinand I of Aragon who took Antequera (cf. Lorenzo Valla, *La conquista de Antequera* [Antequera, 1957]).

7. I.e., Yūsuf III himself.

10. The *Dīwān* reads *ḥaqqa rabbati*, a misprint.

13 Should the rights pertaining to God's covenants not be respected, as well as [those pertaining to] one who has taken into account an enemy difficult to aim at?
14 For, by God, there is one repelled [by them], upon whom they have prevailed, yet whenever they shot, their arrows turned back against them.
15 Moreover, how many men caught unawares and proudly strutting in their coats of mail did [those arrows] transpierce!
16 I clung to the easy part of matters as well as to the hard, preparing the weapons of war at the time of peace.
17 And to how many have I not graciously granted my favor while omitting to reprove them, though they are persons who have "become concealed in the darkness of their veils,"
18 So that the tongues of Time revealed the secrets of their condition!
19 It, two-faced Time, is a creature of hypocrisy and its judgments are carried out with hatred for all creatures.
20 Hence, let there be patience and acceptance of what my Creator has willed, for there is no avoiding success and a fitting victory,
21 In spite of him who denies that [we will have] the upper hand over unbelief.
22 Yet surely no man would approve of supporting unbelief, save [one who] has abjured his faith and impugns the superiority of the true religion.
23 The angels of the seven heavens will bear witness against a stubborn man who constantly lapses into error,
24 Remaining cheerful all the while, though Islam is in the clutch of unbelief.
25 I am satisfied with that wherewith my Lord and Helper is satisfied when exerting myself in holy war among the sharp-edged swords,
26 And while I am concerned with my thoughts about the encompassing enemy, I invoke a God who knows [all] secrets.
27 Perhaps there will be a favorable inclination on the part of Him who knows about forbidding evil and commanding good.
28 To Him do I have recourse wherever my riding camels halt; on Him is my reliance in all requests.

---

17. Cf. Koran 38:32: "It [the sun] became concealed by the veil [of night]."

١٣ أَلَيْسَتْ عُهودُ اللّٰهِ يُرْعَى ذِمامُها   ومَن حَسِبَ الأَعْداءَ صَعْبًا مَرامُها

١٤ فَبِاللّٰهِ مَرْدودٌ عليه ٱحْتِكامُها   ومَهْمَا رَمَتْ عادَتْ عليها سِهامُها

١٥ فَكَمْ أَنْبَتَتْ مِن ساجِبِ دِرْعٍ مُغْتَرِّ

١٦ أَقَمْتُ على سَهْلِ الأُمورِ وصَعْبِها   مُعِدًّا أَوانَ السِّلْمِ أَوْزارَ حَرْبِها

١٧ وَكَمْ دِنْتُ بالعُتْبَى وإِلْغاءِ عَتْبِها   نُفوسًا تَوارَتْ فى غَياهِبِ حُجْبِها

١٨ فَأَبْدَتْ خَفايا حالِها أَلْسُنُ الدَّهْرِ

١٩ هُوَ الدَّهْرُ ذُو وَجْهَيْنِ فِعْلُ مُنافِقِ   وأَحْكامُهُ تَجْرِى بِكَرْهِ الخَلائِقِ

٢٠ فَصَبْرًا وتَسْلِيمًا لِما شاءَ خالِقِي   فلا بُدَّ مِن ظَفَرٍ ونَصْرٍ مُوافِقِ

٢١ على رَغْمِ مَن يَأْبَى الظُهورَ على الكُفْرِ

٢٢ وهَلْ يَرْتَضِى أَنَّ الكُفورَ مُؤَيَّدُ   سِوَى مُلْحِد فَضْلَ الهِدايَةِ يَجْحَدُ

٢٣ مَلائِكَةُ السَّبْعِ السَّمَواتِ تَشْهَدُ   على جامِعٍ فى غَيِّهِ يَتَرَدَّدُ

٢٤ ويَرْتاحُ والإِسْلامُ فى قَبْضَةِ الكُفْرِ

٢٥ رَضِيتُ بِما يَرْضاهُ رَبِّى وناصِرِى   مُجاهَدَةً بَيْنَ السُّيوفِ البَواتِرِ

٢٦ وبين ٱفْتِكارِى فى العَدُوِّ المُحاصِرِ   أُنادِى إِلَاهًا عالِمًا بالسَّرائِرِ

٢٧ عَسَى عَطْفَةٌ مِن عالِمِ النَّهْىِ والأَمْرِ

٢٨ إِلَيْهِ ٱسْتِنادِى حَيْثُ حَلَّتْ رَكائِبِي   عَلَيْهِ ٱعْتِمادِى فى جَمِيعِ المَطالِبِ

29 While the best of intercessors descends from Luʾaiy ibn Ghālib and his followers, both those bold to attack and the companions,
30 As also that which has come down in the Sacred Book distinguishing between good and evil; by "the even and the odd."

29. Luʾaiy ibn Ghālib was the ancestor of Quraish, and therefore of Muhammad. The "companions" of the Prophet are the Aṣḥāb, those who fled with him from Mecca to Medina.

٢٩ وَخَيْرُ شَفِيعٍ مِن لُؤَيِّ بْنِ غَالِبِ   وَأَتْبَاعِهِ ما بَيْنَ سِبْطٍ وَصَاحِبِ

٣٠ وما جاءَ فى الفُرْقانِ و الشَّفْعِ و الوِتْرِ

30. Cf. Koran 89:3: "By the even and the odd."

42 Yūsuf III

1	O you who have aimed	At my heart with the dart	Of a piercing glance:
2	Meet one who's dying,	One whose eye is shedding	Fast-flowing tears!
3	Who will claim justice		From an alluring fawn
4	Slender of body		As is the fresh, green bough,
5	Who has insisted		On distance and shunning?
6	He has no fear	For the sin there's in that	Since he repeats it.
7	I'm unrecovered;	My body's exhausted,	My face has turned wan.
8	Decked in all beauties		Then who can vie with him?
9	A sweet one; fair prey,		Yet he falsely accuses.
10	Full of perfections;		Glory to his Maker!
11	A high rising full moon.	The night of its waxing	On a slender reed,
12	Has risen above	A soft plump body;	A well-nurtured fawn.
13	He has seduced me		With the spell of his eyelids.
14	Had it been allowed		—Yet he shuns me ever—

42. SOURCE: Yūsuf III, *Dīwān*, ed. ʿAbd Allāh Kanūn (Cairo, 1965), pp. 184–185.
FORM: *muwashshaḥa.*
METER: *rajaz.* Rhyme: a–b–a–b–a–b *m–n–o–m–n–o*

٤٢

يوسف الثالث

١ يَا مَنْ رَمَى   قَلْبِي على سَهْمِ   لَحْظٍ مُصِيبْ

٢ صِلْ مُدْنِفَا   ذَا مُقْلَةٍ تَهْمِي   دَمْعًا سَكِيبْ

٣ مَنْ مُنْصِفِي   مِن شادِنٍ غُرِّ

٤ مُهَفْهَفِ   كالغُصْنِ النَّضِرِ

٥ قَدْ لَجَّ فِي   بُعْدِي وَفِي هَجْرِي

٦ لَمْ يَخْشَ مَا   فِي ذاكَ مِن إِثْمِ   أَمَا يُنِيبْ

٧ ولا آشْتَفَى   مِن ناحِلِ الجِسْمِ   بَادِي الشُّحُوبْ

٨ حازَ الجَمالْ   فَمَن يُسامِيهِ

٩ حُلْوٌ حَلالْ   لَوْ لا تَجَنِّيهِ

١٠ وَافِي الكَمالْ   سُبْحانَ بارِيهِ

١١ بَدْرٌ سَمَا   فِي لَيْلَةِ التِّمِّ   على قَضِيبْ

١٢ قَدْ أَشْرَفَا   فِي نَاعِمٍ ضُخْمِ   ظَبْيًا رَبِيبْ

١٣ قَدْ فُتِنَّا   بِسِحْرِ أَجْفانِهْ

١٤ لَوْ أُمْكِنَا   والصَّدُّ مِن شانِهْ

---

11. The source reads *lam samā* which makes no sense in this context. The present emendation is suggested by the editor of the *Dīwān*.

15 I'd have won my desires   By undoing his sash.
16 He quenched all the thirst   That is lodged in my breast   In spite of the spy.
17 Moreover he healed   All the sickness in me,   And my aching heart.
18 How many a night   Did he keep faith with me
19 While by our union   He lodged me in Eden!
20 He cured the disease   Of my languishing heart,
21 With deep red lips   Whose white snow doth taste sweet,   Pleasantly cool.
22 Oft did he heal   With a peaceful embrace   My broken heart
23 He lovingly gazed   Like a fawn without peer
24 —Though my foe had sinned   By intent in my death—
25 And then he bent down;   I exclaimed out of love:
26 "O you who have aimed   At my heart with the dart   Of a piercing glance:
27 Meet one who's dying,   One whose eye is shedding   Fast-flowing tears!"

١٥ نِلْتُ المُنَى   مِنْ حَلِّ هِمْيانِهْ

١٦ أَرْوَى ظِمَا   صَدْرِى على رَغْمِ   أَنْفِ الرَّقِيبْ

١٧ فَهْوَ شَفَا   ما بى مِن سُقْمِ   ومِن وَجِيبْ

١٨ كَمْ مِن لَيَالْ   أَنالَنِى الأُمْنَا

١٩ وَبالوِصالْ   أَحلَّنِى عَدْنَا

٢٠ أَبْرَى آعْتِلَالْ   فُؤادِيَ المُضْنَى

٢١ بِذِى لَمَا   مُسْتَعْذَبِ الظَّلْمِ   عَذْبٍ شَنِيبْ

٢٢ وكَمْ شَفَا   باللَّثْمِ والضَمِّ   قَلْبِى الكَئِيبْ

٢٣ لَمَّا رَنَا   كالشّادِنِ الفَرْدِ

٢٤ وَقد جَنَا   قَتْلِى على عَمْدِ

٢٥ ثُمَّ آنْثَنَى   نادَيتُ مِن وَجْدِ

٢٦ يَا مَنْ رَمَى   قَلْبِى على سَهْمِ   لَحْظٍ مُصِيبْ

٢٧ صِلْ مُدْنِفَا   ذَا مُقْلَةٍ تَهْمِى   دَمْعًا سَكِيبْ

43 Anonymous

1 A noble, enduring, ever-renewed peace do I attribute exclusively to his highness, the best of Caliphs.

2 Peace be upon his highness, the possessor of glory and lofty stature, who has clothed the infidel in a robe of humility;

3 Peace be upon him whose kingship God has expanded, supporting him with victory in every region;

4 Peace be upon his majesty, the capital of whose realm is Constantinople. What a noble city it is!

5 Peace be upon him whose kingdom God adorned with armies and subject populations of Turks;

6 Peace be upon you. May God exalt your rank and may He also make you a king over every nation.

7 Peace be upon the judge and upon whomsoever of the noble, exalted men of learning resemble him;

8 Peace be upon the men of religion and piety and upon whomsoever among the counselors is gifted with sound judgment.

9 Peace be upon you on behalf of some slaves who have remained in a land of exile, in Andalus in the west,

10 Whom the swelling sea of Rūm as well as a deep, gloomy, and fathomless ocean encompasses.

11 Peace be upon you on behalf of some slaves smitten by a dire misfortune. What a misfortune it was!

12 Peace be upon you on behalf of some old men whose white hair has come to be torn from [much] plucking, after [they have enjoyed a life of] glory;

13 Peace be upon you on behalf of some faces that have been bared to the company of non-Arabs after having been veiled;

14 Peace be upon you on behalf of some young girls whom the priest drives by force to a bed of shame;

---

43. SOURCE: al-Maqqarī, *Azhār ar-riyāḍ* (Cairo, 1939), I, 108–115.
METER: *ṭawil.*

When Granada surrendered to the army of Ferdinand and Isabella in 1492, the treaty of capitulation granted the Muslims the right freely to practice their religion, to live according to their own laws and customs, and if they preferred, to be freely allowed to emigrate to Africa with their belongings. Religious friction soon developed between Christians and Muslims, however. Matters reached a climax in 1499 and led to an uprising in the Moorish quarter of Granada known as the Albaicín. It was supported by the towns in the mountainous district of Las Alpujarras. The revolt was crushed in 1501, and soon after the unfortunate

٤٣

لشاعر مجهول

١ سَلامٌ كَريمٌ دائِمٌ مُتَجَدِّدٌ   أَخُصُّ بِهِ مَوْلايَ خَيْرَ خَليفَةِ
٢ سَلامٌ على مَوْلايَ ذِى المَجْدِ والعُلا   ومَنْ أَلْبَسَ الكُفّارَ ثَوْبَ المَذَلَّةِ
٣ سَلامٌ على مَن وَسَّعَ اللّٰهُ مُلْكَهُ   وأَيَّدَهُ بالنَّصْرِ فى كُلِّ وِجْهَةِ
٤ سَلامٌ على مَوْلايَ مَنْ دارُ مُلْكِهِ   قُسَنْطِينَةُ أَكْرِمْ بِها مِن مَدينَةِ
٥ سَلامٌ على مَن زَيَّنَ اللّٰهُ مُلْكَهُ   بِجُنْدٍ وأَتْراكٍ مِن أَهْلِ الرِّعايَةِ
٦ سَلامٌ عليكُمْ شَرَّفَ اللّٰهُ قَدْرَكُمْ   وَزادَكُمُ مُلْكًا على كُلِّ مِلَّةِ
٧ سَلامٌ على القاضِى ومَن كانَ مِثْلَهُ   مِن العُلَماءِ الأَكْرَمِينَ الأَجِلَّةِ
٨ سَلامٌ على أَهْلِ الدِّيانَةِ والتُّقَى   ومَن كانَ ذا رَأْيٍ مِنَ آهْلِ المَشْوَرَةِ
٩ سَلامٌ عليكُمْ مِن عَبِيدٍ تَخَلَّفُوا   بِأَنْدَلُسٍ بالغَرْبِ فى أَرْضِ غُرْبَةِ
١٠ أَحاطَ بِهِمْ بَحْرٌ مِنَ الرُّومِ زاخِرٌ   وبَحْرٌ عَميقٌ ذو ظَلامٍ ولُجَّةِ
١١ سَلامٌ عليكُمْ مِن عَبِيدٍ أَصابَهُمْ   مُصابٌ عَظيمٌ يالَها مِن مُصِيبَةِ
١٢ سَلامٌ عليكُمْ مِن شُيُوخٍ تَمَزَّقَتْ   شُيُوبُهُمْ بالنَّتْفِ مِن بَعْد عِزَّةِ
١٣ سَلامٌ عليكُمْ مِن وُجوهٍ تَكَشَّفَتْ   على جُمْلَةِ الأَعْلاجِ مِن بعد سَتْرَةِ
١٤ سَلامٌ عليكُمْ مِن بَناتٍ عَواتِقٍ   يَسُوقُهُمُ اللَّبّاطُ قَهْرًا لِخَلْوَةِ

Moriscos were ordered either to convert to Christianity or to quit Spanish soil, leaving their property behind them. This was in direct violation of the conditions agreed to in the treaty of surrender. Soon after, an unknown Granadan Morisco sent this ode as an appeal for help to the Ottoman emperor Bāyazīd II [r. 1481–1512]. The poem is of historical interest, for it shows that long before the naval engagement of Lepanto (1571), while the Ottoman empire was still in its zenith, the Moriscos were already attempting to gain Turkish support in order to restore Muslim rule in the peninsula. This led to their final expulsion in the seventeenth century.

15 Peace be upon you on behalf of some old women who have been compelled to eat pork and flesh not killed according to ritual prescriptions.

16 We all kiss the ground of your royal court and we call down blessings upon you at all moments.

17 May the Lord cause your royal power and life to endure, and may He preserve you from every trial and misfortune;

18 May He strengthen you with support and victory over the enemy, and lodge you in the abode of [His] pleasure and regard [for you].

19 We have complained to you, your majesty, of the harm, the misfortune and the enormous calamity that has afflicted us.

20 We have been betrayed and converted to Christianity; our religion has been exchanged for another; we have been oppressed and treated in every shameful way.

21 Yet under the Prophet Muhammad's religion we used to oppose the agents of the Cross with our inner intentions,

22 Facing grave dangers in Holy War because of killing and capturing, hunger and dearth.

23 But the Christians attacked us from all sides in a vast torrent, company after company

24 Smiting us with zeal and resolution like locusts in the multitude of their cavalry and weapons.

25 Nevertheless, for a long time we withstood their armies and killed group after group of them,

26 Although their horsemen increased every moment, whereas ours were in a state of diminution and scarcity,

27 Hence, when we became weak, they camped in our territory and smote us, town after town,

28 Bringing many large cannons that demolished the impregnable walls of the towns,

29 Attacking them energetically during the siege for many months and days; with zeal and determination.

30 So when our cavalry and foot soldiers had perished and we observed that no rescue was forthcoming from our brethren,

31 And when our victuals had diminished and our lot had become hard indeed, we complied, against our will, with their demands, out of fear of disgrace,

32 And fearing for our sons and daughters, lest they be taken captive or cruelly slaughtered,

١٥ سَلامٌ عليكُمْ مِن عَجَائِزَ أُنْرِهَتْ على أَكْلِ خِنْزِيرٍ ولَحْمٍ لِجِيفَةِ
١٦ نُقَبِّلُ نَحْنُ الكُلُّ أَرْضَ بِسَاطِكُمْ ونَدْعُو لَكُمْ بالخَيْرِ فى كُلِّ سَاعَةِ
١٧ أَدامَ الإلٰهُ مُلْكَكُمْ وحَيَاتَكُمْ وعَافَاكُمُ مِنْ كُلِّ سُوءٍ وَمِحْنَةِ
١٨ وأَيَّدَكُمْ بالنَّصْرِ والظَّفْرِ بالعِدَا وأَسْكَنَكُمْ دارَ الرِّضَا والكَرامَةِ
١٩ شَكَوْنَا لَكُمْ مَوْلاَىَ ما قد أَصابَنَا مِن الضُّرِّ والبَلْوَى وعَظْمِ الرَّزِيَةِ
٢٠ غُدِرْنَا ونُصِّرْنَا وبُدِّلَ دِينُنَا ظُلِمْنَا وعُومِلْنَا بِكُلِّ قَبِيحَةِ
٢١ وكُنَّا على دِينِ النَّبِىِّ مُحَمَّدٍ نُقاتِلُ عُمَّالَ الصَّلِيبِ بِنِيَّةِ
٢٢ ونَلْقَى أُمورًا فى الجِهادِ عَظِيمَةً بِقَتْلٍ وأَسْرٍ ثُمَّ جُوعٍ وقِلَّةِ
٢٣ فجَاءَتْ علينا الرُّومُ مِن كُلِّ جانِبٍ بِسَيْلٍ عَظِيمٍ جُمْلَةً بَعْدَ جُمْلَةِ
٢٤ وَمَالُوا علينا كَالجِرادِ بِجَمْعِهِمْ بِجَدٍّ وعَزْمٍ مِن خُيُولٍ وعُدَّةِ
٢٥ فَكُنَّا بِطُولِ الدَّهْرِ نَلْقَى جُموعَهُمْ فَنَقْتُلُ فيها فِرْقَةً بَعْدَ فِرْقَةِ
٢٦ وفُرْسانُهُمْ تَزْدادُ فى كُلِّ سَاعَةٍ وفُرْسانُنَا فى حالِ نَقْصٍ وَقِلَّةِ
٢٧ فلَمَّا ضَعُفْنَا خَيَّمُوا فى بِلادِنا ومَالُوا علينا بَلْدَةً بَعدَ بَلْدَةِ
٢٨ وجَاءُوا بِأَنْفاطٍ عِظَامٍ كَثِيرَةٍ تَهْدِمُ أَسْوارَ البِلادِ المَنِيعَةِ
٢٩ وشَدُّوا عليها فى الحِصارِ بِقُوَّةٍ شُهورًا وأَيَّامًا بِجَدٍّ وعَزْمَةِ
٣٠ فلَمَّا تَفَانَتْ خَيْلُنَا ورِجالُنَا ولَمْ نَرَ مِن إخْوَانِنَا مِن إغَاثَةِ
٣١ وقَلَّتْ لَنَا الأَقْوَاتُ واشْتَدَّ حالُنا أَطَعْنَاهُمُ بالكُرْهِ خَوْفَ الفَضِيحَةِ
٣٢ وخَوْفًا على أَبْنَائِنَا وبَنَاتِنَا مِن أَنْ يُؤْسَرُوا أَوْ يُقْتَلُوا شَرَّ قِتْلَةِ

33 On the condition that we were to remain like the Mudéjars before us, namely the inhabitants of the old territory,

34 And that we were to be allowed to remain in enjoyment [of the right] to call to prayer and [to celebrate] our ritual oration, while we were not [to be required] to abandon any of the prescriptions of the Religious Law;

35 And that whosoever among us desired [to cross] the sea was to [be allowed to] do so in safety, to the land on the [African] coast with all the property he wished [to take],

36 As well as many other stipulations, surpassing fifty by the number of five.

37 Then their Sultan and grandee said to us: "What you have stipulated is granted to you in more than its entirety,"

38 Showing us documents containing a pact and a treaty, saying to us: "This is my amnesty and my protection [over you],

39 So remain in enjoyment of your possessions and homes as you were before, unharmed."

40 Yet when we came under their treaty of protection, their treachery toward us became apparent for [he] broke the agreement.

41 He broke the compacts he had deceived us with and converted us to Christianity by force, with harshness and severity,

42 Burning the books we had and mixing them with dung or with filth,

43 Though each book was on the subject of our religion. Yet they were cast into the fire with scorn and derision,

44 Nor did they spare a single volume belonging to any Muslim, or any tome which one could read in solitude.

45 Whosoever fasted or prayed and his state came to be known, was in every instance cast into the fire,

46 And whosoever of us failed to go to their place of unbelief, him did the priest severely punish,

47 Slapping him on both cheeks, confiscating his property, and imprisoning him in a wretched state.

48 Moreover, during Ramadan, they spoiled our fast time after time with food and drink,

---

33. The Mudéjars were those Muslims living in Christian Spain. They had been permitted to keep their property and had been granted freedom of worship in medieval times.

36. L. del Mármol Carvajal, in his *Historia del rebelión y castigo de los moriscos del reino de Granada*, Biblioteca de autores españoles, XXI (Madrid, 1946) lists forty-nine stipulations.

37. The Sultan is Ferdinand of Aragon.

٣٣ على أَنْ نَكُونَ مِثْلَ مَن كانَ قَبْلَنا   مِنَ الدَّجْنِ مِن أَهْلِ البِلادِ القَدِيمَةِ

٣٤ ونُبْقِى على آذانِنا وصَلاتِنا   ولا نَتْرُكَنْ شَيْئًا مِنَ آمْرِ الشَرِيعَةِ

٣٥ ومَنْ شاءَ مِنَّا البَحْرَ جازَ مُؤَمَّنًا   بِمَا شاءَ مِن مالٍ إلى أَرْضِ عُدْوَةِ

٣٦ إلى غَيْرِ ذاكَ مِن شُروطٍ كَثِيرَةٍ   تَزِيدُ على الخَمْسِينَ شَرْطًا بِخَمْسَةِ

٣٧ فقالَ لَنا سُلْطانُهم وكَبِيرُهُمْ   لَكُمْ ما شَرَطتُّمْ كامِلاً بالزِّيادةِ

٣٨ وأَبْدَى لَنا كُتْبًا بعَهْدٍ ومَوْثِقٍ   وقالَ لَنا هذا أَمانِى وذِمَّتِى

٣٩ فَكُونُوا على أَمْوَالِكُمْ ودِيارِكُمْ   كَمَا كُنْتُمُ مِن قَبْلُ دُونَ أَذِيَّةِ

٤٠ فلَمَّا دَخَلْنَا تَحْتَ عَقْدِ ذِمامِهِمْ   بَدا غَدْرُهُمْ فينا بِنَقْضِ العَزِيمَةِ

٤١ وخانَ عُهودًا كانَ قد غَرَّنا بِها   ونَصَّرَنا كَرْهًا بِعُنْفٍ وسَطْوَةِ

٤٢ وأَحْرَقَ ما كانَتْ لَنا مِن مَصاحِفٍ   وخَلَّطَها بالزِّبْلِ أَوْ بالنَّجاسَةِ

٤٣ وكُلُّ كِتابٍ كانَ فى أَمْرِ دِينِنَا   فَفِى النارِ أَلْقَوْهُ بِهُزْءٍ وحَقْرَةِ

٤٤ ولَمْ يَتْرُكُوا فيها كِتابًا لِمُسْلِمٍ   ولا مُصْحَفًا يُخْلَى به لِلْقِرَاءَةِ

٤٥ ومَن صامَ أَوْ صَلَّى ويُعْلَمُ حالُهُ   فَفِى النارِ يُلْقُوهُ على كُلِّ حالَةِ

٤٦ ومَنْ لَمْ يَجِئْ مِنَّا لِمَوْضِعِ كُفْرِهِمْ   يُعاقِبُهُ اللَّبّاطُ شَرَّ العُقُوبَةِ

٤٧ ويَلْطِمُ خَدَّيْهِ ويَأْخُذُ مالَهُ   ويَجْعَلُهُ فى السِّجْنِ فى سُوءِ حالَةِ

٤٨ وفى رَمَضانٍ يُفْسِدُونَ صِيامَنَا   بِأَكْلٍ وَشُرْبٍ مَرَّةً بَعْدَ مَرَّةِ

41. After the revolt in the Albaicín and Las Alpujarras the Spanish sovereigns decreed as a punitive measure that the Moriscos should either convert to Christianity or abandon Spain, *leaving behind their possessions* (Cf. M. Lafuente Alcántara, *Historia de Granada* [Paris, 1852], II, 350).

42. In 1499 Cardinal Jiménez de Cisneros made a public auto-da-fé in Granada, burning 1,025,000 Arabic volumes according to Mármol.

49 And they ordered us to curse our Prophet and to refrain from invoking him in times of ease or hardship.

50 They even overheard a group chanting his name, and the latter suffered a grievous injury at their hands,

51 For their judges and governors punished them with beatings, fines, imprisonment, and humiliation.

52 Whosoever lay dying, and did not have in attendance one who could preach [their religion to him], in their deceit, they would refuse to bury him,

53 Instead, he was left lying prostrate on a dung heap like a dead donkey or [some other] animal.

54 [They committed] many other similar, shameful deeds, as well as numerous wicked acts.

55 Our names were changed and given a new form with neither our consent nor our desire.

56 Therefore, alas for the exchanging of Muhammad's religion for that of the Christian dogs, the worst of creatures!

57 Alas for our names when they were exchanged for those of ignorant non-Arabs!

58 Alas for our sons and daughters who go off every morning to a priest

59 Who teaches them unbelief, idolatry, and falsehood while they are entirely unable to circumvent [the Christians] by any trick!

60 Alas for those mosques that have been walled up to become dung heaps for the infidel after having enjoyed ritual purity!

61 Alas for those minarets in which the bells [of the Christians] have been hung in place of the Muslim declaration of faith [being announced from them]!

62 Alas for those towns and their beauty! Through unbelief they have grown very dark!

63 They have become strongholds for the worshipers of the Cross, and in them the latter are safe against the occurring of raids.

64 We have become slaves; not captives who may be ransomed, nor even Muslims who pronounce their declaration of faith!

65 Hence, were your eyes to see what has become of our lot, they would overflow with abundant tears.

66 So alas! Alas for us! Alas for the misfortune that struck us, namely harm, sorrow, and the robe of oppression!

---

60. Between 1492 and 1499 Archbishop Talavera turned the main mosque of Granada into the Sagrario; that of Albaicín into the church of El Salvador.

٤٩ وقد أَمَرُونا أَنْ نَسُبَّ نَبِيَّنَا ولا نَذْكُرَنْهُ فى رَخَاءٍ وشِدَّةِ

٥٠ وقد سَمِعُوا قَوْمًا يُغَنُّونَ بِاسْمِهِ فَأَدْرَكَهُمْ مِنْهم أَلِيمُ المَضَرَّةِ

٥١ وعاقَبَهُمْ حُكَّامُهُمْ وَوُلَاتُهُمْ بِضَرْبٍ وتَغْرِيمٍ وسَجْنٍ وذِلَّةِ

٥٢ ومَن جاءَهُ المَوْتُ ولَمْ يَحْضُرِ الذى يُذَكِّرُهُمْ لم يَدْفِنُوهُ بِحِيلَةِ

٥٣ ويُتْرَكُ فى زِبْلٍ طَرِيحًا مُجَدَّلاً كَمِثْلِ حِمَارٍ مَيِّتٍ أَوْ بَهِيمَةِ

٥٤ إلى غَيْرِ هذا مِن أُمُورٍ كَثِيرَةٍ قِباحٍ وأَفْعَالٍ غِزَارٍ رَدِيَّةِ

٥٥ وقد بُدِّلَتْ أَسْمَاؤُنَا وتَحَوَّلَتْ بِغَيرِ رِضًا مِنَّا وغيرِ إِرادَةِ

٥٦ فآهًا على تَبْدِيلِ دِينِ مُحَمَّدٍ بِدِينِ كِلابِ الرُّومِ شَرِّ البَرِيَّةِ

٥٧ وآهًا على أَسْمائِنا حِينَ بُدِّلَتْ بِأَسْمَاءِ أَعلاجٍ مِنَ آهْلِ الغَبَاوَةِ

٥٨ وآهًا على أَبْنائِنا وبَنَاتِنَا يَرُوحُونَ لِلْبَّاطِ فى كلِّ غُدْوَةِ

٥٩ يُعَلِّمُهُمْ كُفْرًا وزُورًا وفِرْيَةً ولا يَقْدِرُوا أَنْ يَمْنَعُوهُمْ بِحِيلَةِ

٦٠ وآهًا على تِلْكَ المَسَاجِدِ سُوِّرَتْ مَزَابِلَ لِلْكُفَّارِ بعد الطَّهَارَةِ

٦١ وآهًا على تِلْكَ الصَّوَامِعِ عُلِّقَتْ نَوَاقِيسُهُمْ فيها نَظِيرَ الشَّهَادَةِ

٦٢ وآهًا على تِلْكَ البِلادِ وحُسْنِها لَقَدْ أَظْلَمَتْ بالكُفْرِ أَعْظَمَ ظُلْمَةِ

٦٣ وصارَتْ لِعُبَّادِ الصَّلِيبِ مَعَاقِلاً وقَدْ أَمِنُوا فيها وُقُوعَ الإِغَارَةِ

٦٤ وصِرْنَا عَبِيدًا لا أُسَارَى فَنُفْتَدَى ولا مُسْلِمِينَ نُطْقُهُمْ بالشَّهادَةِ

٦٥ فَلَوْ أَبْصَرَتْ عَيْنَاكَ ما صارَ حالُنَا إليه لَجادَتْ بالدُّموعِ الغَزِيرَةِ

٦٦ فَيَا وَيْلَنَا ، يا بُؤْسَ ما قد أَصابَنَا مِنَ الضُّرِّ والبَلْوَى وثَوْبِ المَذَلَّةِ

Three other mosques were converted into the churches of San Juan, San Nicolás, and San José (cf. *ibid.*, p. 344).

67 We besought you, your majesty, by the Lord our God, and by the chosen, the elect, the best of creatures,

68 And by those goodly lords, the family of Muhammad and his companions—what noble companions are they!—

69 And by the lord al-ᶜAbbās, our Prophet's paternal uncle, by his white hair, the most excellent white hair,

70 By those upright ones who grant recognition to their Lord, and by every excellent saint endowed with nobility.

71 Perchance you will look upon us and what has smitten us; perhaps the God of the Throne will bring mercy,

72 For your speech is hearkened to and your order is effective, while everything you command is swiftly executed.

73 As for the Christian faith, its [place of] origin is ruled by your authority, and it was from there that it spread to them in every region.

74 So, by God, your highness, be pleased to favor us with some advice or some words of protest,

75 For you possess excellence, glory, rank, and [the power] to rescue God's worshipers from all evil.

76 Therefore ask their Pope, that is to say, the ruler of Rome, why they permitted treason after having [granted] amnesty,

77 And why they harmed us with their betrayal with no wrong or crime on our part?

78 When their people who had been conquered [by us] were under the safeguard of our religion and the protection of [our] glorious kings who fulfilled their promises,

79 Neither were they converted from their faith, nor expelled from their homes, nor did they suffer betrayal or dishonor.

80 As for him who grants a treaty and then betrays it, that is a deed forbidden by every faith,

81 Especially on the part of kings, for it is a disgraceful, infamous deed; unlawful everywhere.

82 Your letter to them arrived, yet they did not heed one single word of it all;

83 It only increased their enmity and boldness against us as well as their perseverance in all kinds of wicked deeds.

---

82. Diego Hurtado de Mendoza relates that at an early date (around 1501?) the Moriscos had sought the intercession of the Ottoman emperor. This

٦٧ سألناك يا مولاى بالله ربنا　　　وبالمصطفى المختار خير البرية

٦٨ وبالسادة الأخيار آل محمد　　　وأصحابه أكرم بهم من صحابة

٦٩ وبالسيد العباس عم نبينا　　　وشيبته البيضاء أفضل شيبة

٧٠ وبالصالحين العارفين بربهم　　　وكل ولى فاضل ذى كرامة

٧١ عسى تنظروا فينا وفيما أصابنا　　　لعل إله العرش يأتى برحمة

٧٢ فقولك مسموع وأمرك نافذ　　　وما قلت من شىء يكون بسرعة

٧٣ ودين النصارى أصله تحت حكمكم　　　ومن ثم يأتيهم إلى كل كورة

٧٤ فبالله يا مولاى منوا بفضلكم　　　علينا برأى أو كلام بحجة

٧٥ فأنتم أولو الإفضال والمجد والعلا　　　وغوث عباد الله فى كل آفة

٧٦ فسل بابهم أعنى المقيم برومة　　　بماذا أجازوا الغدر بعد الأمانة ؟

٧٧ ومالهم مالوا علينا بغدرهم　　　بغير أذى منا وغير جريمة

٧٨ وجنسهم المغلوب فى حفظ ديننا　　　وأمن ملوك ذى وفاء أجلة

٧٩ ولم يخرجوا من دينهم وديارهم　　　ولا نالهم غدر ولا هتك حرمة

٨٠ ومن يعط عهدا ثم يغدر بعهده　　　فذاك حرام الفعل فى كل ملة

٨١ ولا سيما عند الملوك فإنه　　　قبيح شنيع لا يجوز بوجهة

٨٢ وقد بلغ المكتوب منكم إليهم　　　فلم يعملوا منه جميعا بكلمة

٨٣ وما زادهم إلا اعتداء وجرأة　　　علينا وإقداما بكل مساءة

---

poem seems to corroborate his item of information (cf. *Guerra de Granada*, Biblioteca de autores españoles, XX [Madrid, 1946], p. 72).

84 The envoys of Egypt reached them and they were not treated with treachery or dishonor,

85 Yet [the Christians] informed those envoys on our behalf, that we had voluntarily accepted the religion of unbelief,

86 And they brought out some [token] conversions to idolatry, of those who had submitted to them; yet, by God, we will never accept that declaration of faith!

87 They have lied about us with the greatest of falsehood in their words and arguments in saying that.

88 Rather, it was the fear of death and of burning that caused us to convert. We speak just as they spoke [to us]. It happened contrary to our intention,

89 While the faith of God's Prophet has not been extinguished among us, since in every glance our recognition of God's monotheism can be observed.

90 Moreover, by God, we accept neither our change of religion nor what they say on the subject of the Trinity,

91 And if they claim that we have accepted their religion unharmed by them,

92 Then ask Huéjar about its inhabitants: how they became captives and slaughterlings under [the burden] of humiliation and misfortune,

93 And ask Belefique what was the outcome of their affair: they were cut to pieces by the sword after undergoing anxiety.

94 As for Munyāfa, its inhabitants were sundered by the sword. The same was done to the people of Alpujarra.

95 As for Andarax, its people were consumed by fire. It was in their mosque that they all became like charcoal.

96 Lo, your majesty, we complain to you, what we have encountered is the worst form of estrangement.

97 Could our religion not be left to us as well as our ritual prayer, as they swore to do before the agreement was broken?

---

84. Some emissaries from Mamluk Egypt were sent to Spain in 1500 after the Egyptian Sultan had been urged to interfere on behalf of the Moriscos. They informed the Spanish monarchs that if the Moriscos were forced to convert to Christianity, the Mamluk Sultan would retaliate by persecuting the Christian populations of his realm (cf. Mármol Carvajal, *op. cit.*, p. 156).

92. Huéjar was a town where rebellion was suppressed by the Christians in 1501. Its inhabitants were all massacred (cf. P. Boronat y Barrachina, *Los moriscos españoles y su expulsión* [Valencia, 1901], I, 111; Mendoza, *op. cit.*, p. 70).

٨٤ وقد بَلَغَتْ أَرْسالُ مِصْرَ إليهِمْ ... وما نالَهُمْ غَدْرٌ ولا هُتْكُ حُرْمَةِ

٨٥ وقالوا لِتِلْكَ الرُّسْلِ عَنَّا بأَنَّنا ... رَضِينا بِدِينِ الكُفْرِ مِن غيرِ قَهْرَةِ

٨٦ وساقوا عُقودَ الزُّورِ مِمَّنْ أَطاعَهُمْ ... ووَاللهِ ما نَرْضَى بِتِلْكَ الشَّهادَةِ

٨٧ لقد كَذَبُوا فى قَوْلِهِمْ وكَلامِهِمْ ... علينا بِهذا القَوْلِ أَكْبَرَ فِرْيَةِ

٨٨ ولٰكِنَّ خَوْفَ القَتْلِ والحَرْقِ رَدَّنا ... نَقولُ كَمَا قالُوهُ مِن غيرِ نِيَّةِ

٨٩ ودِينُ رَسُولِ اللهِ ما زالَ عندَنا ... وتَوْحِيدُنا لِلّهِ فى كُلِّ لَحْظَةِ

٩٠ وَوَاللهِ ما نَرْضَى بِتَبْدِيلِ دِينِنا ... ولا بالذى قالوا مِنَ أَمْرِ الثَّلاثَةِ

٩١ وإنْ زَعَمُوا أَنَّا رَضِينا بِدِينِهِمْ ... بِغيرِ أَذًى منهمْ لنا ومَساءَةِ

٩٢ فَسَلْ وَحْرًا عن أَهْلِها كَيْفَ أَصْبَحُوا ... أُسارَى وقَتْلَى تَحْتَ ذُلٍّ ومَهْنَةِ

٩٣ وسَلْ بِلِفِيقَا عن قَضِيَّةِ أَمْرِهَا ... لَقَدْ مُزِّقُوا بالسَّيْفِ مِن بعد حَسْرَةِ

٩٤ وَمُنْيَافَةُ بالسَّيفِ مُزِّقَ أَهْلُهَا ... كذا فَعَلُوا أَيْضًا بأَهْلِ البُشَرَّةِ

٩٥ وَأَنْدَرَشُ بالنارِ أُحْرِقَ أَهْلُها ... بِجامِعِهِمْ صارُوا جَمِيعًا كَفَحْمَةِ

٩٦ فَها نَحْنُ يا مَوْلاىَ نَشْكُو إليكُمْ ... فهذا الذى نِلْناهُ مِن شَرِّ فُرْقَةِ

٩٧ عَسَى دِينُنَا يَبْقَى لَنا وصَلاتُنا ... كَمَا عاهَدُونا قَبْلَ نَقْضِ العَزِيمَةِ

---

93. Belefique was another center of insurrection in Las Alpujarras. The Count of Cifuentes had its men massacred and its women sold as slaves (cf. Lafuente Alcántara, *op. cit.*, II, 348).

94. Munyāfa is an unidentified site.

95. In 1500 the Count of Lerín laid siege to the fortress of Laujar in Andarax. He used gunpowder to blow up a mosque where the Muslim women and children had sought refuge (*ibid.*).

98 If not let them allow us to emigrate from their land to North Africa, the homeland of our dear ones, with our belongings.

99 For expulsion is better for us than remaining in unbelief, enjoying power but having no religion.

100 This is what we hope for from the glory of your rank. May every need of ours be satisfied by you!

101 From you do we hope for an end to our anxieties and to the evil lot and humiliation that have overcome us,

102 For you, praise be to God, are the best of our kings while your glory rises above all other glories.

103 Therefore we ask our Lord to prolong your life in kingship and glory, in joy and prosperity;

104 And [to grant you] peace in your realms, victory over your enemies, abundant troops, wealth, and magnificence,

105 Finally, may God's peace, followed by His mercy, be ever upon you for the duration of Time!

---

98. On the Moriscos' belongings, cf. n. 41.

٩٨ وإلَّا فَيُجْلُونَا جَمِيعًا مِنَ آرْضِهِمْ   بِأَمْوالِنَا لِلْغَرْبِ دارِ الأَحِبَّةِ
٩٩ فَإِجْلاؤُنَا خَيْرٌ لَنا مِن مُقامِنَا   على الكُفْرِ فى عِزٍّ على غيرِ مِلَّةِ
١٠٠ فهذا الذى نَرْجُوهُ مِن عِزِّ جاهِكُمْ   ومِنْ عندكُمْ تُقْضَى لَنَا كُلُّ حاجَةِ
١٠١ ومِنْ عندكُمْ نَرْجُو زَوَالَ كُرُوبِنَا   وما نَالَنَا مِن سُوءِ حالٍ وذِلَّةِ
١٠٢ فأَنْتُمْ بِحَمْدِ اللّٰهِ خَيْرُ مُلوكِنَا   وعِزَّتُكُمْ تَعْلُو على كُلِّ عِزَّةِ
١٠٣ فنَسْأَلُ مَوْلانا دَوَامَ حَياتِكُمْ   بِمُلْكٍ وعِزٍّ فى سُرُورٍ ونِعْمَةِ
١٠٤ وتَهْدِينِ أَوْطانٍ ونَصْرٍ على العِدَا   وكَثْرَةِ أَجْنَادٍ ومالٍ وثَرْوَةِ
١٠٥ وثُمَّ سَلامُ اللّٰهِ تَتْلُوهُ رَحْمَةٌ   عليكُمْ مَدَى الأَيَّامِ فى كُلِّ ساعَةِ

Glossary

of Technical Terms Applied to Arabic Poetry

aghṣān (*cf. ghuṣn*).

asmāṭ (*cf. simṭ*).

azjāl (*cf. zajal*).

badīᶜ. The art of complicated rhetorical ornamentation based on word play and alliterative sound effects, greatly cultivated by Neoclassical poets such as Abū Tammām and Buḥturī.

fakhr. The section of a *qaṣīda* devoted to boasting and self-magnification.

ghazal. A short poem devoted to the poet's amorous exploits.

ghuṣn (pl. *aghṣān*). Lit. "branch." The part of a *muwashshaḥa* formed by lines with independent rhyme, as opposed to the *simṭ*.

Ḥaufī. Short, popular love poems sung in Tlemcen, the words of which are put into the mouths of women and express the feminine viewpoint in love, very much like the *kharjas*.

ḥusn at-taᶜlīl. "Ingenious assignment of cause." A rhetorical figure much used in Arabic poetry ("Pass round the glass for the breeze has arisen and *the stars have slackened the reins of night travel*" [**10**, l. 1]).

Khafājī. Garden poetry written in the style of Ibn Khafāja of Alcira.

khamriyya (pl. *khamriyyāt*). A wine song, or a section of a *qaṣīda* devoted to the bacchic theme.

kharja (pl. *kharjāt*). The envoi or final line in a *muwashshaḥa*, also called *markaz* by Ibn Bassām, which was originally in the colloquial language (either Romance or Arabic) and constituted the direct speech of a woman.

madīḥ. The panegyrical section of a *qaṣīda*.

markaz. Ibn Bassām's technical term for the refrain and *kharja* in a *muwashshaḥa*.

Modernist. A school of poets of whom Abū Nuwās was the greatest exponent, who in Baghdad ironized the traditional themes of pre-Islamic poetry taken from Bedouin life, and attempted to adapt the latter to the new urban taste.

Muᶜallaqa. Term applied to any one of seven (or according to some, ten) pre-Islamic *qaṣīdas* considered to be the greatest masterpieces of early Arabic poetry.

mukhammasa. A strophic form derived from the *qaṣīda* but with internal rhymes in each line that divide the latter into five (*khamsa*) segments with the rhyme scheme *bbbba cccca dddda*, and so on.

muqābala. A pair of contrasting ideas elaborated in a balanced compound. A rhetorical device used by Arab poets ("The dawn has bestowed upon us its camphor after the night has claimed back [its] ambergris" [**10**, l. 2]).

musammaṭ (cf. *tasmīṭ*).

muwashshaḥa (pl. *muwashshaḥāt*). A strophic poem invented in al-Andalus in the late ninth or early tenth century. It is written in classical Arabic, but not originally in classical meters, appearing to be syllabic rather than quantitative, and has from five to seven strophes with complicated rhyme schemes, all of which may, however, be reduced to the basic form ababab *mn* cdcdcd *mn* efefef *mn*, and so on. Each strophe contains a part with rhymes peculiar to that strophe (ababab), called *ghuṣn*, and another with rhymes common to the whole poem (*mn*) called *simṭ* (or *qufl*). In the final strophe the *ghuṣn* introduces the words of a girl who expresses herself in colloquial language in the final *simṭ* known technically as *kharja*, "exit, envoi," or as *markaz*. If the poem begins with an odd *simṭ* the latter is called *maṭlaᶜ* "prelude." Otherwise the *muwashshaḥa* is called *aqraᶜ* (lit., "bald") or "acephalous." A typical rhyme scheme is that of **25** by Ibn Baqī, in which the first strophe has the following pattern:

a–b–a–b–a–b *m–n–o–n*
6 5 6 5 6 5 5 5 7 5

The roman letters (ababab) represent the *ghuṣn* and the italics (*mnon*) the *markaz* or *simṭ*, while the numerals below indicate the number of syllables in each segment.

nasīb. The opening section of a *qaṣīda*, traditionally occupied in pre-Islamic poetry by an elegy over a past love affair.

nauriyya. A short poem devoted to the floral theme.

Neoclassical. A term applied to poets such as Abū Tammām, Buḥturi, and Mutanabbī, who revolted against the Modernist school in the East and restored the traditional themes of pre-Islamic and early Umayyad poetry, but treating them with a new style complicated by the use of *badīᶜ*.

Nūniyya. The poem "rhymed in Nūn" is the title of a famous ode (**9**) written by Ibn Zaidūn.

qāṣid. An author of *qaṣīdas*.

qaṣīda. A type of monorhymed ode developed in pre-Islamic times and comprising the following traditional parts: (*a*) *nasīb* or love prelude; (*b*) *raḥīl* or journey theme; (*c*) *fakhr*, theme of self-glorification; (*d*) *madīḥ*, panegyrical theme (or: *hijāʾ* "invective").

Qaṣīda Maqṣūra. The name of a long poem composed by Ḥāzim al-Qarṭājannī on the fall of al-Andalus into Christian hands.

qaṣīda simṭiyya (cf. *tasmīṭ*).

raḥīl. The journey theme in a *qaṣīda*.

simṭ (pl. *asmāṭ*). Lit. "string of pearls." The part of a *muwashshaḥa* formed by lines with a rhyme common to the whole poem.

taḍfīr. "Plaiting, interweaving" is the use of internal rhyme in the *aghṣān* of a *muwashshaḥa*, a practice first introduced by ʿUbāda ibn Māʾ as-Samāʾ.

takāfuʾ. A rhetorical figure used in Arabic poetry, in which two words of opposite meaning are used in a metaphorical sense in the same line ("The dawn has bestowed upon us its *camphor* [= white] after the night has claimed back [its] *ambergris* [= black]" [**10**, l. 2]).

tasmīṭ. The insertion of internal rhyme in the lines of a *qaṣīda* to produce four segments per line with the rhyme scheme *bbba ccca ddda*, and so on.

ṭibāq. A rhetorical figure consisting of the use of two words of opposite meaning in the same line ("The *dawn* has bestowed upon us its camphor after the *night* has claimed back its ambergris" [**10**, l. 2]).

ʿUdhrite. A style of love poetry attributed to early Islamic poets such as Jamīl and ʿUrwa ibn Ḥizām, but much cultivated in ninth-century Baghdad. It expressed a pure love characterized by sexual denial which could lead to the death of the lover.

urjūza. A poem written in *rajaz* meter, in which both hemistichs in each line rhyme together. The whole poem may be monorhymed as occurs in shorter, more ancient pieces (*aa–aa–aa–aa* and so on), or each line may form a separate rhyming couplet, as occurs in longer, historical *urjūzas* (*aa–bb–cc–dd* and so on).

zajal (pl. *azjāl*) A strophic form appearing in early twelfth century al-Andalus structurally related to the *muwashshaḥa*, from which it differs in being entirely in the colloquial language. In it the *kharja* disappears in favour of the *maṭlaʿ* while the *asmāṭ* repeat only half the rhymes of the former.

Bibliography

General

ᶜAbbās, Iḥsān. *Taʾrikh al-adab al-Andalusī.* Beirut, 1960.

Arberry, A. J. *Arabic Poetry: A Primer for Students.* Cambridge, 1965.

———. *Moorish Poetry: A Translation of The Pennants. An Anthology Compiled in 1243 by the Andalusian Ibn Saᶜīd.* Cambridge, 1953.

Biberstein Kazimirski, A. de. *Dictionnaire arabe-français.* 2d ed. Paris, 1960. 2 vols.

Bosworth, C. E. *The Islamic Dynasties.* Edinburgh, 1967.

Corbin, Henry. *Histoire de la philosophie islamique.* Paris, 1964.

Cruz Hernández, M. *Filosofía hispano-musulmana.* Madrid, 1957. 2 vols.

Dozy, R. *Spanish Islam: A History of the Moslems in Spain.* Trans. F. G. Stokes. New York, 1913.

———. *Supplément aux dictionnaires arabes.* Leiden, 1881; reprinted Leiden and Paris, 1967. 2 vols.

Encyclopaedia of Islam, 1st ed. Leiden, and London 1913–1942. 4 vols.

Encyclopaedia of Islam, Supplement. Leiden and London, 1938.

Encyclopaedia of Islam, New ed. Leiden and London, 1954. 2 vols. appeared.

García Gómez, E. *Cinco poetas musulmanes: Biografías y estudios.* Madrid, 1945.

———. *Poemas arábigoandaluces.* Madrid, 1940.

———. *Poesía arábigoandaluza: Breve síntesis histórica.* Madrid, 1952.

Gibb, H. A. R. *Arabic Literature.* 2d ed. Oxford, 1963.

Gómez Moreno, M. *El arte español hasta los almohades. Arte mozárabe.* Ars Hispaniae, III. Madrid, 1951.

González Palencia, A. *Historia de la literatura arábigo-española.* 2d ed. Barcelona, 1945.

Hitti, P. K. *History of the Arabs.* 7th ed. London, 1961.

Huici Miranda, A. *Traducción expañola de un manuscrito anónimo del siglo XIII sobre la cocina hispano-magribī.* Madrid, 1966.

Ibn Saᶜīd al-Maghribī. *Kitāb Raiyāt al-mubarrizīn: Libro de las banderas de los campeones.* Ed. and trans. E. García Gómez. Madrid, 1942.

Imamuddin, S. M. *Some Aspects of the Socio-Economic and Cultural History of Muslim Spain.* Leiden, 1965.

Lane, E. W. *Arabic-English Lexicon.* London, 1863–1885. 8 vols.

Lévi-Provençal, É. *La civilization arabe en Espagne: Vue générale.* Cairo, 1938.

Lewis, A. R. *Naval Power and Trade in the Mediterranean: A.D. 500–1100.* Princeton, 1951.

al-Maqqarī. *History of the Mohammedan Dynasties in Spain.* Trans. Pascual de Gayangos. London, 1840–1843. 2 vols.

MONROE, JAMES, T. *Islam and the Arabs in Spanish Scholarship (XVIth Century to the Present)*. Leiden, 1969.
NICHOLSON, R. A. *A Literary History of the Arabs*. Cambridge, 1962.
NYKL, A. R. *Hispano-Arabic Poetry and Its Relations with the Old Provençal Troubadours*. Baltimore, 1946.
———. *Mukhtarāt min ash-shiʿr al-Andalusī: Selections from Hispano-Arabic Poetry*. Beirut, 1949.
PAREJA, F. M. *Islamología*. Madrid, 1952–1954. 2 vols.
AR-RIKĀBĪ, JAUDAT. *Fī l-adab al-Andalusī*. Cairo, 1960.
TERÉS SÁDABA, E. "Literatura arábigoespañola," in F. M. Pareja, *Islamología*, Madrid, 1954, II, 979–998.
TERRASSE, H. *Islam d'Espagne: Une rencontre de l'orient et de l'occident*. Paris, 1958.
TORRES BALBÁS, L. *Arte almohade, arte nazarí, arte mudéjar*. Ars Hispaniae, IV. Madrid 1949.
TRABULSĪ, AMJAD. *La critique poétique des arabes jus'au Vè siècle de l'hégire (XIè siècle de J. C.)*. Damascus, 1956.
VERNET, J. *Literatura árabe*. Barcelona, 1968.
VON GRUNEBAUM, G. E. "Arabic Poetics." In *Indiana University Conference on Oriental-Western Literary Relations*. Bloomington, Ind., 1955. Pp. 27–46.
———. *A Tenth-Century Document of Arabic Literary Theory and Criticism: Translation and Annotation of the Sections on Poetry of al-Baqillānī's Iʿjāz al-Qurʾān*. Chicago, 1950.
VON SCHACK, A. T. *Poesie und Kunst der Araber in Spanien und Sicilien*. 2d ed. Stuttgart, 1877.
WATT, W. MONTGOMERY, and PIERRE CACHIA. *A History of Islamic Spain*. Edinburgh, 1965.
WRIGHT, W. *A Grammar of the Arabic Language*. 3d. ed. Cambridge, 1951. 2 vols.
YĀQŪT. *Muʿjam al-buldān*. Cairo, 1906–1907. 10 vols.
YŪSUF ʿALĪ, A. *The Holy Qur-an*. Cambridge, Mass. 1946. 2 vols.

History of Hispano-Arabic Poetry From the Islamic Conquest of Hispania to the Caliphate

ABDEL BADI, LUTFI, *La épica árabe y su influencia en la épica castellana*. Santiago, Chile, 1964.
ANTUÑA, MELCHOR M. *La corte literaria de Alháquem II en Córdoba: Conferencia*. San Lorenzo de El Escorial, 1929.
BLACHÈRE, R. "La vie et l'oeuvre du poète-épistolier andalou Ibn Darrāğ al-Kasṭallī," *Hesperis*, XVI (1933), 99–121.
DABBĪ. *Bughyat al-multamis*. Ed. F. Codera and J. Ribera. Bibliotheca Arabico-Hispana, III. Madrid, 1885.
DOZY, R. *Notices sur quelques manuscrits arabes*. Leiden, 1847–1851. 1 vol.
GARCÍA GÓMEZ, E. "El príncipe amnistiado y su dīwān." *Cinco poetas musulmanes*. Madrid, 1945. Pp. 67–93.
———. "La poésie politique sous le califat de Cordoue," *Revue des études islamiques*, n.v. (1949), 5–11.

ḤIMYARĪ, ABŪ L-WALĪD. *Kitāb al-Badīʿ fī waṣf ar-rabīʿ*. Ed. Henri Pérès, Publications de l'Institut des Hautes Études Marocaines, VII. Rabat, 1940.
IBN ʿABD RABBIHI. *Kitāb al-ʿIqd al-farīd*. Ed. Aḥmad Amīn. Cairo, 1962. 10 vols.
IBN DARRĀJ AL-QASṬALLĪ. *Dīwān*. Ed. Maḥmūd ʿAlī Makkī. Damascus, 1961.
IBN HĀNIʾ. *Dīwān*. Ed. Karam al-Bustānī. Beirut, 1964.
IBN ʿIDHĀRĪ AL-MARRAKUSHĪ. *Bayān al-mughrib*. Trans. E. Fagnan. Algiers, 1904. 2 vols.
IBN AL-KHAṬĪB. *Kitab Aʿmāl al-aʿlām*. Ed. É. Lévi-Provençal. Beirut, 1956.
IBN SAʿĪD AL-MAGHRIBĪ. *ʿUnwān al-murqiṣāt wa-l-muṭribāt*. Ed. ʿAbd al-Qādir Maḥdād. Bibliothèque arabe-française, IV. Algiers, 1949.
LÉVI-PROVENÇAL, É. *España musulmana hasta la caida del califato de Córdoba (711–1031 de J.C.)*. Trans E. García Gómez. *Historia de España*, directed by R. Menéndez Pidal, IV–V. Madrid, 1950–1957.
LÉVI-PROVENÇAL, É., and E. GARCÍA GÓMEZ, eds. *Una crónica anónima de ʿAbd al-Raḥmān III al-Nāṣir*. Madrid and Granada, 1950.
AL-MAQQARĪ. *Analectes sur l'histoire et la littérature des arabes d'Espagne*. Ed. R. Dozy, G. Dugat, L. Krehl, W. Wright. Leiden, 1855–1861. 2 vols.
———. *Nafḥ aṭ-ṭib min ghuṣn al-Andalus ar-raṭib*. Ed. Muḥammad Muḥyī d-Din ʿAbd al-Ḥamīd. Cairo, 1949. 10 vols.
MILES, G. C. *The Coinage of the Umayyads in Spain*. New York, 1950.
MONROE, JAMES T. "A Tenth-Century Hispano-Arabic Epic Poem: The Urjūza of Ibn ʿAbd Rabbihi of Cordova," *Journal of the American Oriental Society*, XCI (1971), 67–95.
RIBERA Y TARRAGÓ, J. *Disertaciones y opúsculos*. Madrid 1928. 2 vols.
———. *Huellas, que aparecen en los primitivos historiadores musulmanes de la peninsula, de una poesía épica romanceada que debió florecer en Andalucía en los siglos IX y X: Discurso leido ante la Real Academia de la Historia*. Madrid, 1915.
TERÉS SÁDABA, E. "Préstamos poéticos en al-Andalus," *Andalus*, XXI (1956), 415–418.
ULLMAN, MANFRED. *Untersuchungen zur Ragazpoesie*. Wiesbaden, 1966.

Córdoba in Transition

CORBIN, HENRY. *Avicenne et le récit visionnaire*. Tehran, 1952. 2 vols.
COUR, A. *Un poète arabe d'Andalousie: Ibn Zaïdoûn*. Constantine, 1920.
DICKIE, J. "Ibn Shuhaid. A Biographical and Critical Study," *Andalus*, XXIX (1964), 243–310.
DRONKE, PETER. *Medieval Latin and the Rise of European Love-Lyric*. Oxford, 1965. 2 vols.
FACKENHEIM, E. L. "A Treatise on Love by Ibn Sīnā," *Medieval Studies*, VII (1945), 208–228.
FRINGS, THEODOR. *Die Anfänge der europäischen Liebes-Dichtung im 11 und 12 Jahrhundert*. Munich, 1960
———. *Minnesinger und Troubadours*. Berlin, 1949.

GARCÍA GÓMEZ, E. "Bagdad y los reinos de Taifas," *Revista de Occidente*, CXXVII (1934), 1–22.
HELL, J. "Al-ᶜAbbās ibn al-Aḥnaf, der Minnesänger am Hofe Hārūn ar-Rashīds," *Islamica*, II (1926), 271–307.
IBN ḤAZM. *El collar de la paloma*. Trans. E. García Gómez. 2d ed. Madrid, 1967.
———. *Ṭauq al-ḥamāma*. Ed. Ibrahīm al-Abyarī. Cairo 1959.
———. *Ṭauq al-ḥamāma*. Ed. Léon Bercher. Algiers, 1949.
———. *The Ring of the Dove*. Trans. A. J. Arberry. London, 1953.
IBN KHAQĀN. *Qalā'id al-iqyān*, Bulaq, 1866.
IBN SHUHAID. *Dīwān*. Ed. Charles Pellat. Beirut, 1963.
———. *Risālat at-Tawābiᶜ wa z-zawābiᶜ*. Ed. Buṭrus al-Bustānī. Beirut, 1951.
IBN ZAIDŪN. *Dīwān*. Ed. ᶜAlī ᶜAbd al-ᶜAẓīm. Cairo, 1957.
———. *Dīwān*. Ed. Karam al-Bustānī. Beirut, 1960.
MENÉNDEZ PIDAL, R. *La España del Cid*. Madrid, 1924.
MONROE, JAMES T. *The Shuᶜūbiyya in al-Andalus: The Risāla of Ibn García and Five Refutations*. University of California Publications, Near Eastern Studies, XIII. Berkeley and Los Angeles, 1969.
———. *Risālat at-Tawābiᶜ wa z-zawābiᶜ: The Treatise of Familiar Spirits and Demons by Abū ᶜĀmir ibn Shuhaid al-Ashjaᶜī, al-Andalusī*. University of California Publications, Near Eastern Studies, XV. Berkeley. Los Angeles. London, 1971.

The Mulūk aṭ-Ṭawā'if

ᶜABBĀS, IḤSĀN. *Al-Muwashshaḥāt al-ındalusiyya: Nash'atu-hā wa taṭāuwuru-hā*. Beirut, 1965.
ABŪ ISḤĀQ. *Un alfaquí español: Abū Isḥāq de Elvira*. Ed. and trans. E. García Gómez. Madrid and Granada, 1944.
BARGEBUHR, F. P. *El palacio de la Alhambra en el siglo XI*. Mexico, 1966.
CONTINENTE, J. M. "La muwashshaḥa: Visión de conjunto sobre los problemas que plantea, con una contribución al estudio de los principales washshāḥ." Madrid, University of Madrid, June 26, 1969. Unpublished dissertation.
DOZY, R. *Scriptorum Arabum Loci de Abbadidis*. Leiden, 1846–1863. 3 vols.
GARCÍA GÓMEZ, E. "Abū Isḥāq de Elvira, un alfaquí español." In *Cinco poetas musulmanes*. Madrid, 1945. Pp. 97–138.
———. "Estudio del Dār aṭ-Ṭirāz, preceptiva egipcia de la muwashshaḥa," *Andalus*, XXVII (1962), 21–104.
———. "La ley de Mussafia se aplica a la poesía estrófica arábigoandaluza," *Andalus*, XXVII (1962), 1–20.
———. "La lyrique hispano-arabe et l'apparition de la lyrique romane," *Arabica*, V (1958), 113–143.
———. *Qasidas de Andalucía* Madrid, 1940.
———. "Una pre-muwashshaḥa atribuída a Abū Nuwās," *Andalus*, XXI (1956), 406–414.
———. "Veinticuatro kharjas romances en muwashshaḥas árabes," *Andalus*, XVII (1952), 57–127.
HARTMANN, M. *Das arabische Strophengedichte. I. Das Muwashshaḥ*. Weimar, 1897.

HEGER, K. *Die bisher veröffentlichten Ḫarǧas und ihre Deutungen.* Tubingen, 1960.

IBN BASSĀM. *Dhakhīra.* Cairo, 1942. 3 vols. appeared.

IBN ḤAMDĪS. *Dīwān.* Ed. Iḥsān ᶜAbbās. Beirut, 1960.

IBN KHALDŪN. *The Muqaddimah.* Trans. Franz Rosenthal. New York, 1958. 3 vols.

IBN SANĀ' AL-MULK. *Dār aṭ-ṭirāz fī ᶜamal al-muwashshaḥāt.* Ed. Jaudat ar-Rikābī. Damascus, 1949.

AL-MARRAKUSHĪ, ᶜABD AL-WĀḤID. *Kitāb al-Muᶜjib fī talkhīṣ akhbār al-Maghrib.* Ed. Muḥammad Saᶜīd al-ᶜAryān and Muḥammad al-ᶜArabī al-ᶜIlmī. Cairo, 1949.

MONROE, JAMES T. "The Muwashshaḥāt." In *Collected Studies in Honor of Américo Castro's Eightieth Year.* Oxford, 1965, Pp. 335–371.

AL-MUᶜTAMID IBN ᶜABBĀD. *Dīwān.* Ed. Aḥmad Badawī and Ḥamīd ᶜAbd al-Majīd. Cairo, 1951.

PÉRÈS, HENRI. *La poésie andalouse en arabe classique au XIè siècle.* Paris 1937.

PRIETO Y VIVES, A. *Los reyes de taifas: estudio histórico-numismático de los musulmanes españoles en el siglo V de la hégira (XI de J.C.).* Madrid, 1926.

RIBERA Y TARRAGÓ, J. *Music in Ancient Arabia and Spain.* Trans. E. Hague and M. Leffingwell. Palo Alto, Calif., 1929.

SALAZAR, ADOLFO. "Poesía y música en las primeras formas de versificación rimada en lengua vulgar y sus antecedentes en lengua latina en la Edad Media," *Filosofía y Letras,* VIII (1942), 287–349.

SMITH, DULCIE L. *The Poems of Muᶜtamid, King of Seville.* New York, 1915.

SPITZER, LEO. "The Mozarabic Lyric and Theodor Frings' Theories," *Comparative Literature,* IV (1952), 1–22.

STERN, S. M. "Four Famous Muwashshaḥas from Ibn Bushrā's Anthology," *Andalus,* XXIII (1958), 339–369.

———. *Les chansons mozarabes: Les vers finaux (kharjas) en espagnol dans les muwashshaḥs arabes et hébreux.* Palermo, 1953.

———. "Muḥammad ibn ᶜUbāda al-Qazzāz, un autor de 'muwashshaḥas'," *Andalus,* XV (1950), 79–109.

VON GRUNEBAUM, G. E. *Medieval Islam.* Chicago, 1961.

The Almoravids

AL-AᶜMĀ AT-TUṬĪLĪ. *Dīwān.* Ed. Iḥsān ᶜAbbās. Beirut, 1963.

AL-AHWĀNĪ, ᶜABD AL-AZĪZ. *Az-Zajal fī l-Andalus.* Cairo, 1957.

CODERA Y ZAIDÍN, F. *Decadencia y desaparición de los almorávides de España.* Saragossa, 1899.

COLIN, G. S. "Spanish Arabic," *Encyclopaedia of Islam.* 2d ed. I, 501–503.

GARCÍA GÓMEZ, E. "Abén Guzmán, una voz en la calle." In *Cinco poetas musulmanes.* Madrid, 1945. Pp. 142–167.

———. *Las jarchas romances de la serie árabe en su marco.* Madrid, 1965.

———. *Un eclipse de la poesía en Sevilla: La época almorávide.* Madrid, 1945.

GUNZBURG, DAVID DE. *Le Divan d'Ibn Quzmān.* Berlin, 1896.

HOENERBACH, W. "La teoría del zéjel segun Ṣafī al-Dīn Ḥillī," *Andalus*, XV (1950). 297–334.
———. *Die vulgärarabische Poetik al-Kitāb al-ʿĀṭil al-ḥalī wa l-muraḫḫaṣ al-ghalī des Ṣafiyaddīn Ḥillī.* Wiesbaden, 1956.
IBN ʿABDŪN. *Sevilla a comienzos del siglo XII: El tratado de Ibn ʿAbdūn.* Trans. É. Lévi-Provençal and E. García Gómez. Madrid, 1947.
IBN BADRŪN. *Sharḥ qaṣīdat ibn ʿAbdūn: Commentaire historique du poème d'Ibn ʿAbdoun.* Ed. R. Dozy. Leiden, 1846.
IBN BĀJJA. *Tadbīr al-mutawaḥḥid: El régimen del solitario.* Ed. and trans. M. Asín Palacios. Madrid and Granada, 1946.
IBN KHAFĀJA. *Dīwān.* Ed. Karam al-Bustānī. Beirut, 1961.
IBN QUTAIBA. *Introduction au livre de la poésie et des poètes.* Ed. and trans. M. Gaudefroy-Demombynes. Paris, 1947.
IBN AZ-ZAQQĀQ. *Dīwān.* Ed. ʿAfīfa Dairānī. Beirut, 1964.
———. *Poesías.* Ed. and trans. E. García Gómez. Madrid, 1956.
MUIR, W. *The Caliphate.* Reprinted, Beirut, 1963.
NYKL, A. R., ed. and trans. *El cancionero de Abén Guzmán:* Madrid and Granada, 1933.
RIBERA Y TARRAGÓ, J. *El cancionero de Abén Guzmán: Discurso leído ante la Real Academia Española.* Madrid, 1912.
ASH-SHAQUNDĪ. *Elogio del Islam español.* Trans. E. García Gómez. Madrid, 1954.
STERN, S. M. "Studies on Ibn Quzmān," *Andalus*, XVI (1951), 379–425.
TUULIO, O. J., ed. and trans. *Ibn Quzmān: poète hispano-arabe bilingue.* Helsinki, 1941.

The Almohads

AFFIFI, A. *The Mystical Philosophy of Muḥyī d-Dīn ibn al-ʿArabī.* Cambridge, 1939.
ARBERRY, A. J. *Doctrines of the Sufis.* Cambridge, 1916.
———. *Sufism: An Account of the Mystics of Islam.* London, 1956.
ASÍN PALACIOS, M. *Abenmasarra y su escuela, orígenes de la filosofía hispano-musulmana: Discurso leído ante la Real Academia Española.* Madrid, 1914.
———. *El Islam cristianizado.* Madrid, 1931.
———. *Huellas del Islam.* Madrid, 1941.
———. "Un precursor hispanomusulmán de San Juan de la Cruz," *Andalus*, I (1933), 7–79.
———. *Vidas de santones andaluces.* Madrid, 1933.
BADAWĪ, ʿABD AR-RAḤMĀN. *Aristoteles de Poetica.* Cairo, 1953.
———. *Ḥāzim al-Qarṭājannī wa naẓariyyāt Arisṭū fī l-balāgha wa sh-shiʿr.* Cairo, 1961.
BROWNE, E. G. *A Literary History of Persia.* Cambridge, 1956. 2 vols.
CAGIGAS, ISIDRO DE LAS. *Sevilla almohade y últimos años de su vida musulmana.* Madrid, 1951.
CORBIN, HENRY. *L'Imagination créatrice dans le soufisme d'Ibn ʿArabī.* Paris, 1958.
GARCÍA GÓMEZ, "Observaciones sobre la Qaṣīda Maqṣūra de Ḥāzim al-Qarṭājannī," *Andalus*, I (1933), 81–103.

AL-HALLĀJ. *Dīwān*. Ed. and trans. Louis Massignon. Paris, 1955.
ḤĀZIM AL-QARṬĀJANNĪ. *Dīwān*. Ed. ᶜUthmān al-Kaᶜāᶜk. Beirut, 1964.
HOSSEIN NASR, S. *Three Muslim Sages: Avicenna, Suhrawardy, Ibn ᶜArabī*. Cambridge, Mass., 1964.
HOURANI, GEORGE F. *Averroes: On the Harmony of Religion and Philosophy*. E. J. W. Gibb Memorial Series. London, 1962. 2 vols.
HUICI MIRANDA, A. *Historia política del imperio almohade*. Tetuán, 1956. 2 vols.
IBN AL-ᶜARABĪ. *Tarjumān al-ashwāq*. Beirut: Dar Sader, 1961.
———. *The Tarjumān al-Ashwāq*. Ed. and trans. R. A. Nicholson. London, 1911.
IBN AL-ᶜARĪF. *Maḥāsin al-majālis*. Ed. and trans. M. Asín Palacios. Paris, 1933.
IBN SAHL. *Dīwān*. Ed. Aḥmad Ḥusain al-Qarnī. Cairo, 1926.
IBN ṬUFAIL. *El filósofo autodidacto*. Trans. F. Pons Boïgues. 2d ed. Madrid, 1954.
IBN TŪMART. *Le livre de Mohammed Ibn Toumert: Mahdi des Almohades*. Ed. and intro. I. Goldziher. Algiers, 1903.
JULIEN, A. *Histoire de l'Afrique du Nord*. 2d ed. Paris, 1964. 2 vols.
MASSIGNON, L. "Investigaciones sobre Shushtarī: Poeta andaluz, enterrado en Damieta," *Andalus*, XIV (1949), 29–57.
NICHOLSON, R. A. *Studies in Islamic Mysticism*. Cambridge, 1921.
PRIETO Y VIVES, A. "La reforma numismática de los almohades." *Miscelánea de estudios y textos árabes*. Madrid, 1915, 13–114.
AR-RUṢĀFĪ. *Dīwān*. Ed. Iḥsān ᶜAbbās. Beirut, 1960.
SHUSHTARĪ. *Dīwān*. Ed. ᶜAlī Sāmī an-Nashshār. Alexandria, 1960.
SOUALAH, M. *Ibrāhīm ibn Sahl: Poète musulman d'Espagne*. Algiers, 1914–1918.

The Naṣrids

BLACHÈRE, R. "Le visir-poète Ibn Zumruk et son oeuvre," *Annales de l'Institut d'Études Orientales* (Paris), II (1936), 291–312.
BORONAT Y BARRACHINA, P. *Los moriscos españoles y su expulsión*. Valencia, 1901. 2 vols.
CABANELAS RODRÍGUEZ, D. *El morisco granadino Alonso del Castillo*. Granada, 1965.
CARO BAROJA, J. *Los moriscos del reino de Granada*. Madrid, 1957.
CARRASCO URGOITI, MARÍA S. *El moro de Granada en la literatura (del siglo XV al XX)*. Madrid, 1956.
GARCÍA GÓMEZ, E. "Ibn Zamrak: El poeta de la Alhambra." In *Cinco poetas musulmanes*. Madrid, 1945. Pp. 171–271.
LAFUENTE ALCÁNTARA, E. *Inscripciones árabes de Granada*. Madrid, 1859.
LAFUENTE ALCÁNTARA, M. *Historia de Granada*. Paris, 1852. 2 vols.
LÓPEZ ESTRADA, F. *La toma de Antequera: Textos de Ben al-Jatib, Fernán Pérez de Guzmán, Alvar García de Santa María y Ghillebert de Lannoy*. Antequera, 1964.
LÓPEZ ORTIZ, J. "Fatwas granadinas de los siglos XIV y XV." *Andalus*, VI (1941), 73–127.

LUNA, MIGUEL DE. *The History of the Conquest of Spain by the Moors.* London, 1687.

AL-MAQQARĪ. *Azhār ar-riyāḍ.* Cairo, 1939. 3 vols.

MÁRMOL CARVAJAL, L. del. *Historia del rebelión y castigo de los moriscos del reino de Granada.* Biblioteca de autores españoles, XXI. Madrid, 1946.

MENDOZA, DIEGO HURTADO DE. *Guerra de Granada.* Biblioteca de autores españoles, XXI. Madrid, 1946.

MONROE, JAMES T. "A Curious Morisco Appeal to the Ottoman Empire," *Andalus,* XXI (1966), 281–303.

PRIETO Y VIVES, A. *Formación del reino de Granada: Discurso leído ante la Real Academia de la Historia.* Madrid, 1929.

Romancero español. Ed. L. Santullano. Madrid, 1935.

SOUALAH, M. *Une élégie andalouse sur la guerre de Grenade.* Algiers, 1914.

VALLA, LORENZO. *La conquista de Antequera.* Ed. J. López de Toro. Antequera, 1957.

YŪSUF III OF GRANADA. *Dīwān.* Ed. ᶜAbd Allāh Kannūn.